Law Questions &

LANDLORD
& TENANT

Questions and Answer Series

Titles in the Series

'A' Level Law
Company Law
Constitutional and Administrative Law
Conveyancing
Criminal Law
EC Law
English Legal System
Equity and Trusts
Family Law
Land Law
Landlord and Tenant
Law of Contract
Law of Evidence
Law of Torts
Wills, Probate and Administration

Other titles in preparation

Law Questions & Answers

LANDLORD & TENANT

Second Edition

MARK PAWLOWSKI
LLB(Hons), BCL(Oxon), ACIArb, Barrister
Professor of Property Law, University of Greenwich

JAMES BROWN
LLB(Hons), ACIArb, Barrister
Senior Lecturer in Law, South Bank University

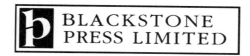

BLACKSTONE
PRESS LIMITED

Published by
Blackstone Press Limited
Aldine Place
London W12 8AA
United Kingdom

Sales enquiries and orders
Telephone +44-(0)-20-8740-2277
Facsimile +44-(0)-20-8743-2922
e-mail: sales@blackstone.demon.co.uk
website: www.blackstonepress.com

ISBN 1-84174-098-5
© Mark Pawlowski and James Brown, 1995, 2000
First edition 1995
Second edition 2000

British Library Cataloguing in Publication Data
A catalogue record for this book is available from the British Library

Typeset in 10/12pt Times
by Montage Studios Limited, Tonbridge, Kent
Printed and bound in Great Britain by Antony Rowe Limited,
Chippenham and Reading

Contents

Preface   v

Table of Cases   ix

Table of Statutes   xxi

1   Introduction   1

2   The Landlord and Tenant Relationship   6

3   Enforceability of Covenants   29

4   Implied and Usual Covenants   54

5   Assignment, Sub-letting, Parting with Possession   71

6   Leasehold Dilapidations   89

7   Express Covenants   116

8   Termination of Leases   134

9   The Rent Act 1977   160

10 Part I of the Housing Act 1988   178

11 Leasehold Enfranchisement   189

Contents

12   Business Tenancies   198

13   Agricultural Holdings and Agricultural Tied Cottages   227

14   Secure Tenancies   243

15   Pick and Mix Questions   253

Index   281

Preface

We were delighted to have been asked by the publishers to produce a second edition of this book. Since the last edition (in 1995), there have been several important developments in the field of landlord and tenant law. Most notably, the Landlord and Tenant (Covenants) Act 1995 has fundamentally altered the enforcement of leasehold covenants producing a complex 'duality' of rules on enforceability; the new legislation does not have retrospective effect and leases granted before 1 January 1996 continue to be enforced under the pre-1995 Act law. We have included two questions on the workings of the 1995 Act in **Chapter 3**. Another important piece of new legislation affecting the enforceability of leasehold covenants is the Contracts (Rights of Third Parties) Act 1999, which came into force in November 1999. Accordingly, we have also included an essay-type question on the 1999 Act in **Chapter 3**. A major new piece of legislation now also governs agricultural tenancies granted on or after 1 September 1995, namely, the Agricultural Tenancies Act 1995. We have added a new question on the workings of this Act in **Chapter 13**.

Unfortunately, however, in other areas of leasehold law, reform has been slow and unrewarding. Over 15 years have now elapsed since the publication of the Law Commission's Report 'Forfeiture of Tenancies' (Law Com. No. 42, 1985), but there is still little expectation that the Law Commission's recommendations (now in modified form) will become law in the foreseeable future. In the meantime, there have been several judicial developments seeking to extend purely contractual doctrines into the leasehold context, in particular, the doctrine of repudiatory breach. We have added a new question on this interesting topic in **Chapter 8**: see Question 4.

There has also been little progress in implementing the Law Commission's proposals for the reform of leasehold dilapidations since its Report, 'Landlord and Tenant, Responsibility for State and Condition of Property' (Law Com. No. 238, 1996). The current workings of Pt II of the Landlord and Tenant Act 1954 also remain unchanged despite the Law Commission's recommendations in this regard contained in its 1992 Report, 'Business Tenancies: A Periodic Review of the Landlord and Tenant Act 1954 Part II' (Law Com. No. 208, 1992). On a more positive note, however, the Queen's Speech last year announced the Government's intention to publish a draft bill on commonhold and leasehold reform in 2000, so there is the prospect of a major new piece of legislation on leasehold law.

We have also been conscious of the new civil justice reforms and how these are likely to impact on landlord and tenant law. We have, therefore, included a new question (in **Chapter 12**) on the workings of Professional Arbitration on Court Terms (PACT) in the lease renewal context, with particular emphasis on its contemporary significance in the light of the Woolf reforms.

We have added a number of new questions to cover recent developments in the case law, in particular, *Bruton* v *London and Quadrant Housing Trust* [1999] 3 All ER 418 (**Chapter 2**), *Southwark London Borough Council* v *Mills* [1999] 4 All ER 449 (**Chapter 4**), *Hemingway Securities Ltd* v *Dunraven Ltd* [1995] 09 EG 322 (**Chapter 5**), *British Telecommunications plc* v *Sun Life Assurance Society plc* [1995] 4 All ER 44 (**Chapter 6**), *Mannai Investment Co. Ltd* v *Eagle Star Life Assurance Co. Ltd* [1997] 24 EG 122 (**Chapter 8**), *Graysim Holdings Ltd* v *P. & O. Property Holdings Ltd* [1996] 1 AC 329 (**Chapter 12**), and *Hammersmith and Fulham London Borough Council* v *Monk* [1992] 1 AC 478 (**Chapter 15**). In total, there are 14 new questions in this edition. In addition, we have substantially revised a number of existing answers in order to bring them into line with recent case law and statutory provisions (e.g., Question 1, **Chapter 10**, dealing with the new statutory changes to assured shorthold tenancies introduced by the Housing Act 1996, and Question 1, **Chapter 15**, concerning the effect of the Unfair Terms in Consumer Contracts Regulations 1999 on the tenant's right of set-off against rent). New cases incorporated into the text include: *Hindcastle Ltd* v *Barbara Attenborough Associates Ltd* [1996] 1 All ER 737 and *Co-operative Insurance Society Ltd* v *Argyll Stores* (Holdings) Ltd [1997] 3 All ER 297 (**Chapter 3**), *Footwear Corporation Ltd* v *Amplight Properties Ltd* [1998] 3 All ER 52 (**Chapter 5**), *Jervis* v *Harris* [1996] 1 EGLR 78 (**Chapter 6**), *Nynehead Developments Ltd* v *R.H. Fibreboard Containers Ltd* [1999] 02 EG 139 and *Brown & Root Technology Ltd* v *Sun Alliance & London Assurance Co. Ltd* [1997] 18 EG 123

(**Chapter 8**), *Dolgellau Golf Club* v *Hett* (1998) 34 EG 87, *Esselte AB* v *Pearl Assurance plc* [1997] 1 WLR 89 and *Bacchiocchi* v *Academic Agency Ltd* [1998] 2 All ER 241 (**Chapter 12**), *Barrett* v *Morgan* [2000] 1 All ER 481 (**Chapter 13**), *Fitzpatrick* v *Sterling Housing Association Ltd* [1999] 4 All ER 705(**Chapter 14**), and *Savva* v *Houssein* [1996] 47 EG 138 (**Chapter 15**). The list is not exhaustive.

We wish to thank our publishers for their diligent efforts in bringing this latest edition to print before the start of the new academic session in October 2000. We also wish to express our deepest gratitude to our respective partners, Lidia and Julie, who have been very tolerant of our obsessive work habits!

We have endeavoured to present the law accurately in our suggested answers as at 1 June 2000.

Mark Pawlowski
James Brown

For Alex

Mark

For Julie

James

Table of Cases

Aberdeen Steak Houses Group Ltd v Crown Estate Commissioners [1997] 2 EGLR 107   201
Abernethie v A.M. & J. Kleiman Ltd [1970] 1 QB 10   206
Abrahams v Wilson [1971] 2 QB 88   176
Acuba v Allied Shoe Repairs [1975] 3 All ER 782   122
Adami v Lincoln Grange Management Ltd [1998] 17 EG 148   106, 274
Addiscombe Garden Estates v Crabbe [1958] 1 QB 513   206
Adelphi (Estates) Ltd v Christie (1983) 47 P & CR 650   24
Adler v Blackman [1953] 1 QB 146, [1952] 2 All ER 945   17, 21, 277
AG Securities v Vaughan/ Antoniades v Villiers [1990] 1 AC 417,
     [1988] 3 WLR 1205   9, 12, 182, 277
AGB Research plc, Re [1994] EGCS 73   157
Air India v Balabel [1993] 30 EG 90   72, 83
Al Hassani v Merrigan (1988) 20 HLR 238   114
Al Saloom v Shirley James Travel Service Ltd (1981) 259 EG 420   120
Aldin v Latimer Clark, Muirhead & Co. [1894] 2 Ch 437   274
Ali v Knight (1984) 272 EG 1165   203, 208
Allnatt London Properties Ltd v Newton [1984] 1 All ER 423   72
Amherst v James Walker Goldsmith and Silversmith Ltd [1983] 3 WLR 334   121
Amsprop Trading Ltd v Harris Distribution Ltd [1997] 1 WLR 1025   51
Anderson v Oppenheimer (1880) 5 QBD 602   63
Anderton & Milner's Contract, Re [1890] Ch D 476   65
Arlesford Trading Co. Ltd v Servansingh [1971] 1 WLR 1080   34
Artemiou v Procopiou [1966] QB 878   205
Artesian Residential Investments Ltd v Beck [1999] 22 EG 145   184
Asco Developments Ltd v Gordon (1978) 248 EG 683   100, 254, 257
Ashburn Anstalt v Arnold [1989] Ch 1   6, 17
Ashgar v Ahmed (1984) 17 HLR 25   59
Ashworth Frazer Ltd v Gloucester City Council [2000] 12 EG 149   78
Aslan v Murphy (No. 1)/Aslan v Murphy (No. 2)/Duke v Wynne [1990] 1 WLR 766   13
Associated British Ports v C.H. Bailey plc [1990] 2 AC 703   98

Bacchiocchi v Academic Agency Ltd [1998] 2 All ER 241   218
Bagettes Ltd v G.P. Estates Ltd [1956] Ch 290   204, 205, 221
Bahamas International Trust Co. Ltd v Threadgold [1974] 1 WLR 1514   230

Bairstow Eves (Securities) Ltd v Ripley [1992] 2 EGLR 47   129
Bandar Property Holdings Ltd v JS Darwen (Successors) Ltd [1968] 2 All ER 305   131
Barclays Bank Ltd v Ascott [1961] 1 WLR 717   202
Barclays Bank v Stasek [1957] Ch 28   155
Bardrick v Haycock (1976) 31 P & CR 420   181
Barnes v Gorsuch (1981) 43 P & CR 294   181
Barrett v Lounova [1990] 1 QB 348   105, 106, 107, 234, 274
Barrett v Morgan [2000] 1 All ER 481   232, 233
Bass Holdings Ltd v Morton Music Ltd [1987] 3 WLR 543   130
Bassairi Ltd v Camden London Borough Council [1998] EGCS 27   205
Basset v Whiteley (1982) P & CR 87   129
Bates v Donaldson [1896] 2 QB 241   76
Bathurst v Fine [1974] 1 WLR 905   141
Battlespring Ltd v Gates (1983) 268 EG 355   173
Baynes & Co. v Lloyd & Sons [1895] 2 QB 610   274
Beacon Carpets Ltd v Kirby [1984] 3 WLR 489   132
Beck v Scholz [1953] 1 QB 570   169
Bell v Alfred Franks and Bartlett Co. Ltd [1980] 1 WLR 340   207
Bell v General Accident Fire & Life Assurance Corporation Ltd [1998] 17 EG 144   256
Berkeley v Poulett (1976) 241 EG 911   151
Bernays v Prosser [1963] 2 QB 592   231
Berrycroft Management Co. Ltd v Sinclair Gardens Investments (Kensington) Ltd
   [1997] 22 EG 141   132
Betty's Cafes Ltd v Phillips Furnishing Stores Ltd [1959] AC 20   201, 247
Bickel v Duke of Westminster [1977] QB 517   75
Bickmore v Dimmer [1903] 1 Ch 158   123
Billson v Residential Apartments Ltd [1992] 2 WLR 15, [1991] 3 WLR 264   139, 140
Bishop v Consolidated London Properties Ltd (1933) 102 LJ KB 257   112, 115
Blackmore v Butler [1954] 2 QB 171   230, 232
Blanway Investments Ltd v Lynch [1993] EGCS 8   169
Blumenthal v Gallery Five Ltd (1971) 220 EG 483   269
Bocardo SA v S & M Hotels Ltd [1980] 1 WLR 17   72
Boyer v Warbey [1953] 1 QB 234   16
Bracey v Read [1963] Ch 88   207, 230
Bradshaw v Pawley (1980) 253 EG 693   268
Branchett v Beaney/Branchett v Swale Borough Council [1992] 3 All ER 910   59
Breams Property Investment Co. Ltd v Stroulger [1948] 2 KB 1   27
Brew Bros Ltd v Snax (Ross) Ltd [1970] 1 QB 612, [1969] 1 WLR 657   94, 264
British Anzani (Felixstowe) Ltd v International Marine Management (UK) Ltd [1980] QB 137,
   [1979] 2 All ER 1063   100, 111, 254, 257
British Bakeries (Midlands) Ltd v Michael Testler & Co. Ltd (1986) 277 EG 1245   78, 79
British Telecommunications plc v Sun Life Assurance Society plc
   [1995] 4 All ER 44   90, 112, 113, 115
Broggi v Robbins (1899) 15 TLR 224   114
Bromley Park Garden Estates Ltd v Moss [1982] 1 WLR 1019   83
Brown & Root Technology Ltd v Sun Alliance & London Assurance Co. Ltd
   [1997] 18 EG 123   127, 130
Brown v Brash [1948] 2 KB 247   161, 185
Brown v Draper [1944] KB 309   164, 166, 185
Brown v Gould [1972] Ch 53   118, 128
Browne v Flower [1911] 1 Ch 219   62, 68
Bruton v London and Quadrant Housing Trust [1999] 3 All ER 481,
   [1998] QB 834   6, 9, 11
Buchmann v May [1978] 2 All ER 993   164, 166, 181

Buckland v Butterfield (1802) 2 Brod & Bing 54 — 151
Burton v Camden London Borough Council [2000] EGCS 23 — 249, 270
Bush Transport Ltd v Nelson (1987) 1 EGLR 71 — 155
Butler Estates Co. v Bean [1942] 1 KB 1 — 45
Button's Lease, Re [1964] 1 Ch 263 — 130

Cadogan v McCarthy & Stone Developments Ltd [1996] EGCS 94 — 201, 209
Caerphilly Concrete Products Ltd v Owen [1972] 1 WLR 372 — 128
Cafeteria (Keighley) Ltd v Harrison (1956) 168 EG 668 — 206, 211
Calabar Properties Ltd v Stitcher [1984] 1 WLR 287 — 99, 100
Calcott v J. S. Bloor (Measham) Ltd [1998] 40 EG 180 — 231
Calthorpe v McOscar [1924] 1 KB 716 — 109
Camden London Borough Council v Shortliffe Community Housing (1992) 25 HLR 330 — 11
Canas Property Co. Ltd v KL Television Services Ltd [1970] 2 QB 433 — 144
Cardshops Ltd v Davies [1971] 1 WLR 591 — 210
Carradine Properties v Aslam [1976] 1 WLR 442 — 158
Carter v SU Carburreter Co. [1942] 2 KB 288 — 168, 169
Cavalier v Pope [1906] AC 428 — 103
Centaploy Ltd v Matlodge Ltd [1974] Ch 1 — 6, 27
Central Estates (Belgravia) Ltd v Woolgar (No. 2) [1972] 1 WLR 1048 — 138
Centrovincial Estates plc v Bulk Storage Ltd (1983) 268 EG 59 — 34
CH Bailey v Memorial Enterprises Ltd [1974] 1 WLR 728 — 17, 268, 269
Chamberlain v Farr [1942] 2 All ER 567 — 255
Chapman v Freeman [1978] 1 WLR 129 — 205
Chartered Trust plc v Davies [1997] 2 EGLR 83 — 148, 149, 264
Chelsea Estates Ltd v Kadri [1970] EGD 1356 — 117
Cheshire Lines Committee v Lewis & Co. (1880) 50 LJ QB 121 — 27
Chester v Buckingham Travel Ltd [1981] 1 WLR 96 — 65
Cheverell Estates Ltd v Harris [1998] 02 EG 127 — 48
Chiswell v Grifton Land and Estates Ltd [1975] 1 WLR 1181 — 208
Choidi v DeMarney (1989) 21 HLR 6 — 100, 107
Christina v Seear (1985) 275 EG 898 — 205, 211, 213
Church of England Building Society v Piskor [1954] Ch 553 — 256
City of London Corporation v Fell [1993] 3 WLR 1164 — 32, 33, 37
Climie v Wood (1869) LR 4 Ex 328 — 153
Co-operative Insurance Society v Argyll Stores (Holdings) Ltd [1997] 3 All ER 297 — 52
Coatsworth v Johnson (1886) 55 LJ QB 220 — 15
Colchester Estates (Cardiff) v Carlton Industries plc [1986] Ch 80 — 99, 273
Connaught Restaurants Ltd v Indoor Leisure Ltd [1994] 4 All ER 834 — 254, 257
Cooper's Lease, Re (1968) P & CR 541 — 75
Cornillie v Saha (1996) 28 HLR 561 — 261
Coronation Street Industrial Properties Ltd v Ingall Industries [1989] 1 WLR 304 — 41, 43
Cosh v Fraser (1964) 108 SJ 116 — 75
Cosh's Contract, Re [1897] 1 Ch 9 — 80
Costain Property Developments Ltd v Finlay & Co. Ltd [1989] 1 EGLR 237 — 52
Crago v Julian [1992] 1 WLR 372 — 7, 269
Crawford v Elliott [1991] 13 EG 163 — 234
Crawley Borough Council v Sawyer (1987) 20 HLR 98 — 243
Crawley Borough Council v Ure [1995] 1 FLR 806 — 276, 278
Crayford v Newton (1886) 36 WN 54 — 96
Credit Suisse v Beegas Nominees Ltd [1994] 4 All ER 803 — 93
Creska Ltd v Hammersmith and Fulham London Borough Council [1998] 37 EG 165 — 96
Cricklewood Property and Investment Trust Ltd v Leighton's Investment Trust Ltd [1945] AC 221 — 148

Cunliffe v Goodman [1950] 2 KB 237   201, 247
Curl v Angelo [1948] 2 All ER 189   163, 164

David Blackstone Ltd v Burnetts (West End) Ltd [1973] 1 WLR 1487   137, 138
Dawncar Investments Ltd v Plews (1993) 25 HLR 639   173
Deen v Andrews (1986) 52 P & CR 17   152
Deverall v Wyndham [1989] 01 EG 70   75
Di Palma v Victoria Square Property Ltd [1986] Ch 150   142
Dinefwr Borough Council v Jones (1987) 284 EG 58   114
Diploma Laundry Ltd v Surrey Timber Co. Ltd [1955] 2 QB 604   209
Doe d Ambler v Woodbridge (1829) 9 B & C 376   260
Doe d Calvert v Frowd (1828) 4 Bing 557   67
Doe d Ellenbrock v Flynn (1834) 1 CM & R 137   66
Doe d Murrell v Milward (1838) 3 M & W 328   154
Doe d Rigge v Bell (1793) 5 Durn & E 471   21
Doe d Warner v Browne (1908) 8 East 165   21
Dolgellau Golf Club v Hett [1998] 34 EG 87   209
Dong Bang Minerva (UK) Ltd v Davina Ltd [1994] EGCS 104   82
Dover District Council v Farrar (1980) 2 HLR 35   90, 104
DR Evans & Co. v Chandler (1969) 211 EG 1381   260
Drane v Evangelou [1978] 1 WLR 455   58, 59, 68
Drebbond Ltd v Horsham District Council (1979) 37 P & CR 237   120
Duke of Westminster v Birrane [1995] 3 All ER 416   191
Duke of Westminster v Guild [1985] QB 688   274
Duke of Westminster v Swinton [1948] 1 KB 524   123, 140
Duke v Wynne [1990] 1 WLR 766   9, 12
Dunn v Fidoe [1950] 2 All ER 685   230
Dunraven Securities Ltd v Holloway (1982) 264 EG 709   260

Eastern Telegraph Co. Ltd v Dent [1899] 1 QB 835   74, 137
Egerton v Esplanade Hotels, London Ltd [1947] 2 All ER 88   141, 260
EH Lewis v Morelli [1948] 2 All ER 1021   256
Eichner v Midland Bank Executor and Trustee Co. Ltd [1970] 1 WLR 1120   201, 262
Electricity Supply Nominees Ltd v IAF Group Ltd [1993] 1 WLR 1059   254, 258
Elite Investments Ltd v TI Bainbridge Silencers Ltd (1986) 280 EG 1001   94
Elitestone Ltd v Morris [1997] 1 WLR 687   152
Elliston v Reacher [1908] 2 Ch 374   52
Elmcroft Developments Ltd v Tankersley- Sawyer (1984) 270 EG 140   95
Elwes v Maw (1802) 3 East 38   152, 154
Esselte AB v Pearl Assurance plc [1997] 1 WLR 891   204, 221
Esso Petroleum Co. Ltd v Kingswood Motors (Addlestone) Ltd [1974] QB 142   87
Esso Petroleum Ltd v Anthony Gibbs Financial Services Ltd (1983) 267 EG 351   122
Estavest Investments Ltd v Commercial Express Travel Ltd [1988] 49 EG 73   170
EWP Ltd v Moore [1992] 1 QB 460   231
Expert Clothing Service & Sales Ltd v Hillgate House Ltd [1986] Ch 340   85, 138

Family Housing Association v Jones [1990] 1 WLR 779   10
Family Housing Association v Miah (1982) 5 HLR 94   244
Famous Army Stores v Meehan [1993] 09 EG 114   254, 257
Farr v Ginnings (1928) 44 TLR 249   75
Featherstone v Staples [1986] 1 WLR 861   233
Fitzpatrick v Sterling Housing Association Ltd [1999] 4 All ER 705   248, 251
Flairline Properties Ltd v Hassan [1998] 169 EGCS 169   204
Flexman v Corbett [1930] 1 Ch 672   65

Footwear Corportion Ltd v Amplight Properties Ltd [1998] 3 All ER 52 83
Foreman v Beagley [1969] 1 WLR 1387 177
Foster v Robinson [1951] 1 KB 149 155
Foyner v Weeks [1891] 2 QB 31 98
Frederick Platts Co. Ltd v Grigor [1950] WN 194 176
Friends' Provident Life Office v British Railways Board [1996] 1 All ER 336 34
Frish Ltd v Barclays Bank Ltd [1951] 2 QB 541 206
Fuller v Judy Properties Ltd [1992] 14 EG 106, [1992] 1 EGLR 75 85, 139
FW Woolworth & Co. Ltd v Lambert [1937] Ch 37 117, 124, 125, 260

Gaidowski v Conville and Caius College Cambridge [1975] 1 WLR 1066 192
Garston v Scottish Widow's Fund and Life Assurance Society [1998] 3 All ER 596 158
Gatwick Parking Service Ltd v Sargent [2000] EG 11 209
Gladstone v Bower [1960] 2 QB 384 231
Glass v Kencakes Ltd [1966] 1 QB 611 260
GLC v London Borough of Tower Hamlets (1983) 15 HLR 54 90
GMS Syndicate Ltd v Gary Elliott Ltd [1982] Ch 1 32
Gold v Brighton Corporation [1956] 1 WLR 1291 210
Gold v Jacques Amand Ltd [1992] 27 EG 140 230
Goldstein v Sanders [1915] 1 Ch 549 75
Governors of Rugby School v Tannahill [1935] 1 KB 87 260
Granada TV Network v Great Universal Stores (1963) 187 EG 391 78
Graysim Holdings Ltd v P & O Property Holdings Ltd
 [1996] 1 AC 329 204, 205, 219, 220, 221
Greater London Council v Connolly [1970] 2 QB 100 269
Greater London Council v London Borough of Tower Hamlets (1984) 15 HLR 54 104
Greater London Properties Ltd's Lease, Re [1959] 1 WLR 503 80
Greenwich London Borough Council v McGrady (1982) 6 HLR 36 277
Gregson v Cyril Lord Ltd [1963] 1 WLR 41 209
Greville v Parker [1910] AC 335 129
Griffin v Pillet [1926] 1 KB 17 114
GS Fashions Ltd v B & Q plc [1995] 09 EG 324 144
Guardian Assurance Co. Ltd v Gants Hill Holdings Ltd (1983) 267 EG 678 117, 126
Guppy's (Bridport) Ltd v Brookling (1984) 269 EG 846 68
Gurton v Parrott [1991] 18 EG 161 206
GUS Management Ltd v Texas Homecare Ltd [1993] 27 EG 130 34

Hafton Properties Ltd v Camp [1993] EGCS 101 68
Hagee (London) Ltd v Erikson (A.B.) and Larson [1976] QB 209 255
Haines v Florensa [1990] 09 EG 70 117, 123, 125
Hall v Howard [1988] 44 EG 83 115
Hammersmith and Fulham LBC v Monk [1992] 1 AC 478 277
Hammersmith and Fulham LBC v Creska Ltd [1999] PLSCS 159 99
Hammersmith and Fulham London Borough Council v Monk [1992] 1 AC 478 276
Hamp v Bygrave (1983) 266 EG 720 151, 154
Hampshire v Wickens (1878) 7 Ch D 555 64, 65
Hankey v Clavering [1942] 2 KB 326 158
Hansom v Newman [1934] Ch 298 98
Haringey London Borough Council v Stewart (1991) 2 EGLR 252 246
Harmer v Jumbil (Nigeria) Tin Areas Ltd [1921] 1 Ch 200 274
Harris v Swick Securities [1969] 3 All ER 1131 192
Harrogate Borough Council v Simpson [1986] 2 FLR 91 251
Hart v Emelkirk Ltd [1983] 1 WLR 1289 101
Havant International Holdings Ltd v Lionsgate (H) Investment Ltd [1999] EGCS 144 158

Havenridge Ltd v Boston Dyers Ltd [1994] EGCS 53 — 131
Hayes v Caryll (1702) 1 Bro Parl Cas 126 — 24
Healing Research Trustee Co. Ltd, Re (1992) 2 EGLR 231 — 35
Hedgedale Ltd v Hards (1991) 15 EG 107 — 177
Hemingway Securities Ltd v Dunraven Ltd [1995] 09 EG 322 — 73, 85, 86, 87, 88
Henry Smith's Charity Trustees v AWADA Trading and Promotion Services Ltd
   (1984) 269 EG 279 — 120
Herbert Duncan Ltd v Cluttons [1993] 2 All ER 449 — 33, 37
Herbert v Lambeth London Borough Council (1993) 90 LGR 310 — 104
Heslop v Burns [1974] 1 WLR 1241 — 255
Hildebrand v Moon (1989) 37 EG 123 — 177
Hill v Rochard [1983] 1 WLR 478 — 172
Hiller v United Dairies (London) Ltd [1934] 1 KB 57 — 169, 182
Hillil Property & Investment Co. Ltd v Naraine Pharmacy Ltd (1979) 252 EG 1013 — 206
Hills (Patents) Ltd v University College Hospital Board of Governors [1956] 1 QB 90 — 206
Hilton v Plustitle [1989] 1 WLR 149, [1988] 3 All ER 1051 — 170, 182
Hindcastle Ltd v Barbara Attenborough Associates Ltd [1996] 1 All ER 737 — 36
Holding & Management Ltd v Property Holding & Investment Trust plc [1990] 05 EG 75 — 93
Holiday Flat Co. v Kuczera (1978) SLT 47 — 165
Holland v Hodgson (1872) LR 7 CP 328 — 151, 154
Holme v Brunskill (1878) 3 QBD 495 — 35
Hopcutt v Carver (1969) 209 EG 1069 — 200
Hopwood v Rugeley Urban District Council [1975] 1 WLR 373 — 107
Horowitz v Ferrand [1956] CLY 4843 — 201
Hounslow London Borough Council v Pilling [1994] 1 All ER 432 — 278
Howard v Midrome Ltd [1991] 03 EG 135 — 101
Howkins v Jardine [1951] 1 KB 614 — 230
Hugall v M'Lean (1885) 53 LT 94 — 114
Hughes v Waite [1957] 1 All ER 603 — 80
Hunt v Decca Navigator Co. Ltd (1972) 222 EG 625 — 202
Hurstfell Ltd v Leicester Square Property Co. Ltd [1988] 37 EG 109 — 200
Hussein v Mehlman [1992] 32 EG 59 — 87, 111, 135, 147, 148, 150, 264, 265
Hyman v Rose [1912] AC 623 — 141
Hynes v Twinsectra Ltd [1995] 35 EG 136 — 144

I. and H. Caplan Ltd v Caplan (No. 2) [1963] 1 WLR 1247 — 204
Industrial Properties (Barton Hill) Ltd v Associated Electrical Industrial Ltd
   [1977] QB 580 — 14, 256
Ingram v Inland Revenue Commissioners [1997] 4 All ER 395 — 20
International Drilling Fluids Ltd v Louisville Investments (Uxbridge) Ltd [1986] Ch 513 — 72
Issa v Hackney London Borough Council [1997] 1 All ER 999 — 104

Jackson v Pekic [1989] 47 EG 141 — 164, 166
Jenkin R. Lewis & Son Ltd v Kerman [1971] Ch 477 — 155
Jenkins v Jackson (1888) 40 ChD 71 — 62, 68
Jervis v Harris [1996] 1 EGLR 78 — 99, 273
Jeune v Queens Cross Properties Ltd [1974] Ch 97 — 100
Joan Barrie v GUS Property Management Ltd (1981) 259 EG 628 — 203, 208
Johnsey Estates Ltd v Lewis Manley (Engineering) Ltd (1987) 284 EG 1240 — 45
Johnson v Moreton [1980] AC 37 — 232
Jones v Llanrwst Urban Council [1911] 1 Ch 393 — 86
Joseph v LCC (1914) 111 LT 276 — 123

Kaye v Massbetter Ltd [1991] 39 EG 129 — 170

Keen v Holland [1984] 1 EGLR 9   231
Kelson v Imperial Tobacco Co. Ltd [1957] 2 QB 334   88
Kennealy v Dunne [1977] QB 837   175
Kenny v Preen [1963] 1 QB 499   68
Kiddle v City Business Properties Ltd [1942] 1 KB 269   62, 70
Killick v Second Covent Garden Property Co. Ltd [1973] 1 WLR 658   78
King, Deceased, Robinson v Gray, Re [1963] Ch 459   30, 34, 132, 269
King's Motors (Oxford) Ltd v Lax [1970] 1 WLR 426, [1969] 3 All ER 665   118, 128, 129
King v Jackson [1998] 03 EG 138   56, 60
Kingston upon Thames RLBC v Prince [1998] EGCS 179   252
Kingswood Estate Co. Ltd v Anderson [1963] 2 QB 169   15
Kitney v MEPC Ltd [1977] 1 WLR 981   130
Kleinwort Benson Ltd v Lincoln City Council [1998] 3 WLR 1095   268
Knight,, Re ex parte Voisey (1882) 21 Ch D 442   17, 21
Kumar v Dunning [1987] 3 WLR 1167   33, 35, 41, 42

Lace v Chantler [1944] KB 368   21, 26
Lam Kee Ying v Lam Shes Tong [1975] AC 247   85
Lambert v FW Woolworth & Co. Ltd (No. 2) [1938] Ch 883   117, 124
Land Reclamation Ltd v Basildon District Council (1979) 250 EG 549   207
Lander and Bagley's Contract, Re [1892] 3 Ch 41   65
Langford Property Co. Ltd v Tureman [1949] 1 KB 29   160, 164, 166, 169, 186
Laurence v Lexcourt Holdings Ltd [1978] 2 All ER 810   24
Lee-Parker v Izzet [1971] 1 WLR 1688   100, 254, 257
Lee v K Carter [1949] 1 KB 85   75
Lee-Verhulst (Investments) Ltd v Harwood Trust [1973] 1 QB 204   204, 221
Leeds v Cheetham (1827) 1 Sim 146   133
Leek and Moorlands Building Society v Clark [1952] 2 QB 788   278
Leigh v Taylor [1902] AC 157   152
Lemmerbell Ltd v Britannia LAS Direct Ltd [1998] 48 EG 188   159
Lewis v Weldcrest Ltd [1978] 1 WLR 1107   207
Linden v Department of Health and Social Security [1986] 1 WLR 164   205, 221
Lister v Lane [1893] 2 QB 212   93
Liverpool City Council v Irwin [1977] AC 239   274
Lloyds Bank Ltd v City of London Corporation [1983] Ch 192   218
London & County (A & D) Ltd v Wilfred Sportsman Ltd [1971] Ch 764   23, 34, 269
London & Manchester Assurance Co. Ltd v GA Dunn & Co. (1983) 265 EG 39   122
London Borough of Enfield v McKeon (1986) 18 HLR 330   246
Loria v Hammer [1989] 2 EGLR 249   113
Lory v Brent London Borough Council [1971] 1 WLR 823   231
Luganda v Service Hotels [1969] 2 Ch 209   162
Lurcott v Wakeley and Wheeler [1911] KB 905   95
Lyttleton Times Co. Ltd v Warners Ltd [1970] AC 476   63

M. W. Kellog Ltd v F. Tobin (unreported, 8 April 1999)   46
Mackley v Nutting [1949] 2 KB 55   256
Malpas v St Ermin's Property Co. Ltd (1992) 24 HLR 537   191
Malzy v Eicholz [1916] 2 KB 308   70
Manchester Brewery Co. v Combs [1901] 2 Ch 608   16
Manfield & Sons Ltd v Botchin [1970] 2 QB 612   255
Mannai Investment Co. Ltd v Eagle Star Life Assurance Co. Ltd
    [1997] 2 WLR 945   157, 158, 159
Mason v Nwokorie [1994] 05 EG 155   55, 60
Matania v National Provincial Bank Ltd [1936] 2 All ER 633   70

Matthews v Smallwood [1910] 1 Ch 777   138, 261
Maugham, Re, ex parte Monkhouse (1885) 14 QBD 956   14
McAuley v Bristol City Council [1992] 1 All ER 749   90, 105, 107, 108
McCombie v Grand Junction Co. Ltd [1962] 1 WLR 581   210
McDougall v Easington District Council [1989] 25 EG 104   93
McEacham v Colton [1902] 2 AC 104   86
McGreal v Wake (1984) 269 EG 1254   99, 113, 114, 115
McHale v Daneham (1979) 249 EG 969   164, 166
McNerny v Lambeth London Borough Council [1989] 19 EG 77   90, 102, 103
Meadows v Clerical, Medical and General Life Assurance Society [1981] Ch 70   144
Meah v Sector Properties Ltd [1974] 1 WLR 547   203, 208
Mecca Leisure Ltd v Renown Investments (Holdings) Ltd (1984) 271 EG 989   121
Melles & Co. v Holme [1918] 2 KB 100   112, 113, 115
Melville v Bruton [1997] 29 EG 319   56
Methuen-Campbell v Walters [1979] QB 525   192
Metropolitan Properties Co. (FGC) Ltd v Barder [1968] 1 WLR 286   164
Micrografix Ltd v Woking 8 Ltd [1995] 37 EG 179   158
Midland Bank plc v Chart Enterprises Inc [1990] 44 EG 68   82
Midland Railways Co.'s Agreement, Re [1971] Ch 725   6, 21, 26, 27
Mikeover Ltd v Brady [1989] 3 All ER 618   13
Milmo v Carreras [1946] KB 306   23, 25
Minja Properties Ltd v Cussins Property Group plc [1998] 30 EG 114   96
Mistry v Isidore [1990] 31 EG 43   175
Monmouth Borough Council v Marlog [1994] 44 EG 240   13
Monson v Bound [1954] 1 WLR 1321   230
Moore and Hulm's Contract, Re [1912] 2 Ch 105   24
Moore Properties (Ilford) Ltd v McKeon [1976] 1 WLR 1278   86
Morcom v Campbell-Johnson [1956] 1 QB 106   109
Morgan v Murch [1970] 1 WLR 778   177
Morrisons Holdings Ltd v Manders Property (Wolverhampton) Ltd [1976] 1 WLR 533   204
Mosley v Cooper [1990] 1 EGLR 124   125
Moss Bros Group plc v CSC Properties Ltd [1999] EGCS 47   76
Moule v Garrett (1872) LR 7 Ex 101   35, 39, 45
Mount Cook Land Ltd v Hartley [2000] EGCS 26   85
Mumford Hotels Ltd v Wheler [1964] Ch 117   133
Murphy v Sawyer-Hoare (1993) 27 EG 127   36
Murray v Aslam (1995) 27 HLR 284   60

Naishe v Curzon (1984) 273 EG 1221   175
Narcissi v Wolfe [1960] Ch 10   210
National Carriers Ltd v Panalpina (Northern) Ltd [1981] AC 675   133, 135, 147, 148, 265
Nelson Developments Ltd v Taboada [1992] 34 EG 72   160, 163, 165
New England Properties plc v Portsmouth New Shops Ltd [1993] 23 EG 130   94
New Zealand Government Property Corporation v HM and S Ltd [1982] 1 All ER 624   156
Newman v Keedwell (1977) 35 P & CR 393   233
Norfolk Capital Group Ltd v Kitway Ltd [1977] QB 506   75
Northampton Borough Council v Lovatt [1998] 07 EG 142   247
Norwich Union Life Insurance v Low Profile Fashions (1992) 64 P & CR 187   33, 44
Nozari-Zadeh v Pearl Assurance plc (1987) 283 EG 457   205, 211
Nurdin & Peacock plc v DB Ramsden & Co. Ltd (No. 2) [1999] 1 All ER 941   268
Nynehead Developments Ltd v RH Fibreboard Containers Ltd [1999] 02 EG 139   149

O'Brien v Robinson [1973] AC 912   113
O'Cedar Ltd v Slough Trading Co. [1927] 2 KB 123   55

O'May v City of London Real Property Co. Ltd [1983] 2 AC 726 210, 225
Old Grovebury Manor Farm Ltd v W. Seymour Plant Sales & Hire Ltd (No. 2)
[1979] 1 WLR 1397 87, 139
Orlando Investments Ltd v Grosvenor Estate Belgravia (1989) 59 P & CR 21 75, 78
Otter v Norman [1989] AC 129 160, 163, 165
Owen v Gadd [1956] 2 QB 99 68

P & A Swift Investments v Combined English Stores Group plc
[1988] 3 WLR 313 35, 41, 42, 43
Packaging Centre v Poland Street Estate [1961] EG 189 78
Palmiero, Re [1999] 38 EG 195 152
Palser v Grinling [1948] AC 291 165
Parc Battersea Ltd v Hutchinson [1999] 22 EG 149 7, 23, 25
Parkins v Westminster City Council [1998] 13 EG 145 163, 164
Parrish v Kinsey (1983) 268 EG 1113 235
Passley v London Borough of Wandsworth (1997) 61 Conv 59 115
Peabody Donation Fund Governors v Grant (1982) 264 EG 925 251
Pegler v Craven [1952] 2 QB 69 211
Pellatt v Boosey (1862) 31 LJ CP 281 260
Pembery v Lamdin [1940] 2 All ER 434 94, 95, 109
Pennell v Payne [1995] QB 192 234
Perera v Vandiyar [1953] 1 WLR 672 68
Pimms v Tallow Chandlers [1964] 2 QB 547 82
Pocock v Steel [1985] 1 WLR 229 174
Poland v Earl of Cadogan [1980] 3 All ER 544 192, 193
Poppet's (Caterers) Ltd v Maidenhead BC [1971] 1 WLR 69 247
Port v Griffith [1938] 1 All ER 295 54
Post Office v Aquarius Properties Ltd [1987] 1 All ER 1055 103, 109
Premier Rinks v Amalgamated Cinematograph Theatres Ltd (1912) 56 Sol Jo 536 78
Preston Borough Council v Fairclough (1982) 8 HLR 70 155, 266
Propert v Parker (1832) 3 My & K 280 64
Proudfoot v Hart (1890) 25 QBD 42 92, 96, 109
Proudreed Ltd v Microgen Holdings plc [1996] 12 EG 127 155
Prudential Assurance Co. Ltd v London Residuary Body [1992] 3 WLR 279 6, 19, 21, 25, 26

Quick v Taff Ely Borough Council [1986] QB 809 62, 103, 109

R v Bristol City Council, ex parte Everett [1998] 3 All ER 603 107
R v Crown Court at Liverpool, ex parte Cooke [1996] 4 All ER 589 104
R v London Borough of Croydon, ex parte Toth (1986) 18 HLR 493 155, 157, 266
R v Phekoo [1981] 1 WLR 1117 56
R v Plymouth City Council and Cornwall City Council, ex parte Freeman
(1987) 19 HLR 328 243
R v Rent Officer for London Borough of Camden, ex parte Plant (1980) 257 EG 713 164, 166
R v Yuthiwattana (1984) 16 HLR 49 56, 58
Rainbow Estates Ltd v Tokenhold Ltd [1998] 3 WLR 980 99, 109, 111
Ramdath v Oswald Daley [1993] 20 EG 123 59
Ravenseft Properties Ltd v Davstone (Holdings) Ltd [1980] QB 12 93, 94, 96, 264
Reading Borough Council v Isley [1981] CLY 1323 248, 251
Receiver for the Metropolitan Police District v Palacegate Properties Ltd [2000] 13 EG 187 199
Redspring v Francis [1973] 1 WLR 134 170, 171, 172
Reed Personnel Services plc v American Express Ltd [1997] 1 EGLR 229 129
Regalgrand Ltd v Dickerson [1996] EGCS 182 56
Rendall v Roberts and Stacey (1959) 175 EG 265 82

Reohorn v Barry Corporation [1956] 1 WLR 845 — 209
Reynolds v Phoenix Assurance Co. Ltd (1978) 247 EG 995 — 133
Richmond v Savill [1926] 2 KB 530 — 156
Rimmer v Liverpool City Council [1985] QB 1 — 90, 102, 103
Roberts v Church Commissioners for England [1972] 1 QB 278 — 192
Roberts v Macilwraith-Christie (1987) 1 EGLR 224 — 173
Robinson v Kilvert (1889) 41 ChD 88 — 70
Roland House Gardens v Cravitz (1975) 29 P & CR 432 — 169
Romulus Trading Co. Ltd v Comet Properties Ltd [1996] 2 EGLR 70 — 54
Rookes v Barnard [1964] AC 1129 — 59
Ropemaker Properties Ltd v Noonhaven Ltd (1989) 2 EGLR 50 — 260
Rose v Gossman (1966) 201 EG 767 — 82
Ross Auto Wash Ltd v Herbert (1978) 250 EG 971 — 206, 211
Rous v Mitchell [1991] 1 All ER 676 — 236
Rowe v Truelove (1977) 241 EG 533 — 175
Royal Life Saving Society v Page [1978] 1 WLR 1329 — 206
Rutherford v Maurer [1962] 1 QB 16 — 230, 231
Rye v Rye [1962] AC 496 — 20

S. Schneiders and Sons Ltd v Abrahams [1925] 1 KB 301 — 176
Sampson v Wilson [1995] 3 WLR 455 — 59
Sarson v Roberts [1895] 2 QB 395 — 102
Savva v Houssein [1996] 47 EG 138 — 138, 261
Scala House & District Property Co. Ltd v Forbes [1974] 1 QB 575 — 85, 137, 139, 261
Segal Securities Ltd v Thoseby [1963] 1 QB 887 — 138, 141, 260
Selous Street Properties Ltd v Oronel Fabrics Ltd (1984) 270 EG 643 — 34, 35, 45
Sharpe v Duke Street Securities (1987) 2 EGLR 106 — 191
Shaw v Lomas (1888) 59 LT 477 — 156
Sheldon v West Bromwich Corporation (1973) 25 P & CR 360 — 114
Shelfer v City of London Electric Lighting Co. [1895] 1 Ch 287 — 86
Shepherds Bush Housing Association Ltd v HATS Co-operative [1992] 24 HLR 176 — 244
Shiloh Spinners Ltd v Harding [1973] AC 691 — 140
Shine v Freedman [1926] EGD 376 — 176
Shirclar Properties Ltd v Heinitz (1983) 268 EG 362 — 122
Shortlands Investments Ltd v Cargill plc [1995] 08 EG 163 — 98
Siddiqui v Rashid [1980] 1 WLR 1018 — 172
Sight & Sound Education Ltd v Books etc. Ltd [1999] 43 EG 161 — 218
Smedley v Chumley & Hawke Ltd (1981) 261 EG 775 — 264
Smirk v Lyndale Developments Ltd [1975] Ch 317 — 155
Smith v Bradford Metropolitan Council (1982) 44 P & CR 171 — 108
Smith v Cardiff Corporation (No. 2) [1955] Ch 159 — 269
Smith v Jenkins (1979) 129 NLJ 198 — 59
Smith v Marrable (1843) 11 M & W 5 — 102, 274
Somma v Hazelhurst [1978] 1 WLR 1014 — 12
Southern Depot Co. Ltd v British Railways Board [1990] 2 EGLR 39 — 85, 141
Southwark London Borough Council v Mills [1999] 4 All ER 449 — 55, 60, 61, 63, 68, 69, 70
Sparkes v Smart [1990] 2 EGLR 245 — 233
Spencer's Case (1583) 5 Co Rep 16a — 44
Spiro v Glencrown Properties Ltd [1990] 1 All ER 600 — 128
Spyer v Phillipson [1931] 2 Ch 183 — 153
Stacey v Hill [1901] 1 QB 660 — 36
Standard Pattern Co. Ltd v Ivey [1962] Ch 432 — 142
Star Rider Ltd v Inntrepreneur Pub Co. [1998] EGLR 53 — 254, 258
Staves v Leeds City Council [1992] 29 EG 119 — 103

Steadman v Steadman [1976] AC 536 — 7, 15, 18
Stent v Monmouth District Council (1987) 282 EG 705 — 103
Stone v Whitcombe (1980) 40 P & CR 296 — 231
Stratford v Syrett [1958] 1 QB 107 — 256
Street v Mountford [1985] AC 809 — 9, 10, 11, 182, 276
Stumbles v Whitley [1930] AC 544 — 207
Swanbrae Ltd v Elliott (1987) 281 EG 916 — 177
Swanson v Forton [1949] Ch 143 — 75

Tagro v Cafane [1991] 1 WLR 378 — 55, 60
Tandon v Trustees of Spurgeons Homes [1982] AC 755 — 192
Taylor Fashions v Liverpool Victoria Trustees [1982] QB 133 — 130
The Royal Borough of Kensington and Chelsea v Hayden (1985) 17 HLR 114 — 244
Thomas Bookman Ltd v Natham [1955] 1 WLR 815 — 75
Thorn EMI Pension Trust Ltd v Quinton Hazell plc (1984) 269 EG 414 — 120
Tickner v Hearn [1960] 1 WLR 1406 — 161
Torrens v Walker [1906] 2 Ch 166 — 114
Total Oil Great Britain Ltd v Thompson Garages (Biggin Hill) Ltd [1972] 1 QB 318 — 135, 264
Trane (UK) Ltd v Provident Mutual Life Assurance [1995] 1 EGLR 33 — 130
Transworld Land Co. v J. Sainsbury plc [1990] 2 EGLR 255 — 52
Tredegar v Harwood [1929] AC 72 — 132
Trustees of Henry Smith's Charity v Willson [1983] QB 316 — 138
Tulk v Moxhay (1848) 2 Ph 774 — 86, 87

Unchained Growth plc v Granby Village (Manchester) Management Co. Ltd
   [1999] EGCS 116 — 254, 258
United Scientific Holdings Ltd v Burnley Borough Council [1978] AC 904 — 116, 121
Universities Superannuation Scheme Ltd v Marks & Spencer plc [1990] 04 EG 158 — 268
Upsons Ltd v E. Robins Ltd [1956] 1 QB 131 — 210

Van Haarlam v Kasner Charitable Trust [1992] 36 EG 135 — 138, 260
VCS Carpark Management Ltd v Regional Railways North East Ltd [2000] 1 All ER 403 — 209
Venetian Glass Gallery Ltd v Next Properties Ltd [1989] 30 EG 92 — 79
Voisey, Ex parte (1882) 21 ChD 442 — 277

Walker v Ogilvy (1974) 28 P & CR 288 — 160, 169
Wallace v Manchester City Council (1998) 30 HLR 1111 — 100
Wallis Fashion Group Ltd v General Accident Life Assurance Ltd [2000] EGCS 45 — 39, 73
Walrond v Hawkins (1875) LR 10 CP 342 — 137
Walsh v Lonsdale (1882) 21 Ch D 9 — 13, 14, 18, 23, 24, 25
Wandsworth London Borough Council v Fadayomi [1987] 3 All ER 474 — 248
Wandsworth London Borough Council v Osei-Bonsu [1999] 1 All ER 265 — 55, 56
Wansbech District Council v Marley (1988) 20 HLR 247 — 247
Wardell v Usher (1841) 3 Scott NR 508 — 153
Warmington v Miller [1973] QB 877 — 15
Warner v Sampson [1959] 1 QB 297 — 66
Warnford Investments Ltd v Duckworth [1979] Ch 127 — 36
Warren v Keen [1954] 1 QB 15 — 90, 246, 275
Warren v Marketing Exchange for Africa Ltd [1988] 2 EGLR 247 — 79
Webb v Pollmount Ltd [1966] 1 All ER 481 — 130
Webb v Sandown Sports Club Ltd [2000] EGCS 13 — 204
Welch v Birrane (1975) 29 P & CR 102 — 137
Weller v Akehurst [1981] 3 All ER 411 — 120
West Country Cleaners (Falmouth) Ltd v Saly [1966] 3 All ER 210 — 118, 129

West Layton Ltd v Ford [1979] 1 QB 593   75
Westminster City Council v Clarke [1992] AC 288, [1992] 1 All ER 695   10, 11, 244
Wetherall v Smith [1980] 1 WLR 1290   230
WG Clark (Properties) Ltd v Dupre Properties Ltd [1991] 3 WLR 579   66
WH Smith Ltd v Wyndham Investments Ltd [1994] EGCS 94   36
Wheeldon v Burrows (1879) 12 Ch D 31   16
Wheeler v Mercer [1957] AC 416   255
White and Carter (Councils) Ltd v McGregor [1963] AC 413   157
Whitworth v Lipton [1993] EGCS 172   175
Whycer v Urry [1956] JPL 365   70
Wilkes v Goodwin [1923] 2 KB 86   165
William Boyer & Sons Ltd v Adams (1976) 32 P & CR 89   204
Williams v Earle (1868) LR 3 QB 739   86, 137
Wisbech St Mary Parish Council v Lilley [1956] 1 WLR 121   66
Woking Borough Council v Bystram [1993] EGCS 208   247
Wolff v Waddington [1989] 47 EG 148   166, 185
Wolmer Securities Ltd v Corne [1966] 2 QB 243   161
Wood Factory Property Ltd v Kiritos Property Ltd [1985] 2 NSWLR 105   150
Woods v Pope (1895) 6 C & P 732   98
Woodspring District Council v Taylor (1982) 4 HLR 95   247
Wright v Mortimer (1996) 72 P & CR D36   206

Yank Ltd v Havering London Borough Council [1998] EGCS 75   55
Yanover v Romford Finance & Development Co. Ltd (1983), unreported   95
Yates v Morris [1950] 2 All ER 577   176
Yaxley v Gott [2000] 1 All ER 711   15

Zenith Investments (Torquay) Ltd v Kammins Ballrooms Co. Ltd (No. 2)
    [1971] 1 WLR 1751   203

Table of Statutes

Administration of Justice Act 1985
  s. 55(5) 142
Agricultural Holdings Act 1948 233, 242
  s. 1(2) 230
Agricultural Holdings Act 1986
  227, 229, 231, 232, 233, 239, 240,
  241, 242
  Part I 241
  s. 1(1) 229
  s. 1(4) 229
  s. 1(5) 230
  s. 2 229, 230, 231
  s. 2(2) 230
  s. 2(2)(a)–(b) 230
  s. 2(3)(a) 231
  s. 3 230
  s. 10 153
  s. 25(1) 232
  s. 26 234
  s. 26(1) 232
  s. 26(2) 234
  s. 27(2)–(3) 235
  s. 27(4) 236
  s. 28 235
  s. 28(5) 235
  s. 60 242
  s. 96(1) 229
  Sch. 3, Part I
    Case A (smallholdings) 234
    Case B (planning consent) 234, 236
    Case C (certificate of bad
      husbandry) 234
    Case D (non-compliance to pay rent or
      to remedy breaches) 234, 235
    Case E (irredeemable breaches) 234
    Case F (insolvency) 234
    Case G (death of tenant) 234
    Case H (ministerial certificates)
      234

Agricultural Tenancies Act 1995
  v, 227, 239, 240, 241, 242
  s. 9 241
Apportionment Act 1870
  s. 3 156
Arbitration Act 1996 224
  s. 34(2)(d) 224
  s. 34(2)(f) 224

Chancery Amendment Act 1858 88
Common Law Procedure Act 1852
  s. 210 141, 142
  s. 211 141
  s. 212 141, 142
Contracts (Rights of Third Parties)
    Act 1999 v, 31, 49, 50, 51, 52, 53
  s. 1 51
  s. 1(7) 52
County Courts Act 1984
  s. 9A 142
  s. 138 49, 184
  s. 138(3)–(4) 142
  s. 138(9A) 142
  s. 139 49
Criminal Law Act 1977 56
  s. 6(1) 56
  s. 6(3) 59
  s. 7 56
  s. 12(3) 56

Defective Premises Act 1972
  s. 4 90, 105, 107
  s. 4(1) 107
  s. 4(4) 107, 108
Distress for Rent Act 1737
  s. 16 266

Environmental Protection Act 1990 67, 104
  s. 79 90, 104

Environmental Protection Act 1990
    — *continued*
  s. 79(1)(a)   104, 107
  ss. 80–81   90, 104
  s. 82   90, 104

Fires Prevention (Metropolis) Act 1774
    133
  s. 83   133

Housing Act 1957
  s. 6   102, 274
Housing Act 1961
  s. 32   106, 274
Housing Act 1980   166
  s. 69   162, 167
Housing Act 1985   165, 243, 247,
      248, 249, 251, 252,
      270, 278
  Part IV   243, 245
  Part V   250
  s. 79(1)   243, 245
  s. 79(3)–(4)   244
  s. 80   243, 245
  s. 81   243, 246
  s. 82(1)   246
  s. 83(2)   246
  s. 84(2)(b)   246
  ss. 87–90   250
  s. 91   249
  s. 91(1)   270
  s. 92   249
  s. 93   249
  s. 93(1)(a)–(b)   249
  s. 94   249, 82
  s. 94(2)   250
  s. 95   249
  s. 96   100, 249
  s. 96(1)   250
  s. 97   249, 250
  s. 97(3)   250
  ss. 98–101   249, 250
  ss. 102–103   250
  s. 113(1)   251
  s. 604   63, 110
  Sch. 1   244, 246
  Sch. 2   245
      ground 1   246, 247
      ground 2   246, 247
      grounds 3–9   246
      ground 10   246, 247, 248
      grounds 11–16   246
      Parts I–IV   246
  Sch. 3   249

Housing Act 1988   56, 57, 58, 59, 60, 74, 75,
      168, 169, 177, 179, 180, 181, 182, 184,
      186, 187, 228, 236, 237, 238, 239, 276,
      278, 279
  Part I   3, 160, 164, 178–88, 228, 236, 239,
      268, 270
  s. 1   184
  s. 1(1)(a)   182
  s. 5(1)   183, 184, 270
  s. 5(2)   181, 184, 185
  s. 5(3)   186
  s. 5(4)   185
  s. 7(3)   184
  s. 7(4)   238
  s. 8   184, 270, 271
  s. 8(3)   184, 270
  s. 13   57, 187, 188
  s. 13(1)   186
  s. 14   187
  s. 14(1)–(3)   187
  s. 20(4)   185
  s. 21   279
  s. 21(1)   180, 185
  s. 21(1)(b)   279
  s. 21(2)   180
  s. 21(3)   185
  s. 22   188
  s. 22(1)   188
  s. 22(2)   188
  s. 22(2)(a)   188
  s. 22(3)(a)   188
  s. 22(3)(b)–(c)   188
  s. 24(3)   238
  s. 25(1)(b)   238
  s. 25(2)   238
  s. 27   55, 59, 60, 238
  s. 27(3)   55, 59, 60
  s. 27(6)   60
  s. 27(7)   60
  s. 27(7)(a)   56
  s. 27(8)(a)   55
  s. 28   56, 59, 60
  s. 28(1)   55, 60
  s. 28(3)(a)   56
  s. 29   162
  s. 36(1)   162
  s. 39   168
  s. 39(5)–(6)   177
  s. 45(3)   278
  s. 45(4)   184
  s. 66   161
  s. 76   168, 176
  s. 116   90, 104, 274
  Sch. 1   180, 181, 279

Housing Act 1988 — *continued*
    paras 9–10   181
    para. 22   181
  Sch. 2   184, 270
    grounds 1–2   184
    grounds 5–7   184
    ground 8   184, 185, 270, 271
    ground 9   184
    ground 10   184, 185, 270
    ground 11   184, 185, 270, 271
    ground 16   184, 238
  Sch. 2A
    para. 9   239
  Sch. 4   168, 176
  Sch. 7   161
  Sch. 17
    para. 33   185
Housing Act 1996   vi, 178, 195, 236, 239,
    276, 278
  s. 96   178, 180, 279
  s. 99   179, 180
  s. 106   192
  s. 144   247
  Sch. 9   192

Insolvency Act 1986
  s. 178   36
  s. 178(4)   36
  s. 181   36

Judicature Acts 1873–1875
    14

Land Charges Act 1972   19, 130
  s. 2(4)   15
Land Registration Act 1925
  s. 24   39
  s. 24(1)   35, 45
  s. 48   15
  s. 70(1)(g)   15, 18, 130
Landlord and Tenant Act 1927   198, 202,
    216, 217
  Part I   126, 216
  s. 9   126
  s. 17   216
  s. 18   90, 98, 201
  s. 18(1)   98, 272
  s. 19(1)   39, 71, 72, 74, 78, 81,
    137, 260
  s. 19(2)   117, 123, 124, 125
  s. 19(3)   117, 123, 126
Landlord and Tenant Act 1954   147, 150,
    198, 199, 212, 216, 218, 219, 223, 224,
    225

Landlord and Tenant Act 1954 — *continued*
  Part II   vi, 22, 25, 32, 33, 75, 147, 150,
    198, 199, 200, 204, 205, 207, 209,
    212, 213, 218, 219, 220, 221, 222,
    223, 225, 231, 255, 256, 259, 261,
    263, 265
  s. 23   203, 206, 220, 221
  s. 23(1)   203, 204, 207, 211, 213, 220
  s. 23(2)   203, 206
  s. 23(3)   209
  s. 23(4)   207
  s. 24   37, 198, 199, 204, 208, 219, 221,
    261, 265
  s. 24(1)   33, 202, 219
  s. 24(2)   150
  s. 24A   37
  s. 25   199, 202, 203, 208, 209, 214, 215,
    217, 218, 220, 261, 262
  s. 26   199, 214, 215, 218, 220, 222
  s. 28   199
  s. 29   203, 210, 223
  s. 29(3)   208
  s. 30   200, 220, 223
  s. 30(1)   198, 202, 262
  s. 30(1)(a)   223, 262
  s. 30(1)(b)   200, 223, 262
  s. 30(1)(c)   201, 223, 262
  s. 30(1)(d)   210, 223
  s. 30(1)(e)   210, 217, 218, 223, 262
  s. 30(1)(f)   201, 202, 207, 209, 210, 217,
    218, 223, 262
  s. 30(1)(g)   202, 207, 209, 210, 213, 217,
    218, 223, 262
  s. 30(1)(h)   213
  s. 30(3)   202, 213
  s. 31   223
  s. 31(2)   201
  s. 32   203, 210, 223
  s. 32(2)–(3)   210
  ss. 33–35   203, 210, 223
  s. 37   202, 218
  s. 37(1)   217, 262
  s. 37(2)   217
  s. 38   218
  s. 38(1)   72
  s. 40   213, 214
  s. 41   211
  s. 41(2)   202
  s. 42   206
  s. 42(3)   202
  s. 47   217
  s. 53   73, 77, 80, 81
  s. 53(1)(b)   125
  s. 64   203, 262

Landlord and Tenant Act 1985   70
  s. 8   62, 63, 70, 90, 102, 110, 274
  s. 8(3)   102
  s. 8(4)   274
  s. 10   102
  s. 11   62, 69, 70, 90, 103, 104, 105, 106,
    107, 110, 114, 148, 264, 274
  s. 11(1)(a)   103
  s. 11(1A)(a)   104, 275
  s. 11(1A)(b)   275
  s. 11(1B)   275
  s. 13   103
  s. 17(1)   100
Landlord and Tenant Act 1987
  Part II   101
Landlord and Tenant Act 1988   72, 74, 81,
    82, 83, 84
  s. 1   73, 78, 80
  s. 1(3)   83
  s. 1(4)   77, 79
  s. 1(6)   82
  s. 2   82
  s. 3   83
  s. 4   73, 82
Landlord and Tenant (Covenants) Act 1995
    v, 29, 30, 33, 34, 35, 37, 38, 39, 40, 42,
    43, 44, 46, 47, 48, 49, 50, 51, 52, 72
  s. 3(5)   51
  s. 5   47
  s. 7   40
  s. 16   47
  s. 17   29, 38, 39, 44, 45, 48, 49
  s. 18   35, 48
  ss. 19–20   48
Law of Property Act 1922
  Sch. 15   128
Law of Property Act 1925
  s. 26(3)   278
  s. 40   6, 15, 18, 128, 129, 155
  s. 52   7
  s. 52(1)   13, 17, 154
  s. 52(2)   13, 157
  s. 52(2)(c)   155
  s. 53   7
  s. 53(1)(a)   269
  s. 54   7
  s. 54(2)   13, 17, 18, 21, 180, 269, 270,
    273, 277
  s. 62   16
  s. 72   20
  s. 72(3)–(4)   20
  s. 77   39
  s. 77(1)   45
  s. 77(1)(c)   35, 45

Law of Property Act 1925 — *continued*
  s. 79(1)   43
  s. 82(1)   20
  s. 136(1)   42
  s. 139   156
  s. 141   34
  s. 141(1)   42, 269
  s. 144   80
  s. 146   23, 85, 90, 97, 136, 138, 140, 260,
    261
  s. 146(1)   97, 273
  s. 146(2)   85, 98, 139, 140, 141, 260
  s. 147   96, 98, 141
  s. 149(6)   230
  s. 150(1)   156
  s. 205(1)   20
  s. 205(1)(ii)   15, 17
  s. 205(1)(xxvii)   255
Law of Property Act 1969   198
Law of Property (Miscellaneous Provisions)
    Act 1989   15
  s. 2   7, 15, 18, 24, 129, 155
  s. 2(1)   15
  s. 2(5)   15
  s. 2(5)(a)   18
Leasehold Property (Repairs) Act 1938
    90, 97, 98, 99, 273
  s. 1(5)   98
Leasehold Reform Act 1967   75, 137, 144,
    189, 190, 191, 192, 193
  s. 1   191, 192
  s. 2   191
  s. 2(1)   191
  s. 2(3)   192
  s. 3   192
  s. 4   192
  s. 4A   192
  s. 8(1)   194
  s. 9   193
  s. 9(4)   194
  ss. 17–18   193
Leasehold Reform Acts 1967–1982   127
Leasehold Reform, Housing and Urban
    Development Act 1993   127, 189, 190,
    192, 194, 195, 196, 197, 250
  Part I   189, 194
  Part II   194
  s. 13   196
  s. 65   192
  s. 66   194
  s. 121   100
  Sch. 15   194
Limitation Act 1980
  s. 15   256

Matrimonial Homes Act 1983
  s. 1(5)–(6)   185

Occupiers' Liability Act 1957   90

Powers of Criminal Courts Act 1973
  s. 35   104
Protection from Eviction Act 1977
  58, 59, 162, 167
  s. 1   55, 56
  s. 1(1)–(3)   58
  s. 2   56, 58
  s. 3   56
  s. 5   57, 176
Public Health Act 1936
  Part III   104

Race Relations Act 1976
  s. 24   71
Rent Act 1977   3, 12, 160–77, 178, 179,
    181, 182, 185, 187, 236, 237, 251, 255,
    256
  s. 2(1)   168
  s. 2(1)(a)   160
  ss. 4–6   180
  s. 7   165, 180
  s. 7(2)   163, 165
  ss. 8–11   180
  s. 12   165, 175, 180
  ss. 13–16   180
  s. 19   162, 167, 180
  s. 98   176
  s. 98(1)   161
  s. 106A   162, 167
  Sch. 1   168, 176
  Sch. 2
    para. 5   164

Rent Act 1977 — *continued*
  Sch. 15   161, 169
    case 2   175, 176
    case 11   173, 174, 175
    Part I   161
    Part II   161
    Part III   161
    Part IV   161, 171
      para. 5(1)(a)   173
      para. 5(1)(b)   172, 173
Rent Acts   75
Rent (Agriculture) Act 1976   228, 236, 237
  Part IV   238
  s. 2(4)   237
  s. 3   237
  s. 4   237
  s. 4(1)   237
  s. 6   237
  s. 7(2)   237
  s. 16   237
  Sch. 4   237
Rent (Amendment) Act 1985   174
Rentcharges Act 1977
  s. 2   268

Sex Discrimination Act 1975
  s. 31   71
Supreme Court Act 1981
  s. 37   101
  s. 38(1)   141, 142
  s. 50   88

Unfair Contract Terms Act 1977   257
  Sch. 1   258
    para. 1(b)   257

Validation of War Time Leases Act 1944   21

1   Introduction

This book has been written by two university lecturers who, apart from teaching landlord and tenant law at degree level to both law and non-law students, have also practised in this field for many years. Its aim is to give students detailed examples of suggested solutions to examination questions in landlord and tenant law, and to further their understanding and appreciation of the subject. It is also an attempt to give guidance on examination technique. One academic writer has described landlord and tenant law as a 'labyrinth of technicality, complexity and difficult concepts' Mitchell, B., *Landlord and Tenant Law*, Oxford: BSP Professional Books, 1987, Preface). It is true that many students who embark on the study of this subject do so with a sense of dread or, at best, unease. The student is faced with the double hurdle of mastering not only the basic common law rules but also the highly complex statutory codes which govern most forms of letting (i.e., residential, business, agricultural).

In landlord and tenant law, as with other law subjects, there exists no substitute for hard work. You will not pass the examination if you do not know the substance of the course. A student who hopes to do well must attend lectures and seminars and read the recommended textbooks and source materials (e.g., cases, statutes and articles). Knowledge of source material is vital to achieving good class 2:1 answers. For example, read the judgments of the cases, not just the headnotes! Devote time during the week to *reading* your lecture notes. As an aid to understanding and learning each topic, you may find it useful to draw a flowchart summarising how the various aspects of cases and statutory provisions within a topic fit together. Essentially, our advice is to think in terms of the examination *right from the start* of your course, and not just during the last few weeks when you hope to 'cram' everything into a brief revision period.

Plan your learning strategy well in advance so that your revision topics cover material you have already learnt and understood in depth during the months prior to the examination.

A good idea when you begin your course is to ensure that you thoroughly understand your syllabus. Check the various topics and, as the course progresses, earmark the key areas which are likely to come up and in which you feel you can do well in the examination. We would like to stress the importance of looking at past papers at an early stage in your course so that you 'get a feel' for the examiner's style and what standard of knowledge is expected of you. Past papers are usually available from your university/college bookshop or library. We also cannot stress enough the importance of attending any revision classes held by your subject lecturer. Such classes are likely to contain invaluable hints. You can expect any topical (controversial) subjects to be included in the examination (see, e.g., Question 5, **Chapter 6** and Question 2, **Chapter 11**).

Acquiring knowledge and understanding the subject is only part of the process of achieving success in examinations. To do well and to guarantee success, it is also necessary to *apply* your knowledge correctly to the question set. This book contains examination questions and answers covering several possible question variations within each topic. All the suggested answers are intended to be of a length which a student could reasonably be expected to produce within the time restraints of an examination. There is a mixture of problem and essay-type questions, both of which require a logical and structured approach which many students find difficult. The essay-type question may ask you to explain the meaning of a particular doctrine or principle (i.e., purely factual), or it may ask you to discuss a certain proposition which, sometimes, will be derived from a quotation. In either case, you should produce a well-structured answer explaining the meaning or significance of the doctrine, principle or proposition and its origin in common law, equity or statute, and cases which illustrate its application to the branch of law concerned (see, e.g., Question 2, **Chapter 2**). The problem type of question requires different skills. You may well be asked to advise one (or more) of the parties, or merely to discuss the legal consequences of the facts raised in the question.

In either case, you should devote some time to reading the question very carefully. Do not stray outside the boundaries of the question — irrelevant material will not gain you any marks! Answer the question set, not the question you wish had been set! Avoid long-windedness and waffle — your answer should be a clear, succinct piece of advice referring to the relevant case law and statutory provisions (see, e.g., Question 1, **Chapter 3**). Essentially, your initial task will be to identify the key issues and set out the fundamental principles involved. You must then apply your knowledge of the law to the specific issues posed, raising alternative arguments as part of a logical sequence of reasoning. Remember that the examiner is testing your ability to understand the issues and lucidly argue the case from the point of view of your client(s) on the established law. Make sure you have grasped the legal significance of all the factual data. There will usually be little in the way of superfluous material. A good tip (often used by the writers when reading solicitors' instructions) is to use a highlighting pen to pick out the salient factual points. Virtually all landlord and tenant law problems contain data which are time-significant. For example, the date of a residential letting may be crucial to determining whether the tenancy falls within the security of tenure provisions of the Rent Act 1977 or Pt I of the Housing Act 1988 (see, e.g., Question 1, **Chapter 9**). You should, therefore, pay particular attention to dates and times.

The examination paper will require you to answer a certain number of questions in a limited period of time. The questions, with possibly some exceptions, will carry equal marks. Read the instructions at the top of the examination paper carefully. Read the individual questions carefully. In your institution, you may be given a period of reading time prior to the actual start of the examination itself. Use this time wisely. Read the *whole* of the examination paper before selecting the questions you want to answer. Try to identify which areas of the syllabus are covered by which questions. Analyse the problem questions — jot down, as part of your rough work, what the examiner is looking for in your answer. Plan your answers — make a list of key cases and/or statutory provisions. You may be very thankful for this list during the examination when, for example, you are under pressure to complete an answer. Check the rubric — do not 'discuss' if you are asked to 'compare and contrast'. Above all, do not panic if some of the questions seem unfamiliar to you on first reading. Read the question(s) again and a few pennies may start to drop! Keep calm and do not be put off by the person sitting in front of you who has already started scribbling furiously. The chances are that he or she has not spent sufficient time digesting the question before putting pen to paper. Sadly, the writers commonly find the first side of an examination script contains nothing of any real relevance. Invariably, this turns out to be a script from a candidate who started writing from the first moment, allowing very little time for prior thought.

One of the great dangers during an examination is to spend too much time on any question. If you are running out of time, then complete your answer in note form. This will, at least, gain you some marks. A good tip is to mark down on your rough paper the various times at which you should be starting each question. If you stick to the timetable, you will avoid over-running and save yourself a lot of nerves!

We have already mentioned that your answers should be clear and concise. One common error among students is to write down the nature of every case that happens to deal with the topic concerned and then recite all the facts that he or she can remember. This will, undoubtedly, fill a lot of space on your answer booklet but will not gain you much respect from the examiner. You should cite only relevant cases, and no more facts should be stated than are absolutely essential to establish the relevance of each case. Remember, the more relevant authority you cite properly, the better your answer. If you cannot recall the name of the case, use some such phrase as 'in a decided case' or 'in a recent case'. Some questions, however, may hinge on only one or two cases where it may be appropriate to consider the facts in more detail (see, e.g., Question 4, **Chapter 8**). If you are citing a statute, be precise and try to refer to the section number(s).

As a matter of good style, use paragraphs to separate the various sections of your answer and write simple, straightforward sentences as much as possible. Sometimes, it may be useful to identify the fundamental problem in your opening paragraph (see, e.g., Question 3, **Chapter 2**). A clear conclusion is also helpful in your final paragraph (see, e.g., Question 2, **Chapter 5**). If the question specifically asks you to 'advise' one (or more) of the parties, it is sometimes useful actually to give the advice required in your concluding sentence (see, e.g., Question 4(b), **Chapter 6**). Another good tip regarding style (often ignored by students) is to underline the title of statutes or the name of cases. From our own experience, this makes the examiner's job much easier because he or she can see at a glance whether or not the relevant material has been covered in your script. In fact, anything that makes your paper easier to read will be much appreciated! Always write as neatly as you can; space out your answers sensibly; number your answers (including each part) clearly; begin a new answer on a fresh page. If you *plan* your answer carefully before putting pen to paper, you should be able to produce a well-written, tidy script. Increasingly, external examiners are stressing the importance of good presentation not only in students' assessed coursework but also in examinations. In order to do yourself justice, you should always try to get the examiner on your side by following the basic rules regarding legibility, spelling and presentation outlined above.

If you are dyslexic, or suffer from some other impairment which may affect your ability to write, do not hesitate to mention this to your personal tutor at an early stage in your course. You should not feel any shame in claiming any allowance to which you may be entitled (e.g., extra time, use of a word-processor, private room etc.). If you suffer from 'exam stress' generally, you should contact your student counsellor, who will be able to provide you with various strategies for coping with exam nerves. He or she will know a great deal about exam worries and how to overcome them. If you have any personal, financial or other problems which might affect your exam performance, you should also make these known to your tutor at an early stage. At the very least, a sympathetic ear may go some way towards relieving your anxieties.

A final word — try and keep up with recent cases and articles in your chosen revision topics. You should, for example, consult the *Estates Gazette*, *Landlord and Tenant Review* and the *Conveyancer and Property Lawyer* on a regular basis to see whether there have been any new developments in the case law and academic literature. Your examiner will obviously be impressed if you can show you are acquainted with any recent developments.

Good luck in your endeavours!

2   The Landlord and Tenant Relationship

INTRODUCTION

In this chapter, we have included six questions on a variety of subjects (i.e., leases and licences, certainty of term, the formalities of a lease, and types of tenancies) which loosely come under the heading of 'the landlord and tenant relationship'.

The lease/licence distinction has produced a welter of case law and academic discussion in articles and elsewhere — it is, therefore, a popular topic with examiners, especially now with the recent House of Lords ruling in *Bruton* v *London and Quadrant Housing Trust* [1999] 3 All ER 481 (see Question 1(a)).

Certainty of term has also been the subject of interesting case law (*Prudential Assurance Co. Ltd* v *London Residuary Body* [1992] 3 WLR 279, overruling *In Re Midland Railway Co.'s Agreement* [1971] Ch 725 and *Ashburn Anstalt* v *Arnold* [1989] Ch 1 on this point). You may, therefore, expect a question on this topic which may be coupled with the doctrine of repugnancy (see, e.g., *Centaploy Ltd* v *Matlodge Ltd* [1974] Ch 1): Question 6.

The subject of the formalities of a lease has become complicated by the fact that there are now two separate statutory provisions governing the validity of contracts for the disposition of interests in land. The Law of Property Act 1925, s. 40, continues to apply to contracts for the grant of a lease entered into before 27 September 1989. Note that a party to an oral agreement for the grant of a lease (entered into before this date) may be able to enforce the same in equity if he or she can establish a sufficient act of part performance made on the faith of the agreement (*Steadman* v *Steadman* [1976] AC 536). The Law of Property (Miscellaneous Provisions) Act 1989, s. 2, now governs contracts made on or after 27 September 1989. Under s. 2, a contract for the sale or other disposition of an interest in land can only be made in writing, and therefore the doctrine of part performance has been effectively abolished in relation to contracts made after this date. You should also be familiar with the provisions of the Law of Property Act 1925, ss. 52, 53 and 54, and the Court of Appeal decision in *Crago* v *Julian* [1992] 1 WLR 372, to the effect that the assignment of any tenancy at law (including an oral periodic tenancy) will not be valid unless made by deed (save in the case of assignments by operation of law: *Parc Battersea Ltd* v *Hutchinson* [1999] 2 EG 149).

Lastly, it is possible that you may be faced with a question on types of leases and tenancies. Below we have set out three straightforward questions on various aspects of this topic which we hope you will find it useful to work through during your revision programme:

1.   You act for Mr Gold, who is the tenant of 15 Wellington Avenue. He holds under a lease, dated 1 January 1920, for a term of 99 years from 25 December 1919. In 1994, Lord Wealth, the freeholder, granted a second lease of the property to Acreland Properties Ltd for a term of 21 years subject to and with the benefit of the existing lease granted to Mr Gold. Consider the position of the parties under these two leases.

2.   What is the legal effect of the following arrangements?:

    (a)   L agrees to sell his freehold farm to T. Before completion, L lets T into possession.

    (b)   L mistakenly thinks he owns Blackacre and agrees to let it to T.

    (c)   L lets land to T with an option 'to renew on the same terms including this option'.

    (d)   L allows T to occupy his land in return for a payment of £100 per year payable in monthly instalments.

3.   Albert holds over after the expiry of his 14-year lease. At first, his landlord, Nigel, is unaware of Albert's continued possession but later he writes to Albert saying that he is prepared to allow him to continue as tenant but failing to mention for what period he is to hold under him. Later, Albert tenders a

quarter's rent which is duly accepted by Nigel. Discuss Albert's current legal status and that existing during each stage of his period of holding over.

See also Question 5(a) (below).

Landlord and tenant courses vary as to the emphasis they give to the various subject areas dealt with in this chapter. The best advice we can give you is to be guided by your lecturer as to how much time you should devote to any one or more of these topics in preparing for your exam.

QUESTION 1

(a)   Assess critically the legal significance of the recent House of Lords' ruling in *Bruton* v *London and Quadrant Housing Trust* (1999).

(b)   Tom, Dick and Harriet are three law students who have recently approached Acrecrest Estates Ltd with a view to renting a flat for their use during the next academic session. They have each been handed a separate (but identical) document for signature headed 'Licence Agreement', which states that 'the Licensor shall grant and the Licensee shall accept a licence to share with two others each to be separately licensed by the Licensor and to the intent that the Licensee shall not have exclusive possession of the premises, for a term of 6 months at a monthly licence fee of £240'. Tom, Dick and Harriet are unhappy about the document they have been asked to sign and seek your advice as to their legal position.

Advise Tom, Dick and Harriet.

Commentary

The first part of this question requires a critical analysis of the surprising unanimous decision of the House of Lords in *Bruton*. Unfortunately, you will not score good marks if you simply regurgitate the facts of the case and outline the ruling. The question asks you to *assess critically* the legal significance of the decision, so you must be prepared to give an incisive commentary on the case. Show the examiner that you have read (and understood) some of the academic literature on the decision: see, for example, Pascoe, S., '*Street* v *Mountford* Gone too Far — *Bruton* v *London and Quadrant Housing Trust*' [1999] *Journal of Housing Law*, pp. 87–91.

Part (b) treads more familiar territory and gives you ample opportunity to regurgitate the House of Lords decision in *AG Securities* v *Vaughan/ Antoniades* v *Villiers* [1990] 1 AC 417, and the subsequent Court of Appeal decision in *Duke* v *Wynne* [1990] 1 WLR 766.

There is a wealth of reading on the subject of the lease/licence distinction. Of particular interest are Martin, J.E., *Residential Security*, London: Sweet & Maxwell, 1989, Ch. 2; Harpum, C., 'Leases, Licences, Sharing and Shams' [1989] CLJ 19; Hill, J., 'Shared Accommodation and Exclusive Possession'

(1989) 52 MLR 408 and Murdoch, S., 'The Lease/Licence Distinction' [1989] EG 8911, 22.

Suggested Answer

(a)   The House of Lords in *Bruton* has confirmed the principle that an agreement will confer on the occupier the status of a tenant if it gives a right to exclusive possession for a term, notwithstanding that the agreement was intended by the parties to create only a licence. Thus in *Bruton* itself, the agreement gave the occupant a right to exclusive possession because there was nothing to suggest that the occupant was to share possession with the Housing Trust or any other party. Mr Bruton did not fall to be classified as a lodger in the *Street* v *Mountford* sense since the Housing Trust had not retained an unlimited right to enter the accommodation for the purpose of providing attendance or services: see, *Westminster City Council* v *Clarke* [1992] AC 288 (HL), where the licence agreement was upheld on the basis that the council could change the subject accommodation without notice or require the occupant to share with any other person, and the council's representative was entitled to enter the property at any time pursuant to the terms of the agreement. An express reservation of *limited* rights to enter for certain defined purposes only (as in *Bruton*) served only to fortify the conclusion that the Housing Trust had granted exclusive possession. The grant of a tenancy will be displaced only where there are 'special circumstances' which are capable of negativing this result: see *Street* v *Mountford* [1985] AC 809, *per* Lord Templeman.

The cental issue in *Bruton*, therefore, was whether the fact that the Housing Trust was a charitable organisation charged with the function of providing short-term accommodation for the homeless pursuant to a licence agreement with the Council (which by its terms prohibited the grant of any tenancies) was sufficient to constitute special circumstances so as to displace the presumption of a tenancy. On this point, the House of Lords, following the earlier Court of Appeal decision in *Family Housing Association* v *Jones* [1990] 1 WLR 779 (which was largely indistinguishable from *Bruton* on the facts), rejected the notion that performance of socially valuable functions could amount to circumstances capable of negativing the general rule in favour of a tenancy. Moreover, the fact that the Housing Trust had agreed with the Council not to create tenancies (and that it had no estate out of which it could grant them) was considered immaterial where the agreement had clearly conferred exclusive possession on the occupier.

The House of Lords' ruling has been criticised on a number of grounds. First, it rejects the notion that a more flexible approach (exemplified by earlier case law, in particular, *Westminster City Council* v *Clarke* [1992] AC 288 (HL) and *Camden London Borough Council* v *Shortliffe Community Housing* (1992) 25 HLR 330) is more appropriate in determining the rights of the parties in the context of public sector housing for the homeless. In *Bruton*, there was no attempt by the parties to create an artificial or sham transaction, or to evade statutory protection. Secondly, it is apparent in *Bruton* that the Housing Trust, being itself only a licensee of the property, could never have had the power to exclude the Council from possession and, consequently, was not in a position to confer such a right on Mr Bruton. This, it is submitted, is a compelling argument and one that should have been decisive of the appeal. The point was addressed by Millet LJ in the Court of Appeal in *Bruton* [1998] QB 834, at 845, where his Lordship concluded that 'if the grantor has no power to exclude the true owner from possession, he has no power to grant a legal right to exclusive possession and his grant cannot take effect as a tenancy'. Thirdly, the House of Lords, it is submitted wrongly, refused to extend the category of 'special circumstances' to include organisations offering accommodation to the homeless. In this connection, Lord Templeman in *Street* instanced the situation where the occupier is an 'object of charity' as displacing the intention to create a tenancy. This would have provided a 'neat solution' (see Cowan, D., [1993] Conv 157, at 160) to the problem of admitting evidence of background features (characterised also as a category of exceptional circumstances relying on the intention of the parties not wishing to enter into legal relationships) in determining the issue of exclusive possession.

The effect of the House of Lords ruling is that a grantor may create a tenancy despite having no proprietary interest in the land and irrespective of any factors giving rise to a tenancy by estoppel. This is a startling proposition, not least because it assumes the existence of a lease which does not have any proprietary characteristics. If Mr Bruton's tenancy did not give rise to a proprietary interest, the question is, what is it? If Mr Bruton's tenancy is purely contractual then surely the very essence of a tenancy, namely, exclusive possession, is lacking unless exclusive possession in this context may now mean exclusive possession as between grantor and grantee only. The conclusion must be that the House of Lords has unwittingly created an entirely new species of tenancy which is purely contractual in nature, personal to the contracting parties, and which cannot be assigned to or bind third parties. But the whole point of the lease/licence distinction is to draw a clear dividing line between personal and proprietary rights. It is now very difficult to distinguish between a contractual tenancy and a licence since both operate *in personam* and create no interest in land.

(b) The question is whether, as a matter of law, the three separate agreements will confer joint exclusive possession on Tom, Dick and Harriet, or merely a right to share the flat as licensees. The point was considered in the House of Lords decision in *AG Securities* v *Vaughan/Antoniades* v *Villiers* [1990] 1 AC 417, involving two separate appeals.

In *Vaughan*, four individual occupants each had a short-term licence agreement granting a right to use the flat in common with others with a like right and expressly negativing a right to exclusive possession of any part of the flat. The licence agreements began at different dates, were for different periods and varied to some extent in the rents charged. The four occupants had replaced earlier ones when vacancies occurred. On these facts, the House of Lords held that the agreements were *independent* of each other and did not confer a right to exclusive possession on any one occupant but merely a right to share the flat with others. Because the agreements had been made on different dates and with different terms and rents, they could not be construed as creating a joint tenancy (i.e., in the absence of the four unities for a joint tenancy).

In *Antoniades*, on the other hand, the occupants were a young man and his girlfriend who wanted to live in the flat as husband and wife. The couple had each signed an agreement which stated that it conferred a personal licence only and expressly negatived the grant of exclusive possession. The agreements were, in fact, modelled on those in the earlier case of *Somma* v *Hazelhurst* [1978] 1 WLR 1014. The House of Lords held that the two agreements were *interdependent* in that it was unreal to regard them as separate and independent licences. The couple had applied jointly to rent the flat and sought and enjoyed joint exclusive occupation of the whole flat. The result was, therefore, a joint tenancy protected by the Rent Act 1977. See also *Duke* v *Wynne* [1990] 1 WLR 766, where the Court of Appeal stressed that the labelling which parties agree to attach to their agreements is never conclusive.

Thus, where there is a steady turnover of occupants who move in at different times and pay different rents and stay for different periods, the agreements are likely to be classified as genuine and conferring 'licence' status only. (This, however, is subject to the argument that there may be a tenancy of an individual bedroom coupled with the right to share the communal parts of the flat, a point not canvassed in *Vaughan*.)

Alternatively, agreements which arise where the occupants seek accommodation together (as in the present case) and sign separate but identical agreements at the same time, paying the same rent and for the same period of time, would, it is submitted, almost certainly point to a sham and confer joint tenancy status on the occupants. One difficulty, however, may relate to the payment of rent. In *Mikeover Ltd* v *Brady* [1989] 3 All ER 618, the court held that the obligation to pay separate monthly sums, being several (as opposed to joint obligations) destroyed unity of interest in order to create a joint tenancy.

Subject to this point, the advice to Tom, Dick and Harriet is to sign the agreements on the basis that they will acquire a joint tenancy of the flat. The fact that they purport to agree to a sharing of the flat with each other will not affect their statutory protection (*Aslan* v *Murphy (No. 1)/Aslan* v *Murphy (No. 2)/Duke* v *Wynne* [1990] 1 WLR 766). In this case all three sharers will be treated as tenants. The position would be different, however, if one of the sharers had been named as tenant with the others merely contributing to the rent. Here, the natural inference would be that what was intended was a contractual flat-sharing arrangement under the tenancy of one of them only (*Monmouth Borough Council* v *Marlog* [1994] 44 EG 240).

QUESTION 2

'Equity treats an agreement for a lease as being as good as a lease.'

Discuss.

Commentary

This is a typical essay question on the meaning of an equitable lease. Apart from explaining equity's willingness to enforce the terms of an intended lease by an order for specific performance (*Walsh* v *Lonsdale* (1882) 21 Ch D 9), you should also refer to the main differences between a legal and an equitable lease. In the main, these relate to third-party rights.

It may be that your lecturer has not covered this topic in the course. If that is the case, it is unlikely that you will be expected to deal with a question of this sort.

Suggested Answer

A lease not made by deed (subject to the exceptions contained in the Law of Property Act 1925, s. 52(2)), or not falling within the concession contained in s. 54(2) (leases taking effect in possession for a term not exceeding three years at a full economic rent) is void at law: s. 52(1). If, however, the tenant goes into possession and pays rent, there will be an implied grant of a periodic tenancy on the terms of the void lease which are consistent with such a tenancy. Alternatively, the void lease at law may be recognised in equity. Irrespective of any rights which the tenant may have acquired at law (i.e., by going into possession and paying rent), equity will enforce the terms of the intended lease if they are specifically enforceable. This is because 'equity looks on that as done which ought to be done' and, hence, the expression 'equitable lease'. In principle, equity regards an informal lease (intended to take effect as a legal lease) as a contract for a lease which is then capable of being enforced by specific performance.

Until the court orders the landlord to grant a lease by deed, equity regards the 'tenant' as an equitable lessee. Equally, the tenant is bound by the covenants in the informal lease, even though it is informal. This is because equity looks to the intention of the parties rather than simply to the form of their agreement. In *Walsh* v *Lonsdale* (1882) 21 Ch D 9, the defendant agreed to grant and the plaintiff to accept a lease of a mill for seven years at a rent payable quarterly in arrears, but with a year's rent payable in advance if demanded. No lease was executed but the plaintiff went into possession and paid rent quarterly in arrears. The defendant then demanded a year's rent in advance, which the plaintiff refused to pay. The court held that the defendant was entitled to demand the rent as the plaintiff held on the same terms as though a lease had actually been granted, since the agreement was one of which the court would order specific performance. Moreover, the court concluded that equity prevailed over legal rules in all courts (since the passing of the Judicature Acts 1873–1875), with the result that the plaintiff's equitable lease prevailed over any yearly tenancy at law. More recently, the doctrine has been extended to enforce repairing covenants in an equitable lease (*Industrial Properties (Barton Hill) Ltd* v *Associated Electrical Industrial Ltd* [1977] QB 580).

The effect of the decision in *Walsh* v *Lonsdale* has been to blur the distinction between equitable leases of this nature and legal leases. Hence, the quote that 'equity treats an agreement for a lease as being as good as a lease'. See, e.g., *Re Maugham, ex parte Monkhouse* (1885) 14 QBD 956, *per* Field J at p. 958. However, there are still important differences between the two types of lease:

First, an equitable lease is dependent upon the court granting specific performance, which is itself discretionary. This is illustrated by the maxim that 'equity grants a right where there is a remedy'. Thus, there must be a contract which complies with the requisite legal formalities (i.e., complying with either the Law of Property Act 1925, s. 40 (if the contract was made before 27 September 1989) or the Law of Property (Miscellaneous Provisions) Act 1989, s. 2 (if the contract was made on or after this date)). A party to an *oral* contract to a lease entered into before 27 September 1989 may be able to rely on the doctrine of part performance to enforce the contract (*Steadman* v *Steadman* [1976] AC 536 and *Kingswood Estate Co. Ltd* v *Anderson* [1963] 2 QB 169). However, this doctrine has no application to contracts falling within the 1989 Act. Because the remedy of specific performance is discretionary, the courts may not grant it where, for example, to do so would result in the landlord being in breach of a covenant contained in the headlease (*Warmington* v *Miller* [1973] QB 877). An order may also be refused if the tenant is himself in default by being in breach of covenant (*Coatsworth* v *Johnson* (1886) 55 LJ QB 220).

It has been held recently that the doctrine of proprietary estoppel may operate to perfect an informal agreement despite non-compliance with s. 2 of the 1989 Act. In *Yaxley* v *Gott* [2000] 1 All ER 711, involving an informal agreement for a rent-free lease of residential premises which did not comply with s. 2(1) of the 1989 Act, the Court of Appeal recognised that, in appropriate cases, the doctrine of proprietary estoppel may be used to circumvent the statutory provisions regarding writing where the facts of the case also ground a claim based on constructive trust principles. In this connection, s. 2(5) of the 1989 Act expressly excludes the creation or operation of resulting, implied or constructive trusts from the formal requirements of s. 2.

Secondly, an equitable lease is binding and enforceable between the parties, but as against third parties it suffers the weakness of all equitable rights — they are good against all persons except a bona fide purchaser of a legal estate without notice. An agreement for a lease is, however, registrable as an estate contract (Class C(iv) land charge) under the Land Charges Act 1972, s. 2(4). If the land is unregistered, therefore, an equitable tenant has no protection against an assignee of the landlord's reversion in the absence of registration. In the case of registered land, the equitable tenant can protect his equitable right by entering a notice on the register under the Land Registration Act 1925, s. 48. Moreover, if he goes into possession, he will be protected against third parties by his occupation, because he will thereby have an overriding interest under the Land Registration Act 1925, s. 70(1)(g).

Thirdly, an agreement for a lease is not a 'conveyance' within the meaning of the Law of Property Act 1925, s. 205(1)(ii), and thus an equitable tenant will not have the benefit of any easements, rights etc. which would be deemed to be included on a conveyance under s. 62 of the 1925 Act. He may, however, acquire easements under the rule in *Wheeldon* v *Burrows* (1879) 12 Ch D 31.

Fourthly, the benefits of covenants and rights in an equitable lease which run with the land are assignable (*Manchester Brewery Co.* v *Combs* [1901] 2 Ch 608). The burdens seem to bind an assignee if capable of running with the land (*Boyer* v *Warbey* [1953] 1 QB 234).

Lastly, an agreement for a lease entitles the landlord to the usual covenants. By contrast, usual covenants will not be implied into a lease.

QUESTION 3

In October 1999, Mandy advertised on her local parish church noticeboard for a tenant for her vacant property at 16 Bumble Road, Bigglestown. John, having seen the advertisement, wrote to Mandy expressing an interest in the property.

In November 1999, Mandy met John and took him round to view the house. Mandy told him that the letting was his for £55 per week and that he could move in, in three months' time. John agreed to these terms.

After the expiration of the three months, John telephoned Mandy to inform her that he was ready to move into the property. Mandy replied, 'Sorry, I've changed my mind about the letting, and anyway I've sold the house with vacant possession to David for £85,000'.

Advise John as to his rights (if any) in relation to the property.

Commentary

This is a tricky question concerned with the formalities of a lease and the enforceability of an agreement for a lease against a third party. To score high marks, your answer should display a detailed knowledge of the relevant statutory provisions and case law.

You may find it useful to begin with a brief introduction identifying the legal issues and explaining the relevancy of the rules governing the formalities of leases. This will then pave the way for a more detailed analysis of the problem.

Suggested Answer

This question is concerned with the law governing the formalities for the creation of leases. The Law of Property Act 1925, s. 52(1), states that 'all conveyances of land or of any interest therein are void for the purposes of conveying or creating a legal estate unless made by deed'. By virtue of s. 205(1)(ii) of the 1925 Act, a conveyance of land includes a legal lease. A lease may, however, be valid at law even though not created by deed. Section 54(2) of the 1925 Act provides an exception to s. 52(1) in that any lease which takes effect in possession for a term not exceeding three years at the best rent which can reasonably be obtained without taking a fine, is exempted from the requirement of a deed and will take effect as a legal lease.

A lease will normally arise where a landowner (the landlord) grants to another (the tenant) the right exclusively to possess land for a fixed or ascertainable period while himself retaining a reversionary estate (i.e., a freehold estate, or a leasehold estate of longer duration than that demised to the tenant).

Even though it is possible for a landlord to grant a tenant a lease in return for no consideration in the form of a rent or premium (see *Ashburn Anstalt* v *Arnold* [1989] Ch 1), the vast majority of leases are granted in return for the payment of a rental sum by the tenant. (The term 'rent' has been defined as 'a payment which a tenant is bound by his contract to make to his landlord for the use of the land', *per* Lord Denning MR in *CH Bailey* v *Memorial Enterprises Ltd* [1974] 1 WLR 728.) In so far as the tenant provides consideration for the use and occupation of the land, there necessarily arises a contract between landlord and tenant. Thus, a void lease at law (i.e., not complying with the legal formality of a deed under s. 52(1)) may still take effect as a contract for a lease which equity may enforce by means of a decree of specific performance.

It can be assumed that both Mandy and John intended to enter into landlord and tenant relations and create a weekly periodic tenancy in favour of John at an agreed rental of £55 per week. A weekly tenancy will be presumed from the fact that the agreed rental is referable to a weekly period (*Adler* v *Blackman* [1953] 1 QB 146). At first glance, it may appear that John's tenancy takes effect as a legal lease under the exception contained in s. 54(2). In this connection, it has been held that periodic tenancies (e.g., weekly, monthly, yearly etc.) fall within the s. 54(2) exemption as being for less than three years (*Re Knight, ex parte Voisey* (1882) 21 Ch D 442). The difficulty, however, in the present case is that John's tenancy does not 'take effect in possession', in so far as it was agreed that John would not move in immediately but in three months' time.

Accordingly, the tenancy does not fall within the s. 54(2) concession and is void at law in the absence of a deed.

Does John have an equitable lease (i.e., recognised in equity)? An equitable lease, from the perspective of the common law, is a mere contract for an estate in land, but in equity it is treated in many ways as being 'as good as a lease' (see *Walsh* v *Lonsdale* (1882) 21 Ch D 9). This is because a contract for a lease may be enforceable in equity by a decree of specific performance. To be so enforceable, however, the contract must comply with the requisite legal formalities as to writing.

A contract for the sale or other disposition of an interest in land (e.g., a contract to enter into a lease) must either be reduced to a written document, all its terms contained therein, and signed by both parties, or merely be evidenced in writing and signed by the person to be charged. If the contract was made before 27 September 1989, the latter rule applies by virtue of the Law of Property Act 1925, s. 40. If, on the other hand, the contract is made on or after this date, the former rule applies by virtue of the Law of Property (Miscellaneous Provisions) Act 1989, s. 2. (Section 40 also permits an oral contract to be enforced by virtue of the doctrine of part performance: see, e.g., *Steadman* v *Steadman* [1976] AC 536.)

The oral agreement in the present case was made in November 1999, and hence the provisions of s. 2 of the 1989 Act will apply. The absence of any signed written instrument containing all the terms of the proposed tenancy suggests that the agreement is void for want of formality, but reference should be made to s. 2(5)(a) of the 1989 Act which provides that the requirement of a written instrument is obviated in the case of contracts for short leases made pursuant to s. 54(2) of the 1925 Act.

Assuming, therefore, that John's oral agreement is valid despite the lack of writing, the question arises as to whether it is enforceable against David as an assignee of the reversion. It is unclear whether the house forms registered or unregistered land. If the house is registered, David, as assignee, will only be bound by John's equitable lease if John had registered the same as a minor interest against Mandy's reversionary title prior to the sale of the house by means of a notice on the register. (There is no suggestion that John moved into occupation of the house prior to the completion of the sale to David so as to render his interest an 'overriding interest' under the Land Registration Act 1925, s. 70(1)(g).) If, on the other hand, the house is unregistered, John's agreement for a lease, being an 'estate contract', was registrable as a Class

C(iv) land charge under the Land Charges Act 1972. The effect of non-registration of the contract as against Mandy's title, prior to the sale of the freehold to David, will be that David (as a purchaser) will take the freehold estate free of John's interest, irrespective of whether he (David) actually knew of the equitable lease or not (*Midland Bank Trust Co. Ltd* v *Green* [1981] AC 513).

QUESTION 4

In 1997, Arnold entered into partnership with his brother, Jake, for the purpose of carrying out public relations work. The partnership was called 'Communicate Associates'. In the same year, Communicate Associates purchased the freehold title to some office space.

In 1998, Arnold and Jake fell into disagreement and decided that, while they would formally carry on the partnership from the office premises for fiscal reasons, the day to day running of the business would be Arnold's responsibility. To make full use of the office premises, however, it was agreed that the partnership would grant Jake a lease of half of the office space, from which Jake would run another business in his own right. Both parties agreed and executed a lease (in 1999) which contained the following wording:

> ... that the Lessee shall from this day be entitled to exclusively possess the premises demised herein for five years, or in any event until such time as the Communicate Associates partnership ... shall cease to exist ... at a rental of £16,000 per year ... payable on the unusual quarter days.

Since taking up possession, Jake has been paying Communicate Associates £1,000 per month rental in advance, which Arnold has paid into the business account of Communicate Associates.

Jake is keen to demonstrate that the 1999 lease is void and that there exists instead a periodic monthly tenancy because, by so doing, he would be able to escape liability to pay the higher rent under the lease.

Advise Jake.

Commentary

This question is concerned with the doctrine of certainty of term (*Prudential Assurance Co. Ltd* v *London Residuary Body* [1992] 3 WLR 279) and the law relating to the capacity of a party to grant a lease of land to himself (*Rye* v *Rye* [1962] AC 496 and the Law of Property Act 1925, s. 72). The facts do not readily bring these issues to mind and so, if you have not carefully revised the case law and statutory provisions, the question may prove somewhat baffling!

Suggested Answer

In order to succeed in his contention, Jake must establish that the 1999 lease is void and that, as a matter of law, he holds the premises under a periodic (monthly) tenancy at the lower rent of £1,000 per month.

It is trite law that there must exist two separate parties to a lease (i.e., it is not possible for a person to grant a lease of land to himself). Although the Law of Property Act 1925, s. 72(3) expressly states that 'a person may convey land to or vest land in himself' (for this purpose, a legal lease is a 'conveyance' of land within the meaning of s. 205(1) of the 1925 Act), the subsection has been judicially interpreted as not having this effect (*Rye* v *Rye* [1962] AC 496). In this case, Lord Denning held that it was impossible for a person to grant a lease to himself, invoking the maxim *nemo potest esse tenens et dominus* (a person cannot be, at the same time, both landlord and tenant of the same premises). In *Rye*, the appellant and his brother acquired a freehold property which they co-owned in equity as tenants in common. The brothers were in partnership as solicitors and agreed that the firm should be run from the premises they had purchased. As a firm, they agreed to pay themselves an annual rent of £500. The House of Lords held that no lease was ever created because the same parties existed on either side of the landlord and tenant relationship. However, Lord Denning did expressly confirm that two lessors could properly grant a lease to one of themselves because, in such an arrangement, there would exist different individuals on either side of the lease. Such an arrangement would be a conveyance pursuant to s. 72(4) of the 1925 Act and the convenants contained in the agreement would be enforceable under s. 82(1) of the 1925 Act just as if the lessee had covenanted with the lessors alone.

The decision in *Rye* was applied in *Ingram* v *Inland Revenue Commissioners* [1997] 4 All ER 395, where the Court of Appeal held that the purported grant of a lease by a nominee to his principal was of no effect since a person could not contract with himself.

In the present case, Jake and Arnold have granted a lease to Jake alone. This is permissible under s. 72(4) of the 1925 Act and the lease cannot, therefore, be attacked on this ground.

Crucial to the existence of a valid lease is the requirement that the term of the lease is for a certain or an ascertainable period. A classic illustration of this doctrine is to be found in the case of *Lace* v *Chantler* [1944] KB 368, where a tenancy 'for the duration of the war' was held invalid as being for an uncertain term. It is interesting to observe that there was, in fact, an exchange of a weekly sum in that case and, consequently, the court was able to infer the existence of a weekly periodic tenancy independently of the void lease at law. (The case, in fact, prompted the enactment of the Validation of War Time Leases Act 1944, which rendered such leases valid as leases for 10-year terms determinable by a month's notice on either side given after the end of hostilities as fixed by Order in Council.) The current leading authority is *Prudential Assurance Co. Ltd* v *London Residuary Body* [1992] 3 WLR 279, in which the House of Lords, overruling *Re Midland Railways Co.'s Agreement* [1971] Ch 725, re-affirmed that the doctrine applies to both fixed and periodic tenancies.

If the 1999 lease is void for uncertainty of term, Jake will be in a position to claim that there exists (between himself and the partnership) a less onerous monthly periodic tenancy arising by implication of law from the payment and acceptance of a monthly rent. (See *Adler* v *Blackman* [1946] 1 QB 146, where the landlord granted a one-year term at a rent of £2 per week. On the expiry of the fixed term the tenant held over, continuing to pay £2 a week. It was held that the tenant was a weekly tenant.)

Such a periodic tenancy will be valid at law (despite the absence of a deed or writing) because it will fall within the Law of Property Act 1925, s. 54(2), which applies to leases taking effect in possession for a term of less than three years (this includes periodic tenancies: *Re Knight, ex parte Voisey* (1882) 21 Ch D 442) at the best rent obtainable.

Is, however, the 1999 lease void for uncertainty of term? The doctrine of certainty of term dictates that the maximum period for which a lease is to run must be calculable with certainty. In the *Prudential* case (see above) the landlords demised the land until such time as it was required by the landlords for the purposes of widening the highway. The House of Lords held that no estate in land had been granted because the purported lease was uncertain as to duration. However, in view of the tenant's entry into possession of the land and payment of a yearly rent, the court was able to infer the creation of a yearly tenancy on such terms as were not inconsistent with the void lease at law. (See also, *Doe d Warner* v *Browne* (1908) 8 East 165 and *Doe d Rigge* v *Bell* (1793) 5 Durn & E 471.)

In the present case, the 1999 lease provides that Jake should be entitled to exclusive possession of the premises 'for five years, or in any event until such time as the Communicate Associates partnership ... shall cease to exist'. If the term granted was simply for five years, the lease would, undoubtedly, be certain as to its duration as from the outset and, hence, valid. However, the additional words 'or in any event until such time as the ... partnership shall cease', render the lease uncertain as to its maximum duration since it is unknown when the partnership (and hence the lease) will end. The lease is, therefore, void for uncertainty. (If the lease was expressed in terms of a five-year term, subject to a power of the landlord to determine earlier upon the partnership ceasing during the term, this would be valid because from its outset the maximum duration of the lease would be certain (i.e., a determinable certain term of five years).

Assuming, therefore, that the monthly tenancy governs the relationship between Jake and the partnership, Jake is under no obligation to pay the higher rent under the void lease since this would be inconsistent with the terms of the periodic tenancy.

QUESTION 5

(a)   What is a 'concurrent lease'?

(b)   In 1999, Plucker Estates Ltd agreed in writing to grant Lorna a 15-year lease of Fir Tree Mansion to take effect from 1 January 2000. Due to an oversight on the part of Plucker Estates Ltd's solicitors, the lease was never executed. The written agreement provided, *inter alia*, that 'the rent payable shall be the sum of £36,000 per annum payable in advance (whether formally demanded or not)'. In December 1999, before Lorna had taken up possession of the premises, Plucker Estates Ltd wrote to her requesting payment of the first year's rent. Lorna ignored this request. On 1 January 2000, Lorna moved into the property and commenced paying a monthy rent of £3,000 in arrears, which Plucker Estates Ltd have accepted. Lorna contends that she has a legal periodic yearly tenancy, under which the rent is payable in arrears.

Plucker Estates Ltd now wish to pursue Lorna for the balance of the rental sums payable in advance. Advise Plucker Estates Ltd.

(c)   On 1 May 1995, Buckle granted Sharp Ltd a six-year lease of a factory. The parties expressly excluded Pt II of the Landlord and Tenant Act 1954 (affording security of tenure to business tenants) so that there would be no automatic continuance of the tenancy after the expiry date of the lease. On

1 May 1997, Sharp Ltd purported to sub-let the factory to Witherall Ltd for a term of five years. The sublease contains a repairing covenant on the part of the tenant and a landlord's right of re-entry for breach of the tenant's covenants.

In November 1999, Sharp Ltd (as a preliminary to commencing forfeiture proceedings) served on Witherall Ltd a s. 146 notice alleging a breach of the covenant to repair. Advise Witherall Ltd.

Commentary

This question is divided into three parts. Part (a) is in the form of a mini-essay question, and parts (b) and (c) are legal problems.

Part (a) asks you to explain what is meant by a concurrent lease (also known sometimes as a lease of the reversion, which is not to be confused with a reversionary lease!). The leading authority on this topic is *London & County (A & D) Ltd* v *Wilfred Sportsman Ltd* [1971] Ch 764.

Part (b) is solely concerned with the rule in *Walsh* v *Lonsdale* (1882) 21 Ch D 9.

Part (c) is concerned with the principle that the relationship of landlord and tenant depends on privity of estate existing between the parties (*Milmo* v *Carreras* [1946] KB 306). It also requires you to mention the recent case of *Parc Battersea Ltd* v *Hutchinson* [1999] 22 EG 149: see further, Brown, J., 'Avoiding Part II of the Landlord and Tenant Act 1954 by Default' [1999] RRLR 246.

Where you find a question in multiple parts such as this, you can assume that each section carries equal marks unless, of course, there is a contrary indication.

Suggested Answer

(a) A concurrent lease (or a lease of the reversion as it is also sometimes known) will arise where the landlord grants a lease to T1 and subsequently grants a lease to T2 of the same premises for a term to commence before the expiry of the lease in favour of T1. The two leases, even though staggered in time, run concurrently with or parallel to one another.

So long as the leases are concurrent, the disposition in favour of T2 operates as a part assignment of the landlord's reversion entitling T2 to the rent reserved in the previous lease and the benefit of the covenants given by T1 (see *London & County (A & D) Ltd* v *Wilfred Sportsman Ltd* [1971] Ch 764).

If T1's lease is prematurely determined before T2's lease has expired, T2 is entitled to possession. Moreover, forfeiture by the landlord of T2's lease cannot affect T1 for, although T1's lease is akin to a sub-tenancy, it is not derived out of T2's lease.

A concurrent lease is a useful device whereby, for a defined period, T2 becomes a temporary owner of the reversionary estate of the landlord. Such a lease may provide security in favour of T2 for a fixed period in return for T2 advancing credit or other commercial benefit to T1. Thus, a landlord, in return for money borrowed from T2, may grant T2 a concurrent lease whereby T2 is entitled to the benefit of the rental payments issuing out of the land paid by T1 (*Re Moore and Hulm's Contract* [1912] 2 Ch 105 and *Adelphi (Estates) Ltd* v *Christie* (1983) 47 P & CR 650).

   (b)   This part of the question is concerned with the rule in *Walsh* v *Lonsdale* (1882) 21 Ch D 9, which establishes that equity may enforce an agreement for a lease by means of an order for specific performance. In this case, the defendant agreed to grant and the plaintiff to accept a lease of a mill for seven years at a rent payable quarterly in arrears but with a year's rent payable in advance if demanded. No lease was executed but the plaintiff went into possession and paid rent quarterly in arrears. The defendant then demanded a year's rent in advance which the plaintiff refused to pay. It was held that the defendant was entitled to demand the rent since the plaintiff held on the same terms as though a lease had actually been granted. The agreement was one of which the court would, in its discretion, order specific performance and equity would in such cases 'look upon that as done which ought to be done'.

In Lorna's case, although no formal (legal) lease was ever executed, the written agreement to grant her a lease on the terms stated therein will take effect as an equitable lease. The requirement of writing for such an agreement appears to have been complied with (see the Law of Property (Miscellaneous Provisions) Act 1989, s. 2) and, provided Plucker Estates Ltd have themselves acted equitably, they may seek to enforce the agreement by means of an order for specific performance. The remedy of specific performance is discretionary, and although it may be ordered in relation to contracts for the grant of a lease (damages in such cases providing an inadequate remedy) it may be barred by delay on the part of the party seeking relief or where such party has not acted in good faith (see, e.g., *Hayes* v *Caryll* (1702) 1 Bro Parl Cas 126 and *Laurence* v *Lexcourt Holdings Ltd* [1978] 2 All ER 810). It is important, therefore, that Plucker Estates Ltd act promptly in seeking specific performance of the agreement.

This equitable lease will override any periodic (monthly) tenancy arising by operation of law from the payment and acceptance of the monthly rent of £3,000 (see *Walsh* v *Lonsdale*, above) and, consequently, Lorna will be obliged to pay the balance of the advance rental sums owing.

(c) In this case, Sharp Ltd were granted a lease for a term of six years. They, in turn, two years on, purported to grant a five-year sublease to Witherall Ltd (i.e., for a term longer than the unexpired residue of the headlease). The rule in *Milmo* v *Carreras* [1946] KB 306 dictates that, where a tenant by a document in the form of a sublease divests himself of his entire leasehold interest (which will occur when a mesne landlord transfers to his sub-tenant an estate as great as or greater than his own), the relationship of landlord and tenant cannot exist between him and the purported sub-tenant. The sublease will, in fact, operate as an assignment by operation of law of the remainder of the tenant's interest in the premises. This is what has effectively happened in this case with the result that no privity of estate exists between Sharp Ltd and their purported sub-tenant, Witherall Ltd.

In the absence of any reversionary interest vested in Sharp Ltd, the s. 146 notice served on Witherall Ltd is void and of no legal effect. Moreover, Sharp Ltd have no right to possession of the premises. After the execution of the purported sublease, they effectively became a stranger to the premises.

The assignment of the headlease by operation of law will also mean that Witherall Ltd will be bound by the provisions and limitations contained in the headlease — one of them being that Pt II of the 1954 Act should not apply. Witherall Ltd are, therefore, without protection under Pt II and will be required to give up possession on the expiry date of the lease (i.e., in 2001): *Parc Battersea Ltd* v *Hutchinson* [1999] 22 EG 149.

QUESTION 6

To what extent does the doctrine of certainty of term apply to periodic tenancies? What is the 'doctrine of repugnancy' in this context? (Illustrate your answer by reference to the decided cases.)

Commentary

The doctrine of certainty in relation to periodic tenancies was discussed by the House of Lords in *Prudential Assurance Co. Ltd* v *London Residuary Body* [1992] 3 WLR 279. For a good summary of the law of certainty of term in the context of the *Prudential* case, see Biles, M., 'One Thing is Certain and the Rest is Lies' (1994) NLJ, 4 February, 156.

Suggested Answer

The common law has always required that, for a lease to be valid, its maximum duration must be ascertained, or ascertainable, at the time when it comes into effect. The famous case on this point is *Lace* v *Chantler* [1944] KB 368, where the Court of Appeal ruled that a lease which had been granted 'for the duration of the war' was void for uncertainty.

The doctrine appears to come unstuck when applied to periodic tenancies where, in reality, the maximum duration is not clear from the outset and simply depends on when, or whether, one of the parties serves a notice to quit. An illusion of certainty can be achieved, however, by arguing that the maximum term is ascertainable in that its duration can be fixed by an act of one of the parties. The difficulty with this approach is that the right of one (or both) of the parties to serve notice may be contractually tied to an event which may or may not happen. In *Re Midland Railway Co.'s Agreement* [1971] Ch 725, the Court of Appeal recognised this difficulty and concluded that the requirement of certainty of term had no direct relevance to periodic tenancies.

This view, however, has recently been exploded by the House of Lords in *Prudential Assurance Co. Ltd* v *London Residuary Body* [1992] 3 WLR 279. In this case, the House of Lords, overruling the *Re Midland Railway* case on this point, held that it was a requirement of *all* leases and tenancy agreements that the term created was of certain duration. Lord Templeman, who gave the leading speech, reasoned that a periodic tenancy is saved from being uncertain because each party has power by notice to determine at the end of any period of the tenancy. The relevant term continues until determined as if both parties made a new agreement at the end of each period for a new term for the next ensuing period. It is interesting to note, however, that Lord Browne-Wilkinson observed that no satisfactory rationale for the rule existed and expressed the hope that the Law Commission would look at the subject afresh to see whether there was, in fact, any good reason for maintaining the rule which operates to defeat in many cases the contractually agreed arrangements between the parties. In the *Prudential* case itself, the parties had, in fact, intended to create a lease on terms that it should continue until the subject land was required by the landlord for the purposes of the widening of a highway. In the result, this purported lease was held void for uncertainty and the land was deemed to be held on a yearly tenancy created by virtue of the tenant's possession and payment of a yearly rent. Moreover, since the term preventing the landlord from determining the tenancy until the land was required for road widening purposes was inconsistent with the right of either party under a yearly tenancy to terminate it on notice, it was considered repugnant to such periodic tenancy and of no effect.

The doctrine of repugnancy is closely related to the rule regarding certainty of term. The basic proposition is that a clause totally precluding a party from determining a periodic tenancy is repugnant to the nature of such a tenancy and void. A leading case is *Centaploy Ltd* v *Matlodge Ltd* [1974] Ch 1, where an agreement to let a garage contained the following words: 'Received the sum of £12, being one week's rent ... and to continue until determined by the lessee ...' Whitford J held that the document provided for a weekly tenancy and, although the term making the tenancy determinable only by the lessee did not make the periodic tenancy thus created void for uncertainty, nevertheless, a term whereby a landlord would never have the right to terminate a periodic tenancy was repugnant to the nature of such a tenancy and void. The practical significance of this finding was that, despite the terms of the agreement, the landlord was free to serve a notice to quit on the tenant bringing the weekly tenancy to an end.

A partial fetter, however, on the right to serve a notice to quit will not be considered as repugnant to the grant of a periodic tenancy. Thus, in *Re Midland Railway Co.'s Agreement* (above), it was suggested by Russell LJ (at p. 733) that a curb for 10, 20 or 50 years should not be rejected as repugnant to the concept of a periodic tenancy.

In *Cheshire Lines Committee* v *Lewis & Co.* (1880) 50 LJ QB 121, the plaintiffs, a railway company, let premises to the defendants on a weekly tenancy to be determined by a week's notice on either side. The parties entered into a collateral agreement that the tenant could occupy the premises 'until the railway company require to pull them down'. The Court of Appeal held that this collateral agreement was void as being repugnant to a periodic tenancy. The case may be contrasted with *Breams Property Investment Co. Ltd* v *Stroulger* [1948] 2 KB 1, where various agreements for quarterly tenancies contained a clause to the effect that the landlords would not, during the period of three years from the beginning of the tenancies, serve notice to quit on the tenants except in the event of the landlords requiring the premises for their own occupation and use. The Court of Appeal held that, as the clause merely attached a condition to the quarterly right to give notice (by suspending it during the first three years of the tenancies except in the event of the landlords requiring possession for their own use), it was not repugnant to the nature of a quarterly tenancy. In effect, the doctrine of repugnancy was side-stepped by construing the lease in a particular way.

3   Enforceability of Covenants

INTRODUCTION

Who can enforce a covenant in a lease, and against whom? This is a difficult topic because it abounds with technical rules and the student may be obliged to consider the liability of a number of different parties (i.e., original tenant, original landlord, assignee of lease, assignee of reversion, a surety). For a collection of cases in this area, the student is referred to Pawlowski, M., and Brown, J., *Casebook on the Law of Landlord and Tenant*, London: Sweet & Maxwell Ltd, 1994, Ch. 3.

The law now differs depending on whether the lease was granted before, or on or after 1 January 1996, when the Landlord and Tenant (Covenants) Act 1995 came into force. One of the main provisions of the 1995 Act, which applies to *all* leases (including those entered into before 1 January 1996), requires that if the landlord wishes to sue the original tenant for fixed charges (i.e., arrears of rent, service charges or liquidated damages, including interest on any of these sums) he must give notice of his intention to do so within six months of the liability arising: s. 17. Another important provision under the 1995 Act, which is common to both old and new leases, relates to the former tenant's entitlement to an 'overriding lease'. The Act entitles the former tenant, if he satisfies an obligation of an assignee following assignment, to call for the grant to him (within 12 months) of an overriding lease from the landlord for a term equal to the unexpired residue of the actual lease (plus a nominal reversion). This has the effect of inserting the former tenant as an intermediate landlord between the landlord and the defaulting assignee. The advantage of the overriding lease to the former tenant is that he will be able to forfeit the assignee's interest and regain possession of the demised premises with a view to marketing them. The rationale behind the overriding lease is, therefore, to give the former tenant the opportunity to recoup his expenditure in discharging his liability to the landlord. If you are faced with a question involving a pre-1996 lease, it is important that you make mention of these changes brought about by the 1995 Act. See Question 1 and 3.

With regard to leases created on or after 1 January 1996, the position is now governed by the 1995 Act. The basic principle under the Act is that, on assignment, the original tenant will be automatically released from his liabilities and only the tenant for the time being will be liable to the landlord. There is one situation, however, in which the former tenant will continue to be liable under the covenants in the lease following an assignment. This is where the landlord requires the tenant to enter into an authorised guarantee agreement (AGA), whereby the tenant guarantees performance of the covenants in the lease by his immediate assignee. The AGA must release the tenant from liability under the agreement on a further assignment of the lease. If the tenant is not so released, the agreement is not an AGA and is void under the Act. See Question 2(a) and 4.

It is frequently overlooked that the privity of contract rule applies to landlords just as it does to tenants. Thus, in relation to pre-1996 leases, the original landlord will remain liable to the tenant on his covenants (express or implied) in the lease despite an assignment of the lease. It is also well-established that the original landlord, although he can no longer sue, can still be sued after the reversion has been assigned: *Re King, (dec'd), Robinson* v *Gray* [1963] Ch 459. Under the 1995 Act, in respect of post-1996 leases, the landlord may seek to be released from his covenants in the lease when he assigns the reversion by serving notice on the tenant giving details of the proposed assignment and indicating that he wishes to be released. The tenant then has four weeks within which to object to the proposed release. If he does not object within that period then, on completion of the assignment, the landlord will be released. If there is an objection (e.g., the tenant may fear that the premises will decline under the new landlord), the landlord can apply to the county court for a declaration that it is reasonable for him to be released. See Question 2(b).

The provisions of the 1995 Act apply to original tenants and landlords, and also to those who become tenants or landlords by virtue of an assignment of the tenancy or reversion.

You should also be aware that the Contracts (Rights of Third Parties) Act 1999 may be relevant in the leasehold context. The Act provides that a third party may enforce directly a contractual term where the contract expressly provides that right, or where the contractual term confers a benefit on him. The Act, therefore, allows for the inclusion of sub-tenants, as a named class of future persons, as the beneficiaries of covenants in a headlease granted after the Act became law. In other words, the sub-tenant may be able to enforce the head landlord's covenants directly against the superior landlord: see further, Porter, R., 'Third Party Benefits', [1999] EG 9950, 72–73. We have included an essay-type question on the 1999 Act in this chapter: see Question 5.

Our advice is to plan your answer carefully, since problem questions in this area seek to test not only your knowledge of the principles but also your ability to write clearly and concisely. If you are thinking of taking up a career at the bar, a problem question on this highly technical topic is definitely for you! Good luck!

QUESTION 1

In 1986, Bakewell Ltd was granted a 30-year lease of a shop in Eltham, London. Two years later, Bakewell Ltd requested consent to an assignment of the unexpired residue of the lease to Babyfoods Ltd. Pursuant to a term of the licence to assign granted by the landlord, Mr Brown entered into a covenant with the landlord to guarantee payment of the rent by Babyfoods Ltd.

In 1990, the landlord sold the freehold of the shop to Property Developments Ltd. Babyfoods Ltd recently went into liquidation owing £15,000 rent, the rent having been increased on review in 1997 (i.e., since the assignment of the lease).

Advise Bakewell Ltd as to its rights and liabilities in respect of the shop. How would your advice differ (if at all) if the lease had been granted to Bakewell Ltd for a term of 10 years (as opposed to 30 years)?

Commentary

This is, without doubt, a difficult question. Even the bright and well-motivated student will find it challenging! It raises a number of complex issues and you will need a clear head to tackle this question successfully. The secret is to plan your answer carefully, jotting down the key points and case names (i.e., what should be included). Use this rough plan to balance the material in your answer so as to avoid writing excessively on one point to the detriment of others. For a good summary of the subject, see Murdoch, S., 'Tenants, Assignees and Sureties' (1984) 272 EG 732 and 857. See also Pawlowski, M., *Leasing Commercial Premises* (Oxford: Chandos Publishing (Oxford) Ltd, 1999), Ch. 6, for a good summary of the interrelation between the common law and the Landlord and Tenant (Covenants) Act 1995.

As to the second part of the question, the widely held view, prior to the decision in *City of London Corporation* v *Fell* [1993] 3 WLR 1164, was that the liability of an original tenant did not cease on the expiry of the contractual term of the lease but extended into any statutory continuation of the tenancy under the Landlord and Tenant Act 1954, Pt II. See, Pawlowski, M., 'Liability of an Original Tenant and his Surety' [1990] EG 9050, 38. The principal authority relied upon for this view was the judgment of Nourse J in *GMS Syndicate Ltd* v *Gary Elliott Ltd* [1982] Ch 1.

In *City of London Corporation* v *Fell*, Mr Desmond Perrett QC at first instance (in which one of the writers appeared as counsel for the City of London: [1992] 3 All ER 224) held that the obligations of the respondents, as original tenants, ceased on the expiration of the contractual term and did not extend into the period of the statutory continuation of the tenancy under Pt II of the 1954 Act. The Court of Appeal ([1993] 2 All ER 449) confirmed this decision, holding that where an original tenant had assigned the tenancy before the end of the contractual term, 'the tenancy' (which s. 24(1) of the 1954 Act provides shall not come to an end) could only mean the tenancy of the assignee. Thus, if the original tenant contracted to pay rent only during the contractual term (as in *Fell*), the landlord could not recover from him any rent payable in respect of any period after that date. The House of Lords ([1993] 3 WLR 1164) reiterated this principle, concluding that there is nothing in Pt II of the 1954 Act to impose liability on an original tenant who has ceased to have any interest in the demised premises. For a short note on the House of Lords decision, see 'Liability of an Original Tenant' (Legal Notes) [1993] EG 9349, 112. Contrast, however, *Herbert Duncan Ltd* v *Cluttons* [1993] 2 All ER 449, where the word 'term' was expressly defined to include 'any period of holding over or extension thereof whether by statute or common law'.

Lastly, our suggested answer contains a reference to *Kumar* v *Dunning* [1987] 3 WLR 1167 and the doctrine of subrogation. If you are mystified as to what this doctrine entails, see Brown, J., and Pawlowski, M., 'Rights of Subrogation and Non-Payment of Rent' [1994] 14/4 RRLR, 22.

Suggested Answer

In view of Babyfoods Ltd's liquidation, it is likely that Property Developments Ltd will pursue Bakewell Ltd for the arrears of rent. (It appears that an original tenant has no power to force the landlord to sue the current assignee in breach before pursuing its remedy against it: *Norwich Union Life Insurance* v *Low Profile Fashions* (1992) 64 P & CR 187.)

As original tenant, Bakewell Ltd is liable on all the covenants in the lease for the duration of the term, and such liability will continue notwithstanding the assignment of the term to Babyfoods Ltd. The Landlord and Tenant (Covenants) Act 1995 does not abrogate the privity of contract rule in respect of leases granted before 1 January 1996. Since Bakewell Ltd's lease was granted in 1986, it would not have been released from its obligations under the lease upon the assignment to Babyfoods Ltd.

Bakewell Ltd's liability will also continue despite an assignment of the freehold reversionary interest in the shop to Property Developments Ltd. Under the Law of Property Act 1925, s. 141, the obligation to pay rent (and the benefit of other tenant's covenants which have reference to the subject matter of the lease) runs with the freehold reversion. Thus, Property Developments Ltd may sue to recover the arrears of rent from Bakewell Ltd notwithstanding the assignment of the freehold.

However, the effect of s. 141 is that, once the reversion has been assigned, it is only the assignee of the reversion who can sue on the real covenants in the lease, whether the breach took place before or after the date of the assignment (*Re King, Deceased, Robinson* v *Gray* [1963] Ch 459 and *London & County (A & D) Ltd* v *Wilfred Sportsman Ltd* [1971] Ch 764, *per* Russell LJ, at pp. 782–4). Moreover, in *Arlesford Trading Co. Ltd* v *Servansingh* [1971] 1 WLR 1080, it was held that the ability to enforce the covenants in the lease against the original tenant passed to the assignee of the reversion although there had never been privity of estate between the parties. In that case (as in the facts here), the original tenant had assigned the lease before the new landlord had acquired the reversion so that the two had never been in any direct relationship of landlord and tenant.

The position prior to the enactment of the Landlord and Tenant (Covenants) Act 1995 was that the liability of the original tenant continued even where the terms of the lease were subsequently varied by the original landlord and an assignee of the lease. In *Selous Street Properties Ltd* v *Oronel Fabrics Ltd* (1984) 270 EG 643 and 743, for example, the landlord brought an action for arrears of rent against the original tenants, who contested their liability on the ground that the rent review (under which the unpaid rent arose) had been carried out on a basis different from that to which the original tenants had agreed. The court held that any increase in the rental value of the premises for rent review purposes did not discharge the liability of the original tenant. The assignee stood in the shoes of the original tenant and was the owner of the whole leasehold estate and, hence, could deal with it so as to alter it or its terms: see also *GUS Management Ltd* v *Texas Homecare Ltd* [1993] 27 EG 130. The principle was also applied in *Centrovincial Estates plc* v *Bulk Storage Ltd* (1983) 268 EG 59, where it was held that the original tenant was liable to pay rent at the rate fixed under a rent review clause even though this took place after it had parted with the lease. Similarly, in *Friends' Provident Life Office* v *British Railways Board* [1996] 1 All ER 336, a substantial increase in rent did not affect the original tenant's liability. The 1995 Act has altered the law by providing (in s. 18) that no former tenant (or his surety) is liable to pay any sum resulting from a 'relevant variation' to the terms of the lease effected after the enactment of the Act (i.e., 1 January 1996). Essentially, the liability of former tenants (and their sureties) will be increased by subsequent variations only if either (1) it is contemplated in the lease, or (2) it is permitted under the general law. An increase in rent under a rent review clause is not covered by s. 18 because the former tenant would have agreed to such a covenant and the covenant itself would not have been altered. Accordingly, Bakewell Ltd will remain liable on the covenant to pay rent, notwithstanding the increase of rent on review since the assignment of the lease.

To what extent may Bakewell Ltd seek to claim an indemnity in respect of the arrears of rent against its assignee? In the absence of an express indemnity covenant, there is implied into any assignment for valuable consideration a covenant under which the assignee will indemnify the assignor in respect of any liability incurred for any breach of covenant committed during the remainder of the term (Law of Property Act 1925, s. 77(1)(c) (unregistered land) and Land Registration Act 1925, s. 24(1) (registered land)). The effect of these provisions is that Bakewell Ltd will have a right of indemnity against its immediate assignee (Babyfoods Ltd) in respect of the £15,000 rent arrears it may be called upon to pay to Property Developments Ltd. The indemnity may not be worth very much in view of Babyfoods Ltd's liquidation but Bakewell Ltd should make a formal claim in the liquidation in case the company has any assets worth realising.

In addition to this statutory right, Bakewell Ltd will also have an implied right of indemnity at common law against the assignee in breach (*Moule* v *Garrett* (1872) LR 7 Ex 101; *Selous Street Properties Ltd* v *Oronel Fabrics Ltd* (1984) 270 EG 643 and 743 and *Re Healing Research Trustee Co. Ltd* (1992) 2 EGLR 231).

In *Kumar* v *Dunning* [1987] 3 WLR 1167, it was held that the benefit of a surety covenant may pass to an assignee of the reversion: see also, *P & A Swift Investments Ltd* v *Combined English Stores Group plc* [1988] 3 WLR 313. Accordingly, in the present case, Property Developments Ltd may seek to claim the arrears of rent from Mr Brown subject to the point that any variation in the terms of the lease between the landlord and the tenant which could prejudice the surety will discharge the latter from his obligations (*Holme* v *Brunskill* (1878) 3 QBD 495).

It also appears from the *Kumar* case that, if Babyfoods Ltd is called upon to pay the rent, then it would be entitled to the benefit of Mr Brown's surety covenant under the doctrine of subrogation. In other words, it would be able to recover the rent arrears from Mr Brown by being subrogated to the rights of the landlord under the surety covenant.

Upon the liquidation of Babyfoods Ltd, the lease will vest in the liquidator of the company, who may disclaim the lease under the Insolvency Act 1986, s. 178. If the bankruptcy (or liquidation) is that of an *assignee* of the lease (as in the present case), the disclaimer will not end the term and the liability of the original tenant will not be discharged, although it will determine the assignee's interest in the term, which continues to subsist although apparently having no owner until a vesting order is made (*Warnford Investments Ltd* v *Duckworth* [1979] Ch 127; *WH Smith Ltd* v *Wyndham Investments Ltd* [1994] EGCS 94 and *Hindcastle Ltd* v *Barbara Attenborough Associates Ltd* [1996] 1 All ER 737 (HL)). Under the Insolvency Act 1986, s. 181, Bakewell Ltd may apply to the court for an order vesting the lease in its name.

A disclaimer of the lease will also not affect the obligations to the landlord of a surety of the original (insolvent) tenant. Under s. 178(4) of the 1986 Act, the interest of the insolvent tenant in the disclaimed property is determined by the disclaimer and the lease extinguished so far as he is concerned, but the lease is deemed to continue in respect of the rights and obligations of other persons: *Hindcastle Ltd* v *Barbara Attenborough Associates Ltd* [1996] 1 All ER 737 (HL), overruling *Stacey* v *Hill* [1901] 1 QB 660. (See [1997] Conv 24 for a commentary on the House of Lords ruling.) However, where it is the *assignee* who is in liquidation, the effect of a disclaimer on the assignee's guarantor will depend on the wording of the guarantee covenant. If Mr Brown's obligations (set out in the licence to assign) are stated to be independent of the covenants of Babyfoods Ltd, then it is clear that they will survive the disclaimer and Mr Brown will continue to be liable. If, however, the liability of Mr Brown is stated to arise only on a *default* of Babyfoods Ltd, then the situation is different. The decision in *Warnford Investments* makes it clear that, after a disclaimer, the assignee has no liability to pay the rent reserved by the lease. So, in *Murphy* v *Sawyer-Hoare* (1993) 27 EG 127, the liability of the assignee's surety arose upon the default of the assignee. After the date of the disclaimer, there could be no such default so it was held that the surety had no liability from then on. This would not, of course, absolve Mr Brown from the £15,000 arrears of rent due up to the date of the disclaimer.

What if the lease had been granted for only a 10-year term? If this were the case, the issue would be whether Bakewell Ltd's liability was limited to the contractual term of the lease (which would have expired in 1996), or whether it extended into the statutory continuation of the tenancy (being a business tenancy) under the Landlord and Tenant Act 1954, s. 24. A great deal will depend upon the wording of the original tenant's covenant to pay rent in the lease and the definition of the word 'term' in the reddendum. In *City of London Corporation* v *Fell* [1993] 3 WLR 1164, the House of Lords held that an original tenant's liability did not extend beyond the original contractual term. However, in *Herbert Duncan Ltd* v *Cluttons* [1993] 2 All ER 449, the wording of the lease expressly defined the term to include 'any period of holding over or extension thereof whether by statute or common law'. The Court of Appeal held that, where the term expressly covers any continuation, the original tenant cannot escape liability beyond the term date. Even so, he will be liable only for the contractual rent, not any higher interim rent which may be payable under s. 24A of the 1954 Act.

QUESTION 2

(a)   In what circumstances may a landlord require the tenant to enter into an authorised guarantee agreement under the Landlord and Tenant (Covenants) Act 1995?   [15 marks]

(b)   The Earl of Leamington holds the freehold title to a pet shop in Coventry. The current tenant is Bernard, who holds a 10-year lease which was granted to him in 1997. The lease includes a covenant on the part of the landlord to maintain a policy of insurance in relation to the demised premises with the Balmoral Insurance Co. Ltd and to pay them the yearly insurance premium of £750.

The Earl now wishes to sell his freehold reversionary interest to a property investment company and seeks your advice as to how (it at all) he may be released from his insurance liability under the lease upon assignment of the reversion. Advise him.   [10 marks]

Commentary

This is a two-part question on the workings of the 1995 Act. The first part requires you to give an overview of the mechanics of the authorised guarantee agreement (AGA). Try to be succinct and informative in your answer. Don't dwell on one aspect to the exclusion of other important points. Imagine you are giving a short seminar presentation to your fellow students on this topic. Your objective is to demonstrate to the examiner that you have a good basic understanding of how the AGA operates in practice.

The second part of the question requires an examination of the rules which permit an original landlord to seek a release from his covenants under the lease in accordance with the statutory procedure laid down by the 1995 Act.

Suggested Answer

(a)   The Landlord and Tenant (Covenants) Act 1995 introduced a new regime of landlord and tenant covenant liability into leases granted on or after 1 January 1996. It also modified existing leases from that date by introducing procedures (notably, the s. 17 notice procedure and overriding leases) to assist former tenants with continuing leasehold liability.

The basic principle under the Act is that, on assignment, the former tenant will be automatically released from his liabilities and only the tenant for the time being will be liable to the landlord. However, under a lease granted after 1 January 1996, a former tenant will remain liable for the defaults of his immediate assignee if the landlord obtains an authorised guarantee agreement (AGA) from him guaranteeing performance of the tenant's covenants by his immediate assignee. The landlord may require such an agreement from the former tenant either (1) automatically as one of the conditions for assignment set out in the covenant in the lease, or (2) because it is reasonable to do so.

Under (1), the parties to a new lease are given the right (under the 1995 Act) to agree in advance the conditions which the former tenant or prospective assignee must meet as a precondition of the landlord's consent to the assignment. A typical condition may be that the assignee must have net profits before tax in its most recent accounts of at least three times the rent, or that the assignee must provide a rent deposit or guarantor. Another condition may be that the former tenant enter into an AGA. So far as the latter is concerned, any form of commercial guarantee is permissible under the Act, so long as no term of the guarantee prevents the former tenant's statutory rights to be released from the guarantee upon a further assignment by his immediate assignee. (To the extent that the former tenant is not so released, the agreement is not an AGA and is void under the Act.)

As to (2), this will apply where the landlord's consent is required to the assignment and the landlord gives the consent on condition that the former tenant enters into an AGA. The condition must be lawfully imposed, and so this situation will arise in either of two cases:

(a)   where the lease contains an absolute prohibition against assignment, but the landlord decides in his discretion to permit the assignment if the former tenant offers a guarantee; or

(b)   (more commonly) where the lease requires the landlord's consent which cannot be unreasonably withheld (whether as a result of s. 19(1) of the Landlord and Tenant Act 1927 or because of an express proviso to that effect) and it is reasonable for the landlord to require a guarantee from the former tenant as a condition of granting his consent. Whether it is reasonable for the landlord to insist on an AGA as a precondition of granting consent will depend on all the circumstances of the case. These circumstances remain uncertain in the absence of any judicial guidance (to date) on this issue: but see *Wallis Fashion Group Ltd* v *General Accident Life Assurance Ltd* [2000] EGCS 45 in the context of a business tenancy renewal. It is also unclear to what extent the landlord can insist on additional security (e.g., in the form of a rent deposit) from the prospective assignee.

It is important to stress that the former tenant's liability under the AGA is entirely different from his previous liability as tenant under the lease before the assignment. The tenant liability is released and replaced by a new liability which is that of a surety only under the AGA. Thus, his liability will be discharged, for example, upon a subsequent variation of the lease terms.

The default notice procedure under s. 17 of the 1995 Act applies in the context of recovering arrears of rent, service charge and liquidated damages (including interest thereon) from the former tenant under his liability arising by virtue of an AGA. Equally, the former tenant is entitled to call for an overriding lease if he satisfies his immediate assignee's obligations under the lease by virtue of his AGA commitment. Apart from this, the original tenant may still seek an indemnity for his expenditure from his immediate assignee (under s. 77 of the Law of Property Act 1925 or s. 24 of the Land Registration Act 1925), or from the assignee in breach by way of indemnity under the common law rule in *Moule* v *Garrett* (1872) LR 7 EX 101.

(b)   Prior to the introduction of the 1995 Act, the original landlord remained liable on his real covenants in the lease throughout the whole term despite any assignment of his reversionary interest. This, in effect, mirrored the position of the original tenant under the privity of contract doctrine.

Given that tenants do not generally have any control over the assignment of the landlord's interest, a landlord who assigns his reversion post-1995 Act is not subject to the automatic release of his covenants like the original tenant. Instead, the landlord can apply to be released under the Act by serving a notice on the tenant either before or within four weeks after the assignment. If a tenant objects, the landlord can apply to court seeking a declaration that his release is reasonable. If there is no objection, the landlord will be released on completion of the assignment. But in the event that the landlord does not apply for a release or accepts the tenant's objection, or the court does not declare the release to be reasonable, the landlord will remain liable on his covenants following the assignment. He will, however, have another opportunity to apply for a release when there is a further assignment of the reversion by his assignee: s. 7 of the 1995 Act.

In the present case, the lease is a post-1995 Act lease (i.e., created after 1 January 1996) and so is caught by the new regime under the Act. Although, as we have seen, there is no mechanism for automatic release in the event of a landlord wishing to assign his reversion, the Earl can apply by notice to the tenant, Bernard, seeking a release from his leasehold liablities. If Bernard objects, the Earl should be advised to apply to the court for an order for release on the ground that Bernard's objections are unreasonable. This will depend on all the circumstances of the case.

If the Earl is unsuccessful in obtaining a release, he will continue to remain liable to Bernard as original landlord (by virtue of privity of contract) despite the sale of his freehold interest. He should be advised, however, to obtain a covenant from the purchaser (to be included in the deed of assignment) to the effect that the latter will inform him of any future assignment of the reversion, thus affording the Earl with another opportunity to seek a release of his liabilities at a future date.

QUESTION 3

   (a) In 1992, Hogan Estates Ltd granted to Tomkins Ltd a 20-year commercial lease of 200 sq. m. of office space at a rent of £12,000 per year, payable on the usual quarter days. The directors of Tomkins Ltd are Bob and Jane, who covenanted with Hogan Estates Ltd to pay all losses, costs, damage and expenses occasioned to the landlord by the non-payment of rent or breach of any obligation by the tenant.

In 1993, Hogan Estates Ltd sold their reversionary interest to the Duke of Hackney without expressly assigning the benefit of the surety covenant. A year later, Tomkins Ltd ran into financial difficulties and stopped paying the rent.

There is now £6,000 due, representing two quarters' rent unpaid. The Duke has made several formal demands for the rent from Tomkins Ltd but these have been to no avail. The Duke does not wish to forfeit the lease, but is keen to recover the rent from Bob and Jane.

Advise the Duke of Hackney.

(b)   In 1990, Fox Property Ltd granted Simon a 10-year lease of commercial premises at a rent of £8,000 per year payable in quarterly instalments.

In 1992, Simon assigned the lease to Brook Ltd. In 1995, Brook Ltd assigned the lease to Sherry, and she in turn (in 1998) assigned the lease to Tony. The lease expired in 2000 and Tony vacated the premises having failed to pay the last two instalments of rent due (i.e., £4,000). Tony has recently been declared bankrupt and has no assets of any value. Since Fox Property Ltd are unlikely to recover any of the unpaid rent from Tony as creditors in his bankruptcy, they have decided to pursue Simon instead for the rent arrears.

Advise Simon.

Commentary

Part (a) is concerned with the liability of a surety under a guarantee covenant and, in particular, the extent to which the benefit of such a covenant is capable of passing to an assignee landlord in the absence of any express assignment of the benefit. A good knowledge of case law is essential in order to achieve a high mark (see, *Kumar* v *Dunning* [1987] 3 WLR 1167; *P & A Swift Investments* v *Combined English Stores Group plc* [1988] 3 WLR 313 and *Coronation Street Industrial Properties Ltd* v *Ingall Industries* [1989] 1 WLR 304). For further reading, see Brown, J., 'The Enforceability of Surety Covenants' [1994] 14/2 RRLR, 18.

Part (b) is concerned with the liability of an original tenant and his assignees for non-payment of rent and, in particular, the ability of an original tenant to claim an indemnity from subsequent assignees of the term.

Questions on enforceability of covenants may be factually complex, involving not only the original landlord and tenant but also subsequent assignees of the term and (possibly) the reversion. It is sometimes worth spending a few minutes drawing a simple diagram to help you identify the respective parties. For the purposes of part (b), we would suggest something along the lines set out in Figure 3.1.

Figure 3.1   The parties involved

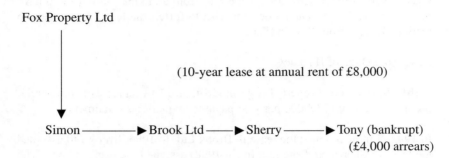

Fox Property Ltd

(10-year lease at annual rent of £8,000)

Simon ─────────▶ Brook Ltd ───▶ Sherry ──────▶ Tony (bankrupt)
                                                            (£4,000 arrears)

Suggested Answer

   (a)   In this case, Hogan Estates Ltd have sold their reversionary interest to
the Duke of Hackney without expressly assigning the benefit of the surety
covenant. The question therefore arises whether the Duke (as an assignee of the
reversion) may enforce this covenant against the two sureties, Bob and Jane.

Bob's and Jane's liability under their surety covenant, being only secondary, is
dependent upon liability being established against the party primarily in default
(i.e., Tomkins Ltd). In this connection, by virtue of the Law of Property Act
1925, s. 141(1), the Duke has inherited the benefit of (and right to sue upon) all
those tenant's covenants which have 'reference to the subject-matter of the
lease', including the covenant to pay rent. Thus, the Duke can sue Tomkins Ltd
(as original tenant) for the rental sums owing, the only difficulty being that the
company is in financial difficulties and, accordingly, unlikely to meet the sum
due. (The privity of contract rule applies to the present case since the lease was
granted in 1992, prior to the enactment of the Landlord and Tenant (Covenants)
Act 1995.)

But has the benefit of the surety covenant passed to the Duke? In the absence
of an express assignment of the benefit of the covenant (complying with the
formalities laid down in the Law of Property Act 1925, s. 136(1)) it might seem,
at first glance, that the Duke has not inherited the benefit of the right to sue upon
this covenant. However, authority suggests that, in certain circumstances, it is
possible for an assignee landlord to acquire the benefit of a surety covenant,
even though given to a predecessor in title, in circumstances where there has
been no express assignment, and thus enforce the same against the surety in
question (*Kumar* v *Dunning* [1987] 3 WLR 1167; *P & A Swift Investments Ltd*

v *Combined English Stores Group plc* [1988] 3 WLR 313 and *Coronation Street Industrial Properties Ltd* v *Ingall Industries plc* [1989] 1 WLR 304).

In the *Swift* case, the House of Lords held that a benefit under a covenant could be enforced by the assignee of the reversion without express assignment if the covenant touched and concerned the land. Whether a covenant touched and concerned the land depended on the covenant satisfying three conditions, namely: (i) that it was beneficial only to the reversioner for the time being; (ii) that it affected the nature, quality, mode of user or value of the reversioner's land; and (iii) that it was not personal in nature. If those three conditions were satisfied, a covenant for the payment of a sum of money could touch and concern the land if it was connected with something to be done on, to, or in relation to the land. A covenant by a surety guaranteeing that a tenant's covenants which touched and concerned the land would be performed and observed was itself a covenant which touched and concerned the land. Accordingly, in that case, the assignee landlord was entitled to recover unpaid rent from the surety.

In the present case, the tenant's covenant is a covenant to pay a sum of money (i.e., rent). This covenant, clearly, 'touches and concerns' the land (i.e., the freehold reversionary estate) and the surety covenant appears to meet all the above requirements (i.e., it is not expressed to be exclusively for the personal benefit of Hogan Estates Ltd, it clearly affects the nature, quality, mode of user or value of the reversioner's land and, as a covenant, is beneficial to the reversioner for the time being). The benefit of the surety covenant has, therefore, passed to the Duke, who may thus hold Bob and Jane to account for the arrears of rent of Tomkins Ltd.

(b) The original parties to the lease are Fox Property Ltd (as landlord) and Simon (as tenant). Simon, as original tenant, is as a matter of contract legally liable on all the covenants in the lease (including the covenant to pay rent) for the duration of the term, even where he subsequently assigns his interest. The position is unaffected by the Landlord and Tenant (Covenants) Act 1995 since, here again, the lease was granted (in 1990) prior to the enactment of the Act (i.e., 1 January 1996). The doctrine of privity of contract continues to apply to old tenancies granted before this date. Invariably the tenant will covenant expressly on behalf of himself and his successors in title, but even where this is not the case he will be deemed to do so in respect of those covenants which relate to the land (e.g., a covenant to pay rent) by virtue of the Law of Property Act 1925, s. 79(1), unless a contrary intention appears in the lease.

It follows, therefore, that Simon (as original tenant) remains liable to Fox Property Ltd in contract to pay the rent throughout the term of the lease, irrespective of the subsequent assignments of the leasehold term. In this connection, it has been held that the original tenant has no power to force the landlord to sue the current assignee in breach before pursuing his remedy against him (*Norwich Union Life Insurance* v *Low Profile Fashions* (1992) 64 P & CR 187).

In order, however, for Fox Property Ltd to recover the arrears of rent from Simon, it must give notice of its intention to do so within six months of the liability arising: s. 17 of the Landlord and Tenant (Covenants) Act 1995. This provision, which applies to all tenancies (including those entered into before 1 January 1996), requires that if the landlord wishes to sue the original tenant for fixed charges (i.e., arrears of rent, service charge or liquidated damages, including interest thereon) it must give the requisite notice within the prescribed time-limit. Failure to do so means that the landlord loses the right to recover from the original tenant to the extent that the sums fell due more than six months prior to any notice served. Another important provision under the 1995 Act, which is common to both old and new leases, relates to the former tenant's entitlement to an overriding lease. The Act entitles Simon, if he satisfies Tony's obligations to the landlord, to call for the grant to him (within 12 months) of an overriding lease from Fox Property Ltd for a term equal to the unexpired residue of the current lease (plus a nominal reversion). This would have the effect of inserting Simon as an intermediate landlord between Fox Property Ltd and the defaulting assignee, Tony. Although this may ultimately enable Simon to recoup his expenditure in discharging his liability to the landlord, it also has several disadvantages, namely, the overriding lease will attract stamp duty and, by taking up such a lease, Simon may become liable for significant landlord's covenants (e.g., to repair, insure, perform maintenance services, etc.).

As between Fox Property Ltd and the subsequent assignees (Brook Ltd, Sherry and Tony), there exists privity of estate while each assignee is in possession. Thus, since Tony is the current assignee in possession, privity of estate exists between him and the original landlord. (There is no longer any relationship of estate as between Fox Property Ltd and Brook Ltd or Sherry.) As the current assignee of the lease, Tony can sue or be sued on the covenants in the lease which relate to the land demised (e.g., a covenant to pay rent) under the rule in *Spencer's Case* (1583) 5 Co Rep 16a. The difficulty here is that Tony is bankrupt and has no assets of any value with which to meet the arrears of rent.

If Simon is liable for all the rent owing from Tony (for the reasons mentioned earlier), it may be possible for him to claim reimbursement, by way of indemnity. Such an indemnity may arise in several ways, namely: (i) by way of an express covenant for indemnity; (ii) by way of implication under statute (the Law of Property Act 1925, s. 77(1)(c)); or (iii) by implication under the rule in *Moule* v *Garrett* (1872) LR 7 Ex 101.

As to (i), a tenant, on assigning the unexpired residue of the term, may oblige his assignee to enter into an express covenant for indemnity with him. Clear words are required to achieve this (see, e.g., *Butler Estates Co.* v *Bean* [1942] 1 KB 1). In the present case, however, it seems that Simon has not extracted any such express right of indemnity from his assignee, Brook Ltd.

As to (ii), there is implied into any assignment for value a covenant under which the assignee will indemnify the assignor in respect of any liability incurred for any breach of covenant committed during the remainder of the term (s. 77(1)(c) of the 1925 Act (unregistered land) and the Land Registration Act 1925, s. 24(1) (registered land)). The effect of s. 77(1) is that the original tenant will have a right of indemnity against his immediate assignee and each subsequent assignor will also have a similar right of indemnity against his assignee, thereby creating a chain of indemnity covenants. Thus, it is open to Simon to claim an indemnity from his immediate assignee (Brook Ltd) for the rent arrears owed by Tony. Similarly, Brook Ltd could claim an indemnity from its immediate asignee, Sherry, who in turn could seek reimbursement from Tony. In this connection, it has been held that an assignee who accepts the liabilities and responsibilities attached to the lease gives valuable consideration for the assignment within the meaning of s. 77(1) of the 1925 Act (*Johnsey Estates Ltd* v *Lewis Manley (Engineering) Ltd* (1987) 284 EG 1240).

As to (iii), in addition to the statutory right under s. 77(1), the original tenant has an implied right of indemnity at common law against the assignee in breach (see, e.g., *Selous Street Properties Ltd* v *Oronel Fabrics Ltd* (1984) 270 EG 643 and 743, where the original tenant was held entitled to be indemnified by the current assignee in breach under the principle in *Moule* v *Garrett*, above, and to be subrogated to the rights of the landlord against such assignee). The rule would therefore permit Simon to sue Tony directly so as to recoup the arrears which Simon is contractually liable to pay to Fox Property Ltd.

Since Tony is not worth suing, Simon's practical recourse is by way of indemnity against Brook Ltd under s. 77(1) of the 1925 Act. In this connection, the original tenant is not required to serve a s. 17 notice on his assignee in order to recover payments from him (*M. W. Kellog Ltd* v *F. Tobin* (unreported, 8 April 1999)).

QUESTION 4

In 1997, Blake Ltd granted Peter a 10-year lease of a restaurant in Pimlico, London. The annual rent was £80,000 per annum payable in quarterly instalments. The lease contained a forfeiture clause allowing the landlord to re-enter upon the premises in the event of rent default or any other tenant's breach of covenant. The lease also contained a tenant's qualified covenant against assignment. This covenant stated, *inter alia*, that the prior written consent of the landlord was required in the event of an assignment, and that the tenant enter into an authorised guarantee agreement with the landlord guaranteeing performance of the tenant's covenants in the lease by the tenant's assignee as a precondition of granting such consent.

In 1998, with the prior written consent of Blake Ltd, Peter assigned the unexpired residue of the lease to Boris. Peter also entered into an authorised guarantee agreement with Blake Ltd, thereby standing as guarantor for Boris's leasehold obligations. Since taking up possession, Boris has been operating a Polish restaurant from the premises.

In 1999, Boris's restaurant business came upon hard times. Custom fell away and Boris was plunged into financial insolvency. As a consequence, Boris has fallen into arrears with the rent due under the lease. The last quarterly instalment received by Blake Ltd was in March 1999. No payments have been received since this quarter.

Advise Blake Ltd as to it rights and remedies against Peter. (Peter has not been given any written warning or other indication of the fact that Boris has fallen into rent arrears).

Commentary

This question focuses specifically on some of the changes to the law effected by the Landlord and Tenant (Covenants) Act 1995. A good answer will mention the old law relating to the original tenant's liability under the privity of contract rule, and the changes which have been introduced by the 1995 Act (i.e., the abolition of the doctrine of privity, the introduction of authorised guarantee agreements, the default notice procedure and overriding leases).

There has been little case law to date on the workings of the 1995 Act so your answer will inevitably concentrate on detailing the relevant provisions of the Act. This is an easy question provided you have mastered how the Act operates in practice. For further reading, see Elvidge, S. and Williams, P., 'Overriding Importance' [1996] EG 9647 132 and Walter, P., 'The Landlord and Tenant (Covenants) Act 1995: A Legislative Folly' [1996] Conv. 432.

Suggested Answer

It is important to note at the outset that Peter's lease was granted in 1997 (i.e., after the coming into force of the Landlord and Tenant (Covenants) Act 1995 on 1 January 1996).

For new leases entered into on or after 1 January 1996, the Act provides that that all leasehold covenants, irrespective of whether they 'touch and concern' the land, are fully enforceable between landlord and tenant, except where the covenant is expressed to be purely personal. The basic rule is that a tenant is liable on the covenants in the lease only while he remains tenant — upon assignment of the lease, he is automatically discharged from further liability under the lease. The Act therefore effectively abolishes the enduring contractual liability of original tenants, but only in respect of new leases granted on or after 1 January 1996.

While a tenant will automatically be released on assignment of the term in most cases (see s. 5 of the 1995 Act), the landlord can require the outgoing tenant to give a guarantee as to future performance of the tenant's obligations by its immediate assignee. In this connection, the Act states that the assigning tenant may be required to enter into an authorised guarantee agreement (AGA) with the landlord as a condition of granting consent to the assignment: s. 16. It is noteworthy, however, that where an assignment is made in breach of a covenant (e.g., where the tenant has failed to secure the landlord's prior written consent, where required), the assigning tenant remains liable despite the (unlawful) assignment.

The Act also allows landlords of new leases to incorporate stricter assignment conditions in qualified covenants against assignment. In short, landlords can require that incoming assignees satisfy factual and discretionary conditions (e.g., that the incoming tenant has, in his most recent accounts, a net profit before tax of at least three times the ground rent).

The Act has also introduced several new measures which apply to both old (i.e., granted before 1 January 1996) and new leases. Of particular significance in the present context is the introduction of the 'default notice' and 'overriding lease' procedures: see ss. 17–20. The default notice procedure is designed as an 'early warning system' for former tenants (and guarantors: see *Cheverell Estates Ltd* v *Harris* [1998] 02 EG 127) who may be obliged to make good to the landlord the financial default of the current tenant. In this connection, s. 17 of the Act states that the landlord must serve on such a party a default notice detailing any fixed charges unpaid by the current tenant, within six months of the relevant sums falling due. These fixed charges are defined in the Act as rent arrears, service charges, insurance fees, and liquidated damages (including interest thereon). In order, therefore, for a landlord to be able to recover any such charges either from an original tenant in an old lease (under the doctrine of privity of contract), or as against a former tenant in a new lease who has entered into an AGA, he must first serve the requisite s. 17 notice in respect of each payment within six months of the charge falling due. (It is noteworthy, however, that a single notice could cover more than one payment, provided that each sum was due less than six months previously.) In the event that the landlord fails to serve such a notice within six months, the charge becomes irrecoverable.

Hand-in-glove with the default notice procedure, the 1995 Act introduced the novel concept of the overriding lease, which is intended to benefit former original tenants (who may be liable for the current tenant's default under the doctrine of privity of contract) and former tenants in new leases (who may be so obliged under an AGA). The Act states that former tenants (or their guarantors) who have paid up under a default notice have 12 months from the date of payment in which to claim 'an overriding lease' from the landlord. Such a lease is inserted above the existing lease, thus creating a direct landlord and tenant relationship between the former tenant (or guarantor) and the assignee in default. In other words, the claimant of the overriding lease becomes the current assignee's landlord and can determine what action, including forfeiture, to take against him. Such an overriding lease will generally be on the same terms as the defaulting tenant's lease, and of a term equivalent to the residue of such lease save that a small reversionary period (typically, three days) will be added. The main advantage, therefore, of acquiring an overriding lease is that the former tenant (or his guarantor) can regain possession of the premises (through forfeiture proceedings) with a view to marketing the property afresh in order to recoup the monies paid to the landlord in discharging its liability under a s. 17 notice.

In the present case, because Peter's lease is a new lease under the Act, the enduring contractual liability of Peter, as original tenant, has been effectively abolished. However, Peter still remains liable to underwrite the financial default and other leasehold obligations of Boris by virtue of his liability under the AGA, which he entered into with Blake Ltd as a condition of the latter granting consent to the assignment. This, in principle, is quite lawful, and indeed encouraged by the Act. However, Peter can be held liable for Boris's rent arrears only upon receipt of a valid s. 17 notice claiming the arrears due. We are told that Blake Ltd received the last quarterly payment in respect of rent in March 1999. Blake Ltd can pursue Peter for those rent arrears only if it gave Peter the appropriate notice within six months of that charge becoming due. In this respect, s. 17 provides a statutory limitation period of six months in relation to landlords who are seeking to claim arrears of rent or other fixed charges from former tenants/guarantors. Since Blake Ltd has clearly not served any such notice on Peter, it will be barred from recovering those arrears from him. This, however, will not preclude Blake Ltd from recovering more recent rent arrears provided it serves the requisite s. 17 notice within the prescribed time-limit. Should Peter then discharge his liability in respect of those arrears to the landlord, he will be able to claim an overriding lease of an equivalent length of the residue of the current lease, plus three days. Save as to this, the overriding lease will be on the same terms and conditions as the existing lease.

Peter will be liable on the overriding lease for the rent to Blake Ltd, and will become Boris's landlord. If Boris fails to pay the rent to Peter (as his new landlord) then Peter will be able to seek possession of Boris's lease by instigating forfeiture proceedings against him for non-payment of rent. This is possible because we are informed that Boris's lease (and, consequently, the overriding lease) contains a forfeiture clause, which allows the landlord to re-enter the premises in the event, *inter alia*, of non-payment of rent. If Peter does seek to forfeit Boris's lease, the waiver rules relating to forfeiture will apply as normal, as will the rules relating to relief against forfeiture for non-payment of rent: see ss. 138 and 139 of County Courts Act 1984. If Peter is successful in his forfeiture action against Boris, he will be in a position to obtain a new tenant for the restaurant premises by either subletting or assigning the same with Blake Ltd's consent in accordance with the terms of his overriding lease.

QUESTION 5

What impact will the Contracts (Rights of Third Parties) Act 1999 have on the enforceability of covenants in commercial leases? Give specific examples to illustrate your answer.

Commentary

This is a topical question in view of the fact that the 1999 Act came into force on 11 November 1999. It does not have retrospective effect, but is subject to a six-month opt-in period (i.e., it applies to all contracts entered into on or after 11 May 2000, but contracts entered into from 11 November 1999 to 10 May 2000 could be made subject to the Act if the parties so agreed).

The question requires you to give an overview of the Act and, more specifically, to give examples of how the legislation will affect the enforceability of leasehold covenants in commercial leases. One obvious example relates to covenants by subtenants which may be for the benefit of superior landlords, or covenants given by superior landlords (e.g., to provide maintenance services for the benefit of tenants) which may be enforced by subtenants. In addition, the Act is likely to affect covenants which are taken to benefit adjoining owners or other tenants in a development. You will also score higher marks if you are able to show how the 1999 Act operates in conjunction with the Landlord and Tenant (Covenants) Act 1995 — by no means an easy task, if your knowledge of the 1995 Act is only superficial!

Suggested Answer

The doctrine of privity of contract provides that a contract under English law cannot generally confer rights or impose obligations arising under it on persons who are not parties to the contract. In essence, it prevents someone, not a party to the contract, from taking its benefit; and it also protects that person from burdens being imposed on him, without his consent, by the parties to the contract. The rule has given rise to much criticism because, in principle, there is no reason why rights in favour of non-parties should not be created, if the parties so desire.

The 1999 Act allows a third party to enforce a term of a contract, despite not being a party to it, if the contract expressly provides that he may, or purports to confer a benefit on him. The third party need not be individually named in the contract and need not even be in existence at the time the contract is made, provided he is identified by description. For example, a covenant in a lease purporting to confer benefits on subtenants can now be enforceable by any subtenant of the demised property. The intention of the Act is, therefore, to place the third party in the same position as if he had been a party to the contract, so that he has all the same remedies as the contracting parties and is subject to all the same restrictions and exclusions. So far as the parties themselves are concerned, they have all the defences against claims by the third party that they would have had if he had been a party to the contract. They are not, however, entitled to rescind the contract or vary its terms so as to deprive the third party of its benefit, without obtaining the third party's consent. It is, however, possible to exclude the application of the Act by agreement.

Under the Landlord and Tenant (Covenants) Act 1995, a subtenant has no ability directly to enforce a superior landlord's covenant contained in a headlease which is a new tenancy (i.e., granted on or after 1 January 1996). (If the headlease is an old tenancy, the subtenant can directly enforce the superior landlord's covenants, provided they relate to the sublet premises.) The 1999 Act now permits direct enforcement of such covenants (e.g., a covenant to insure or repair the building) by a subtenant, provided the lease expressly so provides or the covenant in question purports to confer such a benefit on him: s. 1. In the latter case, however, the subtenant will not be able to enforce the covenant if, on a proper construction of the headlease, it appears that the head landlord and head tenant did not intend the covenant to be enforceable by the subtenant. Quite apart from this, it is also open to the parties to state expressly that they do not want any other persons (e.g., subtenants) to have a right to enforce any part of the headlease. As already mentioned, in order to have the right of enforcement under s. 1, the third party must be identified expressly in the contract either by name, or as a member of a class or as answering a particular description, although it need not be in existence at the time the contract is entered into.

Under s. 3(5) of the 1995 Act, a superior landlord is able to enforce a covenant restricting user against a subtenant, but not any other covenant. In *Amsprop Trading Ltd* v *Harris Distribution Ltd* [1997] 1 WLR 1025, for example, it was held that, although the sublease expressly referred to the superior landlords as persons for whose benefit the repairing covenants in the sublease were given, the covenants were not made with the superior landlords and, accordingly, the latter could not enforce them directly against the subtenant. Under the 1999 Act, however, subleases can now contain covenants (e.g., to repair or permit access) expressed to be for the benefit of any superior landlord, which can then be directly enforceable against the subtenant. Although the same effect can be achieved by imposing direct covenants in the licence to sublet, the new Act will provide a much simpler mechanism for direct enforcement as between superior landlord and subtenant.

Under the 1999 Act, it is also possible for covenants in relation to say, nuisance, noise, etc. by one tenant to be taken for the benefit of other tenants in a development such as a shopping centre. Prior to the Act, such covenants would normally only have been enforceable by virtue of a building scheme under the rule in *Elliston* v *Reacher* [1908] 2 Ch 374. A recent example of the problems associated with the enforcement of leasehold covenants in the context of a shopping centre is the case of *Co-operative Insurance Society* v *Argyll Stores (Holdings) Ltd* [1997] 3 All ER 297, where the House of Lords held that a covenant in a lease of retail premises to keep open for trading during business hours was not, other than in exceptional circumstances, specifically enforceable by a landlord: see, Bailey, P., 'When Shops Go AWOL' [1997] EG 9723, pp. 137–39. More strikingly, in *Transworld Land Co.* v *J. Sainsbury plc* [1990] 2 EGLR 255, the landlord sought to claim damages in respect of the adverse effect on other tenants of J. Sainsbury having closed their store in the landlord's shopping centre: see also, *Costain Property Developments Ltd* v *Finlay & Co. Ltd* [1989] 1 EGLR 237. Clearly, a more direct route to the enforcement of the keep-open covenant in the *Transworld* case would have been for the other tenants within the centre to be able to claim their trading losses against Sainsbury. The 1999 Act now makes this possible.

The interrelation between the 1995 and 1999 Acts is likely to give rise to some problems in the future. What, for example, is the position if a tenant, who undertakes a repairing obligation for the benefit of other tenants in a development, subsequently assigns his lease? Under the 1995 Act, he will be released (in the absence of an authorised guarantee agreement) from further performance of the tenant's covenants in the lease. He cannot, therefore, be sued by other tenants on the repairing covenant after the assignment. But what is the position of the assignee? Under the 1995 Act, the landlord can enforce the covenant against him, but what about the other tenants? Under the 1999 Act, they are able to enforce the covenant against 'the promisor', defined in s. 1(7) as 'the *party to the contract* against whom the term is enforceable by the third party'. The obvious difficulty here is that the assignee is not a party to the contract (i.e., the lease) but has merely acquired the leasehold estate by assignment. One solution to this problem is ensure that the assignee covenants (in the licence to assign) not only with the landlord but also with other tenants to observe the tenant's covenants in the lease. This, of course, involves reverting to the pre-1999 Act practice of requiring direct covenants from the assignee.

As mentioned earlier, it is permissible for the parties expressly to contract out of the Act for contracts made on or after 11 May 2000. This, it is suggested, is likely to be common practice in the leasehold context. For example, a superior landlord granting a headlease will usually be reluctant to undertake onerous obligations (e.g., to repair) to a class of subtenants. This reluctance is all the more likely given that the 1999 Act does not specifically state whether or not rights acquired pursuant to it are assignable. The danger here is that the superior landlord may have little or no control over who is within the potential class. It also seems unlikely that subtenants would wish to expose themselves to greater liability under their covenants in favour of superior landlords. Practically speaking, therefore, the new Act may have only limited impact on commercial leases. In the majority of new leases, the expectation amongst practitioners is that there will be an express clause excluding the operation of the Act. By contrast, in the residential field, the enforcement of nuisance and noise covenants will be more relevant to adjoining tenants in, say, a block of flats, and so a decision to retain the provisions of the Act is more likely.

4 Implied and Usual Covenants

INTRODUCTION

In this chapter, we have included four questions covering the following topics:

(a)   the landlord's implied covenant for quiet enjoyment and nuisance;

(b)   the landlord's implied covenant not to derogate from grant;

(c)   unlawful eviction and harassment;

(d)   usual covenants;

(e)   a tenant's denial of his landlord's title.

(Implied obligations to repair are covered in **Chapter 6** under the heading 'Leasehold Dilapidations'.)

Problem questions on quiet enjoyment and non-derogation from grant are popular with examiners. Since the publication of the first edition of this book, there have been several important developments in this area. Note, for example, that the decision in *Port* v *Griffith* [1938] 1 All ER 295 (see pp. 48–49 of the first edition), concerning a landlord who let adjoining premises to the tenant's trade rival, has been applied by Garland J in *Romulus Trading Co. Ltd* v *Comet Properties Ltd* [1996] 2 EGLR 70. The upshot of both these decisions is that a landlord will not be in derogation from grant where, having let premises to the tenant for a particular purpose, he then lets adjoining property for a substantially similar purpose. The fact that this makes the tenant's business on the demised property more expensive (or less convenient) to carry on is irrelevant: *O'Cedar Ltd* v *Slough Trading Co.* [1927] 2 KB 123. The landlord will be held liable in these circumstances only if he has expressly covenanted not to let neighbouring premises for a competing use. A good example of a recent case applying the doctrine of non-derogation from grant is *Yank Ltd* v *Havering London Borough Council* [1998] EGCS 75, where the defendant council had failed to keep various activities on their land within reasonable limits even though they were contemplated by the parties at the time the lease was executed. If a permitted activity is carried on in an unreasonable way, it will constitute a breach of the covenant.

You should, of course, be aware of the recent House of Lords ruling in *Southwark London Borough Council* v *Mills* [1999] 4 All ER 449, on the liability of a landlord for inadequate sound insulation. This is an important decision and one likely to feature in a landlord and tenant or housing law exam paper. We have included an essay-type question on the case: see Questions 2 and 4.

Most importantly, you should be aware of the Housing Act 1988, s. 27(3), which imposes a statutory liability to pay damages on a landlord who personally, or through his agents, has committed acts which amount to the offences of unlawful eviction or harassment under the Protection from Eviction Act 1977, s. 1. This liability is incurred by acts occurring after 9 June 1988 and arises irrespective of whether or not there has actually been a conviction for the offence. Section 28(1) of the 1988 Act provides that the measure of damages for the purpose of s. 27(3) is the difference between the value of the landlord's interest subject to the residential occupier's right, and its value in the absence of the occupier's right (*Tagro* v *Cafane* [1991] 1 WLR 378). Note also that the tenant is entitled to damages under s. 27 of the 1988 Act or at common law for wrongful eviction, but not both (*Mason* v *Nwokorie* [1994] 05 EG 155). For a brief summary of these provisions, see de Havillande, J., 'Damage Limitation' [1998] EG 9837; Madge, N., 'Harassment and Eviction' 1993 143 *New Law Journal*, pp. 844–46 and 880–82. See Question 1.

In the recent case of *Wandsworth London Borough Council* v *Osei-Bonsu* [1999] 1 All ER 265, the Court of Appeal held that a mistaken belief as to the law on the part of the landlord could be relevant as a defence under s. 27(8)(a) of the 1988 Act. However, if the landlord has no 'reasonable cause' for that mistaken belief, this defence will not succeed. The *Wandsworth* case also indicates that, when considering mitigation of damages on account of the occupier's conduct (under s. 27(7)(a)), it is necessary to look at that conduct in the light of all the surrounding facts. Thus, in *Wandsworth* itself, the reality was that the landlord's eviction was the culmination of an unbroken chain of events starting with the occupier's violence towards his wife. In the circumstances, the Court felt it appropriate to reduce damages by two-thirds. It seems also that a wilful withholding of rent amounts to conduct which the court can take into account in reducing damages (*Regalgrand Ltd* v *Dickerson* [1996] EGCS 182). As to the question of assessment of damages generally under s. 28(3)(a), the Court of Appeal also confirmed the generally held view that s. 28 requires valuation on a factual, as opposed to a notional, basis. In other words, the assessment must take account of the *actual* situation in the premises which are being valued. In *Melville* v *Bruton* [1997] 29 EG 319, for example, two tenants remained in occupation of the property after the eviction of a third tenant. As a result, no award under s. 28 could be made to the evicted tenant. Similarly, damages will be low in cases where the tenant has limited security of tenure regardless of the eviction. In *King* v *Jackson* [1998] 03 EG 138, only a small award was made because the tenant, who was holding under an assured shorthold tenancy, had given notice to quit effective just six days after the date of the unlawful eviction.

Apart from the tenant's civil remedies, you should also devote some time to studying the Protection from Eviction Act 1977, ss. 1, 2 and 3 (as amended by the Housing Act 1988). These provisions seek to protect by way of criminal sanction the rights of residential occupiers peaceably to enjoy their property. Notable cases in this area include *R* v *Yuthiwattana* (1984) 16 HLR 49 and *R* v *Phekoo* [1981] 1 WLR 1117. Remember also that the Criminal Law Act 1977 creates criminal offences that are of relevance to the law of unlawful eviction and harassment. Section 6(1) of the 1977 Act states that any person who, without lawful authority, uses or threatens violence to secure entry to premises commits an offence. Under s. 7, an offence is committed by a trespasser refusing to leave when required to do so by or on behalf of a displaced residential occupier. A 'displaced residential occupier' is defined as a lawful occupier who has been excluded from his residence by the trespasser (s. 12(3)). While this provision is primarily intended against squatters, there is no reason why the trespasser should not be a landlord who refuses to leave the demised premises when required to do so by his tenant.

The subject of usual covenants is often omitted from landlord and tenant courses and so be guided by your lecturer as to how much time to devote to this relatively narrow topic. We have included it in this chapter together with a question on the tenant's denial of his landlord's title (see Question 3).

QUESTION 1

Susan has been the weekly tenant of a furnished flat within a block of flats owned by Gerry since 1993. A few weeks ago, Gerry wrote to Susan seeking an increase in rent. Susan wrote back saying she would not pay anything over and above her current rent. Gerry was very irritated by this reply and wrote to Susan demanding that she vacate her flat by 10 a.m. the following morning. Susan did not comply with this demand and went to work as usual.

When she got back in the evening, Susan found that Gerry had changed the lock to her flat and thrown all her belongings out onto the landing. She could not get in and was forced to spend the night at a nearby hotel. Susan has been unable to gain access to the flat ever since.

Advise Susan as to her civil remedies against Gerry.

Commentary

This question covers a variety of legal issues on quiet enjoyment and unlawful eviction. Some reference to the Housing Act 1988 is also required.

Try to give your answer a logical structure. There is a lot to write down so be economical with the facts of the cases. Cite cases to support legal principle and do not dwell on one point to the detriment of others. If you follow this advice, you should be able to score a good mark without too much difficulty!

Suggested Answer

Presumably Susan's tenancy, unless an assured shorthold tenancy, will be assured and Susan will have security of tenure under the Housing Act 1988. Her tenancy is a weekly (periodic) tenancy and must be terminated by a written notice to quit complying with the Protection from Eviction Act 1977, s. 5 (i.e., minimum four week's notice). In any event, the tenancy will continue until the landlord, Gerry, obtains a court order for possession by establishing one or more statutory grounds for possession.

Gerry has sought to increase Susan's rent. This he is entitled to do, provided he has served notice in the prescribed form after the applicable qualifying periods have elapsed under the Housing Act 1988, s. 13. The proposed rent will then take effect unless Susan refers the matter to a rent assessment committee. She is not, however, in breach of any terms of her tenancy by not agreeing to the increased rent; but if she fails to refer the matter to a rent assessment committee then after the requisite period the proposed rent would take effect (from the date of the landlord's notice) and she would be in breach of the tenancy if she simply carried on paying the old rent.

Clearly, however, Susan's apparent lack of cooperation with the landlord does not entitle him to re-enter the flat and change the lock. Even if Susan was in breach of her tenancy, Gerry would not be able to enforce a right of re-entry save by proceedings in court because the premises comprise a dwelling (Protection from Eviction Act 1977, s. 2).

Gerry's eviction of Susan constitutes a breach of her tenancy. Most tenancy agreements will contain an express covenant which provides that the tenant is entitled to quiet enjoyment of the premises demised. In the absence of an express covenant, however, an implied covenant by the landlord for quiet enjoyment will arise from the relationship of landlord and tenant. The implied covenant protects the tenant from acts which cause physical interference with the tenant's enjoyment of occupation (*Drane* v *Evangelou* [1978] 1 WLR 455).

Since Susan enjoys exclusive possession of the flat under her tenancy, Gerry's re-entry also amounts to a trespass.

By way of criminal sanction, the Protection from Eviction Act 1977 seeks to protect the rights of residential occupiers peacefully to enjoy their property. Susan clearly qualifies as a 'residential occupier' within the meaning of s. 1(1) of the Act since she occupies the flat as a residence under an assured tenancy under the Housing Act 1988. Section 1(2) provides that it is an offence for any person unlawfully to deprive a residential occupier of any premises of his occupation of the premises or of any part of them. In *R* v *Yuthiwattana* (1984) 16 HLR 49, the Court of Appeal held that an unlawful deprivation of occupation for this purpose must have the character of an eviction. Clearly, therefore, an offence has been committed by Gerry under s. 1(2) for unlawfully depriving Susan of her occupation of the flat. It may also be that Gerry's demands for an increase in rent (if written in aggressive terms), coupled with a demand that she vacate the flat within 24 hours, amounts to harassment and that an offence has been committed under s. 1(3) of the 1977 Act.

What civil remedies are available to Susan? Clearly, her immediate concern is to get back into her flat as quickly as possible. If the flat is now empty, she could use the remedy of self-help and break back into the flat. If Gerry was still physically in the property, she could use reasonable force to remove him without committing an offence under the displaced residential occupier provisions of the Criminal Law Act 1977, s. 6(3). However, it is likely that Susan would feel uneasy about taking physical action herself, and therefore she should apply to the court for a mandatory injunction ordering Gerry to give her possession of the flat. She should also seek a negative injunction restraining Gerry from further unlawful acts in the future. If Gerry should fail to comply with the terms of the injunction, he will be in contempt of court and liable to imprisonment.

The further remedy available to Susan is damages. Apart from claiming special damages representing any damage caused to her belongings and for the cost of alternative accommodation, she would be entitled to claim general damages for any physical injury, discomfort, inconvenience etc. caused as a result of the unlawful eviction, but not for injured feelings or mental distress for breach of the covenant for quiet enjoyment (*Branchett* v *Beaney/Branchett* v *Swale Borough Council* [1992] 3 All ER 910). Such damages may, however, be awarded in tort based on trespass or nuisance (*Rookes* v *Barnard* [1964] AC 1129 (HL)). Aggravated damages may also be awarded for claims brought in tort, and are appropriate where there has been especially severe suffering caused by the landlord's conduct. She would also be entitled to exemplary damages in tort (*Drane* v *Evangelou* [1978] 1 WLR 455). However, it is a necessary requirement for the award of such damages that the landlord's action was profit motivated in some way (*Ramdath* v *Oswald Daley* [1993] 20 EG 123, where the Court of Appeal held that an action for unlawful eviction could give rise to an award of exemplary damages under the *Drane* principle 'whenever necessary to teach the landlord a lesson'). If Gerry is prosecuted under the Protection from Eviction Act 1977 and receives a fine or is ordered to pay his victim compensation, then such sums may be taken into account when the court comes to award damages in the civil action (*Ashgar* v *Ahmed* (1984) 17 HLR 25 and *Smith* v *Jenkins* (1979) 129 NLJ 198).

Lastly, reference must be made to the Housing Act 1988, ss. 27 and 28, which provide a tenant with a statutory right to damages in cases of unlawful eviction or harassment. Section 27(3) imposes a statutory liability to pay damages on a landlord who personally (or through his agents) has committed acts which amount to the offences of unlawful eviction or harassment. (No claim for damages under the 1988 Act lies against the landlord's agent as a joint tortfeasor: *Sampson* v *Wilson* [1995] 3 WLR 455.) This liability is incurred by acts occurring after 9 June 1988 and arises irrespective of whether or not there has actually been a conviction for the offence. The liability is specifically stated to be in the nature of a tort and to be additional to any other liability in damages (i.e., breach of quiet enjoyment or trespass). By virtue of s. 27(6), the landlord has a complete defence either if the tenant is actually reinstated in the premises before the proceedings are finally disposed of, or if a court makes an order reinstating the tenant. In *Tagro* v *Cafane* [1991] 1 WLR 378, it was held that reinstatement did not consist of handing the tenant back a key to a lock which did not work and allowing her to resume occupation of a totally wrecked room.

Section 27(7) of the 1988 Act provides that any damages awarded against a landlord may be reduced where, prior to the events giving rise to the claim, the conduct of the tenant was such that it would be reasonable to reduce the damages payable, or where, before the proceedings were begun, the landlord offered to reinstate the tenant and the tenant unreasonably refused that offer. It seems that the court may be reluctant to award any damages under the 1988 Act where the tenant is reinstated after only a few hours of the eviction (*Murray* v *Aslam* (1995) 27 HLR 284).

It is apparent that Susan will be entitled to statutory damages unless, prior to the hearing, there is an offer of reinstatement by Gerry and it is unreasonable for her to refuse such an offer. This would not, however, preclude Susan from claiming damages at common law.

Section 28(1) of the 1988 Act provides that the measure of damages for the purpose of s. 27(3) is the difference between the value of the landlord's interest subject to the residential occupier's right and its value in the absence of the occupier's right (*Tagro* v *Cafane* [1991] 1 WLR 378). For these purposes, it is the landlord's interest in the building in which the premises are situated, not just his interest in the demised premises, which has to be valued. The valuation must reflect the true position of the actual tenant. If Susan's security of tenure is limited (for example, because she is an assured shorthold tenant), this will be reflected in the award of damages: *King* v *Jackson* [1998] 03 EG 138, where a nominal award was made under s. 28 because the tenant, under an assured shorthold tenancy, had given notice to quit effective just six days after the date of the illegal eviction. It should also be noted that damages cannot be awarded for the same loss both under s. 27 and under the common law, (i.e., exemplary damages and s. 28 damages) (*Mason* v *Nwokorie* [1994] 05 EG 155).

QUESTION 2

Critically assess the recent House of Lords ruling in *Southwark London Borough Council* v *Mills* [1999] 4 All ER 449. Would the Law Commission's proposals for reform of the law of leasehold dilapidations redress the deficiencies in the law highlighted by the *Southwark* ruling?

Commentary

This is a relatively straightforward essay-type question requiring you to assess the legal impact of the *Southwark* decision. Apart from analysing the case itself, the question requires you to comment on the most recent Law Commission recommendations in this particular area: see the Law Commission's Report, 'The Law of Landlord and Tenant: Responsibility for State and Condition of Property' (Law Com. No. 238, 1996). (See also Question 5, **Chapter 6**.) You will obviously lose marks if you make no reference to the Law Commission's proposals.

Your answer should avoid a simple rehearsal of the facts and ruling in the case. Try to be analytical in your commentary of the judgments and be prepared to make reference to earlier case law which you consider requires re-examination in the light of the House of Lords ruling. In short, demonstrate to the examiner that you have a good understanding of the legal issues raised in the case and how they might be resolved by reform of the law. See further, Rook D., [2000] Conv. 161.

Suggested Answer

The House of Lords in *Southwark* (the leading opinions were given by Lords Hoffmann and Millett) unanimously confirmed that a landlord cannot be liable in nuisance for authorising the activities of his tenant if those activities do not themselves constitute an actionable nuisance. Nuisance involves doing something on neighbouring land that constitutes unreasonable interference with the claimant's enjoyment of his land. In *Southwark*, the tenants complained of inadequate sound insulation between their flats and other flats in the same building, causing them to hear all of the everyday activities of neighbouring tenants. Those activities were not only reasonable but, in the words of Lord Millett, 'the necessary and inevitable incidents of the ordinary occupation of residential property'. They could not, therefore, as a matter of law, constitute an actionable nuisance.

Moreover, the tenants had taken their flats in the knowledge that the neighbouring flats were also occupied as residential flats; they could not, therefore, complain about the normal activities carried on by their neighbouring occupants which, of course, mirrored their own activities. Nor could they complain to the landlord for permitting such activities by letting the neighbouring flats. The tenancy agreements contained no express obligation on the landlord to ensure adequate sound insulation between the flats and no such obligation could be implied under the general law. The obligation to 'keep in repair the structure and exterior of the dwelling-house' (implied by s. 11 of the Landlord and Tenant Act 1985) has no application where the property is not actually in a state of disrepair (i.e., 'disrepair' means deterioration from a previous physical condition: *Quick* v *Taff Ely BC* [1986] QB 809). The statutorily implied condition as to fitness for human habitation (imposed by s. 8 of the 1985 Act) was equally unhelpful in so far as it is constrained by unrealistically low rental limits (unchanged since 1957) which render the provision redundant in virtually all (including the instant) cases. In the absence of any governing contractual or statutory provision, therefore, the principle that the tenant 'takes the property as he finds it' was held to prevail: see, e.g., *Kiddle* v *City Business Properties Ltd* [1942] 1 KB 269, at 274–275, *per* Lord Goddard.

By contrast, the covenant for quiet enjoyment requires a substantial interference with the tenant's lawful possession of the land which, according to their Lordships, did not have to be direct or physical. It could, therefore, cover regular excessive noise, despite contrary *dicta* in *Jenkins* v *Jackson* (1888) 40 ChD 71 and *Browne* v *Flower* [1911] 1 Ch 219. In the former case, Kekewich J pointed out that the word 'quietly' in the covenant 'does not mean undisturbed by noise', and in the latter, Parker J opined that 'a mere interference with the comfort of persons using the demised premises by the creation of a personal annoyance such as might arise from noise ... is not enough'. Considerable doubt must now be cast on the correctness of these earlier judicial pronouncements. In Lord Millett's view, there was nothing in the wording of the covenant to justify such a limitation. According to his Lordship, the covenant for quiet enjoyment is broken if the landlord does anything that substantially interferes with the tenant's title to or possession of the demised premises, or with his ordinary and lawful enjoyment of the property. The interference need not be direct or physical.

Moreover, the covenant for quiet enjoyment, in his Lordship's view, had two broadly similar features in common with the implied obligation not to derogate from grant. First, both operated prospectively (i.e., for the future) in the sense that the landlord undertook not to do anything *after* the date of the grant which would derogate from it or substantially interfere with the tenant's enjoyment of the demised property. Secondly, in both cases, the landlord's obligations were confined to the subject-matter of the grant, namely, the demised premises (including any incidental rights attached to it). In the *Southwark* case, the subject-matter of the grant was the flat having inadequate sound insulation. It was evident, therefore, that the landlord had covenanted not to interfere with the tenant's use and enjoyment of the flat having *that* built-in feature. To import into the covenant an obligation on the landlord to obtain possession of the adjoining flats (and not re-let them) or to install sound insulation would go beyond the operation of the grant. Lord Millett also emphasised the importance of looking at the location of the demised premises, and the use to which adjoining premises are put at the date of the tenancy and the use to which they may reasonably be put in the future. On this basis, it would have made no difference to the House of Lords ruling if the adjoining flats had been let subsequently to the tenants moving in.

Lord Hoffmann also viewed the covenant for quiet enjoyment as being only *prospective* in nature (i.e., it is a covenant that the tenant's lawful possession *will* not be interrupted by the landlord). Accordingly, it did not apply to things done before the grant of the tenancy (even though they may have continuing consequences for the tenant): *Anderson* v *Oppenheimer* (1880) 5 QBD 602. Here again, the principle is that the tenant takes the property as he finds it, in particular, subject to the uses which the parties contemplated would be made of the parts retained by the landlord: *Lyttleton Times Co. Ltd* v *Warners Ltd* [1970] AC 476. In *Southwark*, the tenants must reasonably have contemplated that there would be other tenants living normally in neighbouring flats, and so their sole complaint related to the structural defect (i.e., lack of sound proofing), which was present when they took the premises, and for which the landlord, applying the principle of *caveat lessee*, assumed no responsibility.

Interestingly, the Law Commission, in its Report, 'The Law of Landlord and Tenant: Responsibility for State and Condition of Property' (Law Com. No. 238), recommended that the statutory implied condition as to fitness for human habitation (contained in s. 8 of the 1985 Act) be extended to every lease for less than seven years regardless of rental level. The Commission also recommended that the criteria for determining whether a dwelling-house was fit for human habitation should be those listed in s. 604 of the Housing Act 1985 (as amended), including such matters as dampness, adequate provision for lighting, ventilation, etc. Significantly, however, there is no recommendation to extend the criteria so as to include sound insulation. This obvious gap in the proposed new legislative framework will need to be re-examined if the deficiencies in the law highlighted by the *Southwark* case are to be overcome. The difficulty facing most housing authorities, however, as indicated by Lord Millett, is the allocation of scarce financial resources to a variety of divergent housing needs. It is apparent that the installation of sound-proofing does not

rank as a priority need with most councils, or indeed local residents'
associations. As one academic commentator has observed, 'the boundary line
between law reform and practical politics does become difficult to draw'
(Bridge, S., 'Putting it Right? The Law Commission and the Condition of
Tenanted Property' [1996] Conv 342, at 350).

QUESTION 3

(a)   What are the usual covenants? In what situation are they relevant?

(b)   In what circumstances will a tenant be deemed to deny his landlord's
title? What is the legal consequence of such a denial?

Commentary

This question is concerned with two specific areas, namely: (a) the law relating
to the implication of usual covenants in agreements for leases; and (b) the
implied condition on the part of the tenant not to deny or impugn his landlord's
title.

For a summary of the law relating to the denial of a landlord's title, see
Pawlowski, M., *The Forfeiture of Leases* London: Sweet & Maxwell, 1993,
pp. 48–57.

Suggested Answer

(a)   In some cases, the parties will precede an intended formal lease by an
agreement for a lease (i.e., a contract whereby landlord and tenant agree that a
legal lease will be granted and accepted on certain terms). If an agreement for
a lease is silent as to the covenants to be included, the common law will imply
a term into the agreement that the lease will, when executed, contain the 'usual
covenants' (*Hampshire* v *Wickens* (1878) 7 Ch D 555 and *Propert* v *Parker*
(1832) 3 My & K 280).

The usual covenants to be implied into the agreement will vary according to
prevailing custom and conveyancing practice. However, in *Hampshire* v
Wickens (above) Lord Jessel MR indicated that the following covenants and
conditions are always 'usual': on the part of the landlord, a covenant for quiet
enjoyment in the usual qualified form; and on the part of the tenant, a covenant
to pay rent, a covenant to pay rates and taxes, a covenant to keep the premises
in repair and deliver them up in repair at the end of the term, a covenant to

permit the landlord to enter and view the state and condition of the premises if the landlord has accepted a repairing obligation, and a condition of re-entry for non-payment of rent but not for breach of any other covenant (see *Re Anderton & Milner's Contract* [1890] Ch D 476 and *Re Lander and Bagley's Contract* [1892] 3 Ch 41). However, a covenant not to assign is not a usual covenant to be inferred in an agreement for a lease (*Hampshire* v *Wickens*, above).

The *Hampshire* case is a useful decision in so far as it provides an obvious list of the usual covenants to be implied into agreements for leases, but the list is by no means closed and, as stated earlier, much will depend on the established trade and conveyancing practice relevant to the proposed landlord and tenant relationship. In *Flexman* v *Corbett* [1930] 1 Ch 672, Maugham J indicated that the ultimate question was whether the form of the covenant was such as to constitute a defect in the subject-matter of the agreement. Thus, if it is established that the lease is in the form in which it would be anticipated as being in the great majority of cases, having regard to the nature of the property and to the place where it is situated, and to the purposes for which the premises are to be used, it would not be reasonable to say that there was a defect in the subject-matter of the agreement.

In *Flexman*, it was recognised that the question whether particular covenants are usual covenants is a question of fact, and that the decision of the court would depend on admissible evidence of conveyancers and others familiar with the practice in reference to leases and books of precedents. It is also permissible to obtain evidence with regard to the practice in the particular district in which the premises in question are situated. What is usual in Mayfair may not be usual at all in some other parts of London such as, for instance, Whitechapel.

In *Chester* v *Buckingham Travel Ltd* [1981] 1 WLR 96, an agreement was made in 1971 to grant a lease of a garage and workshop. Some years after the tenant had taken up occupation it was necessary to determine what covenants ought to be implied into the lease. Foster J, upon hearing evidence from conveyancers as to what covenants might be included as 'usual covenants' in such a letting, in the context of the subject-matter of the lease, recognised other covenants (outside the *Hampshire* list) as usual.

The word 'usual' means no more than 'occurring in ordinary use', so that if it is found that in nine out of 10 cases a covenant of a particular sort would be in a lease of premises of a given nature and in a given district, the covenant may be 'usual' for the particular premises in question (*Flexman* v *Corbett*, above).

(b) Implied into every lease is a condition that the tenant should not expressly or impliedly deny the landlord's title to the premises, or prejudice it by any acts which are inconsistent with the existence of the tenancy. If a tenant denies the landlord's title, he will commit a repudiatory breach of the contract of letting entitling the landlord to forfeit the lease. Such a forfeiture may be incurred (without recourse to a proviso for re-entry in the lease) in three distinct circumstances, namely: (i) denial by matter of record; (ii) denial by act *in pais*; and (iii) disclaimer by a yearly or other periodic tenant.

A denial by matter of record will arise when the tenant, in the course of his pleadings, expressly denies the landlord's title and is thereby estopped by the record from reasserting his lease or tenancy (*Warner* v *Sampson* [1959] 1 QB 297, where the Court of Appeal held that a general traverse in the tenant's pleadings did not involve the affirmative setting up by the tenant of a title adverse to that of the landlord as it merely put the landlord to proof of the allegations traversed). In *WG Clark (Properties) Ltd* v *Dupre Properties Ltd* [1991] 3 WLR 579, it was held that a partial disclaimer of the landlord's title is not sufficient to constitute a disclaimer of the whole since it does not show that the tenant has evinced the necessary intention no longer to be bound by his relationship with the landlord.

Once the landlord has commenced proceedings for possession based on disclaimer of his title in the tenant's pleading, the tenant cannot improve his position by amending his pleading to remove the disclaimer notwithstanding that the amendment of a pleading relates back to the date of the original pleading (*WG Clark (Properties) Ltd* v *Dupre Properties Ltd*, above). This is because the landlord's service of proceedings for possession is the equivalent to actual re-entry onto the demised premises which brings the landlord and tenant relationship to an end. The tenant may, however, avoid a forfeiture by retracting his denial of title *before* the landlord re-enters or takes effective proceedings for re-entry in reliance on the denial (*Warner* v *Sampson*, above).

A denial by act *in pais* will arise when the tenant deliberately attempts to set up an adverse (or hostile) title either in himself or in a stranger in the face of the landlord's title (*Doe d Ellenbrock* v *Flynn* (1834) 1 CM & R 137). The rule in *Ellenbrock* must, however, be cautiously applied where the tenant denies his landlord's title by mere words (*Wisbech St Mary Parish Council* v *Lilley* [1956] 1 WLR 121).

A disclaimer of the lease (whether by words or acts) by a yearly or other periodic tenant will operate as a waiver by the tenant of the usual notice to quit.

The effect of such a disclaimer, therefore, is that the landlord may terminate the tenancy forthwith without serving the appropriate notice to quit on his tenant. The principle appears to be founded on the doctrine of estoppel, since the landlord is not obliged to determine the tenancy by notice to quit because the tenant has already asserted by words or conduct that it has no existence (*Doe d Calvert* v *Frowd* (1828) 4 Bing 557). Thus, strictly speaking, an act of disclaimer by a periodic tenant does not give the landlord a right of forfeiture but merely operates to relieve him from serving the appropriate notice to quit to bring the tenancy to an end.

QUESTION 4

Bernard is the freehold owner of two adjacent houses, Nos 15 and 16, High Street, Barchester, Somerset.

In 1996, Bernard let No. 16 to Doris, a psychiatrist, on a monthly tenancy at a rent of £600 per month. She uses No. 16 as a private clinic where she offers therapy and assistance to victims of mental trauma.

Six months ago, Bernard let No. 15 to Tony on a monthly tenancy at a rent of £650 per month. Tony is a freelance concert pianist and uses the property occasionally for rehearsals.

The noise generated by Tony's rehearsals has upset Doris. She is concerned because her counselling sessions are being disrupted because of Tony's piano playing.

Doris has complained to the local authority about the noise level of Tony's rehearsals. The local authority, however, feel that the sound is not so high as to merit any action under the Environmental Protection Act 1990. Doris has also approached Bernard asking him to provide better sound insulation between the two properties, but Bernard has refused.

Advise Doris as to any legal claim she may have against Bernard. (You are not required to consider any potential legal claims against Tony.)

Commentary

This question requires consideration of several legal issues. A solid answer will consider the nature of the landlord's implied covenants of quiet enjoyment and non-derogation from grant. Your answer should also tackle Bernard's potential liability in nuisance following the recent House of Lords ruling in *Southwark LBC* v *Mills* [1999] 4 All ER 449. See further, Rook, D., [2000] Conv. 161.

Suggested Answer

Most leases will contain an express covenant on the part of the landlord that the tenant is entitled to quiet enjoyment of the demised premises. In the absence of an express provision, a covenant for quiet enjoyment will be automatically implied.

As its name suggests, this covenant is designed to ensure that the tenant may peacefully enjoy the demised property without interruption from the landlord or persons claiming under him (e.g., other tenants of the landlord). The interruption may be direct or indirect, physical or non-physical. Examples where the landlord has been held liable under the covenant include the illegal eviction of the tenant (*Drane* v *Evangelou* [1978] 1 WLR 455), physical interference with the tenant's business user by the erection of scaffolding outside the premises (*Owen* v *Gadd* [1956] 2 QB 99), a prolonged course of intimidation and harassment of the tenant (*Kenny* v *Preen* [1963] 1 QB 499), cutting off the tenant's gas and electricity supply (*Perera* v *Vandiyar* [1953] 1 WLR 672) and substantial disruption caused by the landlord's building works (*Guppy's (Bridport) Ltd* v *Brookling* (1984) 269 EG 846). It seems that an omission on the part of the landlord which is a breach of duty (e.g., to repair) may also constitute a breach of the covenant (*Hafton Properties Ltd* v *Camp* [1993] EGCS 101).

In *Jenkins* v *Jackson* (1888) 40 ChD 71, Kekewich J opined that the word 'quietly' in the covenant 'does not mean undisturbed by noise'. Similarly, in *Browne* v *Flower* [1911] 1 Ch 219, Parker J suggested that a 'mere interference with the comfort of persons using the demised premises by the creation of a personal annoyance such as might arise from noise . . . is not enough'. These observations, however, must now be read in the light of the recent House of Lords' decision in *Southwark London Borough Council* v *Mills* [1999] 4 All ER 449, in which Lord Millett concluded that there was nothing in the wording of the covenant to justify such a limitation. Accordingly, the covenant will be broken if the landlord does anything that substantially interferes with the tenant's title or possession of the demised premises, or with his ordinary and lawful enjoyment of the property. The interference need not be direct or physical.

In the *Southwark* case, tenants of flats complained of inadequate sound insulation between their flats and other flats in the same building, causing them to hear all the everyday activities of their neighbours. The House of Lords held unanimously that the covenant for quiet enjoyment (and non-derogation from grant) operated only prospectively (i.e., for the future) and thus it did not apply to things done before the grant of the tenancy even though they may have continuing consequences for the tenant. The landlord's obligation was confined to the subject-matter of the grant, namely, the demised property having inadequate sound insulation. He could not, therefore, be responsible for installing new insulation since that would go beyond the operation of the grant.

The basic principle is that the tenant takes the property as he finds it, in particular, subject to the uses which the parties contemplated would be made of the parts retained by the landlord. In *Southwark*, the tenants must have contemplated that there would be other tenants living in neighbouring flats, and so their sole complaint related to the structural defect (i.e., lack of sound proofing) which was present when they took the premises and for which the landlord, applying the principle *caveat lessee*, assumed no responsibility in the absence of express or implied obligation. In this connection, the tenancy contained no express covenant on the landlord as regards sound proofing. Moreover, the landlord's implied obligation to keep in repair the structure and exterior of a dwelling-house in respect of residential lettings for under seven years (see s. 11 of the Landlord and Tenant Act 1985) had no application in the absence of evidence of disrepair. In short, the House of Lords concluded that the covenant for quiet enjoyment (and non-derogation from grant) was not an appropriate mechanism for importing (through the back door) an improvement to the premises for which the landlord would not otherwise be liable under contract or statute.

The House of Lords also held that a landlord could not be liable in nuisance for authorising the activities of his tenants if those activities did not themselves constitute an actionable nuisance. In *Southwark*, the activities of the other tenants were not only reasonable but, in the words of Lord Millett, 'the necessary and inevitable incidents of the ordinary occupation of residential property'. They could not, therefore, as a matter of law, constitute an actionable nuisance. Interestingly, his Lordship concluded that it would have made no difference if the adjoining flats had been let *subsequently* to the tenants moving in since it must have been within the contemplation of the tenants that the adjoining flats would be let to residential tenants who would live normally in them.

In the present case, it is debatable whether Tony's piano playing constitutes an actionable nuisance. Nuisance involves doing something on neighbouring land that constitutes unreasonable interference with the claimant's enjoyment of his land. A person cannot increase the liabilities of his neighbour by applying his own property to special uses: *Robinson* v *Kilvert* (1889) 41 ChD 88 (ordinary heating damaging paper exceptionally susceptible to heat) and *Whycer* v *Urry* [1956] JPL 365 (practice of ophthalmic optician in a business area too specifically delicate for protection). In any event, it may be that Tony's activities can be characterised as no more than a necessary and inevitable incident of the ordinary occupation of the property, in which case Bernard will not be liable in nuisance in accordance with principles enunciated in the *Southwark* decision. Doris cannot complain about normal activities carried on by Bernard's neighbouring tenants. Nor can she complain to her landlord for permitting such activities by letting the adjoining property to Tony. Her tenancy agreement presumably contains no express obligation on Bernard to ensure adequate sound insulation between Nos 15 and 16 and such obligation, as we have seen, will not be implied under the general law. The implied obligation under s. 11 of the 1985 Act has no application where the property is not actually in a state of disrepair, and the statutorily implied condition as to fitness for human habitation (imposed by s. 8 of the 1985 Act) will not assist Doris in so far as the rent payable under her monthly tenancy is well above the rental limits imposed by that Act. In the absence, therefore, of any governing contractual or statutory provision, the principle that the tenant 'takes the property as [s]he finds it' will prevail (see, e.g., *Kiddle* v *City Business Properties Ltd* [1942] 1 KB 269, at 274-75, *per* Lord Goddard).

Similarly, there will be no liability under the covenant for quiet enjoyment (or non-derogation from grant) since the subject-matter of Doris's grant is the property (No. 16) having inadequate sound insulation. It is evident, therefore, that Bernard has covenanted not to interfere with Doris's use and enjoyment of the property having that built-in feature. Moreover, a landlord will not be liable to his tenant under a covenant for quiet enjoyment (or derogation from grant) for a nuisance caused by another of his tenants simply because he knows that the latter is causing the nuisance and does not himself take any steps to prevent what is being done. In order to render Bernard liable, therefore, there must be active participation on his part, or a sufficiently positive act, amounting to authorisation of the nuisance, so as to make him responsible for it (*Malzy* v *Eicholz* [1916] 2 KB 308 and *Matania* v *National Provincial Bank Ltd* [1936] 2 All ER 633). It seems, on the facts, that Bernard has not authorised or ratified Tony's activities in any way.

5   Assignment, Sub-letting, Parting with Possession

INTRODUCTION

When can the tenant assign, sub-let, etc.? The answer to this question will depend essentially on the terms of the lease. There are five possible situations:

(a)   If the lease contains no restriction, the tenant can freely assign or sub-let without obtaining consent from the landlord.

(b)   The lease may contain an absolute covenant against assigning etc. A simple prohibition, unqualified by any words requiring the consent of the landlord, entitles the landlord to withhold his consent and to impose what conditions he likes. By way of statutory exception, a covenant purporting to restrict prospective assignees or sublessees on grounds of race, nationality or sex is deemed to be qualified (Race Relations Act 1976, s. 24, and Sex Discrimination Act 1975, s. 31).

(c)   The lease may contain a qualified covenant. A covenant not to assign, sub-let etc. without obtaining the consent of the landlord brings into operation the Landlord and Tenant Act 1927, s. 19(1), which provides that, notwithstanding any provision to the contrary, such covenant shall be deemed to be subject to the proviso that such consent shall not be unreasonably withheld.

(d)   The lease may contain an express proviso that consent shall not be unreasonably withheld, in which case the tenant is in the same position as in (c) above.

(e)   The lease may contain a covenant by the tenant to offer a free surrender to the landlord before assigning, sub-letting etc. Such a covenant is not invalidated by s. 19(1) of the 1927 Act (*Bocardo SA* v *S & M Hotels Ltd* [1980] 1 WLR 17). However, a clause requiring the tenant to offer a surrender of the lease before assignment will be void when contained in a business tenancy, since such a clause is contrary to the Landlord and Tenant Act 1954, s. 38(1) (*Allnatt London Properties Ltd* v *Newton* [1984] 1 All ER 423).

Where the lease requires the landlord's consent to the assignment or sub-letting, a mass of case law has arisen as to whether the landlord's consent was reasonably or unreasonably withheld in the particular circumstances. In this connection, the Landlord and Tenant Act 1988 imposes a duty on the landlord to consent to a tenant's application to assign, sub-let etc. unless he has good reason for not doing so. For a summary of the provisions of the 1988 Act, see Austin, J., 'Landlord and Tenant Act 1988' [1989] EG 8912, 55. While the Act reverses the burden of proof so that it is now necessary for the landlord to prove that any refusal is reasonable and provides the tenant with an action for damages for breach of statutory duty, it does not alter the law in any other respect (*Air India* v *Balabel* [1993] 30 EG 90).

It is, in each case, a question of fact, depending upon all the circumstances, whether the landlord's consent to an assignment, sub-letting etc. is being unreasonably withheld. A leading case in this area is *International Drilling Fluids Ltd* v *Louisville Investments (Uxbridge) Ltd* [1986] Ch 513, where Balcombe LJ set out a number of guidelines for determining whether consent was being reasonably or unreasonably withheld, but these must now be read in conjunction with the statutory requirements of the 1988 Act. See further Williams, D., 'Assignment of Leases, Recent Developments' (1986) 279 EG 51; McLoughlin, P., 'To Consent or Not to Consent' [1990] EG 9011, 60 and 'Sureties in Commercial Leases' [1991] EG 9120, 86. For a comprehensive collection of case law in this area, see Pawlowski, M., and Brown J., *Casebook on the Law of Landlord and Tenant*, London: Sweet & Maxwell Ltd, 1994, Ch. 5.

It is also important that you are aware that the Landlord and Tenant (Covenants) Act 1995 has amended s. 19(1) of the 1927 Act in a number of significant respects. Under a lease granted after 1 January 1996, a former tenant will remain liable for the defaults of his immediate assignee if the landlord obtains an 'authorised guarantee agreement' (AGA) from him guaranteeing performance of the tenant's covenants by his immediate assignee. The landlord may require such an agreement from the former tenant either (i) automatically as one of the conditions for assignment set out in the covenant in the lease, or (ii) because it is reasonable to do so. In the latter case, the landlord may impose an AGA as a condition of granting consent where the lease contains an absolute prohibition against assignment, or where the lease contains a qualified covenant against assignment and it is reasonable, in all the circumstances of the case, for the landlord to require an AGA from the former tenant: see *Wallis Fashion Group Ltd* v *General Accident Life Assurance Ltd* [2000] EGCS 45 in the context of a business tenancy renewal. (See further, Question 2(a), **Chapter 3**.)

You should also be aware of the remedies available to a landlord where the tenant has gone ahead and assigned, sub-let etc. in breach of covenant. Apart from damages, the landlord is entitled to forfeit the lease, or to seek an injunction where the tenant threatens to assign or sub-let. In *Hemingway Securities Ltd* v *Dunraven Ltd* [1995] 09 EG 322, the landlord obtained a mandatory injunction against the sub-tenant, requiring him to execute a deed delivering up the unlawful sub-lease to the tenant. (See Question 4.) The tenant's remedies include the seeking of a declaration under the Landlord and Tenant Act 1954, s. 53, that consent has been unreasonably withheld. Additionally, the tenant may bring a claim for damages alleging that the landlord is in breach of his statutory duty under the Landlord and Tenant Act 1988, s. 1 (see s. 4). Such a claim may be combined with a claim for an injunction requiring the landlord to comply with his statutory duty under the Act.

This is a compact area of study and a favourite amongst examiners and examinees alike!

QUESTION 1

A & Co. Ltd is the tenant of a house on the Blackmore Estate owned by Lord Wealth. It wishes to assign its lease of the house to one of its directors for his personal use, but Lord Wealth has written to A & Co. Ltd refusing his consent to the assignment on the grounds that (a) the house has been allowed to fall into disrepair, (b) the proposed assignee would be entitled to claim the benefit of the Housing Act 1988, and (c) the house has already been earmarked for occupation by a caretaker for the purposes of the more efficient management of the Estate. The lease, which expires in three months' time, contains a qualified covenant on the part of the tenant not to assign, sub-let or part with possession of the premises without the prior consent of the landlord.

Advise A & Co. Ltd of its legal position and the steps it may take to challenge the validity of the objections raised by Lord Wealth.

Commentary

The central issue in this question is whether Lord Wealth has unreasonably withheld his consent to the proposed assignment. It therefore requires a thorough discussion of the case law on this point. You will also need to examine the various remedies available to the tenant on the assumption that consent has been unreasonably withheld. If you have revised the cases, a question like this should enable you to score a good 2:1.

Suggested Answer

A covenant not to assign, sub-let etc. without first obtaining the consent of the landlord brings into operation the Landlord and Tenant Act 1927, s. 19(1), which provides, *inter alia*, that, notwithstanding any provision to the contrary, such covenant shall be deemed to be subject to the proviso that such consent shall not be unreasonably withheld. The section does not absolve the tenant from the formality of seeking consent, so that if A & Co. Ltd goes ahead without seeking consent it will commit a breach regardless of the reasonableness of the transaction (*Eastern Telegraph Co. Ltd v Dent* [1899] 1 QB 835).

The Landlord and Tenant Act 1988 imposes a duty on the landlord to consent to the tenant's application to assign, sub-let etc. unless he has good reason for not doing so. The burden of proof is, therefore, on Lord Wealth to show that his refusal of consent is reasonable. In this connection, three grounds have been put forward by Lord Wealth for refusing consent. First, the house is in a state of disrepair. The mere fact that A & Co. Ltd is committing a continuing breach of a covenant to repair does not necessarily entitle the landlord to refuse his consent to the proposed assignment(*Farr* v *Ginnings* (1928) 44 TLR 249; *Cosh* v *Fraser* (1964) 108 SJ 116). However, where the lack of repair is serious, the landlord's position will be much stronger (*Goldstein* v *Sanders* [1915] 1 Ch 549). In *Orlando Investments Ltd* v *Grosvenor Estate Belgravia* (1989) 59 P & CR 21, the Court of Appeal held that where there are extensive and longstanding breaches of a covenant to repair, it is not unreasonable for a landlord to refuse to consent to an assignment unless he can be reasonably satisfied that the proposed assignee will remedy the breaches. Thus, in the present case, much will depend on the nature and extent of the disrepair and whether the proposed assignee is prepared to remedy it.

The second ground for refusal is that the proposed assignee, being an individual, would be entitled to claim the benefit of the Housing Act 1988. It has been held to be reasonable for a landlord to refuse his consent where the proposed assignee would, unlike the assignor, be entitled to statutory protection (*Norfolk Capital Group Ltd* v *Kitway Ltd* [1977] QB 506 and *Bickel* v *Duke of Westminster* [1977] QB 517). In both these cases, the proposed assignee would have become entitled to purchase the freehold under the Leasehold Reform Act 1967. The fact that the proposed assignee would enjoy statutory protection not enjoyed by the current tenant may be a reasonable ground of refusal, particularly if the consent is sought shortly before the expiry of the term for the purpose of giving the assignee the benefit of such protection (*Lee* v *K Carter* [1949] 1 KB 85, where the landlord was held justified in refusing consent to an assignment by a company lessee of a flat to an individual director; similarly, in *Swanson* v *Forton* [1949] Ch 143, where the tenant, who was out of possession and so incapable of enjoying statutory protection under the Rent Acts, proposed to assign 12 days before the expiry of the term). See also *West Layton Ltd* v *Ford* [1979] 1 QB 593, where the effect of a proposed sub-letting would have been to confer statutory protection on the sub-tenant, and *Re Cooper's Lease* (1968) P & CR 541, where the proposed sub-tenant would have acquired statutory protection under the Landlord and Tenant Act 1954, Pt II. These decisions may be contrasted with *Thomas Bookman Ltd* v *Natham* [1955] 1 WLR 815 (where seven and a half months remained unexpired and the object of the assignment had nothing to do with the Rent Acts) and *Deverall* v *Wyndham* [1989] 01 EG 70 (where the risk of the landlord being saddled with statutory tenants was outweighed by other considerations in favour of the tenant). It seems likely, therefore, bearing in mind that the lease has only three months left to run, that Lord Wealth's refusal of consent on this ground will be considered reasonable in all the circumstances.

Lord Wealth's third ground of refusal is that the house has been earmarked for occupation by a caretaker for the purposes of the more efficient management of the Estate. In *Bromley Park Garden Estates Ltd* v *Moss* [1982] 1 WLR 1019, the Court of Appeal held that a landlord's refusal to consent to an assignment will be unreasonable if it is designed to achieve a collateral result unconnected with the terms of the lease, even though the purpose is in accordance with good estate management. In that case, the landlords refused consent on the ground, *inter alia*, that, in the interests of the proper management of their estate, it was their policy not to permit multiple lettings in the same premises because it lowered their investment value. The court held that since the landlords' reason for refusing consent (namely, that a single lease of the whole building would enhance its investment value) was wholly extraneous to, and unconnected with, the bargain made by the parties to the lease when the covenant was granted and accepted, the landlords' refusal of consent was unreasonable. Similar reasoning would apply in the present case, and accordingly Lord Wealth's refusal of consent on the ground that the house has been earmarked for a caretaker for the purpose of more efficient management of the Estate is not justified (as being extraneous to the bargain made between the parties).

By contrast, in *Moss Bros Group plc* v *CSC Properties Ltd* [1999] EGCS 47, the landlord was held to have reasonably withheld consent to an assignment of a lease of a men's fashion store in a major shopping mall to an electronic games retailer on the ground that the assignment and change of use would conflict with its policy of reserving that part of the mall for fashion-related stores. Given such a tenant-mix policy, it was not unreasonable to conclude that the games retailer would attract a clientele that was, for the most part, quite different from the shoppers who would seek out the fashion-related stores. The case is, therefore, authority for the proposition that the landlord's letting policy may be a relevant consideration in determining whether the landlord has acted reasonably.

It is, perhaps, also worth mentioning that a landlord cannot reasonably refuse his consent simply because he desires to obtain possession of the premises for himself (*Bates* v *Donaldson* [1896] 2 QB 241).

As to how A & Co. Ltd may challenge the validity of the objections raised by Lord Wealth, it is open to the tenant to go ahead with the transaction and simply wait for the landlord to sue, and then set up the unreasonable refusal by way of defence and counterclaim for a declaration that the landlord's refusal was unreasonable and that the tenant was entitled, notwithstanding the refusal, to assign. Alternatively, assuming A & Co. Ltd does not want to take the risk of going ahead and assigning without consent, it may apply to the county court for a declaration that the consent has been unreasonably withheld. This jurisdiction is given by the Landlord and Tenant Act 1954, s. 53. Additionally, A & Co. Ltd may bring an action for damages, alleging that Lord Wealth is in breach of his statutory duty under the Landlord and Tenant Act 1988, s. 1(4). Such a claim may be combined with a claim for an injunction requiring Lord Wealth to comply with his statutory duty to grant consent to the proposed assignment.

QUESTION 2

Samuel Printers Ltd is the lessee of shop premises which it holds under a lease granted to it by Acrecrest Properties Ltd for a term of 21 years. A user covenant in the lease prohibits the lessee from using the premises 'for any purpose other than the trade or business of a printer without the lessors' written consent which shall not be unreasonably withheld'. By another clause in the lease, the lessee covenants 'not to assign, underlet or part with possession of the premises or any part thereof without the written consent of the landlords which shall not be unreasonably withheld'. Samuel Printers Ltd is desirous to assign the unexpired residue of the term to a company called London Lettings Ltd, which proposes to use the premises as offices.

The landlords, Acrecrest Properties Ltd, have raised written objections to the proposed assignment on the ground that it will necessarily result in a breach of the user covenant. Moreover, they have serious doubts as to the proposed assignee's ability to meet the obligations under the lease and have, therefore, required a surety as a condition of granting consent. They have also insisted that the proposed assignee pay a substantial rental deposit.

Advise Samuel Printers Ltd.

Commentary

This question has a similar format to Question 1 above, but the issues raised are obviously different. Here again, a good knowledge of the case law will pay dividends!

For an article on the requirement of a surety as a condition of granting consent, see McLoughlin, P., 'Sureties in Commercial Leases' [1991] EG 9120, 86.

Suggested Answer

Since the lease contains a qualified covenant against assignment, sub-letting etc., the provisions of the Landlord and Tenant Act 1927, s. 19(1) will apply to render the covenant subject to the further proviso that the landlords' consent shall not be unreasonably withheld. Moreover, the landlords are under a statutory duty to give consent to the proposed assignment unless they have good reason for refusing it (Landlord and Tenant Act 1988, s. 1).

The objection based on the fact that the proposed assignment will necessarily result in a breach of the user covenant may be reasonable (*Packaging Centre* v *Poland Street Estate* [1961] EG 189 and *Granada TV Network* v *Great Universal Stores* (1963) 187 EG 391). However, in most cases, breach of a user covenant is not a necessary consequence of assignment or sub-letting. In *Killick* v *Second Covent Garden Property Co. Ltd* [1973] 1 WLR 658, the Court of Appeal held that even if, on its true construction, a user covenant precluded the assignee from using the premises, it was not a necessary consequence of the assignment that there would be a breach of covenant as, once the assignment had been made, the landlord would have the same rights to enforce the user covenant against the assignee as it had against the tenant. (See also *Ashworth Frazer Ltd* v *Gloucester City Council* [2000] 12 EG 149 (CA).) Moreover, the words 'without the lessor's written consent which shall not be unreasonably withheld' (which appeared in the covenant in *Killick*) were held to extend to the whole of the covenant so that the landlord could not (in any event) object to any reasonable use of the premises.

In *British Bakeries (Midlands) Ltd* v *Michael Testler & Co. Ltd* (1986) 277 EG 1245, the landlord refused consent on the ground, *inter alia*, of the proposed user of the premises. This ground was rejected by Peter Gibson J, in the light of the *Killick* decision, as being an expectation of a future breach of user covenant, which did not provide a good reason for a refusal of consent.

On this reasoning, the proposed assignment in the present case would not necessarily involve a breach of the user covenant, and accordingly the landlords' objection based on this ground is unreasonable.

As to the requirement of a surety as a condition of granting consent, the imposition of unreasonable conditions amounts to unreasonable refusal of consent. In particular, conditions designed to extort an advantage not otherwise obtainable are unreasonable (*Premier Rinks* v *Amalgamated Cinematograph Theatres Ltd* (1912) 56 Sol Jo 536). In *Orlando Investments Ltd* v *Grosvenor*

Estate Belgravia (1989) 59 P & CR 21, the Court of Appeal held that it was not unreasonable, in the circumstances, for the landlord to require the proposed assignee to carry out essential works of repair to the premises and to provide security for the due execution of the work. This was required as evidence of the proposed assignee's willingness to do the repairs, not his financial ability to do them, and it was not unreasonable (given the past history of breaches) for the landlord to require proof of the proposed assignee's willingness to perform.

Under the Landlord and Tenant Act 1988, s. 1(4), the giving of consent subject to any condition which is not reasonable does not satisfy the statutory duty to give consent.

It is, of course, open to a landlord to consider the financial standing of the assignee in deciding whether or not to consent to the assignment. Apart from the usual references provided by banks, solicitors, accountants etc., the landlord may be entitled to ask for the trading profits of the proposed assignee with a view to satisfying himself of the latter's ability to meet his obligations under the lease (*British Bakeries (Midlands) Ltd* v *Michael Testler & Co. Ltd* (1986) 277 EG 1245, where it was held that the landlord was not acting unreasonably in refusing consent in view of his real doubts as to the proposed assignee's ability to meet the obligations under the lease; see also, *Venetian Glass Gallery Ltd* v *Next Properties Ltd* [1989] 30 EG 92). In *Warren* v *Marketing Exchange for Africa Ltd* [1988] 2 EGLR 247, HH Judge Finlay QC confirmed that a landlord need not be content with references of a qualified or superficial nature.

The trading accounts of the proposed assignee are likely to be a better guide to its financial ability than references. The accounts will show the capital adequacy of the assignee and the general level of profitability. The best indicator of whether the assignee will be able to pay the rent is the profit and loss account. In the *British Bakeries* case, evidence was given that a generally accepted test of the financial standing of any proposed assignee is that his accounts should show a pre-tax profit of not less than three times the amount payable under the lease. (The pre-tax profit is the relevant figure because it is that profit against which the rent will be charged.) This test, however, is only a guide. In the *Venetian Glass* case, the prospective assignee was a limited company whose recent trading profits were poor, but it was improving its trade and other factors (e.g., the availability of a strong guarantee) showed that the company was suitable despite its low profit margin. Another aspect of the accounts which may be relevant is the balance sheet since this will show the net asset value of the assignee, which may be relevant in so far as the landlord may have to sue for rent and rely on a suitable asset base from which to recover its debt.

Moreover, generally speaking, a surety may be reasonably required by the landlord as a condition of granting consent if the proposed assignee is of insufficient financial standing, but ultimately much will depend on the particular circumstances of the case (*In re Greater London Properties Ltd's Lease* [1959] 1 WLR 503). Assuming, therefore, that the financial standing of London Lettings Ltd is genuinely in question, it would be reasonable for the landlords to require a surety.

As to the requirement of a rental deposit, under the Law of Property Act 1925, s. 144, every qualified covenant against assigning, sub-letting etc. without the landlord's consent is deemed, unless the contrary is expressed, to be subject to a proviso that no sum of money in the nature of a fine shall be payable for such consent. The landlord may, however, require the payment of a reasonable sum in respect of legal or other expenses incurred in granting consent. The question here is whether a rental deposit constitutes a 'fine' for the purpose of s. 144. It has been held, in a different context, that a large sum paid at the commencement of a lease and purporting to represent rent paid in advance was a fine for the purpose of deciding whether a lease was at a rent or a premium (*Hughes* v *Waite* [1957] 1 All ER 603). That decision is, however, distinguishable on the basis that the word 'fine' in *Hughes* was being used to describe a single capital payment as opposed to recurrent income payments by way of rent, whereas in s. 144 the word is used to denote a sum in the nature of a penalty. The decision in *Re Cosh's Contract* [1897] 1 Ch 9 also points to the conclusion that, for the purpose of s. 144, a deposit by way of security is not a fine.

Although a rental deposit may not be a fine prohibited by s. 144, it does not mean that a deposit may be demanded by the landlord as a matter of course. The demand must still, in the case of a qualified covenant, have to satisfy the requirement of reasonableness, and whether Acrecrest Properties Ltd are acting reasonably in the present case will again depend upon the financial strength of the proposed assignee.

Samuel Printers Ltd is advised to apply to the county court, under the Landlord and Tenant Act 1954, s. 53, for a declaration that consent has been unreasonably withheld. It should also seek damages, alleging that the landlords are in breach of their statutory duty under the Landlord and Tenant Act 1988, s. 1, and claim an injunction requiring them to comply with their statutory duty by granting consent.

QUESTION 3

(a) To what extent has the Landlord and Tenant Act 1988 altered the law in respect of the granting of consent to a proposed assignment of the demised premises?

[20 marks]

(b) To what extent can a landlord give at the hearing other reasons for objections to the proposed assignment not given to the tenant at the time when the decision to refuse consent was made?

[5 marks]

Commentary

The first part of this question should pose no difficulty to the well-prepared student who has revised this topic for the exam. Apart from referring to the 1988 Act itself, you should make reference to the pre-1998 position and draw appropriate comparisons. There have been several cases on the 1988 Act which should also be mentioned. For a brief outline of the workings of the 1988 Act, see Austin, J., 'The Landlord and Tenant Act 1988' [1989] EG 8912, 55.

The second part of this question is more problematic. It is quite specific, and unless you are familiar with the recent case law in point you will not know where to begin! Frankly, not a very fair question, but some examiners do like to throw one into the exam simply to test your detailed knowledge of one or two cases.

For a summary of the relevant law, see Wilkinson, H. W., 'Reasons not put into Writing' (1999) 149 NLJ 1039.

Suggested Answer

(a) Prior to the enactment of the Landlord and Tenant Act 1988, a restriction on dealings without the landlord's consent was primarily governed by the Landlord and Tenant Act 1927, s. 19(1), which implies a proviso that consent is not to be unreasonably withheld. Such a proviso is often expressly incorporated in a lease.

If a tenant considered that a landlord was unreasonably withholding consent, then the tenant could either seek a declaration, under the Landlord and Tenant

Act 1954, s. 53, that consent was being unreasonably withheld, or alternatively assign without consent and use the unreasonableness as a defence to any subsequent action brought against him by the landlord. To seek a court declaration was time-consuming and costly, and at the end of the day the proposed assignee might not have been around by the time the declaration was received. On the other hand, to go ahead with the assignment without consent was risky for the tenant and, more particularly, for the potential assignee.

Moreover, the tenant did not previously have any right to damages from the landlord, even if the landlord was found to have withheld consent unreasonably (see *Rendall* v *Roberts and Stacey* (1959) 175 EG 265), except where there was an express covenant on the part of the landlord not to withhold consent unreasonably (see *dicta* in *Rose* v *Gossman* (1966) 201 EG 767). Furthermore, there was no obligation on the part of the landlord to give any reasons for his decision (except under the Housing Act 1985, s. 94 in the case of a secure tenancy) and the burden of proof was on the tenant to show that the landlord was acting unreasonably (*Pimms* v *Tallow Chandlers* [1964] 2 QB 547).

The 1988 Act imposes upon the landlord a duty to give consent (unless he has a good reason for withholding it) within a reasonable period, thus giving rise to a claim in damages (under s. 4) if consent is not forthcoming or is unreasonably withheld. It also imposes a duty on the landlord to serve on the tenant written notice of his decision whether or not to give consent, specifying any conditions and, if consent is withheld, the reasons for withholding consent. This must also be done within a reasonable time. Section 1(6) of the Act provides that it is for the landlord to show:

(a)   if he gave consent, that he did so within a reasonable time (see *Midland Bank plc* v *Chart Enterprises Inc* [1990] 44 EG 68, where the landlords were held to have unreasonably delayed in the communication of their decision as to consent to the proposed assignment, and *Dong Bang Minerva (UK) Ltd* v *Davina Ltd* [1994] EGCS 104, where the landlords were held to have unreasonably delayed in granting consent to a proposed sub-tenancy);

(b)   if he gave consent subject to any condition, that the condition was a reasonable condition; and

(c)   if he did not give consent, that it was reasonable not to do so.

Section 2 of the 1988 Act places a further duty on the landlord to take reasonable steps to pass on the tenant's application for consent to anyone he believes may be required to consent to the transaction. Thus, for example, a landlord who receives an application from a tenant, which also requires the consent of the superior landlord, is under a duty to send a copy of the application to the superior landlord.

Although the intention of the Act is obviously to provide the tenant with a quick, safe remedy, it is still open to tenants to seek a declaration that the landlord is acting unreasonably where they do not want to take the risk of going ahead and assigning without consent. As an alternative, they may combine a claim for damages for breach of statutory duty with an application for an injunction requiring the landlord to comply with his statutory duty.

Section 3 of the 1988 Act deals with subleases. It applies in a situation where a tenancy includes a covenant on the part of the tenant not to consent to his sub-tenant's assigning, underletting, charging or parting with possession of the premises comprised in the sub-tenancy without the approval of the landlord, and the covenant is subject to the qualification that the approval is not to be unreasonably withheld. The section provides that the landlord owes a duty to the sub-tenant in terms comparable with the duty he owes to a tenant under the Act.

While the 1988 Act reverses the burden of proof so that it is now necessary for the landlord to prove that any refusal is reasonable, and while it provides the tenant with a claim for damages, it does not alter the law in any other respects. In particular, the Act does not require the landlord, when withholding consent to an assignment, to justify as a matter of fact the matters upon which it relies (*Air India* v *Balabel* [1993] 30 EG 90).

  (b) Prior to the 1988 Act, it was open to a landlord to give at the hearing other reasons for objections to the proposed assignment not given to the tenant originally, provided that they were present in his mind when he made the decision to refuse consent (*Bromley Park Garden Estates Ltd* v *Moss* [1982] 1 WLR 1019, *per* Slade LJ). It is now clear that a landlord can only rely on reasons for withholding consent which are stated in writing within a reasonable time of the tenant's application for consent. In *Footwear Corportion Ltd* v *Amplight Properties Ltd* [1998] 3 All ER 52, the tenant of retail premises wrote to the landlord seeking consent to a sub-letting. Three days later, the landlord's managing director telephoned the tenant's surveyor indicating that consent would not be granted for a variety of reasons. The Court held that the landlord was not entitled to rely on reasons justifying its refusal which had not been communicated to the tenant in *writing* within a reasonable time in compliance with s. 1(3) of the 1988 Act. The upshot of this decision, therefore, is that:

(a)   if the landlord gives *no* reasons within a reasonable time of the tenant's application for consent, he cannot rely in court on any reasons which, in fact, brought about the refusal;

(b)   if the landlord has given *written* reasons for refusal within a reasonable time, he cannot rely on unstated reasons which may also have affected his decision to refuse consent; and

(c)   if the landlord has given *oral* reasons within a reasonable time, he cannot rely on these (or any other) reasons for justifying refusal of consent.

The rationale for the Court's ruling is that, even though there is a contractual duty not to withhold consent unreasonably, the 1988 Act imposes a distinct and separate *statutory* duty on the landlord, who is refusing consent, to respond in writing within a reasonable time giving his reasons for refusal. The Act therefore specifically requires consent or refusal of consent to be in writing, albeit that there may be no such contractual requirement under the terms of the covenant in the lease.

QUESTION 4

Blackhorse Ltd holds the freehold title to a high-street property in Birmingham. Several years ago, it granted a 15-year lease to Dyers Ltd, a company which carries on a stationery business from the property. Under the terms of its lease, Dyers Ltd covenanted, *inter alia*, as follows:

... not to assign, sub-let, charge or otherwise part with possession of the premises or any part thereof, or share occupation of the same or any part thereof, save with the landlord's prior written consent ...

The lease also contains a forfeiture clause in the event of non-payment of rent or non-performance of other tenant covenants. The property comprises a shop with a flat above.

Herman is a managing director of Dyers Ltd. Three months ago, with the consent of the other directors of Dyers Ltd, but without the consent of Blackhorse Ltd, Herman took a sub-lease of the flat, paying Dyers Ltd a monthly rent of £300.

Blackhorse Ltd has recently discovered that Herman is living in the flat. It does not wish to bring forfeiture proceedings against Dyers Ltd, but is keen, nevertheless, to oblige Herman to vacate the flat.

Advise Blackhorse Ltd as to what legal action (other than forfeiture) it can take against Dyers Ltd and Herman.

Commentary

This is an interesting question, which raises a novel point of law. It is concerned with the remedies open to a landlord faced with an illegal sub-letting or sharing of occupation of the demised premises. A good answer will consider the important ruling in *Hemingway Securities Ltd* v *Dunraven Ltd* [1995] 09 EG 322. See further, Luxton, P. and Wilkie, M., 'Who Needs Section 146 Injunctive Relief for a Landlord' [1995] Conv 416.

Suggested Answer

In a case of unauthorised assignment or sub-letting of the demised premises, a landlord will invariably opt to effect a forfeiture of the lease in order to recover the property from the unlawful assignee or sub-tenant. This, however, is usually a lengthy and expensive course of action involving the service of a s. 146 notice and the commencement of proceedings against both the tenant in breach of covenant and the unlawful occupier in possession. Although breach of a covenant against assigning, sub-letting and parting with possession is treated, as a matter of law, as an irremediable breach (see *Scala House & District Property Co. Ltd* v *Forbes* [1974] QB 575 and *Expert Clothing Service & Sales Ltd* v *Hillgate House Ltd* [1986] Ch 340), it is still open to the court to grant relief against forfeiture under s. 146(2) of the Law of Property Act 1925 in appropriate circumstances. An important factor in granting relief is the fact that it would have been unreasonable for the landlord to have withheld consent to the assignment (or sub-letting) of the lease had such consent been sought by the tenant. Thus, where it is clear that consent could not have been refused, it appears that relief against forfeiture will generally be granted (*Lam Kee Ying* v *Lam Shes Tong* [1975] AC 247 (PC)). Moreover, the general trend is for the courts to grant relief where there has been an assignment in breach of covenant, even where the breach is wilful and has resulted in the landlord being misled (*Southern Depot Co. Ltd* v *British Railways Board* [1990] 2 EGLR 39 and *Fuller* v *Judy Properties Ltd* [1992] 1 EGLR 75). In cases involving sub-letting in breach of covenant, the courts adopt the principle of proportionality, taking a number of factors into account in considering whether or not to grant relief, including the value of the lease and the extent of any loss suffered by the landlord (*Mount Cook Land Ltd* v *Hartley* [2000] EGCS 26). In the majority of cases, therefore, relief will be granted and the landlord will not be in a position to forfeit the lease. In such circumstances, the landlord may seek to claim damages for breach of covenant or, alternatively, attempt to regularise the position by taking other steps to oust the unlawful occupier.

The landlord cannot, of course, take direct action against an illegal sub-tenant/occupier of the premises, simply because he has no *locus standi* to sue in trespass during the subsistence of the lease. Because the landlord has divested himself of exclusive possession in favour of the tenant, he no longer retains any right to possession in himself. A reversioner may sue for trespass only if it actually affects his reversionary interest. Accordingly, a mere trespass, unaccompanied by any permanent physical injury to the land, is not actionable by the landlord who must, therefore, wait until his interest falls into possession (*Jones* v *Llanrwst Urban Council* [1911] 1 Ch 393, at 404, and *Shelfer* v *City of London Electric Lighting Co.* [1895] 1 Ch 287, at 318). Thus, in *Moore Properties (Ilford) Ltd* v *McKeon* [1976] 1 WLR 1278, the tenancy had ended so that the landlord was able to bring summary possession proceedings against the defendants, who had taken up occupation by virtue of a sub-tenancy which had been granted in breach of an absolute prohibition against sub-letting and without the landlord's knowledge or consent.

Where, however, the head tenancy subsists, it may be open to a landlord to seek a mandatory injunction against the sub-tenant requiring him to effect a surrender of the unlawful sub-lease. In *Hemingway Securities Ltd* v *Dunraven Ltd* [1995] 09 EG 322 the lease contained a fully qualified covenant against sub-letting and required, as a condition precedent to the landlord's consent, that the prospective sub-tenant enter into a direct covenant with the landlord to observe all the tenant's covenants contained in the head lease. The tenant, without the landlord's consent (and apparently without its knowledge), sub-let the premises to four individuals in partnership, who duly entered into possession of the premises. The landlord sought a mandatory injunction against the tenant alleging a breach of contract, and against the sub-tenants either for inducing a breach of contract, or for breaching the covenant against sub-letting on the basis that it was binding on the sub-tenants under the rule in *Tulk* v *Moxhay* (1848) 2 Ph 774. Jacob J held that the landlord was entitled to a mandatory injunction on both grounds, requiring the sub-tenants to execute a deed delivering up their unlawful sub-lease to the tenant.

In cases such as this, if the landlord acts promptly, he may be able to obtain a prohibitory injunction against the tenant, preventing the latter from assigning or sub-letting, etc. in breach of covenant (*Williams* v *Earle* (1868) LR 3 QB 739). The landlord may also seek such an injunction where the tenant is himself an assignee of the lease (*McEacham* v *Colton* [1902] 2 AC 104 (PC)). However, an unlawful sub-letting or assignment, which has already been executed, will create a valid title which will vest in the unlawful sub-tenant or assignee. The sub-letting or assignment is not void but voidable at the option of the landlord. In other words, the sub-tenant (or assignee) will take a defeasible title (i.e., subject to the landlord's right of forfeiture) (*Old Grovebury Manor Farm Ltd v W. Seymour Plant Sales & Hire Ltd (No. 2)* [1979] 1 WLR 1397). The significance of the decision in *Hemingway*, therefore, is that it gives the landlord a means of actually *undoing* the transaction without recourse to expensive forfeiture proceedings culminating in the potential determination of the lease.

The point was also addressed in *Esso Petroleum Co. Ltd* v *Kingswood Motors (Addlestone) Ltd* [1974] QB 142, where a collusive conveyance was executed to allow the vendors to avoid a solus agreement by which they were bound to buy petroleum only from Esso. The court held that the purchaser's conduct amounted to a deliberate inducement of a breach of the vendor's contract. On this basis, a mandatory injunction was granted against the purchaser requiring it to reconvey the legal estate. The *Esso* case establishes the principle that a party to a contract may obtain an injunction against a third party who induces (or who threatens to induce) the other contracting party to breach the contract. In the *Hemingway* case, Jacob J similarly found that the sub-tenants had intentionally induced a breach of the tenant's contract with the landlord not to sub-let without consent, and so was able to award a mandatory injunction against the sub-tenants to surrender the sub-lease. In so doing, he clearly treated the lease as a species of contract — an approach much in keeping with contemporary judicial trends: see, e.g., *Hussein* v *Mehlman* [1992] 32 EG 59, involving a repudiatory breach of a contract of letting.

The alternative ground relied upon by Jacob J in the *Hemingway* case was based on the application of the rule in *Tulk* v *Moxhay*. Jacob J concluded that a qualified covenant against sub-letting was, in essence, a restrictive covenant enforceable in equity as against the sub-tenants by means of a mandatory injunction. This aspect of the case has, however, been criticised by academic writers on the ground that the breach of covenant against sub-letting was a 'once and for all' breach committed, not by the sub-tenant, but by the tenant: see Luxton, P. and Wilkie, M. [1995] Conv 416.

It is apparent from the foregoing that Blackhorse Ltd should be advised to pursue injunctive relief against Dyers Ltd (alleging breach of contract) and Herman (based on the tort of interference with contract). The jurisdiction to grant an injunction against Herman for inducing a breach of contract will be available if Herman had knowledge that the grant of the sub-lease was a breach of a covenant in the head lease. In this connection, it is more than likely that Herman had notice of the terms of the head lease (in particular, the qualified covenant against assignment) by virtue of his position as a director of Dyers Ltd.

An order should be sought against Dyers Ltd restraining any like breaches in future. The order against Herman should require him to execute a deed of surrender delivering up his unlawful sub-lease to Dyers Ltd. Herman may seek to argue that injunctive relief will operate harshly against him because it will deny him the right to seek relief, which would otherwise be open to him as a sub-tenant if the landlord had invoked forfeiture proceedings against Dyers Ltd. However, the injunction, being a creature of equity, is a discretionary remedy and undue hardship to the defendant, or unreasonable delay or lack of 'clean hands' on the part of the claimant, are grounds upon which the remedy may be refused. In the present case, it would seem that injunctive relief would cause little hardship to Herman. He did not pay a premium on the grant of the sub-lease which, in any event, is only periodic in nature. It seems also that a mandatory injunction can be granted even if the claimant has suffered no serious damage or inconvenience (*Kelson* v *Imperial Tobacco Co. Ltd* [1957] 2 QB 334). In *Hemingway*, Jacob J also thought it wrong in principle that an unlawful sub-tenant should be allowed to stay on at the premises and thereby benefit from his wrongdoing. Similar reasoning would, no doubt, apply in the present case. If the court, however, was minded to exercise its discretion *against* granting an injunction, Blackhorse Ltd would still be entitled to an award of equitable damages in lieu of an injunction (under the Chancery Amendment Act 1858, now s. 50 of the Supreme Court Act 1981), and presumably also damages in tort for inducing a breach of contract. It would also have a claim in damages against Dyers Ltd for breach of covenant.

6 Leasehold Dilapidations

INTRODUCTION

The subject of leasehold dilapidations is vast, and the student may be asked to answer questions on any one or more of the following topics:

(a)   the meaning of repair;

(b)   the standard of repair;

(c)   the rule that a landlord is liable only on notice;

(d)   implied obligations to repair; and

(e)   remedies for breach of a repairing obligation.

Questions in this area tend to take the form of lengthy problems, the student usually being asked to advise a party to the lease as to its legal liability (if any) in respect of a number of alleged defects on the demised premises. You should be aware that liability for defects on the property may arise either in contract or in tort.

In relation to express covenants, the question will invariably require you to consider the case law contrasting a work of repair with renewal and improvement (see, e.g., *Ravenseft Properties Ltd* v *Davstone (Holdings) Ltd* [1980] QB 12). This may be linked with a secondary issue as to what standard of repair should apply.

Sometimes, the question will focus on the landlord's implied obligations to repair in the absence of any express covenant to maintain the premises. Here, the student may be required to consider liability at common law (i.e., fitness for human habitation and maintenance of essential means of access) and under statute (i.e., the Landlord and Tenant 1985, ss. 8 and 11, as amended by the Housing Act 1988, s. 116). This may be contrasted with the tenant's implied obligation to use the premises in a tenant-like manner (*Warren* v *Keen* [1954] 1 QB 15).

With regard to liability in tort, the question may involve an examination of the landlord's liability:

(a)   in negligence (e.g., *Rimmer* v *Liverpool City Council* [1985] QB 1; *McNerny* v *Lambeth London Borough Council* [1989] 19 EG 77);

(b)   under the Defective Premises Act 1972, s. 4 (e.g., *McAuley* v *Bristol City Council* [1992] 1 All ER 749); and

(c)   under the Environmental Protection Act 1990, ss. 79–82 (e.g., *Dover District Council* v *Farrar* (1980) 2 HLR 35 and *GLC* v *London Borough of Tower Hamlets* (1983) 15 HLR 54).

So far as the tenant is concerned, liability may arise under the torts of waste or nuisance, or under the Occupiers' Liability Act 1957.

The rule that the landlord's liability to repair the demised premises arises only after he has been given sufficient notice of the defects has been the subject of recent case law, in particular, the Court of Appeal decision in *British Telecommunications plc* v *Sun Life Assurance Society plc* [1995] 4 All ER 44, where a number of earlier authorities were reviewed. We have included an essay-type question on this topic: see Question 6.

The subject of remedies for disrepair is a complex one. The student may be asked to advise on the landlord's remedies of forfeiture of the lease and/or damages for breach of covenant. Both these remedies are limited by statute and you will need to possess a good understanding of the workings of the Law of Property Act 1925, s. 146, the Leasehold Property (Repairs) Act 1938, and the Landlord and Tenant Act 1927, s. 18. So far as the tenant's remedies are concerned, these will include damages, specific performance, set off against rent, and the appointment of a receiver.

Although a complex area of study, questions on dilapidations tend to be popular with both examiners and students. Most landlord and tenant courses focus on this subject in some depth, and the well-prepared student should have little difficulty in scoring a good mark.

Lastly, it is worth mentioning that the whole topic of leasehold dilapidations has been the subject of consideration by the Law Commission: see Law Commission Report (Law Com. No. 238, 1996), 'Landlord and Tenant: Responsibility for State and Condition of Property', and Bridge, S., 'Putting in Right? The Law Commission and the Condition of Tenanted Property' [1996] Conv 342. It is possible that your examiner may wish to set a question on the Law Commission's proposals, and this will undoubtedly take the form of an essay question. Essay questions give you the chance to show that you have read beyond the basic texts and have understood some of the broader issues affecting your topic of study. See Question 5.

QUESTION 1

By a lease, dated 1 March 1990, the Earl of London demised Flatacre Hall to Albert Smith for a term of 99 years. By clause 2 of the lease, Albert covenanted 'to keep the demised premises and all additions thereto at all times during the said term in good and tenantable repair'. The Earl has now presented Albert with a formidable schedule of dilapidations, the items of which may be summarised under the following headings:

(a) Renew roof of stable block. Estimated cost: £15,000. The wood has rotted and the entire roof structure needs to be replaced;

(b) Eradicate rising damp in basement of main building. Estimated cost: £35,000. There is no damp-course as the building dates from 1850;

(c) Re-build side wall of kitchen. Estimated cost: £12,000. The wall is unsafe due to old age. The work will involve compliance with modern building standards;

(d) Redecorate throughout the main building. Estimated cost: £8,000. The wallpaper is badly stained and worn. The paintwork has faded and turned yellow. Much of the external woodwork has rotted.

Advise Albert as to his legal liability (if any) in respect of each of the alleged defects set out above.

Commentary

This is an example of a multi-part question, where you are asked to advise the tenant as to his liability in respect of a number of alleged defects. Essentially, the question seeks to test your understanding of the meaning of 'repair' and requires you to contrast works of repair with renewal and improvement. Try to avoid giving the examiner a 'mini-lecture' on the subject, and instead concentrate on being selective in your information and actually answering the question as set. Each part of the question revolves around a specific cluster of cases and so a thorough knowledge of the case law will pay dividends!

The fourth part of the question calls for an examination of cases on decorative repairs, in particular, *Proudfoot* v *Hart* (1890) 25 QBD 42.

Suggested Answer

A tenant who has covenanted to *keep* in repair the demised premises during the term must have them in repair at all times during the term, and so if they are at any time out of repair he commits a breach of the covenant. It has been held that a covenant which requires the landlord to keep the building in 'good and tenantable condition' is wide enough to require him to put the building in that condition which, given the property's age, character and locality, would make it reasonably fit for the occupation of a reasonably-minded teanant of the class likely to take it (*Credit Suisse v Beegas Nominees Ltd* [1994] 4 All ER 803). Consequently, the covenant in the present case obliges Albert to *put* the premises in repair (if they are not in repair when the lease begins) and to *leave* them in repair during the currency of the term.

The essential issue is whether, having regard to all the circumstances of the case, the proposed remedial works can fairly be regarded as 'repair' in the context of this particular lease (*Holding & Management Ltd v Property Holding & Investment Trust plc* [1990] 05 EG 75). Three criteria have been established over the years for determining whether a work constitutes repair, namely:

(a) whether the works go to the whole or substantially the whole of the structure, or only to a subsidiary part;

(b) whether the effect is to produce a building of a wholly different character from that which had been let; and

(c) what is the cost of the works in relation to the previous value of the building and what is the effect on the value and life of the building (*McDougall v Easington District Council* [1989] 25 EG 104).

(a) 'Renew roof of stable-block'. As mentioned above, one test to be applied in deciding whether particular works can properly be described as 'repair', as opposed to works of renewal or improvement, is whether they involve giving back to the landlord a wholly different thing from that demised under the lease. This was the test put forward in *Ravenseft Properties Ltd v Davstone (Holdings) Ltd* [1980] QB 12, following the observations of Lord Esher MR in *Lister v Lane* [1893] 2 QB 212. In deciding the question whether the works would involve giving back to the landlord a wholly different thing, regard may be had, as a guide, to the proportion which the cost of the disputed works bear to the value or cost of the whole building.

In *Elite Investments Ltd* v *TI Bainbridge Silencers Ltd* (1986) 280 EG 1001, a case involving a dilapidated roof of an industrial unit, the evidence was that the replacement of the roof would cost around £84,000. In its dilapidated condition, the unit had virtually no value for lettings, but its value as repaired would be about £140,000–£150,000. It is noteworthy that the roof was beyond patching and had come to the end of its useful life and needed to be entirely replaced. The court held, rejecting the tenant's argument based on giving back to the landlord an entirely different thing, that this was not a different thing but merely an industrial building with a new roof. It was also suggested in this case that in a situation where the value of the demised building when repaired (£140,000–£150,000) is very much less than the cost of putting up a new building altogether (£1m), it is the cost of putting up the new building, not the value of the old building when repaired, which should be compared with the cost of the works required to repair the old building (£84,000).

In *New England Properties plc* v *Portsmouth New Shops Ltd* [1993] 23 EG 130, the original design of the roof was inadequate and it was necessary to replace the entire roof at a cost in excess of £200,000. It was held that the lease imposed an obligation on the landlord not simply to repair but also to renew or replace where necessary. It was also suggested *obiter* that, although it was a borderline case, the replacement of the roof fell to be regarded in any event as a work of repair.

In the present case, the information given is that the estimated cost of repairs amounts to £15,000. There is no mention of the value of the stable-block when repaired, or indeed of the cost of erecting a new stable-block altogether. Nevertheless, despite the extensive nature of the remedial works, it seems almost certain that the courts would treat the same as works of repair thereby rendering Albert liable under his covenant.

(b) 'Eradicate damp in basement'. Prior to the decision in *Ravenseft* (above), it had been thought that 'repair' did not include the remedying of an inherent defect in the design or construction of the demised premises. This view has now been exploded and the question, in all cases, is one of degree (*Brew Brothers Ltd* v *Snax (Ross) Ltd* [1969] 1 WLR 657).

The facts here show that there is no damp-course in the basement as the building dates back to 1850. In *Pembery* v *Lamdin* [1940] 2 All ER 434, a case involving a cellar built without a damp-course, it was held that the landlord was not liable under his repairing covenant to carry out remedial works to prevent damp penetrating into the cellar because this would involve ordering him to give the tenant a different thing from that which was demised. Similarly, in *Yanover* v *Romford Finance & Development Co. Ltd* (1983), unreported, Park J held that the proposed remedial work of the installation of a damp-course in a ground-floor flat at a cost of £8,000 was a major building operation which was not within the landlord's covenant relating to external repairs.

These cases may be contrasted with *Elmcroft Developments Ltd* v *Tankersley-Sawyer* (1984) 270 EG 140, where there was evidence of penetrating damp in flats due to the existing damp-course having been positioned below ground level, with consequent 'bridging' causing rising damp in the walls. The remedial work required included insertion of a damp-course by silicone injection. The Court of Appeal held that the landlords were in breach of their covenant to repair since the remedial work did not go beyond repair and did not involve the provision of a wholly different thing from that which was demised. It is to be observed that the *Pembery* case involved premises built in 1840, whereas the more recent decision in *Elmcroft* concerned a modern letting of flats in a high class residential area of Central London.

In the present case, the estimated cost of the remedial work is £35,000. Looking at the matter as one of degree, therefore, Albert should be advised that he is not liable to eradicate the rising damp in the basement.

(c) 'Re-build side wall'. The word 'repair' has been defined as meaning the restoration by renewal or replacement of *subsidiary* parts of the whole, as opposed to the reconstruction of the whole or substantially the whole. In *Lurcott* v *Wakeley and Wheeler* [1911] KB 905, the front wall of a house had to be pulled down due to its dangerous condition. The house was very old and the condition of the wall was caused by old age. The Court of Appeal held that the tenant was liable under his covenant to repair and to replace worn out parts of a house. Essentially, where the remedial works would produce premises of a wholly different character from those which had been let, the works fall to be classified as improvements (as opposed to repair) to the premises. In the words of Cozens-Hardy MR in *Lurcott*, 'is it something which goes to the whole, or substantially the whole, or is it simply an injury to a portion, a subsidiary portion, of the demised property?'

In the present case, Albert should be advised that the side wall of the kitchen is merely a subsidiary portion of the main building, the rebuilding of which would not change the character or nature of the building as a whole. The fact that the work will involve compliance with modern building standards does not, it is submitted, change the position. Albert is obliged to repair the wall in the only sense in which it can be repaired, namely, by rebuilding it according to current building regulations etc. (*Ravenseft Properties Ltd* v *Davstone (Holdings) Ltd* [1980] QB 12, *per* Forbes J., at p. 22). The fact that the repairs will inevitably incorporate some improvement in design and construction does not mean that they cease to be works of repair: *Creska Ltd* v *Hammersmith and Fulham London Borough Council* [1998] 37 EG 165 (repair of an under-floor heating system) and *Minja Properties Ltd* v *Cussins Property Group plc* [1998] 30 EG 114 (replacement of existing rusted single-glazed window frames with double-glazed units).

(d) 'Redecoration throughout main building'. As a general rule, a repairing covenant does not carry with it the obligation to carry out decorative repairs, except painting necessary for the prevention of decay as opposed to mere ornamentation. In *Crayford* v *Newton* (1886) 36 WN 54, the Court of Appeal held that a tenant who agreed to keep the inside of the premises in tenantable repair and who occupied them for 17 years without having painted or papered was only bound to paint and paper so as to prevent the house from going into decay. There seems little doubt, therefore, that Albert is obliged to paint the external woodwork to prevent rot.

In *Proudfoot* v *Hart* (1890) 25 QBD 42, however, the Court of Appeal, while laying down the general rule that the tenant is not bound by a general repairing covenant to do repairs which are merely decorative, also concluded that he is bound to repaper, paint and whitewash walls and ceilings if the condition of the house in those respects is such that it would not be taken by a reasonably minded tenant of the class likely to take it. The court also held that, in determining the standard of repair, regard is to be had to the age, character and prospective life of the premises and the locality in which it is situated. Applying the test of the reasonably minded tenant, it seems that Albert may be liable to repaper and paint the interior of the main building, although it is possible that he may be able to avail himself of the special form of relief available to a tenant in respect of internal decorative repairs under the Law of Property Act 1925, s. 147. This section provides that the court may relieve the tenant from liability for such repairs if, having regard to all the circumstances of the case (including in particular the length of the tenant's term or interest remaining unexpired), the court is satisfied that the landlord's notice is unreasonable.

QUESTION 2

Compare and contrast the remedies available to:

(a) a landlord; and

(b) a tenant

for breach of a covenant to repair.

To what extent are the landlord's remedies limited by statute and the tenant's remedies extended by statute?

Commentary

This is a relatively straightforward question on remedies for disrepair. However, there is a lot of ground to cover and there is a real danger that the student will spend too much time on one particular remedy at the expense of others. Essentially, the question requires a broad outline of the various remedies, but with particular emphasis on statutory intervention. For a good summary of the relevant law, see Williams, D., 'Landlord's Remedies for Disrepair' [1989] EG 8938, 24, and Williams, D., 'Tenant's Remedies for Disrepair' (1984) *Law Society Gazette*, 9 May, p. 1269. See also, more recently, Madge, N., 'Damages for Breach of Repairing Obligations' (1999) 149 NLJ 1643.

Suggested Answer

(a) Landlord's remedies. A landlord faced with a tenant who is in breach of his covenant to repair may elect to forfeit the lease and claim damages for any loss suffered to his reversion. In all cases (other than non-payment of rent), a prerequisite to forfeiture is the service by the landlord of a notice under the Law of Property Act 1925, s. 146(1). He must, in the notice, specify the particular breach complained of and, if the breach is capable of remedy, require the tenant to remedy the same within a reasonable time. In addition, where appropriate, the notice must refer to the landlord's claim for compensation.

Where the lease in question was granted for seven or more years and three years or more remain unexpired at the date of the s. 146 notice, the landlord's remedy of forfeiture (and damages) is further limited by the Leasehold Property (Repairs) Act 1938. Where the Act applies, the landlord cannot proceed without first serving a s. 146 notice, which must also inform the tenant of his right to serve a counternotice claiming the benefit of the Act. If the tenant does serve such a counternotice within 28 days, no further proceedings by action or otherwise can be taken by the landlord without leave of the court establishing a case, on the balance of probabilities, that one or more of the five grounds set out in s. 1(5) of the Act have been fulfilled (*Associated British Ports* v *C.H. Bailey plc* [1990] 2 AC 703).

Under s. 146(2) of the 1925 Act, the tenant is also entitled to apply to the court for relief against forfeiture. The court may grant or refuse relief on terms as it thinks fit, and in the case of a breach of a repairing covenant the court will usually require the tenant to remedy the disrepair and make compensation to the landlord for any damage to the reversion before it grants such relief. A special form of relief is given to the tenant under s. 147 of the 1925 Act in respect of internal decorative repairs. Upon the tenant's application for relief, the court may relieve the tenant from liability for such repairs if, having regard to all the circumstances of the case (including, in particular, the length of the term unexpired), the court is satisfied that the landlord's notice is unreasonable.

Apart from claiming forfeiture, the landlord will invariably seek to claim damages. Where the landlord's claim is brought during the currency of the lease, damages will represent the amount by which the landlord's reversion has depreciated in marketable value by the premises being out of repair. Practically, this is the amount by which the saleable value of the premises is reduced by the neglect bearing in mind the length of the unexpired term. However, by the Landlord and Tenant Act 1927, s. 18(1), damages for breach of a repairing covenant during the currency of a lease are not to exceed the amount (if any) by which the value of the premises is reduced. This, in effect, provides an upper limit to the amount of damages recoverable. At the end of the term, the landlord may bring a claim on the covenant to yield up the premises in repair. The measure of damages is the cost of repair (*Foyner* v *Weeks* [1891] 2 QB 31) plus loss of rental while the repair is being done (*Woods* v *Pope* (1895) 6 C & P 732). Here again, the common law measure is subject to s. 18 of the 1927 Act (*Hansom* v *Newman* [1934] Ch 298 and *Shortlands Investments Ltd* v *Cargill plc* [1995] 08 EG 163).

Section 18(1) of the 1927 Act also provides that no damages are recoverable by the landlord for failure to leave or put premises in repair at the end of a lease if it is shown that they, in whatever condition, would, at or shortly after the end, have been pulled down or such alterations made as to render the tenant's repairs valueless.

It is possible for a landlord to avoid the procedural requirements of the 1938 Act if he has the benefit of a covenant in the lease enabling him to inspect the state of repair of the demised premises and serve notice on the tenant requiring him to execute the necessary repairs. If he fails to do so, the landlord may carry out the work himself and recover the cost from the tenant. In these circumstances, a claim by the landlord to recover the cost of the repairs is, by reason of the express terms of the covenant, either a claim for a *debt* or *rent* due under the lease rather than a claim for damages for breach of covenant within the 1938 Act. Accordingly, the landlord does not require leave under the Act to bring the claim against the tenant (*Colchester Estates (Cardiff)* v *Carlton Industries plc* [1986] Ch 80 and *Jervis* v *Harris* [1996] 1 EGLR 78 (CA)). This self-help remedy, however, may not be available to the landlord if the carrying out of the repairs would be highly disruptive to the tenant's business (*Hammersmith and Fulham London Borough Council* v *Creska Ltd* [1999] PLSCS 159).

In exceptional cases, it may be open to the landlord to seek specific performance of his tenant's repairing obligations: *Rainbow Estates Ltd* v *Tokenhold Ltd* [1998] 3 WLR 980, where specific performance was granted because the lease contained no forfeiture clause nor any right entitling the landlord access to the premises to carry out the repairs with a view to claiming the cost from the tenants as a debt or rent arrears. Moreover, there was evidence of serious disrepair and deterioration to the property. (See further, Pawlowski, M. [1998] Conv 495.)

(b) Tenant's remedies. Where the landlord is in breach of his repairing covenant, the tenant has basically four remedies, namely:

(a) damages;

(b) specific performance;

(c) set off against rent; and

(d) appointment of a receiver.

In addition, the tenant may be able to invoke action by the local authority in extreme cases of disrepair.

Damages may be awarded under the various heads of claim set out in *Calabar Properties Ltd* v *Stitcher* [1984] 1 WLR 287, a decision of the Court of Appeal applied in *McGreal* v *Wake* (1984) 269 EG 1254. In the latter case, the tenant was held to have a valid claim against the landlord for having to live in an unrepaired house for several months, and was entitled to recover costs of redecoration, storing furniture and for alternative accommodation. Substantial damages may also be awarded for distress, discomfort and inconvenience (*Choidi* v *DeMarney* (1989) 21 HLR 6). Usually, such damages are assessed by means of a notional reduction in rent. If the tenant does not remain in occupation because of the disrepair but is forced to sell, he may recover the diminution of the price occasioned by the landlord's failure to repair (*Wallace* v *Manchester City Council* (1998) 30 HLR 1111 (CA)). It appears, however, that damages for diminution in capital value will not be recoverable unless the tenant had acquired the premises with the intention of re-selling (*Calabar Properties* above).

In addition to damages, the tenant may seek to enforce a landlord's repairing obligation by means of a decree of specific performance under the Landlord and Tenant Act 1985, s. 17(1). Section 17(1) provides that in any proceedings in which a tenant of a dwelling alleges a breach on the part of his landlord of a repairing covenant relating to any part of the premises in which the dwelling is comprised, the court may, in its discretion, order specific performance of the covenant whether or not the breach relates to a part of the premises let to the tenant and notwithstanding any equitable rule restricting the scope of that remedy. Apart from this statutory right, the tenant may invoke the court's inherent equitable jurisdiction to make an order where the landlord is in possession of the land where the defect exists (*Jeune* v *Queens Cross Properties Ltd* [1974] Ch 97).

By way of 'self-help', the tenant may also opt to do the repairs himself and deduct the expense from current or future rent. Upon being sued for unpaid rent by his landlord, the tenant will be able to rely upon his own counterclaim against the landlord for breach of the landlord's repairing covenant as effecting a complete defence by way of an equitable set off to the claim for rent (*British Anzani (Felixstowe) Ltd* v *International Marine Management (UK) Ltd* [1980] QB 137). In addition, the tenant has a common law right to deduct the repairing cost from the rent where, having given notice to the landlord, the tenant carries out the repairs which are the landlord's responsibility (*Lee-Parker* v *Izzet* [1971] 1 WLR 1688 and *Asco Developments Ltd* v *Gordon* (1978) 248 EG 683). Reference may also be made to the Housing Act 1985, s. 96 (as substituted by the Leasehold Reform, Housing and Urban Development Act 1993, s. 121), under which secure tenants whose landlords are local housing authorities are entitled to have qualifying repairs carried out, at their landlords' expense, to the dwelling-houses of which they are such tenants.

Lastly, the tenant may seek to rely upon the court's power, either as an interim measure or as part of a final order, to order the appointment of a receiver and manager of the premises. Under the Supreme Court Act 1981, s. 37, the High Court has power to appoint a receiver in all cases where it appears just and convenient to do so. A receiver has, accordingly, been appointed in cases where the landlord was in serious breach of his covenant to repair (*Hart* v *Emelkirk Ltd* [1983] 1 WLR 1289). The function of a receiver in such cases is to receive the rents and service charges from the tenants and to repair and manage the premises (usually a block of flats) during his appointment. In addition to this general jurisdiction, the Landlord and Tenant Act 1987, Pt II provides for the appointment of managers by the county court to assume responsibility for the management of premises containing flats (*Howard* v *Midrome Ltd* [1991] 03 EG 135).

QUESTION 3

North London Properties (NLP) are the freehold owners of Stanley Estate, a tower block, comprising 26 self-contained flats let on weekly tenancies. During the past year, NLP have received various complaints from Arthur, one of the tenants of the block, alleging:

(a)   severe condensation dampness in his flat resulting from poor ventilation, inadequate heating and insulation. In particular, Arthur has drawn attention to the single-glazed metal framed windows which he insists should be replaced. The condensation has caused furniture and fabrics to become rotten, but there is no evidence of physical damage to the property itself. He has also complained of frequent colds and bronchial infections which he attributes to the condensation problem; and

(b)   inadequate hot water supply attributable to a faulty boiler situated in the basement of the block.

NLP have denied liability for any of these defects, pointing to the absence of any express covenants on the part of the landlord to repair or maintain the block.

Advise Arthur:

(a)   whether NLP are liable to remedy the condensation dampness;

[20 marks]

AND

(b)   whether NLP are liable to repair the faulty boiler.

[5 marks]

Commentary

This is a difficult problem concerning a landlord's implied obligations to repair, both at common law and under statute. In addition, the question requires some discussion of a landlord's liability in negligence for inherent defects in the design and construction of the property (*Rimmer* v *Liverpool City Council* [1985] QB 1 and *McNerny* v *Lambeth London Borough Council* [1989] 19 EG 77).

Condensation dampness continues to be a serious problem for tenants of blocks of flats built in the 1960s and 1970s. It is generally thought that the law is quite inadequate in this area. See further, Pawlowski, M., 'Tenant's Remedies for Condensation Dampness' [1993] EG 9335, 108 and (Mainly for Students) 'The Curse of the Black Spot: Condensation and the Law' [1995] EG 9513, 128 and [1995] EG 9515, 103.

Suggested Answer

(a)   A number of causes of action may be open to Arthur despite the absence of any express covenant to repair on the part of NLP. In furnished lettings, there is at common law (under the rule in *Smith* v *Marrable* (1843) 11 M & W 5) an implied condition on the part of the landlord that the demised premises will be fit for human habitation at the commencement of the tenancy. If this condition is not fulfilled on the day the tenancy commences, the tenant is entitled to treat the letting as discharged, quit the premises and sue for damages. However, because the condition relates to fitness only at the *commencement* of the tenancy, it will not protect a tenant if the premises later become unfit during the currency of the term (*Sarson* v *Roberts* [1895] 2 QB 395). Assuming the flats are rented furnished and that the condensation was present at the commencement of the letting, NLP would appear to be in breach of this implied condition.

Alternatively, the Landlord and Tenant Act 1985, s. 8 (formerly the Housing Act 1957, s. 6), implies a condition on the part of the landlord that premises are fit for human habitation at the commencement of the tenancy, and an undertaking that the landlord will *keep* the premises in that condition during the term of the tenancy. The standard of fitness is measured having regard to the condition of the premises in respect of a variety of matters including ventilation and freedom from damp (s. 10). Although s. 8 applies to both furnished and unfurnished lettings, s. 8(3) stipulates that it takes effect only in relation to lettings below certain rent limits (e.g., if the letting was made on or after 6 July 1957, the rent limit is £80 p.a. in London and £52 p.a. elsewhere). These very low limits are far below normal market rents, and therefore it is more than likely that Arthur's letting falls outside the ambit of the section.

The Landlord and Tenant Act 1985, s. 11(1)(a), implies a covenant on the part of the landlord to keep in repair the structure and exterior of a dwelling-house. The section applies in general to any tenancy of a dwelling-house granted on or after 24 October 1961 for a term of less than seven years (s. 13) and includes periodic tenancies. In *Quick* v *Taff Ely Borough Council* [1986] QB 809, the plaintiff was the tenant of a house which suffered from severe condendsation caused by lack of insulation, single-glazed metal frame windows and inadequate heating. The Court of Appeal held that the liability under the implied covenant did not arise because of lack of amenity or efficiency, but only where there existed a physical condition which called for repair to the structure or exterior of the dwelling-house. As there was no evidence to indicate physical damage to the windows or any other part of the structure and exterior, the landlord was not liable to carry out work to alleviate the condensation (see also, *Post Office* v *Aquarius Properties Ltd* [1987] 1 All ER 1055 and *Stent* v *Monmouth District Council* (1987) 282 EG 705, where this same principle was applied). These decisions may be contrasted with *Staves* v *Leeds City Council* [1992] 29 EG 119, where plasterwork in the flat was so saturated that it required complete renewal.

The upshot of this analysis is that NLP will be liable under s. 11 of the 1985 Act only if Arthur can point to some disrepair to the physical condition of the structure and/or exterior of his flat (e.g., the walls, plaster, windows). Mere damage to furniture and fabrics will not be sufficient to render NLP liable.

Apart from liability under statute, it is possible that NLP may be liable in negligence. At common law, a 'bare' landlord is under no duty of care to ensure that the premises are reasonably safe at the time of the letting (*Cavalier* v *Pope* [1906] AC 428). But a landlord who has designed and/or constructed the premises remains liable for faults of construction and design despite having disposed of the property by selling or letting it (*Rimmer* v *Liverpool City Council* [1985] QB 1). In *McNerny* v *Lambeth London Borough Council* [1989] 19 EG 77, the tenant sought to apply the *Rimmer* principle to premises suffering from condensation dampness. Unfortunately, on the facts, the landlord council, being a bare landlord (i.e., a mere owner as opposed to an owner-builder), was held to owe no duty of care, and accordingly the tenant's claim for damages based on negligence failed. The same principles would govern NLP's liability.

Lastly, it is possible that Arthur may have recourse under the Environmental Protection Act 1990, ss. 79–82 (replacing the provisions of the Public Health Act 1936, Pt III). Section 79(1)(a) includes in the definition of a statutory nuisance 'any premises in such state as to be prejudicial to health or a nuisance'. Section 82 empowers a magistrates' court to make an order requiring the defendant, *inter alia*, to abate the nuisance within a specified time and to execute any works necessary for that purpose. The provisions have been applied successfully in the context of premises suffering from condensation dampness (*Greater London Council* v *London Borough of Tower Hamlets* (1984) 15 HLR 54, but contrast *Dover District Council* v *Farrar* (1980) 2 HLR 32). Moreover, in *Herbert* v *Lambeth London Borough Council* (1993) 90 LGR 310, a case involving damp and mouldy accommodation, it was held that the magistrates' court has jurisdiction to make a compensation order under the Powers of Criminal Courts Act 1973, s. 35, on the making of a nuisance order under s. 82 of the 1990 Act. Accordingly, Arthur may have a strong claim based on statutory nuisance. The court, however, will take into account only the loss or damage caused by the continuation of the nuisance from the date when the period stated in the complainant's notice expired to the date of the hearing (*R* v *Crown Court at Liverpool, ex parte Cooke* [1996] 4 All ER 589). It seems also that the relevant provisions of the 1990 Act do not give rise to a *civil* cause of claim entitling Arthur to damages for any loss suffered as a result of the condensation dampness (*Issa* v *Hackney London Borough Council* [1997] 1 All ER 999).

(b) In *Campden Hill Towers Ltd* v *Gardner* [1977] QB 823, the phrase 'structure and exterior' of a dwelling-house in the context of the Landlord and Tenant Act 1985, s. 11, when applied to a flat separately occupied within a block of flats, was held to mean not the exterior of the whole building but anything which would be regarded as part of the structure or exterior of the particular flat in question. Similarly, a central heating boiler situated in the common parts of the block was held not to be an installation *in the dwelling-house* within the meaning of the section. The amendments to s. 11 introduced by the Housing Act 1988, s. 116, overturn the effect of this decision, but only in respect of tenancies entered into after 15 January 1989. Section 116 (which adds s. 11(1A)(a) to the Landlord and Tenant Act 1985, s. 11) provides, *inter alia*, that a landlord is obliged to keep in repair and proper working order an installation which, directly or indirectly, serves the dwelling-house and which either (i) forms part of any part of a building in which the landlord has an estate or interest, or (ii) is owned by the landlord or is under his control. Failure to repair or maintain in working order must, however, affect the tenant's enjoyment of the dwelling-house (or any common parts which he is entitled to use). Accordingly, NLP's liability to repair the faulty boiler will depend on whether Arthur's tenancy was granted on or after 15 January 1989.

QUESTION 4

Albert and Jane Smith are the joint tenants of a terraced house which is let to them by John Jones under an assured tenancy agreement for a fixed term of 10 years. The written tenancy agreement obliges the tenants to repair the interior of the demised premises but places no obligation on the landlord to repair the exterior. Clause 3 of the agreement provides as follows:

> The Tenants shall give the Landlord's agents and workmen access to the demised premises for any purpose which may from time to time be required by the Landlord.

Albert and Jane are in dispute with John Jones over the following matters:

(a) The gutters are in poor condition and allow rainwater to penetrate into the premises. As a result, damage has occurred to the internal plaster and timbers in the upper parts of the house.

(b) A few weeks ago, Albert fell and fractured his arm when an unstable concrete step, sunk in earth at the top of the garden of the demised premises, moved under his weight causing him to lose his footing.

Advise Albert and Jane as to the liability (if any) of John Jones in respect of the above matters of complaint.

Commentary

This question raises a number of specific issues requiring a good understanding of the workings of the Defective Premises Act 1972, s. 4.

As to part (a), because the Landlord and Tenant Act 1985, s. 11, does not apply on the facts (the tenancy is for over seven years), you should consider the principle that an obligation to repair may be implied on the landlord in order to match a *correlative obligation* on the part of the tenant (*Barrett* v *Lounova (1982) Ltd* [1990] 1 QB 348).

The facts of part (b), on the other hand, should trigger a discussion of the Defective Premises Act 1972, s. 4, and the Court of Appeal decision in *McAuley* v *Bristol City Council* [1992] 1 All ER 749. For a good summary of the case, see Murdoch, S., 'Landlord's Liability Under the Defective Premises Act' [1991] EG 9143, 133.

This is a difficult problem and the danger is that the poor student will simply enter into a discussion of the Landlord and Tenant Act 1985, s. 11, without realising that it is largely irrelevant to the question.

Suggested Answer

(a)   Guttering. Although the Landlord and Tenant Act 1985, s. 11 (formerly the Housing Act 1961, s. 32), imposes on a landlord an implied covenant, *inter alia*, to keep in repair the structure and exterior of the dwelling-house (including specifically drains, gutters and external pipes), this section applies only to short, residential lettings granted for *less* than seven years. Accordingly, s. 11 has no application to the present case.

A similar problem arose in the case of *Barrett* v *Lounova* [1990] 1 QB 348, where s. 11 did not apply because the tenancy was created before 24 October 1961. In that case as well, the drains and gutters were in poor condition causing extensive water penetration and damage to the internal plaster and timbers. The tenancy obliged the tenant to repair the interior but placed no obligations on the landlords to repair the exterior. The Court of Appeal held that the ordinary rules for implying terms into contracts also applied to leases, and that there was an implied covenant on the landlords to repair the exterior. In that case, the tenant had repairing obligations in respect of the interior and there would come a time when these could not be performed if the exterior were in disrepair. That raised the question as to who had the correlative obligation to repair the exterior. As the tenant's repairing obligation was enforceable throughout the term, an implied covenant was necessary to give business efficacy to the tenancy agreement. The obligation to repair the exterior could not be upon the tenant as it would be unrealistic to expect the tenant to do such work. A covenant upon both parties would be unworkable and so that left an implied covenant upon the landlord as the only solution that made business sense. It is submitted that a similar argument could be put forward on behalf of Jane and Albert.

The later decision in *Adami* v *Lincoln Grange Management Ltd* [1998] 17 EG 148, in which the *Barrett* case was not applied, may be distinguished on the basis that it concerned a long lease at a nominal rent, which dealt expressly with the repair of the subject premises and imposed an insurance obligation to cover catastrophic damage to the building. In these circumstances, there was no basis on which to presume any intention that the landlord should be obliged to repair the structure.

Since John Jones is in breach of his implied covenant to repair the exterior, he will be liable for the consequential damage caused to the internal plaster and timber. In *Barrett* v *Lounova*, this was agreed at £1,250. In addition, Albert and Jane are entitled to claim damages for distress, discomfort and inconvenience (*Choidi* v *DeMarney* (1989) 21 HLR 6).

Alternatively, it may be that Albert and Jane could make a claim under the Defective Premises Act 1972, s. 4, and seek an injunction compelling John Jones to carry out remedial works to the defective gutters. Had it been necessary to decide this alternative claim in the *Barrett* case, the court would have been prepared to grant the injunction sought.

   (b) Concrete step. Here again, it seems that the Landlord and Tenant Act 1985, s. 11, has no application since (apart from the tenancy being for 10 years) this provision does not extend to the repair of a backyard or garden (*Hopwood* v *Rugeley Urban District Council* [1975] 1 WLR 373). Equally, it has been held recently that premises which are in a state such as to give rise to a danger of accident or physical injury are not capable of being a statutory nuisance within the meaning of s. 79(1)(a) of the Environmental Protection Act 1990 (*R* v *Bristol City Council, ex parte Everett* [1998] 3 All ER 603, involving a steep staircase). Moreover, a physical accident cannot be described as an injury to health in the context of this legislation, which is directed at premises that create a risk of disease and illness. The question, therefore, is whether Albert and Jane can successfully argue that John Jones is in breach of his duty of care under the Defective Premises Act 1972, s. 4.

The effect of s. 4 is to impose on a landlord who has covenanted to repair, an obligation to the tenant (and third parties) to keep them 'reasonably safe from personal injury or from damage to their property' caused by defects in the state of the property. Although s. 4(1) is concerned with a landlord who is in breach of his own repairing covenant, s. 4(4) also operates to impose liability on a landlord despite the fact that, under the terms of the tenancy, it is the tenant who is obliged to repair. Moreover, where personal injury or damage to property is caused by a defect which is outside the express repairing obligations of *both* the landlord and tenant, the case of *McAuley* v *Bristol City Council* [1992] 1 All ER 749 demonstrates that the landlord can become liable to the tenant under s. 4(4).

In *McAuley*, the Court of Appeal held that s. 4(4) of the 1972 Act imposes a duty of care on a landlord towards his tenant where premises are let under a tenancy which expressly or impliedly gives the landlord the right to enter the premises to carry out repairs. In *Smith* v *Bradford Metropolitan Council* (1982) 44 P & CR 171, the Court of Appeal held that a provision in the tenancy agreement to the effect that the tenant should give the landlord's agents reasonable facilities for inspecting the premises and their state of repair and for carrying out repairs, gave the landlord an *express* right of re-entry to carry out repairs to the back yard of the house. Accordingly, the landlord was held liable under s. 4(4) for injuries caused to the tenant when he fell because of the condition of the yard.

In *McAuley*, the tenant fell and broke her ankle on a loose step in the garden of the property. There was no express right on the part of the landlord to enter to repair the garden steps, but instead (as in the question set) there was an express provision which required the tenant to give the landlord's agents reasonable facilities for entering upon the premises for any purpose which may be required by the landlord. In the absence, therefore, of any express right of re-entry to repair the garden step, the central issue was whether such a right should be *implied*. The Court of Appeal came to the conclusion that a right to re-enter to carry out any repair necessary to remove the risk of injury should be implied, and accordingly held the landlord liable.

On this basis, Albert should be advised that he has a good claim against John Jones under s. 4(4) of the 1972 Act.

QUESTION 5

What recent proposals have been put forward for reform of the current law on leasehold dilapidations? Do you agree that the law should be changed in this area?

Commentary

This is a straightforward essay question which seeks to test your knowledge of the broader issues governing the law of dilapidations. Apart from referring to the Law Commission's proposals for reform (i.e., Law Commission Report (Law Com. No. 238, 1996), 'Landlord and Tenant: Responsibility for State and Condition of Property'), you should also try and use some examples of current defects in the law and explain how these would be rectified under the new regime. Remember that the question specifically asks you to comment on whether a change in the law is desirable. For a good analysis of the Law

Commission's proposals, see Bridge, S., 'Putting it Right? The Law Commission and the Condition of Tenanted Property' [1996] Conv 342.

Suggested Answer

In 1996, the Law Commission published its Report, 'Landlord and Tenant: Responsibility for State and Condition of Property' (Law Com. No. 238, 1996). The aim of the Report was to examine the scope of the current obligations to repair and to consider their deficiencies.

One of the main criticisms of the existing law is that it is based on the concept of 'repair', which involves looking at the physical state of the property as opposed to its lack of efficiency or amenity. In particular, it has been held that 'repair' denotes deterioration from a previous physical condition (*Quick* v *Taff Ely Borough Council* [1986] QB 809, a case involving condensation dampness). The consequence is that inherent defects which result in a building being unfit for its intended purpose (e.g., the metal window frames in *Quick*, above), but which do not give rise to a physical deterioration, fall outside the ambit of 'repair'. Thus, a tenant has been held not liable to repair a concrete basement, which had in the past suffered from an ingress of water, because there was at the time of the hearing no physical damage to the concrete walls or floor (*Post Office* v *Aquarius Properties Ltd* [1987] 1 All ER 1055).

Another problem lies in the current distinction between works of repair and improvement which can lead to difficulties in practice. Thus, the insertion of a damp-proof course in a building which was constructed without one is treated as an improvement (*Pembery* v *Lamdin* [1940] 2 All ER 434), but replacing an old two-pipe drainage system with a modern one-pipe system is classified as a repair (*Morcom* v *Campbell-Johnson* [1956] 1 QB 106).

Thirdly, the standard to which property is to be repaired is judged by reference to its age, character and locality at the date of the letting (*Proudfoot* v *Hart* (1890) 25 QBD 42 and *Calthorpe* v *McOscar* [1924] 1 KB 716). Thus, changes in the neighbourhood during the currency of the lease can make the legal standard inappropriate.

Fourthly, there is considerable scope for improving the rules governing the enforcement of repairing obligations. For example, the remedy of specific performance is currently available to a landlord against a defaulting tenant only in exceptional circumstances (*Rainbow Estates Ltd* v *Tokenhold Ltd* [1998] 3 WLR 980).

Lastly, it is generally thought that the existing law is too complicated, in so far as it is full of overlapping obligations and derives from a wide variety of different statutes.

For all these reasons, it is apparent that this area of law is ripe for reform. The Law Commission considers that one of the primary objectives should be to ensure that residential premises are reasonably fit to live in. In addition, it feels that greater emphasis should be placed on the *enforcement* of repairing obligations, given the nation's interest in the quality of its housing stock. Accordingly, greater emphasis should be placed on remedies which ensure that remedial works are actually carried out, and this may mean giving local authorities greater powers of enforcement.

At present, s. 8 of the Landlord and Tenant Act 1985 implies into residential leases let for a term of less than seven years a condition that the dwelling-house be fit for human habitation both at commencement and during the term of the lease. The difficulty with this provision is that it is severely curtailed in its operation by very low rental limits (which have remained unchanged since 1957). The Law Commission proposes to abandon these rental limits and thereby extend s. 8 to all residential leases for less than seven years. This new statutory covenant would stand alongside the existing implied obligations (as to structure and exterior) under s. 11 of the 1985 Act. The definition of 'fitness for human habitation' would also be harmonised with the criteria set out in s. 604 of the Housing Act 1985. Although this recommendation is to be welcomed, it is not what the Law Commission originally proposed in its Consultation Paper (No. 123, 1992). The Commission originally advocated the idea of an implied duty to maintain premises (both commercial and residential) in a condition suitable for their intended use. It was suggested that this new duty would be imposed on the landlord and that it would not be limited to defects of which he had notice. Unfortunately, the proposal has been resisted by the commercial sector and, hence, it has not been adopted in the Commission's Report.

The 1992 Consultation Paper also advocated a new definition of 'repair' so as to include some works of improvement (e.g., those necessary to cure any defect which rendered the premises unfit for their purpose). The Commission has now abandoned this proposal (largely on the basis that it would lead to uncertainty and promote litigation) in favour of a 'default provision' (imposed in all cases where the parties had failed to make express provision for repairs) whereby the landlord would be obliged to put the premises in repair at the commencement of the term, and keep them in repair for its duration. The standard of repair would be that which was appropriate having regard to the age, character, and prospective life of the demised property and to its locality. Essentially, this default covenant would apply principally to commercial leases.

As mentioned earlier, the Commission is anxious that enforcement of repairing obligations is shifted away from compensation towards ensuring that premises are actually repaired. Accordingly, specific performance is seen as the major remedy in this field. Although the recent case of *Rainbow Estates Ltd* v *Tokenhold Ltd* [1998] 3 WLR 980 has acknowledged that a landlord may seek specific performance of his tenant's repairing obligations, it is unlikely that the remedy will be invoked in the majority of cases involving disrepair. The *Rainbow* case had a number of unusual features which favoured the grant of specific performance against the tenants. First, the lease in question contained no forfeiture clause so that a breach of the tenant's repairing covenant did not entitle the landlord to forfeit the lease. Neither did the lease contain a clause entitling the landlord access to the premises to carry out the repairs with a view to claiming the cost from the tenants as a debt or rent arrears. This all pointed to the fact that there was no adequate alternative remedy other than specific performance against the tenants. The recommendation by the Law Commission that the remedy of specific performance be made generally available as a discretionary remedy to enforce repairing obligations in all leases to landlords and tenants alike remains, therefore, a fundamental reform of leasehold law.

The Commission also recommended the abolition of the common law doctrine of waste and the implied covenant of tenant-like user. In their place, the Commission suggests a new covenant to be implied in all leases whereby the tenant would undertake to take proper care of the premises and make good any damage wilfully done or caused to the premises by him (or any other person lawfully in occupation or visiting the premises), and not to carry out any alterations which would result in the destruction or alteration of the character of the premises to the detriment of the landlord's interest.

Although the Commission's proposals are to be welcomed, they have been criticised for failing to provide a comprehensive review of tenant's remedies for the landlord's default, in particular, the tenant's ability to terminate the tenancy at common law (see *Hussein* v *Mehlman* [1992] 32 EG 59) and to set-off the cost of repairs against rent (*British Anzani (Felixstowe) Ltd* v *International Marine Management (UK) Ltd* [1979] 2 All ER 1063). It has also been suggested by one academic commentator that landlords in the private sector will seek to pass on the expense of repairs to their tenants by means of substantial rent increases: see Bridge, S. [1996] Conv 342, at 350. Moreover, if a tenant is minded to initiate proceedings for specific performance in order to compel his landlord to repair the demised property, the likely response from the landlord will be to seek to recover possession from the tenant. As Bridge points out, security of tenure in the private sector is precarious under the assured shorthold tenancy regime and the danger of the landlord pursuing such 'retaliatory eviction' cannot be underestimated. Ultimately, as Bridge explains, little purpose may be served in giving residential tenants rights if they have no security, as any attempt to exercise those rights can be met by the landlord bringing proceedings for the recovery of possession. On this analysis, the Law Commission's recommendations may prove disappointing.

QUESTION 6

> ... a covenant to keep premises in repair obliges the covenantor to keep them in repair at all times, so that there is a breach of the obligation immediately a defect occurs. (*British Telecommunications plc* v *Sun Life Assurance Society plc* [1995] 4 All ER 44 (CA), *per* Nourse LJ).

To what extent does this statement apply to a landlord's obligation to repair defects in the demised premises or outside the landlord's control? (Illustrate your answer by reference to decided cases.)

Commentary

This is a straightforward question on the rule that a landlord is only liable for defects occurring in the demised premises if he has sufficient notice of their existence. The reference to defects outside the landlord's control is more tricky. The point was canvassed in the *Sun Life* case itself and also several earlier authorities, notably, *Bishop* v *Consolidated London Properties Ltd* (1933) 102 LJ KB 257 and *Melles & Co.* v *Holme* [1918] 2 KB 100. The law is unclear as to the landlord's position in the absence of any direct ruling. See further, Smith, P. F. [1997] 61 Conv 59.

You should note that the question requires you to illustrate your answer by reference to case law. This means that you must make reference to the decided cases in order to score a good mark. Most of the relevant cases were reviewed in the *Sun Life* decision, so if you have read the judgment of Nourse LJ carefully, this should not pose any problem.

Suggested Answer

In *British Telecommunications plc* v *Sun Life Assurance Society plc* [1995] 4 All ER 44, the claimant was the tenant of the sixth and seventh floors of a building under a lease which required the defendant landlord to keep the building in repair. The question in issue was whether the landlord became liable to repair immediately any defect which appeared in the building (as contended by the tenant), or only on the expiration of a reasonable period for doing the repairs following the appearance of the defect (as argued by the landlord). The Court of Appeal, accepting the tenant's argument, reiterated the general rule that a covenant to *keep* in repair obliged the landlord to keep the property in repair at all times so that a breach occurs immediately a defect appears.

This basic proposition may be illustrated by a number of authorities. In *Melles & Co.* v *Holme* [1918] 2 KB 100, for example, the landlord was held liable for exterior guttering which had become blocked, even though he had no express notice of the defect from the tenant. The Divisional Court held that the notice rule had no application where the landlord demised only part of the premises and retained in his own control the portion the defective condition of which caused the damage. More recently, in *Loria* v *Hammer* [1989] 2 EGLR 249, a case involving the intrusion of rainwater into the tenant's flat caused by a defective flat roof, the Court held that the landlord's liability to keep his retained premises in repair was not dependent on his receiving notification of the defect. Thus, the moment there was a disrepair, the landlord's duty to keep in repair had been broken.

In the course of his judgment in *Sun Life*, Nourse LJ recognised that there were a number of exceptions to the general rule referred to above. One important exception is where the defect occurs in the demised premises, in which case the landlord is in breach of his obligation only when he has information about the existence of the defect such as would put a reasonable landlord on inquiry as to whether works of repair were needed and he had failed to carry out the necessary works within a reasonable time thereafter.

There are a number of cases which clearly support this exception, although it has not been without its judicial critics: see, for example, *McGreal* v *Wake* (1984) 269 EG 1254, where Sir John Donaldson MR remarked that the rule was 'unfortunate' because it 'penalised the conscientious landlord and rewarded the absentee'. The leading authority is *O'Brien* v *Robinson* [1973] AC 912, where the tenant complained of the noise above his flat and warned the landlord that, is something was not done, the ceiling would collapse. No defects in the ceiling were or became visible and, shortly afterwards, those responsible for the noise moved out. Three years later, the ceiling fell and caused injury to the tenant and his wife. The House of Lords held that liability for breach of the implied covenant to repair under (what is now) s. 11 of the Landlord and Tenant Act 1985 arose only when the landlord had notice of the defect. In the instant case, the landlord was held not to have notice of the defect by reason of the incidents of nuisance and annoyance some three years earlier.

The notice rule has been applied in a number of cases: *Hugall* v *M'Lean* (1885) 53 LT 94 (defective condition of drains); *Broggi* v *Robbins* (1899) 15 TLR 224 (unsafe condition of wooden flooring); *Torrens* v *Walker* [1906] 2 Ch 166 (dangerous outside walls of demised premises); and *McGreal* v *Wake* (1984) 269 EG 1254 (rising damp, wet rot, decayed brickwork and cracked/sagging ceilings). It is well-established that the notice rule applies even though the landlord has expressly reserved a right to inspect the demised premises for disrepair.

As to what constitutes sufficient notice, it is evident that the tenant is not obliged to identify the precise nature or degree of disrepair. For example, in *Griffin* v *Pillet* [1926] 1 KB 17, the tenant's letter to the landlord, stating merely that 'the steps to the front door want attention', was held good notice. In *Al Hassani* v *Merrigan* (1988) 20 HLR 238, however, the tenant's notice was held bad since it stated that the tenant would be ascertaining what was necessary to put matters right and submit estimates. Since the notice told the landlord that he would be informed what was necessary in due course and that he could then either do the remedial work or have the cost deducted from the rent, it was held insufficient to bring into effect the landlord's implied obligations. Actual knowledge, or information about the existence of a defect such as would put a reasonable man on inquiry as to whether works of repair were needed, is sufficient to trigger the landlord's obligation to repair, in the absence of express notice (*Sheldon* v *West Bromwich Corporation* (1973) 25 P & CR 360, where an inspection by the landlord's plumber of an old water tank was sufficient to give the landlord actual knowledge of the need for repair).

It is sufficient if the landlord is given notification of the defect through its agent, for example, a rent collector, officer or employee (*Dinefwr Borough Council* v *Jones* (1987) 284 EG 58, where it was held that knowledge of defects obtained by an official of the landlord's health department constituted notice for the purpose of s. 11 of the 1985 Act). The fact that knowledge was acquired for a different purpose (e.g., in connection with the tenant's right to buy the property) did not prevent it from fixing the landlord with notice of the disrepair. (See also,

Hall v *Howard* [1988] 44 EG 83, where a valuation report, obtained by the tenant in connection with his possible bid for the reversion, specifying items of disrepair, was held sufficient notice.)

The notice rule requires the landlord to execute the remedial works within a reasonable period of time from being given notice of the defect. What is a reasonable time is, of course, a question of fact depending on the urgency of the required repairs: see *McGreal* v *Wake*, above, where two months from the date of notice was considered reasonable on the facts.

In *Sun Life*, Nourse LJ intimated, but without reaching a concluded view on the point, that a further exception to the general rule might arise where a defect is caused by an occurrence wholly outside the landlord's control. He postulated a case where the roof of a house had been damaged by a branch from a tree standing on neighbouring land not in the possession or control of the landlord and rainwater had found its way down into the tenant's rooms by that means. Provisionally, he accepted that such a case could be made the subject of a further exception. It is interesting to observe, however, that in *Bishop* v *Consolidated London Properties Ltd* (1933) 102 LJ KB 257, Du Parq J held that the landlords were nonetheless liable for breach of covenant though they could show that the cause of the defect (a dead pigeon causing an obstruction in a downfall overflow pipe) was fortuitous and occurred through no fault on their part. Similarly, in *Melles & Co.* v *Holme* [1918] 2 KB 100, referred to earlier, there was evidence suggesting that the blockage in the downpipe was caused mainly by refuse which had been thrown into the gutter by another tenant. It is difficult to see how these cases differ from Nourse LJ's example. Interestingly, in *Passley* v *London Borough of Wandsworth* (1997) 61 Conv 59, Hobhouse LJ was sceptical about the possible validity of this exception. If the cause of the defect can be attributed to neither party, one comes back to the meaning of the covenant, as established by the decisions.

A further possible exception to the general rule identified by Nourse LJ is where the covenant is not to keep in repair but simply to repair. Being somewhat of a rarity in modern leases and tenancy agreements, his Lordship expressed no concluded view as to whether such a covenant merited different analysis.

7   Express Covenants

INTRODUCTION

In this chapter, we have set out four questions on express covenants, namely, rent review, alteration and user, option to renew, and insurance. Questions on covenants against assignment, sub-letting etc. and repair will be found in **Chapters 5** and **6**, respectively.

The law relating to the construction and operation of rent review clauses has become a highly specialised subject in its own right. The amount of time you should devote to this topic will depend very much on the emphasis given to it by your lecturer. The aim of rent review clauses has been commented upon judicially (see, e.g., the judgment of Lord Diplock in *United Scientific Holdings Ltd* v *Burnley Borough Council* [1978] AC 904) and it is commonly accepted that the object of such a clause is to provide the landlord with a safeguard against the devaluing effects of inflation on his rental income. A review clause may provide for the rent to be reviewed upwards or downwards, although it is generally more common to find upwards only clauses. Exam questions in this area will usually require the student to analyse the review clause and assess whether the landlord, in seeking to review the rent, has complied with the necessary review machinery. Of particular relevance in this regard is the law relating to the 'timing' and 'notice' requirements which govern the operation of the rent review clause.

Questions on alteration and user of the demised premises tend also to be of the problem variety. Covenants against alteration may take the form of a total prohibition on the tenant's ability to effect structural changes to the property, or may be qualified so that only such alterations as are authorised by the landlord may be effected. In the latter case, the tenant must seek the landlord's formal approval prior to carrying out any work. A qualified covenant may state that the landlord will not unreasonably refuse his consent to the proposed alteration (i.e., a fully qualified covenant). In the absence, however, of any such express requirement of reasonableness, the Landlord and Tenant Act 1927, s. 19(2), provides that a qualified covenant against alterations is subject to the proviso that the landlord's consent to the making of 'improvements' is not to be unreasonably withheld. The term 'improvement' refers to a type of alteration which, from the tenant's perspective, enhances and improves his beneficial user of the demised premises (*FW Woolworth & Co. Ltd* v *Lambert* [1937] Ch 37 and *Lambert* v *FW Woolworth & Co. Ltd (No. 2)* [1938] Ch 883). The landlord, however, is not prevented from seeking a reasonable sum in relation to any damage or diminution in value of his reversionary interest in the property. Moreover, such a sum may take the form of a condition for the granting of consent, and the onus is on the tenant to prove that such conditional consent (or refusal) is unreasonable (*FW Woolworth & Co. Ltd* v *Lambert* [1937] Ch 37 and *Haines* v *Florensa* [1990] 09 EG 70).

Covenants which restrict the tenant's ability to alter the user of the demised premises also provide a fruitful area for examination questions. In the absence of any covenant restricting user, a tenant is free to use the property for whatever purpose he likes, provided no acts of waste are committed and any requisite planning permission has been obtained for a change of use. A well drafted lease, however, will almost certainly contain an express covenant restricting the tenant's ability to change the way in which he uses the demised premises. Such a covenant may take the form of an absolute prohibition on any change of user, or, alternatively, provide that the landlord's consent is required before the tenant may effect any change (i.e., a qualified covenant). The covenant may also expressly declare that the landlord will not withhold consent unreasonably (i.e., a fully qualified covenant). In the case of qualified covenants, the landlord has an unfettered veto over the proposed change of user (*Guardian Assurance Co. Ltd* v *Gants Hill Holdings Ltd* (1983) 267 EG 678) unless the tenant can show that the landlord has waived any breach of the covenant (*Chelsea Estates Ltd* v *Kadri* [1970] EGD 1356). Note also that a qualified covenant against change of user is subject to a proviso that no fine is payable by the tenant for the landlord's consent if no structural alteration of the premises is involved (Landlord and Tenant Act 1927, s. 19(3)). This, however, does not preclude the landlord from requiring payment of a reasonable sum in respect of any damage to, or diminution in the value of, the premises (or any neighbouring premises) belonging to him, and of any legal or other expenses incurred in connection with such consent.

For a review of the case law in this area, see Williams, D., 'User Covenants and Breaches' [1991] EG 9149, 63. For a summary of the Law Commission's recommendations, see Smith, P. F., 'The Law Commission Report on Covenants Restricting Dispositions, Alterations and Changes of User' (1985) 135 NLJ 991 and 1015.

Questions on options to renew/purchase also frequently crop up in the examinations. Here again, much will depend on the emphasis given to the subject by your lecturer. In formally drafted leases, it is not unusual to find that a landlord has granted the tenant either the right to purchase the freehold, or the right to extend the lease for a further term. These rights will exist independently of any statutory rights of enfranchisement. It will invariably be a condition precedent to the exercise of the option to renew that the tenant has abided by all the tenant's covenants in the lease, and even the most minor breach may act as a bar to the right of renewal (*West Country Cleaners (Falmouth) Ltd* v *Saly* [1966] 3 All ER 210). In order to be enforceable, such an option must also be sufficiently certain (*King's Motors (Oxford) Ltd* v *Lax* [1969] 3 All ER 665), but the courts will strive to give a workable interpretation to the wording where this is possible (*Brown* v *Gould* [1972] Ch 53).

It is also noteworthy that options to renew leases and options to purchase are proprietary in their nature, being 'estate contracts', and, if registered correctly, in the context of registered or unregistered land, will bind third party transferees of the leasehold estate.

For the sake of completeness, we have also included a question on the topic of insurance in this chapter.

Lastly, a word of caution! Although you will find, in the various law reports, a plethora of cases concerned with the interpretation of leasehold covenants, you should be aware that many of these will simply turn on their own facts and on the particular wording of the covenant in question. Such cases are time-absorbing and, at the end of the day, may provide little by way of precedent. Our advice is to stick to the leading cases which establish general principles.

QUESTION 1

(a)   How can a tenant ensure that 'time is made of the essence' in relation to the operation of a rent review clause?

(b)   By a lease, dated 1 June 1994, Property (UK) Ltd demised office space to Doubledoor Ltd for a term of 20 years at an initial rent of £2,000 per annum. The rent review clause in the lease provided that the rent was liable to an 'upwards only' review as from the first calendar day in the fifth year calculable as from 1 June 1994, and that during the year preceding the fifth year, the landlord should, within the final calendar month of the said year, serve on the tenant a 'notice of rental increase'.

The increased rental sum was expressed in the review clause to be either one-half of the sum total of the rack rent for the demised premises (as at the time of notice), or £2,200, whichever is the greater.

On 15 July 1999, Property (UK) Ltd served on Doubledoor Ltd a notice of rental increase, which stated that, as from 1 June 1999, Doubledoor Ltd was liable to pay an annual rent of £4,000, this figure representing half of the rack rent for the demised premises.

The notice was headed 'subject to contract'. Doubledoor Ltd maintains that it is not obliged to pay the higher rent.

Advise Property (UK) Ltd as to whether it can demand the higher rent.

Commentary

This question is divided into two parts, but both parts require you to examine the principles governing the timing and operation of rent review clauses. The only real difference between the two parts is that part (a) is in the form of a mini-essay, whereas part (b) is a problem question, designed to test the student's practical application of his or her knowledge of the law.

In answering both parts of the question, you should make reference to case law — a good knowledge of the cases will impress the examiner! Always structure your answer by identifying the key issues and applying the relevant law clearly and concisely. A student who adopts a structured answer is best equipped to score a healthy mark!

On the subject of trigger notices which are headed 'subject to contract' or 'without prejudice', see Brown, J., and Pawlowski, M., 'Without Prejudice Communications' (1993) 13/4 RRLR, 284.

Suggested Answer

(a)   A number of courses of action are open to a tenant who wishes to ensure that time is 'made of the essence' in relation to the operation of a rent review clause.

First, he can insist that the review clause expressly provides that all stipulations as to time in the rent provisions of the lease are to be of the essence of the contract and incapable of enlargement save by agreement between the parties (*Weller* v *Akehurst* [1981] 3 All ER 411). Clear words, however, are needed to make time of the essence (*Thorn EMI Pension Trust Ltd* v *Quinton Hazell plc* (1984) 269 EG 414). For example, where the lease provides for a landlord to serve a trigger notice invoking the rent review process within a certain time 'but not otherwise', a failure to serve the notice within the time-limit will disentitle the landlord from serving the review notice (*Drebbond Ltd* v *Horsham District Council* (1979) 37 P & CR 237).

Secondly, the tenant may insist that the wording of the review clause is such as to evidence a clear intention to make time of the essence. This could be done by setting out a clear timetable for review with provision for what is to happen in the event of non-compliance (see, e.g., *Henry Smith's Charity Trustees* v *AWADA Trading and Promotion Services Ltd* (1984) 269 EG 279).

Thirdly, a tenant may be able to insist that the lease contains a break clause entitling the tenant to determine the lease, within a certain period after the reviewed rent has been determined, if he is not minded to accept the reviewed rent. In relation to such a break clause, time may be held to be of the essence, in which case it would be arguable that, by necessary implication, time was also of the essence in relation to the operation of the rent review clause itself. Thus, in *Al Saloom* v *Shirley James Travel Service Ltd* (1981) 259 EG 420, the presumption that time was not of the essence was rebutted because of the interrelation of the rent review provisions and a break clause in the lease. See also, *Legal and General Assurance (Pensions Management) Ltd* v *Cheshire County Council* (1984) 269 EG 40.

Many review clauses incorporate a provision for the service of a counter-notice by the tenant after such time as a trigger notice has been served on him by the landlord. A counter-notice gives the tenant the opportunity to challenge the proposed new rent, and often encourages the landlord and tenant to come to an agreement as to the proposed rent increase. Even if served late, the counter-notice will operate so as to challenge the proposed new rental because the presumption that time is not of the essence will apply equally to this form of notice, save where there exists a contrary indication (*Mecca Leisure Ltd* v *Renown Investments (Holdings) Ltd* (1984) 271 EG 989). In *Mecca*, it was suggested by Eveleigh LJ that a landlord could make time of the essence as to the service of a tenant's counter-notice by serving on the tenant an express notice to that effect. Although there is no authority directly in point, it may also be open to the tenant, when faced with a landlord who has delayed in serving his trigger notice, to make time of the essence by serving such a formal notice.

(**b**)   The review clause provides for a unilateral 'upwards only' review, so that only the landlord has the power to increase the rent provided he complies with the requisite procedure for triggering the review.

The review clause provides that the existing rent (of £2,000) may be increased either by £200 to £2,200 per year, or to a sum representing half of the rack rental for the property, if this sum is greater than £2,200. The clause also provides that, in order to so increase the rent, the landlord must serve a notice of rental increase within the twelfth month of the year preceding the fifth year of the term. In order, therefore, to comply with the review machinery, Property (UK) Ltd was obliged to serve its notice in December 1998. In this case, however, the notice was actually served some seven months late in July 1999.

In view of the lateness in triggering the review, is the rental increase valid? Since the House of Lords decision in *United Scientific Holdings Ltd* v *Burnley Borough Council* [1978] AC 904, the position is that, save where there exists a contrary indication in the lease, time will not be of the essence in relation to the issue and service of a landlord's notice triggering a rent review. In the present case, there appears to be nothing in the wording of the rent review clause to displace the presumption that time is not of the essence, and accordingly Property (UK) Ltd should be advised that their notice is not invalid despite being late. In this connection, the courts are generally loathe to prevent a landlord from exercising his contractually agreed right to review the rent, even in circumstances where the landlord has delayed unreasonably in serving the relevant trigger notice. (See *Amherst* v *James Walker Goldsmith and Silversmith Ltd* [1983] 3 WLR 334, where the Court of Appeal held that, time not being of the essence of the review clause, mere delay, however lengthy, could not preclude the landlord from exercising his contractual right to invoke the rent review provisions of the lease. Moreover, there was no justification for reading into the lease any implied term that the landlord had to serve his notice within a reasonable time.) See also, *London & Manchester Assurance Co. Ltd v GA Dunn & Co.* (1983) 265 EG 39 and *Acuba v Allied Shoe Repairs* [1975] 3 All ER 782. An estoppel or waiver may, however, preclude the right to a review (see, e.g., *Esso Petroleum Ltd v Anthony Gibbs Financial Services Ltd* (1983) 267 EG 351), but this does not arise on the facts of the present case.

Of greater difficulty is the fact that Property (UK) Ltd's notice was expressly headed 'subject to contract'. In order to be valid, a landlord's trigger notice must be unequivocal and certain in its terms of reference. In *Shirclar Properties Ltd v Heinitz* (1983) 268 EG 362, Davies J held that the landlord's notice, which contained the rubric 'subject to contract', did not constitute an unequivocal notice because it appeared to contemplate discussion and the possibility of ultimate agreement. However, in *Royal Life Insurance v Phillips* [1990] 43 EG 70, the landlord's letter triggering the review was headed 'subject to contract' and 'without prejudice'. Nolan J held that these rubrics made no sense in the context of a document clearly intended to have legal effect. A reasonably-minded tenant receiving such a letter by recorded delivery four days prior to the expiry of the time-limit would have understood it as a notice pursuant to the review clause. Accordingly, the notice was held to constitute a valid notice initiating the review procedure. The upshot of the foregoing is that a notice qualified by the use of the words 'subject to contract' may still be an effective notice if it is clear from the context that the document is a review notice, but if the notice is itself couched in ambiguous language it will be held to be a mere negotiating document and not a formal notice. In the present case, it is submitted that the notice is unambiguous and that, accordingly, Property (UK) Ltd can claim the higher rent.

QUESTION 2

In 1988, Big Estate Ltd granted Sheila a 25-year lease of a small, single-storey retail unit. The lease contains, *inter alia*, the following covenants:

The LESSEE for herself and her assigns hereby covenants:

(i)   not to alter the demised premises in any way whatsoever save with the consent of the Lessor

(ii)   at all times during the said term to use the demised premises only as a florist shop and not to effect any change of user save with the consent of the Lessor.

In 1999, Sheila's florist business began to run into financial difficulties. She now wishes to turn the premises into a wool and hosiery shop. The change of user would require Sheila to demolish an internal wall in the shop, thus converting two rooms into one.

In 1999, she wrote to Big Estate Ltd seeking its consent to the change of user and structural alteration. Big Estate Ltd has replied, stating that it will only agree to the proposed changes if Sheila pays compensation in the sum of £1,000 in relation to the change of user and £5,000 in relation to the alteration.

Advise Sheila.

Commentary

This is a straightforward question on covenants against change of user and alteration of the demised premises. Essentially, you are asked to identify the nature of the two covenants, state the relevant law and apply the same to the particular facts. The question does not require you to draw heavily on any particular cases but seeks to test the understanding of general principles in this area. A good working knowledge of the Landlord and Tenant Act 1927, s. 19(2) and (3) is, however, essential.

An easy question for the well-prepared student!

Suggested Answer

By virtue of covenant (i), it is a term of the lease that Sheila will not alter the demised premises save with the landlord's consent. Covenants such as this are commonly found in well-drafted leases.

An alteration may be defined as a change in the constitution, fabric or form of a building (e.g., the conversion of houses into flats: *Duke of Westminster* v *Swinton* [1948] 1 KB 524). But a change in the constitution or form of the building must necessarily involve something more than just a cosmetic change or a change to the appearance of a building (*Joseph* v *LCC* (1914) 111 LT 276 and *Bickmore* v *Dimmer* [1903] 1 Ch 158). Clear examples of alterations include the conversion of two rooms into one, the subdivision of rooms, the creation and moving of existing doorways and windows, or the demolition of attached outhouses etc. It seems evident, therefore, that Sheila's proposed works would amount to an alteration of the demised premises (*Haines* v *Florensa* [1990] 09 EG 70, where the works involved the conversion of a loft).

Covenants which restrict alterations may come in three forms: first, the covenant may amount to an absolute prohibition against the carrying out of alterations to the property; secondly, the covenant may be qualified in its nature, that is, prohibit alterations save those to which the landlord has consented; and, thirdly, the covenant may be fully qualified in that it prohibits alterations save those in relation to which the landlord has consented, but such consent is not to be unreasonably withheld. In Sheila's lease, the covenant falls into the second category (i.e., it is qualified).

An alteration will be deemed to be in the nature of an 'improvement' if, from the tenant's standpoint, it enhances the tenant's beneficial user of the demised premises even where it diminishes the letting value of the premises (*FW Woolworth & Co. Ltd* v *Lambert* [1937] Ch 37 and *Lambert* v *FW Woolworth & Co. Ltd (No. 2)* [1938] Ch 883). In our case, Sheila's proposed alteration may be termed an improvement since it will clearly assist her to obtain a better user of the premises.

Since the covenant is qualified and her proposed user constitutes an improvement, the provisions of the Landlord and Tenant Act 1927, s. 19(2), will come into play. This subsection, despite any express provision to the contrary, converts a qualified covenant against alterations into a fully qualified one (i.e., subject to a proviso that the landlord's consent to the making of improvements is not to be unreasonably withheld). This proviso, however, does not preclude the landlord from requiring, as a condition of consent, the payment of a reasonable sum in respect of any damage to or diminution in the value of the demised premises or any neighbouring premises belonging to the landlord. Moreover, the landlord is free to claim any legal (or other) expenses properly incurred in connection with such consent. In the case of an improvement which does not add to the letting value of the premises, the landlord may also require, as a condition of consent, where such a requirement would be reasonable, an undertaking from the tenant to reinstate the premises in the condition in which they were before the improvement was executed (s. 19(2)).

The effect of s. 19(2), therefore, is that there is imposed on Big Estate Ltd the requirement of reasonableness in relation to any refusal of consent, or conditional consent, to Sheila's proposed alteration. If the landlord's refusal (albeit in the form of a conditional consent) is reasonable, then Sheila cannot alter the premises except in compliance with the condition. If, however, its refusal of consent (or refusal by way of imposing the condition) is unreasonable, then she may go ahead and carry out the proposed alteration.

If Sheila wishes to challenge the landlord's refusal, two courses are open to her. She may either ignore the landlord's decision, treat it as unreasonable and effect the alteration work, or she may apply to the county court for a declaration (pursuant to the Landlord and Tenant Act 1954, s. 53(1)(b)) that (i) the landlord's refusal is unlawful because the condition stated is unreasonable, and (ii) she be permitted to carry out the alteration despite the refusal (see, e.g., *Haines* v *Florensa* [1990] 09 EG 70). The second course of action is clearly more sensible since it does not expose Sheila to a possible action for forfeiture of her lease and damages for breach of covenant if the landlord's refusal is held to be reasonable. It would also preclude the landlord from seeking a mandatory injunction requiring the tenant to reinstate the premises as they were originally prior to the alteration (*Mosley* v *Cooper* [1990] 1 EGLR 124).

It is for the court to determine whether the condition imposed by Big Estate Ltd is reasonable, but (as mentioned earlier) s. 19(2) dictates that a sum may be lawfully required by a landlord for such consent if it is a reasonable reflection of the amount by which (if at all) the landlord's reversionary interest has diminished, or represents any properly incurred expenses in relation to the consent. In our case, it would be necessary to examine, with the assistance of a surveyor, the basis upon which the landlord arrived at the sum of £5,000 before any firm view could be given as to whether this condition is lawful. If Sheila decided to challenge the landlord's refusal of consent by way of declaration, the burden of proof would lie on her to establish the unreasonableness of the sum sought by Big Estate Ltd (*FW Woolworth* v *Lambert* above).

In relation to the covenant which seeks to restrict Sheila's ability to change the user of the premises, such covenants are commonly known as 'restrictive user covenants' and also come in three forms:

(a)   the covenant may be absolute (i.e., imposing a total prohibition);

(b)   the covenant may be qualified; or

(c)   it may be fully qualified.

If fully qualified, the covenant will expressly state that the landlord's consent for any proposed changes of user will not be unreasonably withheld. If qualified (but not fully qualified), however, the covenant makes no reference to reasonableness and the landlord has an absolute veto over the tenant's proposed change of user. Moreover, unlike qualified covenants against alterations which constitute the making of improvements, no requirement of reasonableness is imposed by law (*Guardian Assurance Co. Ltd* v *Gants Hill Holdings Ltd* (1983) 267 EG 678). In the present case, the covenant against change of user is qualified (as opposed to fully qualified).

However, the Landlord and Tenant Act 1927, s. 19(3), does state that where the change of user does not involve a structural alteration to the premises, no fine or premium can be demanded by the landlord save for sums which reasonably represent compensation for the diminution in value of the premises, or legal or other expenses. In this case, however, Sheila's proposed change of user would involve a structural change and, therefore, in principle, the sum of £1,000 seems to be legitimately demanded, if reasonable. Nevertheless, it is for the court to determine this in the light of expert evidence.

Lastly, it may be mentioned that, since Sheila is a business tenant, she may be entitled to compensation for the improvement under the Landlord and Tenant Act 1927, Pt I, if (before making the improvement) she notifies the landlord of the proposed work. Should Big Estate Ltd then serve a notice of objection, she may apply to the court to have the proposed improvement certified as a proper improvement. Section 9 of the 1927 Act states that Pt I of the Act applies notwithstanding any contract to the contrary.

QUESTION 3

In 1980, the Earl of Dover granted Michelle a 20-year lease of a fishmonger's shop. The lease provides that Michelle should 'maintain and keep the demised premises in good and tenantable repair'. Also included in the lease is an option which confers on Michelle the right:

> after the expiration of 19 years from the date of the demise herein, by notice, to renew the lease of the demised premises for a further term of 20 years as from the expiry date of this demise, on the same terms as this lease, save that the rent for any renewed term shall be fixed having regard to the market value of the demised premises at the time of exercising this option and any renewed lease shall not contain this option to renew but, in any event, this option being conditional on the observance by the tenant of the tenant's covenants in the lease.

The option is expressed as personal to Michelle and incapable of assignment, and that it would cease to have effect on assignment of the lease.

The lease further provides that if Michelle desires to renew the lease, she should serve on the landlord a notice of intention so to do.

In 1997, the Earl of Dover sold his reversionary interest to Buzby Property Ltd. Last year, Michelle contracted to sell her leasehold interest in the shop to Malcolm. Although a formal assignment has been executed, Michelle remains the registered proprietor of the property. In 1999, Michelle served on Buzby Property Ltd a notice of intention to renew, as required under the terms of her lease. Her new landlords, however, have refused to renew the lease on the ground that Michelle, by failing to repair a cracked brick wall at the side of the shop, has breached the tenant's repairing covenant in the lease and is, therefore, barred from exercising the option. They also claim that the option is void for uncertainty and unenforceable as against them for non-registration, and that because Michelle assigned the property the option is no longer exercisable by her under the terms of the lease. Michelle admits to failing to repair the wall but contends that the cracking is *de minimis*.

Advise Michelle.

Commentary

This question is concerned with an option to renew a lease. It is relatively straightforward provided you are familiar with the issues being raised.

Nowadays, statute (in the form of the Leasehold Reform Acts 1967–1982 and the Leasehold Reform, Housing and Urban Development Act 1993) has conferred on many residential tenants the right (either individually or collectively) compulsorily to acquire from their landlords either the freehold or an extension to their existing leases.

Despite the growing availability of statutory enfranchisement, a lease may confer on the tenant a *contractual* right either to purchase the freehold reversion or to acquire some form of leasehold extension. Such privately conferred rights take the form of options to purchase or options to renew, respectively. For a good summary of the law in this area, see Smith, P.F., 'Renewal of Leases by Covenant' (1994) 14/3 RRLR, 31.

One tricky point relates to Michelle's assignment of her leasehold estate to Malcolm. Does she still have the right to exercise the option to renew? See *Brown & Root Technology Ltd* v *Sun Alliance & London Assurance Co. Ltd* [1997] 18 EG 123 (CA).

Suggested Answer

Michelle has been granted a personal option to renew her lease for a further 20 years at a market rent. To be valid, such options must be certain and unequivocal in their terms (*King's Motors (Oxford) Ltd* v *Lax* [1970] 1 WLR 426, where the option was held void on the ground that it provided for the new rent to be agreed between the parties without any reference to arbitration, or some supplementary agreement fixing the rent to be paid). A vaguely worded option to renew will be upheld, however, if it is capable of having some workable meaning. In *Brown* v *Gould* [1972] Ch 53, the option clause provided for the new rent to be fixed having regard to the market value of the premises at the time of exercising the option, taking into account any increased value of the premises attributable to structural improvements made by the tenant during the currency of his lease. Although the clause provided no machinery for fixing the rent, the court held that it was not void for uncertainty since it was not devoid of any meaning; nor could it be said that there was a wide variety of meanings which could fairly be put on the clause so that it was impossible to say which of them was intended.

In our case, the option would seem sufficiently certain in its terms of reference, namely, as to the title to be acquired and relevant procedural mechanisms. So far as the rent is concerned, applying *Brown* v *Gould*, it is submitted that, in the absence of machinery agreed on by the parties, the court would not be precluded from resolving any dispute as to the rent payable, if the parties disagreed as to the quantum, applying the formula laid down in the option clause. The courts are reluctant to hold void for uncertainty any provision that was intended to have legal effect, and in the present case it cannot be doubted that the option was intended to have business efficacy.

However, the wording of the option clearly prevents Michelle from being able potentially to convert the lease into a 2,000-year term as a perpetually renewable lease under the Law of Property Act 1922, sch. 15 (see e.g., *Caerphilly Concrete Products Ltd* v *Owen* [1972] 1 WLR 372).

Whether existing as an integral part of the lease, or as collateral to it, an option to renew is a conditional estate contract (*Spiro* v *Glencrown Properties Ltd* [1990] 1 All ER 600). If the landlord refuses to complete the transaction by renewing the lease as agreed, then prima facie he will be in breach of contract and can be compelled to renew the lease by a decree of specific performance. However, being a contract for the sale of land, the option must comply with the necessary legal formalities and either be evidenced in writing (or partly performed) if entered into before 27 September 1989 (see Law of Property Act

1925, s. 40), or, if entered into on or after this date, actually be reduced to writing with all the terms contained therein and signed by both parties (see Law of Property (Miscellaneous Provisions) Act 1989, s. 2). As the option, in the present case, is contained in the lease (seemingly created in or around 1980), the relevant formalities (s. 40 of the 1925 Act) have been complied with and the option is valid.

Buzby Property Ltd also contend that Michelle is unable to rely on the option because she has breached her repairing covenant and that the option does not bind them as assignees of the reversion because of lack of registration.

As to the first point, the option states that it is only exercisable if Michelle has complied with all the tenant's covenants in the lease. Buzby Property Ltd contend that she has not complied with the repairing covenant by failing to repair the cracked brick wall. It is a question of evidence as to the nature of this breach, and only an expert building surveyor can really determine the extent of the cracking and whether or not the defect is *de minimis*. If a breach has occurred, it would seem that this would be a bar to Michelle being able to exercise the option to renew. In *West Country Cleaners (Falmouth) Ltd* v *Saly* [1966] 3 All ER 210, the tenants were held to be disqualified from exercising their option to renew the lease for an extended term by reason of their breaches of a painting covenant (albeit that the breaches were only trivial). Similarly, in *Bairstow Eves (Securities) Ltd* v *Ripley* [1992] 2 EGLR 47, the Court of Appeal confirmed the proposition that a tenant seeking to enforce an option to renew in a lease, where compliance with repairing obligations was a condition precedent to the exercise of the option, could not excuse himself by saying that the want of repair was trivial or merely a technical breach. The general principle is that where an option is conditional upon the performance by the grantee of some act in a stated manner (or at a stated time), the act must be performed strictly in order to entitle the grantee to exercise the right (*Greville* v *Parker* [1910] AC 335). However, the position will be different where the tenant is under an obligation to 'reasonably perform and observe' the tenant's covenants in the lease as a condition of renewal (*Basset* v *Whiteley* (1982) P & CR 87 and *Reed Personnel Services plc* v *American Express Ltd* [1997] 1 EGLR 229). In such a case, the tenant will be entitled to renew if he has behaved as a reasonable tenant.

The material date for determining whether the tenant has complied with the condition(s) upon which the option to renew is granted is the date of the expiry of the original term and not the date when the tenant gives notice purporting to exercise the option (*King's Motors (Oxford) Ltd* v *Lax* [1970] 1 WLR 426).

Thus, even though she may technically be in breach of the repairing covenant, Michelle may still validly enforce the option provided she remedies the breach prior to the expiry of her lease in 2000 (see *Trane (UK) Ltd* v *Provident Mutual Life Assurance* [1995] 1 EGLR 33 and *Bass Holdings Ltd* v *Morton Music Ltd* [1987] 3 WLR 543 (CA)).

As to the registration point, if the premises comprise registered land, then despite the fact that Michelle should have registered the option (being a minor interest) by way of notice or caution so as to bind any assignees of the Earl of Dover, such an option can, in any event, bind assignees as an 'overriding interest' under the Land Registration Act 1925, s. 70(1)(g), being a proprietary right (see *Re Button's Lease* [1964] 1 Ch 263, 271) belonging to the tenant in actual occupation of the demised premises (*Webb* v *Pollmount Ltd* [1966] 1 All ER 481, involving an option to purchase). If, however, the demised premises comprise unregistered land, Michelle should have registered the option as a Class C(iv) (estate contract) land charge against the Earl of Dover, pursuant to the Land Charges Act 1972, in order to ensure that Buzby Property Ltd (as assignee purchasers) were bound by the same (*Kitney* v *MEPC Ltd* [1977] 1 WLR 981). Thus, it would seem that in the context of unregistered land the option would be void (for lack of registration) as against her current landlords. In this connection, it makes no difference that Buzby Property Ltd may have, in fact, known of the existence of the unregistered option. It may be that Michelle could claim that Buzby were estopped (e.g., by acquiescence) from asserting the invalidity of the option (*Taylor Fashions* v *Liverpool Victoria Trustees* [1982] QB 133), but there is nothing on the facts to suggest this.

Lastly, the landlords contend that the option is no longer exercisable by Michelle because she assigned her leasehold estate to Malcolm last year. Although, undoubtedly, the option is personal to Michelle and ceases to have effect upon assignment under the terms of the lease, we are told that Malcolm has not (to date) been registered as the new proprietor of the property. The point arose in *Brown & Root Technology Ltd* v *Sun Alliance & London Assurance Co. Ltd* [1997] 18 EG 123, where the Court of Appeal held that, in relation to the operation of a tenant's break clause, the assignment of the legal estate in the lease was not effective as the assignee was never registered as the proprietor. The assignment in the break clause meant assignment of the legal estate, which remained with the tenant. On the same reasoning, Michelle is not debarred from exercising the option on this ground because she remains the registered proprietor of the shop.

QUESTION 4

'The separate interest of landlord and tenant in leased buildings present problems which are at their most acute in the considerations relating to insurance, reinstatement of damaged property and the division of insurance moneys if the buildings are destroyed.'

Discuss this proposition and illustrate your answer from the decided cases.

Commentary

There have been several important cases concerning the interpretation and application of covenants to insure. Invariably, the courts will determine such disputes with reference to the wording of the lease and the construction of the particular covenant in question.

Landlord and tenant courses differ as to the amount of time devoted to the topic of insurance. If your lecturer makes only passing reference to the subject, this is a good indication that it is unlikely to feature in the examination.

For a good summary of the case law, see Williams, D., 'The Covenant to Insure' (1985) 274 EG 577.

Suggested Answer

A well-drafted lease will provide for either the landlord or the tenant to execute a policy of insurance for the premises against risks such as fire, vandalism, flooding etc. Often, it will be the landlord who covenants to insure, but it is the tenant who will bear the burden of meeting the cost of the insurance premiums which are often made payable as additional rent. In such cases, the courts will not imply a term to the effect that the landlord should safeguard the tenant's financial interests by placing the insurance with the insurer who provides the lowest quotation. See *Bandar Property Holdings Ltd* v *JS Darwen (Successors) Ltd* [1968] 2 All ER 305, where Roskill J held that a term that the landlord should place the insurance so as not to impose an unnecessarily heavy burden on the tenant would not be implied. The decision was followed in *Havenridge Ltd* v *Boston Dyers Ltd* [1994] EGCS 53, where the Court of Appeal reiterated the principle that it was sufficient for the landlord to prove that the premium paid was no greater than the going rate for that insurer in the normal course of his business at the time (see also, *Berrycroft Management Co. Ltd* v *Sinclair Gardens Investments (Kensington) Ltd* [1997] 22 EG 141 (CA)).

On occasion, where the tenant has undertaken to effect the necessary insurance cover for the property, the landlord reserves in his own favour a power of veto as to the appropriateness of the insurer in question. In such cases, the landlord's power of veto is valid and the landlord's consent is a condition precedent to the insurance being effected; and in the absence of any express provision to the contrary, the landlord is not under any implied obligation to act reasonably in the withholding of consent (*Tredegar* v *Harwood* [1929] AC 72).

If the premises are destroyed or damaged, for example, by fire, the question of the application of the insurance moneys can often pose difficult problems as between landlord and tenant. In *Re King (Deceased) Robinson* v *Gray* [1963] Ch 459, the tenant had covenanted to keep the premises in repair; at her own expense, to insure the premises against fire in the joint names of the landlord and tenant; and to apply the insurance moneys in rebuilding. When the premises were destroyed by fire, the insurance moneys were paid in the joint names of the parties, but reinstatement was not possible owing to a local authority's compulsory acquisition of the property. The Court of Appeal held that the tenant was entitled to the whole of the insurance moneys since the landlord's only interest therein was as security for the performance by the tenant of her obligations to repair and reinstate and that, as the premiums had been paid by the tenant to meet her obligations, the moneys belonged to her.

In *Beacon Carpets Ltd* v *Kirby* [1984] 3 WLR 489, the insurance moneys under a policy effected by the landlord in the joint names of the parties for their 'respective rights and interests' proved insufficient to pay for full reinstatement after a fire destroyed the building. The Court of Appeal held that the basic right of the parties was to have the insurance moneys applied in rebuilding for their respective benefit. However, because the parties had by their own acts released that right without agreeing how the moneys were to be dealt with, it could only be inferred that, in default of agreement, they were treating the insurance moneys as standing in the place of the building which would otherwise have been replaced. It followed that the insurance moneys belonged to the parties in shares proportionate to their respective interests in the property insured. *Re King* was distinguished since that case dealt only with rights in the insurance moneys once the prime purpose of rebuilding had been frustrated by the actions of a third party, and did not affect the case (as in *Beacon*) where the parties were treating the insurance moneys as standing in the place of the building.

Where the landlord's obligation to insure is satisfied at the tenant's expense, it will ensure for the benefit of *both* the landlord and the tenant, and accordingly the landlord will be obliged to use the insurance moneys, if called upon to do so, towards the reinstatement of the demised premises (*Mumford Hotels Ltd* v *Wheler* [1964] Ch 117). In this case, the lease did not contain an express covenant to reinstate. When the premises were destroyed by fire, the insurance moneys were paid to the landlord, who refused to reinstate the property. The court held that the issue was not whether a covenant to reinstate should be implied, but whether the true inference was that the landlord should be treated as insuring on her own behalf or for the joint benefit of herself and the tenant. In the circumstances, the landlord's obligation to insure, at the tenant's expense, was intended to be for the benefit of both the landlord and the tenant, so that the landlord was obliged to use the insurance moneys to reinstate the premises if called upon to do so.

The Fires Prevention (Metropolis) Act 1774, s. 83, provides that where the demised premises are burnt down, demolished or damaged by fire, the party who has not expressly covenanted to insure the property (e.g., the tenant) may require the insurance moneys paid to the insuring party (e.g., the landlord) to be spent on the reinstatement of the premises. In *Reynolds* v *Phoenix Assurance Co. Ltd* (1978) 247 EG 995, the plaintiffs had written to request that the defendant insurers lay out and expend moneys towards reinstating the fire-damaged premises. They made this request in order to bring into effect the provisions of the 1774 Act. The court, however, held that the Act was intended to deal with a different situation, namely, to prevent the insurance moneys being paid to an insured (e.g., the landlord) who might make away with them. It was not intended to apply to a case where the insured and the person serving the notice were one and the same person.

In the event that property has been demised to the tenant on a full-repairing lease and the premises have been destroyed by fire with no notice having been served under the 1774 Act, it seems that the tenant, in the absence of express provision, has no equity to compel his landlord to expend the insurance moneys on the demised premises (*Leeds* v *Cheetham* (1827) 1 Sim 146). Such a tenant also remains bound, despite the fire, to abide by his own repairing and rental obligations. However, today, developments in the doctrine of frustration may offer the tenant a remedy in this regard (*National Carriers Ltd* v *Panalpina (Northern) Ltd* [1981] AC 675). From the standpoint of the tenant, it would seem sensible to include a covenant for insurance moneys to be applied towards reinstatement in the lease which would cover such an eventuality.

8 Termination of Leases

INTRODUCTION

In this chapter, you will find questions on forfeiture of leases, the doctrine of frustration, repudiation, surrender, and tenant's right to fixtures.

Questions on forfeiture are quite popular with examiners. The forfeiture of the lease is, of course, the primary remedy of a landlord faced with a tenant who has defaulted in the payment of his rent or other obligations in the lease. At the same time, the lease will invariably be a valuable asset which the tenant will seek to preserve in most cases by seeking relief from forfeiture. There is a vast body of case law on the subject as well as important statutory provisions. See, generally, Pawlowski, M., *The Forfeiture of Leases*, London: Sweet & Maxwell Ltd, 1993. See Question 1 and 2.

In 1985, the Law Commission, as part of its programme for the codification of the law of landlord and tenant, published a report entitled 'Forfeiture of Tenancies' (Law Com. No. 142, 1985), which examined various defects in the current law and recommended the replacement of the present structure with an entirely new system. In 1994, the Commission published a further Report ('Landlord and Tenant Law: Termination of Tenancies Bill', Law Com. No. 221, 1994) which contained a draft bill implementing the Commission's proposals. In 1998, the Law Commission produced a Consultative Document relating specifically to the landlord's current right to forfeit by actual physical re-entry onto the demised premises. It recommended, contrary to the previously held view, that a right of physical re-entry should be retained under the proposed termination order scheme and should be placed on a statutory footing which would integrate it properly with the rest of the scheme: Pawlowski, M., Termination of Tenancies by Physical Re-entry', (1998) 2 L & T Review, pp. 24–27. It may be some time, however, before the bill actually becomes law. Since this is an important topic of study, we have included an essay question on the Law Commission's proposals. See Question 3.

It was once thought that the doctrine of repudiatory breach (to be found in the law of contract) had no application to leases (*Total Oil Great Britain Ltd* v *Thompson Garages (Biggin Hill) Ltd* [1972] 1 QB 318, *per* Lord Denning MR, at p. 324). This view no longer represents the law (*Hussein* v *Mehlman* [1992] 32 EG 59). However, the extent to which the doctrine may be applied universally to leases has not yet been fully worked out. We have, therefore, included a question on this interesting topic for those students wishing to explore some of the less charted waters of landlord and tenant law! For further reading, see Pawlowski, M., 'Repudiatory Breach in Leases' [1994] Lit. Vol. 14/1, pp. 7–14; 'Repudiatory Breach in the Leasehold Context' [1999] Conv 150; 'The Application of the Doctrine of Mitigation of Damages to Leases' [1995] *Liverpool Law Review*, vol. XVII(2), pp. 173–88; 'Contractual Termination of leases: Unresolved Issues' (1998) 13 JPL 4; (Mainly for Students) 'Ending Fixed-term Leases Early' [1996] EG 9615, 100.

Although the House of Lords has held that the doctrine of frustration applies to leases (*National Carriers Ltd* v *Panalpina Northern Ltd* [1981] AC 675), the actual circumstances in which a lease can be frustrated will be rare. Once again, an interesting topic which we have coupled with a question on repudiatory breach: see Question 4 (and Question 3, **Chapter 8**).

For the sake of completeness, we have also included a problem question on surrender and tenant's fixtures: see Questions 5 and 6. There is also a new question on tenant's break notices: Question 7.

QUESTION 1

In 1990, Lillian acquired the freehold of a shop in a shopping parade. The shop had been let on a 30-year lease in January 1989. The rent under the lease was payable quarterly in advance. The lease contained, *inter alia*, covenants against assignment or sub-letting without consent, with a right of re-entry exercisable on breach of any tenant's covenant. Michael was the original tenant of the shop which he ran as a pizza takeaway.

In 1998, Michael had asked Lillian for consent to assign the lease, but Lillian took so long over the matter that the potential assignee withdrew. In January 2000, he found another assignee, Norma, who had satisfactory references. Not wishing to risk any delay, Michael assigned the lease to Norma without asking Lillian. The following month, Lillian found out about this. Her agent demanded rent by mistake for the March 2000 quarter. The rent was again demanded for the June 2000 quarter but this time qualified by the words 'without prejudice'.

In July 2000, Lillian served notice on Norma under the Law of Property Act 1925, s. 146. One day later, she repossessed the property while it was unoccupied and changed the locks.

Advise Norma as to her rights, if any, in relation to the property.

Commentary

This is a fairly typical question on the forfeiture of leases. It raises a number of issues, each requiring discussion and illustration through statute and case law. If you miss the key point on waiver, your marks will be very low!

Ideally, in a question of this sort, you need to tackle the various issues as they arise chronologically on the facts. It is important that you structure your answer carefully so that it deals with each issue in a logical sequence. The tendency, under exam conditions, is simply to write down the first relevant thing that comes into your head. If you spend a few minutes *planning your answer*, this will undoubtedly pay dividends and earn you higher marks.

Suggested Answer

The central issue is whether Lillian's physical re-entry onto the premises in July 2000 was lawful. If not, Norma will be able to seek a declaration that the lease has not become forfeited and that Lillian's purported re-entry was a trespass.

It is important to stress from the outset that the assignment, despite being made without Lillian's consent, is not void but *voidable* at the option of the landlord. Accordingly, Norma will take a defeasible title (i.e., subject to Lillian's right of forfeiture) (*Williams* v *Earle* (1868) LR 3 QB 739).

The lease contains a qualified covenant against assignment and sub-letting. Such a covenant is subject to the further proviso that the landlord's consent shall not be unreasonably withheld (Landlord and Tenant Act 1927, s. 19(1)). The section, however, does not absolve the tenant from the formality of seeking consent, so that if he goes ahead without seeking consent (as Michael has done in the present case) he commits a breach of the covenant regardless of the reasonableness of the transaction (*Eastern Telegraph Co. Ltd* v *Dent* [1899] 1 QB 835).

Although Michael was clearly in breach of covenant in assigning the lease to Norma without seeking Lillian's consent, the question arises whether Lillian can be said to have waived the breach so as to disentitle her from relying on it as a ground of forfeiture. We are told that Lillian, having actual knowledge of the breach, demanded rent (through her agent) for the March 2000 quarter. The effect of a waiver depends on the nature of the breach giving rise to the landlord's election to forfeit. In this connection, the tenant's breach will be classified either as a 'continuing' breach, or as a 'once and for all breach'. If the breach is of a continuing nature, there is a continually recurring cause of forfeiture and the waiver will operate only in relation to past breaches (i.e., breaches committed in the period prior to the landlord's act which constitutes the waiver). Thus, a landlord who has waived a continuing breach for a period of time will not be precluded from subsequently ending his waiver and enforcing the covenant in the lease. Where, on the other hand, the breach is classified as a 'once and for all breach', the right to forfeit for that breach will be lost upon waiver. A covenant against assigning or sub-letting has been held to be a once and for all breach (*Walrond* v *Hawkins* (1875) LR 10 CP 342 and *Scala House & District Property Co. Ltd* v *Forbes* [1974] 1 QB 575).

Moreover, an unambiguous demand for rent due after the breach constitutes an act of waiver. Thus, in *Welch* v *Birrane* (1975) 29 P & CR 102, the landlords refused the tenant permission to assign his lease to sitting sub-tenants in the demised premises on the ground that the proposed assignee might become entitled to enfranchisement under the Leasehold Reform Act 1967. The tenant, nevertheless, assigned the lease as originally intended. The landlords continued to demand rent from the tenant despite the breach of covenant and claimed forfeiture. Lawson J, following the decision of Swanwick J in *David Blackstone*

Ltd v *Burnetts (West End) Ltd* [1973] 1 WLR 1487, held that the landlords, by demanding rent accruing due *after* the breach of covenant, had effectively waived the forfeiture. See also *Van Haarlam* v *Kasner Charitable Trust* [1992] 36 EG 135.

The fact that the March quarter rent was demanded by Lillian's agent by mistake will not affect the position. Whether a particular act, coupled with the requisite knowledge of the breach, constitutes a waiver is a question of law to be considered objectively without regard to the intention of the landlord, or the belief or understanding of the tenant (*Matthews* v *Smallwood* [1910] 1 Ch 777). Thus, since it is irrelevant *quo animo* an act of waiver was made, knowledge of the breach by the landlord's agent will be sufficient even where the act of acknowledgement of the lease is that of another agent who is unaware of the breach (*Central Estates (Belgravia) Ltd* v *Woolgar (No. 2)* [1972] 1 WLR 1048). In this case, the landlords' managing agents instructed their staff to refuse all rent from the tenant. The instructions failed to reach one of the clerks who sent out a routine demand for the quarter's rent and a subsequent receipt. The Court of Appeal held that the landlord's demand for the rent through their agents, with knowledge of the breach, effected a waiver of the forfeiture. Accordingly, the fact that Lillian's agent did not intend to waive the forfeiture by demanding rent for the March quarter will make no difference to the result.

As to the demand of rent for the June quarter, there is little doubt that a demand for rent qualified by such words as 'without prejudice' or 'under protest' will operate as an effective waiver (*Segal Securities Ltd* v *Thoseby* [1963] 1 QB 887). In order, however, to constitute a waiver, the demand must have been communicated to the tenant. Thus, there will be no waiver if the demand has been prepared and sent by the landlord but never received by the tenant (*Trustees of Henry Smith's Charity* v *Willson* [1983] QB 316 and *David Blackstone Ltd* v *Burnetts (West End) Ltd* [1973] 1 WLR 1487, *per* Swanwick J, at p. 1499). In these circumstances, the uncommunicated rent demand can be withdrawn by the landlord at any time before it is received by the tenant. In the present case, it is assumed that both demands were actually received by Michael.

Quite apart from the waiver of the breach, we are told that Lillian repossessed the property a day after service of the s. 146 notice. Since the breach of a covenant against assignment is technically incapable of remedy as a matter of law (see *Expert Clothing Service & Sales Ltd* v *Hillgate House Ltd* [1986] Ch 340 and contrast *Savva* v *Houssein* [1996] 47 EG 138, involving a breach of a negative covenant not to display signs or alter the premises without the landlord's consent, which was held to be capable of remedy), the s. 146 notice need not require the tenant to remedy it and the landlord may proceed with his action or physical re-entry with little delay. In such circumstances, it has been held that 14 days is a sufficient time to elapse between the service of the notice and the date of re-entry (*Scala House & District Property Co. Ltd* v *Forbes* [1974] QB 575). In *Fuller* v *Judy Properties Ltd* [1992] 14 EG 106, involving a breach of covenant against assignment, seven days was held a reasonable time. In the present case, Lillian has re-entered just one day after the service of her s. 146 notice. This may be held an insufficient time and provide Norma with another basis for invalidating the forfeiture.

In addition to Norma bringing an action alleging trespass, she should be urged to safeguard her position by claiming, in the alternative, relief from forfeiture under s. 146(2) of the 1925 Act. This she can do despite Lillian's physical re-entry onto the premises (*Billson* v *Residential Apartments Ltd* [1992] 2 WLR 15). As assignee of the lease, she is the 'lessee' for the purposes of s. 146 of the 1925 Act (*Old Grovebury Manor Farm Ltd* v *Seymour Plant Sales & Hire Ltd (No. 2)* [1979] 1 WLR 1397) and so she will be concerned to avoid the forfeiture, and not the original tenant, Michael.

QUESTION 2

(a) What are the principles governing relief from forfeiture in the case of failure by a tenant to comply with a covenant other than the payment of rent?

(b) Mary lets commercial premises to Tim at a rent of £35,000 per year. There is a forfeiture clause in the lease. Tim falls into arrears with the rent and Mary brings proceedings in the High Court for forfeiture of the lease.

Advise Tim as to whether he can seek relief from forfeiture.

What would be the position if the proceedings were brought in the county court?

Commentary

This is a question dealing specifically with relief from forfeiture for breach of a covenant to repair and for non-payment of rent. The statutory provisions governing relief, particularly for non-payment of rent, are highly complex and you should attempt this question only if you are reasonably familiar with the relevant principles. The subject of relief from forfeiture is quite popular with examiners, so be warned!

For a brief summary, see Pawlowski, M., *The Forfeiture of Leases*, London: Sweet & Maxwell Ltd, 1993, pp. 10–16.

Suggested Answer

(a)   The court's inherent equitable jurisdiction to relieve against forfeiture of leases for wilful breaches of covenant (other than non-payment of rent), which was retrospectively resurrected by the House of Lords in *Shiloh Spinners Ltd* v *Harding* [1973] AC 691, has been implicitly removed by the Law of Property Act 1925, s. 146, conferring statutory powers of relief in the landlord and tenant context (*Billson* v *Residential Apartments Ltd* [1991] 3 WLR 264). Thus, for example, if a tenant cannot obtain relief under s. 146(2) he has no recourse to any underlying equitable jurisdiction to be relieved against a wilful breach of covenant in order to preserve his lease.

The general statutory provisions relevant to relief against forfeiture from breaches of covenant (other than non-payment of rent) are contained in s. 146(2) of the 1925 Act. Under s. 146(2), the tenant is entitled to apply to the court (in the landlord's action or in an action brought by himself) for relief against forfeiture of his lease. The court may grant or refuse relief on terms as it thinks fit, and in the case of a breach of a repairing covenant the court will usually require the tenant to remedy the disrepair and make compensation to the landlord for any damage to the reversion before it grants such relief.

Section 146(2) provides that the court may grant or refuse relief, having regard to the proceedings and conduct of the parties and to all other circumstances, as it thinks fit. Moreover, in the case of relief, the court may grant it on such terms, if any, as to costs, expense damages, compensation, penalty, or otherwise, including the granting of an injunction to restrain any like breach in the future as, in the circumstances of each case, it thinks fit. The court's discretion to grant or refuse relief is very wide and will usually depend on any one or more of the following factors:

(a)   whether the tenant is able and willing to remedy and/or recompense the landlord for the breach (*Duke of Westminster* v *Swinton* [1948] 1 KB 524);

(b)   whether the breach was wilful (*Shiloh Spinners Ltd* v *Harding* [1973] AC 691);

(c)   the gravity of the breach;

(d)   the extent of the diminution in the value of the landlord's reversionary interest as compared to the value of the leasehold interest threatened with forfeiture (*Southern Depot Co. Ltd* v *British Railways Board* (1990) 2 EGLR 39);

(e)   the conduct of the landlord (*Segal Securities Ltd* v *Thoseby* [1963] 1 QB 887);

(f)   the personal qualifications of the tenant (*Bathurst* v *Fine* [1974] 1 WLR 905);

(g)   the financial position of the tenant; and

(h)   whether the breach involves an immoral/illegal user (*Egerton* v *Esplanade Hotels, London Ltd* [1947] 2 All ER 88).

While there is no doubt that the court's discretion to grant relief under s. 146(2) is very wide, it is equally clear that it must be exercised judicially, having regard to the circumstances of each individual case and to the specific matters referred to in s. 146(2), and with the object of ensuring that the landlord is not substantially prejudiced or damaged by the revival of the tenant's lease (*Hyman* v *Rose* [1912] AC 623).

A special form of relief is available to the tenant in respect of internal decorative repairs under s. 147 of the 1925 Act, which provides that the court may relieve the tenant from liability for such repairs if 'having regard to all the circumstances of the case (including in particular the length of the lessee's term or interest remaining unexpired), the court is satisfied that the landlord's notice is unreasonable'. The court's power under s. 147 is to grant relief not merely from forfeiture but from the need to do the decorative repairs at all.

If relief is granted by the court, the tenant will retain his lease as if it had never been forfeited.

(b)   Tim can seek relief in the High Court under the Common Law Procedure Act 1852, ss. 210–212, and the Supreme Court Act 1981, s. 38(1) and (2).

Under s. 212 of the 1852 Act, Tim is entitled to be relieved in equity if at least six months' rent is in arrears and, at any time before the trial of Mary's action, he pays or tenders all the arrears and costs to Mary or into court. The relief under s. 212 will take the form of a stay of Mary's action and Tim will continue to hold the demised premises under his original lease without any new lease. In *Standard Pattern Co. Ltd* v *Ivey* [1962] Ch 432, it was held that relief under s. 212 only applied where six months' rent was in arrears, and accordingly a tenant could not, by payment of the sums necessary to meet the landlord's claim, compel a stay of proceedings under the section where only one quarter's rent was unpaid. Thus, if less than six months' rent is in arrears in the present case, Tim should be advised to invoke the court's jurisdiction to grant relief under s. 38(1) of the Supreme Court Act 1981.

Under s. 210 of the 1852 Act, Tim will also be entitled to relief in equity at or after the trial of the landlord's action, if he pays all the arrears of rent and costs within six months of the execution of the order for possession.

In the county court, relief is based upon the making of a suspended order for possession. Under the County Courts Act 1984, s. 138(3), where the tenant seeks relief at the trial of the landlord's action, the court is obliged to order possession of the land to be given to the landlord at the expiration of such period, not being less than four weeks from the date of the order, as the court thinks fit, unless within that period the tenant pays into court all the rent in arrears and the costs of the action. The court has power, under s. 138(4), to extend the period for payment at any time before possession of the land is recovered by the landlord. If the tenant pays the rent due and costs within the time fixed under the order (or any extension thereof), he will continue to hold under the lease, but if he fails to pay within the time limit the order for possession will be enforced and the tenant will be barred from all relief (including relief in the High Court — see, *Di Palma* v *Victoria Square Property Ltd* [1986] Ch 150) except that afforded by s. 138(4) and (9A) of the 1984 Act.

Under s. 9A of the 1984 Act (inserted by the Administration of Justice Act 1985, s. 55(5)), the tenant has the right to apply for relief at any time within six months from the date on which the landlord recovers possession of the demised premises.

QUESTION 3

'The Law Commission's proposals for termination proceedings are so obviously such an improvement on the present arrangements for forfeiture and the grant of relief that one is amazed it took twenty years for this solution to the mess to be put forward'.

To what extent are the present arrangements a 'mess'? Do you agree with the comment that the proposals are an obvious improvement on the present arrangements?

Commentary

This is an essay question which is intended to test the student's knowledge of the broader issues surrounding the law of forfeiture of leases. The usual principles apply in tackling such questions in exam conditions — prepare a rough plan, structure your answer, do not waffle, make a series of points, write a conclusion.

For a survey of the Law Commission's proposals, see Peet, C., 'The Termination of Tenancies Bill' [1994] EG 9426, 133. See also Smith, P. F., 'Reform of the Law of Forfeiture' [1986] Conv 165, Pawlowski, M., *The Forfeiture of Leases*, London: Sweet & Maxwell, 1993, Ch. 12, Hutchinson, L., 'Law on Your Side' [1998] EG 9808, 149 and Pawlowski, M., 'Termination of Tenancies by Physical Re-entry' (1998) 2 L & T Review, pp. 24–27.

Suggested Answer

The Law Commission in its report entitled 'Forfeiture of Tenancies' (Law Com. No. 142, 1985) noted three major sources of difficulty under the present law, namely:

(a)   the doctrine of re-entry;

(b)   the doctrine of waiver; and

(c)   the separate regimes for forfeiture for non-payment of rent and all other breaches of covenant.

Essentially, its report recommended abolition of the first two defects and assimilation of the rule of forfeiture for non-payment of rent and other breaches of covenant into a single, comprehensive code. The justification for such a radical change was that the present law is unnecessarily complicated, incoherent and may give rise to injustice.

Under the doctrine of re-entry, a landlord forfeits a lease by re-entry upon the demised premises and the lease terminates on the date on which the re-entry takes place. In cases where the landlord forfeits by bringing court proceedings for possession, a notional re-entry is deemed to take place from the date when the proceedings are served on the tenant (*Canas Property Co. Ltd* v *KL Television Services Ltd* [1970] 2 QB 433). This gives rise to the anomaly that, although the lease is notionally forfeited from that date, nevertheless the tenant remains in possession of the premises for an indefinite period until the final outcome of the landlord's proceedings. Accordingly, the date of the service of the proceedings has no real significance and there is no reason why it should mark the ending of the lease.

Because the lease is deemed to end at the time of re-entry, there is the further difficulty that all the obligations which it imposes upon the tenant terminate also at that time. The tenant will remain in possession for an indefinite period after forfeiture (pending his application for relief), and during this period he will be under no obligation to pay rent or to perform any of his other covenants in the lease unless he is subsequently granted relief from forfeiture. During this 'twilight period' (see *Meadows* v *Clerical, Medical and General Life Assurance Society* [1981] Ch 70, *per* Sir Robert Megarry V-C, at p. 78), the status of the lease is somewhat obscure, the landlord is deprived of his right to claim rent or to seek any equitable remedy (e.g., an injunction) to enforce the tenant's covenants, and any damages payable for breaches by a tenant of his covenant to repair are assessable only down to the service of the proceedings.

The anomalies surrounding the doctrine of re-entry can be illustrated by reference to the case of *Hynes* v *Twinsectra Ltd* [1995] 35 EG 136, where the Court of Appeal held that, despite a forfeiture, there was an existing tenancy sufficient for the purposes of allowing the tenant to make an application to acquire the freehold under the Leasehold Reform Act 1967. The Court reached this decision largely on the basis of a subsisting claim for relief from forfeiture made by the tenant's predecessor in title. Although the landlord is effectively estopped from denying the continued existence of the forfeited lease, the lease remains in existence so far as the tenant is concerned at least until the final outcome of his application for relief: see *GS Fashions Ltd* v *B & Q plc* [1995] 09 EG 324, where it was held that the landlord, who by service of the writ had unequivocally elected to forfeit, was thereby prevented from subsequently disputing the validity of the forfeiture.

In view of these difficulties, the Commission initially recommended the abolition of the doctrine of re-entry and its replacement by a scheme under which (apart from termination by agreement) court proceedings and a termination order would always be necessary to end a lease, and until that time it would simply continue in full force. In its 1998 Consultative Document, however, the Commission recommended, contrary to its previously held view, that a right of physical re-entry should be retained and placed on a statutory footing which would integrate it properly with the rest of the termination order scheme. This change of view was prompted largely by concerns expressed by the commercial property industry that the landlord's right of physical re-entry should not be abolished on the ground that it provides an 'effective management tool' and is commonly used as a means of bringing a tenancy to an end quickly and in a cost-effective way in cases where there is no prospect of the tenant remedying the particular breach complained of. In addition, concern was expressed that a move to a wholly court-based termination regime would result in a large increase in the volume of business for the courts (especially the county courts) which could seriously prejudice their ability to operate the new scheme.

The Commission viewed the doctrine of waiver of forfeiture as equally artificial. At present, the landlord may lose his right of forfeiture for a particular breach by the mere act of a demand or acceptance of rent irrespective of his intention. With the introduction of the scheme of termination orders, the lease would remain in existence until the court decided whether or not, in its discretion, to terminate it and rent would continue to be payable until that time. Accordingly, there would no longer be any justification for inferring a waiver from the mere demand or acceptance of rent, or, moreover, from any conduct by the landlord amounting merely to a recognition of the continued existence of the lease. The Commission would, therefore, replace the current doctrine of waiver with a new rule to the effect that the landlord would lose his right to a termination order only if his conduct, after he had actual knowledge of the event, was such that it would lead a reasonable tenant to believe, and did in fact lead the actual tenant to believe, that the landlord would not seek a termination order on the ground of that event. This would be a question of fact to be decided in the light of the circumstances of each case. Such a formulation, however, has the disadvantage of uncertainty and may be more difficult to apply in some cases than the present doctrine of waiver.

The Commission also noted that the present distinction, in relation to relief against forfeiture, between cases involving non-payment of rent and other breaches of covenant, gave rise to unnecessary complexity in the law. The distinction has an historical basis in so far as, from early times, equity granted relief against non-payment of rent upon payment of the arrears and costs of the action, viewing the landlord's right to forfeit on this ground as no more than security for the payment of a specific sum of money. On the other hand, so far as other breaches of covenant were concerned, the old Court of Chancery considered that the forfeiture clause should be fully enforced (even if the default could be put right) unless there was some element of fraud, accident, mistake or surprise which rendered it inequitable to grant relief. Coupled with this attitude lay equity's inherent inability to compensate the landlord for any loss occasioned by a breach other than non-payment of rent by means of an appropriate award of damages.

While the jurisdiction to grant relief in non-rent cases was considerably extended by legislation during the 19th century, equity's inherent power to relieve in cases of non-payment of rent was also embodied in separate legislative provisions during this period, with the result that there now exist two parallel systems of relief, each operating to produce very similar results. Moreover, unnecessary differences exist between the granting of relief in the High Court and county court in cases involving non-payment of rent.

The Law Commission, accordingly, proposed the removal of these two regimes and their replacement by a much simplified, unified structure. There is no doubt that such a reform is long overdue, particularly because, as can be seen, the reason for having two separate systems for relief is largely historical.

At present, where the landlord is in breach of his obligations under the lease, the tenant may have no means of bringing the relationship of landlord and tenant to an end, because his lease is unlikely to contain a right to terminate on the part of the tenant. The Commission, therefore, proposed the inclusion of a *tenant's* right to terminate in the new scheme. However, in its 1994 report ('Landlord and Tenant Law: Termination of Tenancies Bill', Law Com. No. 221, 1994), the Commission decided not to pursue its 1985 proposal for a new scheme of termination of tenancies by tenants, largely because this would be too innovative and unlikely to receive universal support. This is a pity, because the original structure would have vastly simplified the law by providing a system of termination orders under which either the landlord or the tenant would have been entitled to terminate the tenancy upon the fault of the other.

QUESTION 4

In April 1998, Betty granted Jane a five-year tenancy of a hairdressing salon in Greenwich, London, at an annual rent of £15,000. The lease provided, *inter alia*, that Betty would 'keep and maintain the demised premises in good repair'. The property is approached from a small alleyway which leads to the main Greenwich High Street.

In May 2000, the ceiling to the property collapsed through old age. Jane immediately wrote to Betty and told her of the state of disrepair. To date, Betty has failed to acknowledge Jane's correspondence.

Two weeks ago, the local authority began major construction works to the Greenwich High Street which adjoins the alleyway. Jane has received a letter from the local authority stating that that alleyway will be blocked off for six months to allow the works to be carried out. As a result of the closure of the alleyway, Jane has suffered a 70 per cent reduction in her business.

Two days ago, Jane posted the keys to the premises back to Betty, after packing up her equipment and moving out of the property to a new location.

Advise Jane as to whether she is still liable for the rent to Betty for the remainder of the contractual term of the lease.

Commentary

This question requires you to consider in detail the House of Lords decision in *National Carriers Ltd* v *Panalpina (Northern) Ltd* [1981] AC 675 and the decision in *Hussein* v *Mehlman* [1992] 32 EG 59.

Since Jane's lease is presumably a business tenancy within Pt II of the Landlord and Tenant Act 1954, you will also need to consider briefly the effect (if any) of contractual termination under the Act. This is by no means an easy task since there is no case law (to date) on the interaction of these common law methods of termination and the workings of Pt II. See however, Pawlowski, M., 'Contractual Termination of Leases — Unresolved Issues' (1998) 13 JPL, pp. 4–6.

The temptation is simply to regurgitate the facts and ruling in the two main cases without getting to grips with the various unresolved issues raised by the current case law. This is clearly an area of leasehold law where the courts have yet to give authoritative guidance: see, however, the further reading listed in the Introduction to this chapter. See also Question 3, **Chapter 15**.

Suggested Answer

Recent cases have seen growing judicial acceptance that the contractual doctrines of frustration and repudiatory breach are, as a matter of legal theory, applicable to leasehold law.

In *National Carriers Ltd* v *Panalpina (Northern) Ltd* [1981] AC 675, the House of Lords held that a lease was capable of being discharged by the occurrence of a frustrating event. In this case, a warehouse was demised to the tenants for a term of 10 years from 1 January 1974. The only vehicular access to the warehouse was by a street which the local authority closed on 16 May 1979 because of the dangerous condition of a derelict warehouse nearby. The road was closed for 20 months, during which the tenant's warehouse was rendered useless. In an action by the landlords for the recovery of unpaid rent, the tenants claimed that the lease had been frustrated. The House of Lords, although recognising that the doctrine was, in principle, applicable to leases, held on the facts that the lease had not become discharged. The tenants had lost less than two years of use of the premises out of a total of 10 years. Moreover, the lease would still have nearly three years left to run after the interruption had ceased. Similar reasoning would apply in the instant case, where Jane's business would suffer only six months' of disruption and her lease would still have two and a half years (i.e., half the term) left to run after the works were completed. As against this, we are told that Jane has suffered a 70 per cent reduction in her business as a result of the closure of the alleyway. Although this may have been the primary reason for her relocating elsewhere, it is doubtful whether the blocking of the alleyway would be considered so serious that it goes to the whole foundation of the lease, rendering the leasehold estate worthless or useless (*Cricklewood Property and Investment Trust Ltd* v *Leighton's Investment Trust Ltd* [1945] AC 221 (HL). Accordingly, Jane's lease is unlikely to have been discharged by a frustrating event.

It seems more likely that Jane will be able to rely upon the doctrine of repudiatory breach as determining her lease. In *Hussein* v *Mehlman* [1992] 32 EG 59, it was held that a lease may be terminated by the acceptance of a repudiatory breach of its terms. Here, the landlord granted the tenants an assured shorthold tenancy of a dwelling-house subject to the repairing covenants implied by the landlord under the Landlord and Tenant Act 1985, s. 11. From the commencement of the term, the tenants complained to the landlord about the state of disrepair of the premises; in particular, one of the bedrooms had been made uninhabitable by a ceiling collapse. The landlord refused to carry out this and other repairs. Eventually, the tenants returned the keys and vacated the premises. The court held that the landlord was in repudiatory breach of the contract of letting, and by returning the keys and giving up possession the tenants had accepted the breach and the tenancy was therefore at an end.

The decision in *Hussein* (albeit only at county court level) was treated as apparently correct, without argument, by the Court of Appeal in *Chartered*

Trust plc v *Davies* [1997] 2 EGLR 83. But the most recent case in point, namely, *Nynehead Developments Ltd* v *RH Fibreboard Containers Ltd* [1999] 02 EG 139, suggests that the actual circumstances in which a lease will be effectively brought to an end by acceptance of a landlord's repudiatory breach are likely to be exceptional. Before a breach can be characterised as repudiatory, it must deprive the tenant of substantially the whole of his bargain, just as a supervening event must substantially deprive the tenant of the whole benefit of the contract before it can frustrate the lease. In both the *Hussein* and *Chartered Trust* cases, the tenant was deprived of substantially the whole of his bargain because, in the former, the tenant could not live in the house for the remainder of the term, and in the latter, her business had been effectively destroyed. By contrast, in *Nynehead*, although the breaches were serious, the consequences for the tenant were not such as to deprive the tenant of the essence of his bargain. Interestingly, in *Hussein*, the tenancy was granted for a three-year term commencing in December 1989, and the ceiling collapse and water penetration (which rendered the premises uninhabitable) occurred in March 1991. It was evident that there was no likelihood that the condition of the house would improve before the end of the term and, hence, the landlord's breach was sufficient to vitiate 'the central purpose of the contract of letting'. In *Chartered Trust*, although the lease had still about 20 years left to run, the landlord's conduct in derogating from grant resulted in substantial interference with the tenant's business driving her to bankruptcy. This, in itself, was considered sufficient to deprive the tenant of the whole benefit of her contract and constituted a repudiation of the lease regardless of the unexpired term of the lease.

In the present case, Jane's lease still has over two years left to run. In these circumstances, she may find it difficult to argue that she has been substantially deprived of the whole of her bargain. Applying *Chartered Trust*, however, if the ceiling collapse has seriously disrupted her business, such consequence may be enough substantially to deprive Jane of the benefit of her contract.

Even if Jane is able to rely on the doctrine of repudiatory breach so as to discharge her *contractual* tenancy, this may not be sufficient to determine the actual (leasehold) estate. In *Hussein*, the court allowed the tenants to make use of the doctrine to put an end to the tenancy independently of any proprietary mechanism for termination (e.g., surrender, notice to quit, etc.). The difficulty with using this 'independent' approach is that a lease is both an executory contract and an executed demise. In other words, it may be artificial to regard the parties' rights as governed solely by executory promises where those rights are also properly viewed by reference to their character as an estate in land. It may be, therefore, that an *integrated* approach is required whereby the repudiation is effected by some proprietary measure. For example, it may be possible to employ the fiction of an implied surrender on Jane's behalf in order to give a proprietary basis to the operation of the contractual repudiation. Although the judgments in *National Carriers* and *Hussein* appear to favour an independent approach to the question of contractual termination, any conclusions based on these authorities must remain speculative in the absence of any authoritative guidance on this point.

A further difficulty relates to the interrelation of contractual termination and the provisions for termination contained in Pt II of the Landlord and Tenant Act 1954. Presumably, Jane's lease is a business tenancy falling within Pt II of the 1954 Act. In this connection, s. 24(2) of the Act expressly preserves surrender as a means by which a business tenancy may validly be brought to an end. It may be possible, therefore, to argue that a tenant who accepts his (or her) landlord's repudiatory conduct by vacating the premises and returning the keys to the landlord should be categorised as having effected a common law surrender of the property and thus fall within the ambit of s. 24(2). In *Wood Factory Property Ltd* v *Kiritos Property Ltd* [1985] 2 NSWLR 105, the Supreme Court of New South Wales suggested that it may be possible to classify the acceptance by a *landlord* of a tenant's repudiatory breach as a new species of surrender by operation of law. Unfortunately, the English courts have not yet had the opportunity to consider this issue, so the question whether the 1954 Act would limit Jane's ability to apply contractual principles of repudiation in the context of her business tenancy remains an open one.

QUESTION 5

Barry is the tenant of a house under a lease for seven years which is about to expire. Advise Barry whether he can lawfully remove the following articles before the end of the term, all of which have been fitted and erected by him:

    (a)   Bookshelves in a recess in the sitting-room.

    (b)   A small safe cemented into a cavity in the wall of his study and which is used for storing personal possessions.

    (c)   A stone sundial and statue resting on their own weight in the garden.

Commentary

This is a straightforward question concerning a tenant's right to remove fixtures on the expiry of the lease. In answering the question, you should refer to the two tests (i.e., degree of annexation and purpose of annexation) for determining whether a particular item constitutes a fixture or not. You will also score higher marks if you are able to refer to the cases in point.

You should assume that the lease provides no guidance as to whether the objects are fixtures or not, or in relation to rights of removal. It may also be assumed that Barry and the landlord have not entered into any agreement in relation to the objects.

For further reading, see Haley, M., 'The Law and Fixtures: When is a Chattel not a Chattel?' (1985) 135 NLJ 539 and 588; Williams, D., 'To Have and Have Not' [1994] EG 9738, 143; and Pawlowski, M., 'House: Chattel or Realty' (1997) 1/2 JHL, pp. 23–26.

Suggested Answer

The term 'fixture' is applied to anything which has become so attached to the land as to form part of it in law. In determining whether an object has become a fixture or not, the two main factors a court will consider are:

(a)   the degree of annexation; and

(b)   the purpose of the annexation.

It has been said that the second of these two tests is likely to be more decisive than the first (see *Berkeley* v *Poulett* (1976) 241 EG 911 and *Hamp* v *Bygrave* (1983) 266 EG 720), but ultimately it is always a question of fact in each case whether an object is a fixture (and therefore attached to the land) or a chattel.

The degree of annexation test dictates that if an article is attached to the land in a substantial way, or secured in such a way that any removal would be likely to damage the land, then it will probably be a fixture; whereas if the object merely rests on the land under its own weight, it remains a chattel (*Holland* v *Hodgson* (1872) LR 7 CP 328). Thus, a fireplace and an ornamental chimney piece have been held to be fixtures on the basis that they could not be removed without injuring the land. See also, *Buckland* v *Butterfield* (1802) 2 Brod & Bing 54.

By contrast, articles which are capable of removal without damage to the land, such as a 'Dutch barn' (*Elwes* v *Maw* (1802) 3 East 38), or a greenhouse bolted to a concrete plinth lying on the ground under its own weight (*Deen* v *Andrews* (1986) 52 P & CR 17) have been held to be chattels.

Under the purpose of annexation test, if a chattel substantially attached to the land is only physically so annexed with the purpose of putting it to better use (rather than enhancing the land), then despite appearing to be a fixture it will nonetheless remain a chattel and will thus be capable of removal, if removal is practical and feasible (see, e.g., *Leigh* v *Taylor* [1902] AC 157, concerning a wall tapestry). In relation to this more subjective test, the authorities show no clear line of reasoning, and therefore much will depend on the facts of each individual case.

In *Elitestone Ltd* v *Morris* [1997] 1 WLR 687, the House of Lords confirmed that the answer to the question whether a structure (in that case a wooden bungalow resting on concrete pillars attached to the ground) became part and parcel of the land itself depended on the degree and the object of annexation to the land. In that case, the bungalow could be removed only by being demolished and, accordingly, it was held to form part of the realty.

If an article is classified, as a matter of law, as a chattel, it may be removed by the person bringing it onto the land or his successors in title. This principle applies to tenants of demised land. If, however, the object is deemed a fixture, prima facie it cannot be removed and must be left for the landlord on the basis that it has become part of the freehold land. There are, however, three significant exceptions to this rule where a tenant may remove certain fixtures, namely:

(a)   domestic and ornamental fixtures;

(b)   trade fixtures; and

(c)   agricultural fixtures.

These are known as 'tenant's fixtures'. It has recently been held, however, that a tenant is not entitled to remove tenant's fixtures following forfeiture of the lease by peaceable re-entry (*Re Palmiero: debtor 3666 of 1999* [1999] 38 EG 195).

Domestic and ornamental fixtures may be removed in their entirety by the tenant provided the injury to the land is no more than decorative (*Spyer* v *Phillipson* [1931] 2 Ch 183). Fixtures which permanently improve the premises cannot be removed (e.g., a fitted kitchen). Trade fixtures may be removed by the tenant if they have been installed by him for the purpose of his business or trade. Thus, engine machinery has been held to be removable (*Climie* v *Wood* (1869) LR 4 Ex 328) and so have shrubs planted by a commercial gardener (*Wardell* v *Usher* (1841) 3 Scott NR 508). In relation to agricultural fixtures, agricultural tenants have certain statutory rights to remove fixtures added by them to the demised land, under the Agricultural Holdings Act 1986, s. 10.

The upshot of the foregoing is that Barry may only remove such objects as are classified in law as chattels or amount to tenant's fixtures.

(a) The bookshelves. It would be useful to discover whether the book-shelves are free-standing or built into the wall of the sitting-room. If they are free-standing, applying the degree of annexation test, it may be presumed that the shelves are mere chattels. If the shelves are secured to the recess, it seems that they would be deemed fixtures and would belong to the landlord. This presumption could be rebutted, however. Applying the purpose of annexation test, Barry may be able to show that the securing of the shelves merely enhanced them in their own right. Alternatively, if classified as fixtures, he may be able to demonstrate that the shelves were installed for purely business reasons or were of an ornamental nature. As such, they would rank as tenant's fixtures, entitling Barry to remove them if removal is possible without damaging the recess.

(b) The small safe. Due to the manner in which the safe has been secured (i.e., cemented into a cavity in the wall of the study), there is a strong prima facie presumption that the safe forms part of the land (i.e., it is a fixture). It may be possible for Barry to argue that the safe was cemented simply for purposes of storage, in which case this could rebut the presumption that the safe is a fixture due to its cementation. This would be a question of fact for the trial judge. It is unlikely, however, that this argument would succeed because it would be extremely difficult to remove the safe without severely damaging the cavity in the wall.

If the safe falls to be classified as a fixture, it is unlikely to constitute a tenant's fixture. We are told that Barry uses the safe for storing his personal possessions and not for any business user. Moreover, it is difficult to envisage the safe as being ornamental. It is submitted, therefore, that the safe is a fixture which passes to the landlord.

(c)   The stone sundial and statue. These, we are told, rest on their own weight in the garden. Not being physically secured to the land, these objects would prima facie, applying the degree of annexation test, be regarded as chattels, and hence be removeable by Barry. Under the purpose of annexation test, however, it is also relevant to examine the intention with which he placed these objects in the garden (*Hamp* v *Bygrave*, above). If they were placed to improve the land in a permanent way, they will be regarded as fixtures, but if placed to enhance the objects themselves they will be regarded as chattels. This is a question for the trial judge to determine on the hearing of evidence. The courts have, however, in the light of the *Elwes* and *Holland* cases (above), shown a tendency to treat objects placed on land under their own weight as mere chattels. In the unlikely event that it was held that these items were fixtures, it would still be open to Barry to argue that he has the right to remove them, being tenant's ornamental and domestic fixtures.

QUESTION 6

Discuss the ways in which a tenant may terminate his lease by surrender and consider the possible legal consequences which may flow from a surrender of a lease. (Illustrate your answer by reference to decided cases.)

Commentary

This is a standard type of essay question concerned with the topic of surrender. Students should be familiar with the various forms of surrender (express and implied) and the effects of a surrender on the parties to the lease and any sub-tenants. A structured answer, demonstrating a good knowledge of case law, will contribute to the attainment of a 2:1 mark.

Suggested Answer

A surrender of a lease is the process by which a tenant gives up his (leasehold) estate in the land to his immediate landlord. The lease is essentially destroyed by mutual agreement. The effect of a surrender is to terminate the tenant's liability under his covenants as from the date of the surrender. A surrender may arise expressly or by implication (i.e., by operation of law).

An express surrender must be made by deed (Law of Property Act 1925, s. 52(1)). An express surrender must operate immediately and will be invalid if it is expressed to operate at some future date (*Doe d Murrell* v *Milward* (1838) 3 M & W 328). A future surrender may, however, take the form of an agreement to surrender, in which case it will be valid if made in compliance with the relevant legal formalities necessary for contracts for the disposition of interests in land (i.e., s. 40 of the 1925 Act or the Law of Property (Miscellaneous Provisions) Act 1989, s. 2, depending on whether the contract was made before or on or after 27 September 1989). To be effective, the surrender must be to the immediate landlord. Thus, a transfer of a sub-tenancy not to the mesne tenant but to the head landlord will not operate as a surrender, but rather as an assignment of the benefit of the sub-tenancy to the head lessor.

An implied surrender (i.e., by operation of law) is expressly exempted from the requirement of a deed by virtue of the Law of Property Act 1925, s. 52(2)(c). Such a surrender may arise from any unequivocal conduct of the parties which is inconsistent with the continuation of the lease. A common example of such a surrender is where the tenant abandons the premises and the landlord accepts his implied offer of a surrender by changing the locks and re-letting the premises to a third party (*R* v *London Borough of Croydon, ex parte Toth* (1986) 18 HLR 493). The abandonment must, however, be of a permanent, and not a temporary, nature. A mere temporary abandonment is too equivocal unless the tenant is absent for a long time with large rent arrears owing (*Preston Borough Council* v *Fairclough* (1982) 8 HLR 70). Moreover, although the taking of keys (coupled with other acts) may evidence the taking of possession of the premises by the landlord, this will not be the case where there is no intention to accept a surrender until after the grant of a new lease (*Proudreed Ltd* v *Microgen Holdings plc* [1996] 12 EG 127 (CA)).

Another example of a surrender by operation of law will arise where the tenant agrees with the landlord to replace his existing lease with a new lease on different terms, or with substantially different premises (see, e.g., *Bush Transport Ltd* v *Nelson* (1987) 1 EGLR 71 and *Foster* v *Robinson* [1951] 1 KB 149). In the latter case, a protected tenant accepted a rent-free licence to occupy the same premises to replace his existing tenancy. By contrast, a mere variation in the rent payable will not give rise to a surrender by implication (*Jenkin R. Lewis & Son Ltd* v *Kerman* [1971] Ch 477), nor where there is a replacement of an old rent book with a new one which contains substantially the same terms with only slight variations (*Smirk* v *Lyndale Developments Ltd* [1975] Ch 317).

No surrender of the lease will be implied where the tenant accepts a new lease from the landlord which is void or voidable (*Barclays Bank* v *Stasek* [1957] Ch 28). This is because a surrender by operation of law is subject to an implied condition that the new lease is valid; if it is not, the current lease remains in force.

In surrendering his lease, a tenant cannot prejudice the rights of other parties affected by it. For example, the Law of Property Act 1925, s. 139, provides that, in the event of a surrender of the head lease by a mesne tenant, the head landlord automatically becomes the landlord in relation to the sub-tenant so as to preserve the validity of the sub-lease. By s. 150(1) of the 1925 Act, a lease may be surrendered with a view to the acceptance of a new lease, without any surrender of any sub-lease.

Following a surrender, a tenant may remain liable for past breaches of covenant occurring during the term of his lease (*Richmond* v *Savill* [1926] 2 KB 530). It is possible, however, for the parties to agree that all past (as well as future) liability of the tenant should cease upon surrender.

Prima facie, a surrender includes the right to remove tenant's fixtures in the absence of express contrary agreement. Where there is a surrender by operation of law and the tenant remains in possession under a new lease (see earlier), the right to remove such fixtures continues throughout the tenant's possession (*New Zealand Government Property Corporation* v *HM and S Ltd* [1982] 1 All ER 624).

As regards rent, the tenant is not entitled to recover any part of any rent paid in advance, but rent accruing before the surrender (but not yet due) may be the subject of apportionment under the Apportionment Act 1870, s. 3. The tenant remains liable for any arrears due before the surrender under any personal covenant, if any. If not, the landlord will be able to maintain an action for use and occupation (*Shaw* v *Lomas* (1888) 59 LT 477).

QUESTION 7

In February 1994, Mountbatten Ltd granted to Tolkein Ltd a lease of an office suite in central London for a term of 10 years from and including 19 January 1994. The lease contained, *inter alia*, the following clause:

> ... the tenant may, by serving not less than six months' notice in writing on the landlord, or its solicitors, such notice to expire on the *fifth* anniversary of the term commencement date, determine this lease and upon expiry of such notice this lease shall cease and determine and have no further effect ...

By a letter, dated 21 May 1998, Tolkein Ltd gave notice to Mountbatten Ltd to determine the lease on 17 January 1999.

Shortly after the notice was served, Tolkein Ltd vacated the demised premises. It has not paid any rent since the expiry date of its notice, and the property remains vacant and unoccupied.

Mountbatten Ltd is of the view that the notice of determination served on it by Tolkein Limited is invalid and of no effect. Despite several demands for rent, Tolkein Ltd has refused to make any further payments.

Advise Mountbatten Ltd as to its legal position.

Commentary

This is an interesting question concerning the law relating to break clauses in leases; in particular, the rules governing the validity of a notice where an incorrect break-date has been specified. A good answer will give consideration to the recent House of Lords ruling in *Mannai Investment Co. Ltd* v *Eagle Star Life Assurance Co. Ltd* [1997] 2 WLR 945 and subsequent cases in point.

For further reading, see: Williams, P., 'When Time Runs Out' [1997] EG 9724, 112–14 and Wilkinson, H.W., 'Construing Break Notices' (1997) 147 NLJ 1187.

Suggested Answer

If the notice served by Tolkein Limited is invalid then the lease will remain alive and the premature abandonment by Tolkein Limited and its refusal to pay rent will constitute a repudiatory breach of contract.

It would then be open to Mountbatten Limited to accept the repudiation as terminating the tenancy — effectively bringing about a surrender of the lease by operation of law. Such a surrender is exempt from any legal formality by virtue of s. 52(2) of the Law of Property Act 1925. A surrender by operation of law can be inferred from the parties' conduct where, for example, the tenant abandons the property and the landlord changes the locks and re-lets the premises to a third party (see *R* v *London Borough of Croydon, ex parte Toth* (1986) 18 HLR 493 and *Re AGB Research plc* [1994] EGCS 73). Alternatively, it may be open to Mountbatten Ltd to elect to continue with the lease if there are genuine economic reasons for so doing (see *White and Carter (Councils) Ltd* v *McGregor* [1963] AC 413).

On the other hand, if Tolkein Ltd's notice is valid (despite the incorrect break-date), the lease will have been effectively determined (on 19 January 1999) and Tolkein Ltd's liability to pay rent extinguished from that date.

On the face of it, the notice is clearly incorrect in so far as it specifies 17 January 1999 as the termination date of the lease, whereas the actual termination date (as required under the break clause) is 19 January 1999. Is this error fatal to the validity of the notice? At one time, the rules as to the validity of contractual break notices were very strict. Any error could easily invalidate the notice: see, for example, *Hankey* v *Clavering* [1942] 2 KB 326. However, the House of Lords in *Mannai Investment Co. Ltd* v *Eagle Star Life Assurance Co. Ltd* [1997] 2 WLR 945 has now adopted the more flexible approach to determining the validity of break notices enunciated in the earlier case of *Carradine Properties* v *Aslam* [1976] 1 WLR 442. The question in each case is whether it was obvious to the 'reasonable recipient' of the notice, with knowledge of the terms of the lease (in particular, the relevant anniversary dates), that the tenant wished to determine the lease on that anniversary and not an earlier time. A minor error in the notice will not, therefore, normally detract from the validity of the notice. In *Mannai* itself, applying this objective test, a contractual break notice in a lease, which was one day short of the appropriate anniversary date, was held to be valid.

In *Carradine*, the landlord served a break notice on 6 September 1974, purporting to break the lease on 27 September 1973, instead of 27 September 1975. The court held that this was an obvious slip as the specified date had already passed. The notice was, therefore, held valid. Similarly, in *Micrografix Ltd* v *Woking 8 Ltd* [1995] 37 EG 179, the tenant's break notice specified 23 March 1994 instead of 23 June 1995. This notice was also held valid. Again, in *Garston* v *Scottish Widow's Fund and Life Assurance Society* [1998] 3 All ER 596, a lease, dated 10 July 1985, was granted for a term of 20 years from 24 June 1985. Under a break clause, the tenant had the right to end the lease at the end of the tenth year (i.e., on 24 June 1995). By an error, the tenant's notice purported to end the lease on 9 July 1995. A moment's reflection would have indicated to the landlord (as a reasonable recipient of the notice) that the tenant intended to end the lease at the end of the tenth year but had confused the date of the lease with the date for the commencement of the term. The notice was, therefore, held to be valid. (See also, most recently, *Havant International Holdings Ltd* v *Lionsgate (H) Investment Ltd* [1999] EGCS 144.) In all these cases, the intended purpose and effect of the notice were quite clear to the recipient and it would have been unjust if such a technicality were to render it ineffective. The standard of reference was that of the reasonable man exercising common sense in the context of the particular circumstances of the case.

By contrast to the foregoing, in *Lemmerbell Ltd v Britannia LAS Direct Ltd* [1998] 48 EG 188, the Court of Appeal, applying the *Mannai* test, held that the tenant's break notice was defective. Here, the defects in the notices were more substantial and could not, therefore, be cured by the application of the *Mannai* ruling. On an objective analysis, the reasonable landlord recipient of the notice could not know, in the absence of evidence of an assignment of the lease, whether the notice was given by the tenant (as stated in the notice) or not. It was, accordingly, impossible to cure the defect.

It is evident from the decision in *Lemmerbell* that the *Mannai* test will not avail every party who has served a defective break notice. In *Lemmerbell*, it was by no means obvious that there was an error in the name of the tenant in the notice, nor who the actual tenant was, nor whether the sender of the notice was an authorised agent of the tenant. The obvious conclusion to be drawn from this case is that, while minor errors may be excused, substantive defects remain incurable.

In the present case, the notice served by Tolkein Ltd is two days short of the relevant anniversary date. However, in my view, a reasonable landlord recipient of this notice (who must be taken to be aware of the provisions in the lease) would not be misled by it, since it must have realised that the tenant was seeking to determine the lease in accordance with the relevant break clause in the lease. On this analysis, therefore, the notice was effective to bring the lease to an end on 19 January 1999. If that is right then Tolkein Limited is released from any further obligations in the lease as from that date, in particular, its obligation to pay rent. Mountbatten Limited is, therefore, best advised to endeavour to find another tenant for the property as soon as possible.

9 The Rent Act 1977

INTRODUCTION

A tenancy of residential premises will be a protected tenancy under the Rent Act 1977 if it is granted before 15 January 1989. A residential tenancy granted on or after this date is subject to the Housing Act 1988, Pt I, and will be either an assured or an assured shorthold tenancy (see **Chapter 10**).

To qualify as a protected tenancy, the premises must comprise a dwelling-house and the purpose of the letting must be full residential use as one dwelling. The tenancy may be of part of a house, being a part let as a separate dwelling. There are also a number of excluded tenancies which do not qualify for Rent Act protection. For example, a tenancy is not protected if under the tenancy the dwelling-house is bona fide let at a rent which includes any payments in respect of board or any substantial payments in respect of attendance (s. 7(2); *Otter* v *Norman* [1989] AC 129 and *Nelson Developments Ltd* v *Taboada* [1992] 34 EG 72). Other notable exclusions include holiday lettings, company lettings, and tenancies granted by resident landlords.

After the termination of a protected tenancy, the protected tenant is entitled to be the statutory tenant of the dwelling-house provided he continues to occupy it as his residence (s. 2(1)(a)). The requirement of continuing residence has been the subject of numerous cases, and of particular interest is the tenant who is a genuine 'two-homes' occupant who may claim statutory protection under the Rent Act 1977 despite residing in *both* properties (see, e.g., *Langford Property Co. Ltd* v *Tureman* [1949] 1 KB 29; contrast *Walker* v *Ogilvy* (1974) 28 P & CR 288). You should remember that a tenant's forced absence from the property while, for example, in prison, or in hospital or on military service, does not necessarily destroy a statutory tenancy (*Tickner* v *Hearn* [1960] 1 WLR 1406). However, a long absence from the premises raises an inference of cesser of residence requiring the tenant to show an *animus revertendi* (an intention to return) *and* a *corpus possessionis* (i.e., some symbol of occupation) such as leaving the premises furnished or occupied by someone on the tenant's behalf (*Brown* v *Brash* [1948] 2 KB 247). You may well be asked to answer a question on any of these topics which may also include some discussion of succession rights.

If you decide to revise the Rent Act 1977, make sure you cover the landlord's grounds for possession in some depth. It is almost certain that a problem question on the 1977 Act will require you to consider one or more of the mandatory and/or discretionary grounds listed in sch. 15 to the 1977 Act. Be aware that a landlord who claims possession against a protected or statutory tenant must establish:

(a) the effective termination of the contractual tenancy (e.g., by expiry of time, notice to quit, forfeiture etc.); and

(b) that one or more of the statutory grounds for possession apply.

Thus, a common law forfeiture of the tenancy will only destroy the protected (contractual) tenancy and the tenant will remain a statutory tenant of the premises (*Wolmer Securities Ltd* v *Corne* [1966] 2 QB 243).

The discretionary grounds for possession are contained in sch. 15, Pts I, III and IV of the 1977 Act. A landlord relying on any of these grounds must additionally prove that it is reasonable to make an order for possession (s. 98(1)). The mandatory grounds, on the other hand (which are contained in sch. 15, Pt II of the 1977 Act as amended by the Housing Act 1988, s. 66 and sch. 7), are not subject to any overriding consideration of reasonableness. A landlord who establishes any of the mandatory grounds can claim possession as of right, provided that:

(a) the dwelling-house is let on a protected tenancy; and

(b) not later than 'the relevant date' the landlord gave the tenant written notice that possession might be recovered under the ground in question.

For most tenancies the relevant date is the commencement of the tenancy.

Lastly, a brief word about restricted contracts. A restricted contract is defined in s. 19 of the 1977 Act and may exist where the resident landlord exclusion applies, or where the rent includes payment for the use of furniture or services, provided that, in the latter case, the payments are for board or substantial attendance. A furnished contractual licence may also come within this category (*Luganda* v *Service Hotels* [1969] 2 Ch 209). A restricted contract occupier has no security of tenure other than:

(a)   protection from harassment and unlawful eviction under the Protection from Eviction Act 1977 (as amended by the Housing Act 1988, s. 29);

(b)   the right to apply to a rent tribunal for deferment of a notice to quit for up to six months at a time in respect of a periodic tenancy granted before 28 November 1980, or, alternatively, to apply to the court for deferment of the order for possession for up to three months subject to the imposition of conditions with regard to payment by the tenant of arrears of rent (if any) and rent or mesne profits, in respect of periodic or fixed-term contracts created on or after 28 November 1980 (see Housing Act 1980, s. 69, inserting a new s. 106A into the Rent Act 1977).

As from 15 January 1989, however, no tenancy or other contract is capable of being a restricted contract (Housing Act 1988, s. 36(1)).

There are four problem questions in this chapter which are intended to give you the opportunity to test your broad knowledge of the area. The usual principles apply in tackling such questions in exam conditions — draw up a plan in rough, make a series of points, and list the relevant cases (before you forget them!).

QUESTION 1

Fred is the weekly tenant of a room at 2 Bedsit Lane, owned by Bertram. He has been Bertram's tenant since 1988. He pays a weekly rent of £75 which entitles him to a 'continental breakfast' seven days a week which is served in his room. In addition, the rent includes an amount (£12) in respect of daily cleaning of the room and change of bed linen each week.

Bertram's wife resides on the premises three nights a week in order to fulfil these duties as caretaker. The rest of the time she spends living with her husband in Brighton.

Fred's tenancy agreement is described as a 'holiday let' although it has periodically been renewed.

Bertram now wishes to evict Fred and sell the house with vacant possession.

Advise Bertram.

Commentary

This problem question deals with a number of the well-known exclusions to a protected tenancy. Do not waste time dealing with points which do not cause problems. There is no need, for example, to write at length about the distinction between a tenancy and a licence. You are actually told in the question that Fred is the weekly tenant of the room in question. Instead, begin by considering whether Fred has a tenancy of a *separate dwelling*, which is more to the point (*Curl* v *Angelo* [1948] 2 All ER 189 and *Parkins* v *Westminster City Council* [1998] 13 EG 145). The issue regarding the continental breakfast is now covered by House of Lords authority (*Otter* v *Norman* [1989] AC 129) and your answer should consider the principles emerging from this case in some depth.

The point regarding attendance is more difficult since, unlike board, it must be substantial in the terms of s. 7(2) to avoid statutory protection (*Nelson Developments Ltd* v *Taboada* [1992] 34 EG 72). For a good article, see Rogers, C.P., 'Making a Meal out of the Rent Acts: Board, Attendance and the 'Protected Tenancy' (1988) 51 MLR 642.

The residence of Bertram's wife may also give some students a problem. The key lies in the fact that the test as to what constitutes residence for the purposes of the resident landlord exclusion is the same as that for statutory tenants under the 1977 Act (sch. 2, para. 5; *Jackson* v *Pekic* [1989] 47 EG 141). For a discussion of this point, see Pawlowski, M., 'Residence and the Resident Landlord' [1991] EG 9111/9112, 78 and 52. In the statutory tenant context, a tenant can maintain statutory tenant status by virtue of his wife's occupation (*Brown* v *Draper* [1944] KB 309). Moreover, a statutory tenant has been held to reside in premises where he spends only two nights a week (*Langford Property Co. Ltd* v *Tureman* [1949] 1 KB 29). It may be possible to combine these propositions and apply them in the context of a resident landlord.

As to holiday lets, your answer should refer to some of the cases in this area (*Buchmann* v *May* [1978] 2 All ER 993; *R* v *Rent Officer for London Borough of Camden, ex parte Plant* (1980) 257 EG 713 and *McHale* v *Daneham* (1979) 249 EG 969). For further reading, see Waite, A., 'Dodging the Rent Acts' (1981) 131 NLJ 460, and Lyons, T.J., 'The Meaning of ''Holiday'' under the Rent Acts' [1984] Conv 286. This exclusion will take Fred's tenancy wholly outside the Rent Act 1977. The other exclusions, on the other hand, will deny Fred protected status but will still give him limited protection as a restricted contract tenant.

As with most problem questions of this kind, you are not expected to give a definitive answer to all the issues raised — it is enough that you state the general principles, refer to the relevant cases and apply the law to the particular problem giving a reasoned view. Although there is a lot of ground to cover, this is the sort of question where you could score a high 2:1.

Suggested Answer

Fred has been the weekly tenant of the room since 1988, and accordingly the central issue is whether Fred qualifies as a protected tenant under the Rent Act 1977. Part I of the Housing Act 1988 has no application since the tenancy was granted before 15 January 1989.

We are not told what facilities are available in the room. This may be relevant since the room must be let as a separate dwelling in order to qualify for full Rent Act protection. The word 'dwelling' in the 1977 Act includes all the major activities of life, particularly sleeping, cooking and feeding (*Curl* v *Angelo* [1948] 2 All ER 189). In *Metropolitan Properties Co. (FGC) Ltd* v *Barder* [1968] 1 WLR 286, for example, the room in question (servant's room No. 3) was held not to be let as a separate dwelling because it was used only as an au pair's bedroom. In *Parkins* v *Westminster City Council* [1998] 13 EG 145, a case involving a secure tenancy under the Housing Act 1985, a bedroom was held not to be a separate dwelling because it did not satisfy the requirements of essential living facilities.

We are told that Fred pays a weekly rent of £75 which entitles him to a continental breakfast seven days a week which is served in his room. It has been held that any amount of board which is not *de minimis* is sufficient to exclude statutory protection under s. 7 of the Rent Act 1977 (*Otter v Norman* [1989] AC 129, applying the majority view in *Wilkes v Goodwin* [1923] 2 KB 86). In *Otter*, the House of Lords concluded that the provision of breakfast by itself, with the implicit inclusion of the ancillary services involved in preparing it and the provision of crockery and cutlery with which to eat it, amounted to board for the purposes of the Rent Act 1977. In that case, the landlord let a room to the tenant at a rent which included payment for the provision daily by the landlord of a continental breakfast served in the communal dining room of the building in which the tenant's room was situated. The House of Lords stressed that a *bona fide* obligation to provide board entailed not only the cost of the food and drink provided but also all the housekeeping chores which had to be undertaken in shopping for provisions, preparation and service of meals on the premises, and clearing and washing up after meals. See also *Holiday Flat Co. v Kuczera* (1978) SLT 47, a Scottish case.

Assuming, therefore, that the breakfast is prepared and served by Bertram at the premises (albeit in Fred's room), the board exclusion would prima facie apply rendering Fred's tenancy unprotected under the 1977 Act.

In addition, we are told that Fred's rent includes an amount (£12) in respect of daily cleaning and a change of bed linen each week. In this connection, a tenancy will not be protected under the 1977 Act if the rent includes substantial payments in respect of attendance (s. 7(2)). Attendance has been held to include services in the form of daily room cleaning and weekly laundry (*Nelson Developments Ltd v Taboada* [1992] 34 EG 72 and *Palser v Grinling* [1948] AC 291). In *Nelson*, the initial rent was £55, of which no less than £11 was treated as being attributable to services. Having regard to the county court practice of taking 10 per cent as the lower end of the bracket and 20 per cent as the upper end, the Court of Appeal concluded that the attendance exclusion applied. In Fred's case, the amount of rent attributable to the services is £12, and hence well above the 10 per cent watershed applied in the *Nelson* case.

The next point to consider is that Bertram's wife resides on the premises three nights a week in order to carry out her duties as caretaker. Section 12 of the

Rent Act 1977 (as amended by the Housing Act 1980) sets out four preconditions for the operation of the resident landlord exclusion. First, the tenancy (whether furnished or unfurnished) must have been granted on or after 14 August 1974. Secondly, the tenancy must be of a dwelling-house forming part of a building or flat which, in the former case, is not a purpose built block of flats. These pre-conditions appear to be met in the present case. Thirdly, the tenancy was granted by a person who, at the time when he granted it, occupied as his residence another dwelling-house which forms part of the flat or building. We are not told whether Bertram resided at the premises when he granted the tenancy to Fred in 1988. Fourthly, at all times *since* the tenancy was granted, the interest of the landlord under the tenancy has belonged to a person who, at the time he owned that interest, occupied as his residence another dwelling-house which also formed part of the flat or building. The test of residence for a resident landlord is basically the same as that for a statutory tenant under the 1977 Act (*Jackson* v *Pekic* [1989] 47 EG 141), thus it is possible for a landlord to have two homes on the analogy of the position of a statutory tenant (*Wolff* v *Waddington* [1989] 47 EG 148). Moreover, it is clear that a tenant can maintain statutory tenant status by virtue of his wife's occupation (*Brown* v *Draper* [1944] KB 309) and where he resides on the premises for a minimum of two nights a week (*Langford Property Co. Ltd* v *Tureman* [1949] 1 KB 29). It is arguable, therefore, that Bertram will qualify as a resident landlord on the basis of his wife's limited occupation of the premises, provided the other preconditions are satisfied.

We are told that the agreement is described as a holiday let. Holiday lettings fall outside the protection of the Rent Act 1977 altogether. Since the tenancy agreement expressly states the purpose for which it was made (i.e., a holiday), that statement will stand as evidence of the purpose of the parties unless Fred can establish that it does not correspond with the true purpose (*Buchmann* v *May* [1978] 2 All ER 993, involving a holiday let for three months). In the present case, the court would undoubtedly view the letting as a sham in so far as the tenancy has been periodically renewed. However, in *McHale* v *Daneham* (1979) 249 EG 969, the county court judge held that persons from abroad who signed a six-month holiday letting agreement and then renewed it, first for one month, then for a further two months, had a genuine holiday letting. The tenants were working in this country but the landlord understood that they were on holiday. The case is clearly distinguishable on the ground that Fred has been a weekly tenant of the room since 1988 and is, presumably, working in this country (see *R* v *Rent Officer for London Borough of Camden, ex parte Plant* (1980) 257 EG 713). It is highly unlikely, therefore, that Bertram will be able to avail himself of the holiday let exclusion.

Assuming, however, that one or more of the other exclusions apply, this will mean that Fred will not have protected tenancy status but will still be entitled to the limited protection afforded to a restricted contract tenant under the 1977 Act (s. 19). As such, Fred will have no security of tenure other than:

(a)   protection from harassment and unlawful eviction under the Protection from Eviction Act 1977; and

(b)   since his tenancy was granted after 28 November 1980, the right to apply to the court for deferment of the order for possession for up to three months subject to the imposition of conditions with regard to the payment of arrears of rent (if any) and rent or mesne profits (Housing Act 1980, s. 69, inserting a new s. 106A into the Rent Act 1977).

QUESTION 2

In August 1998, Susan bought from Mark the freehold of a house in London divided into three flats.

(a)   The first floor flat had been let by Mark in January 1986 to James on a monthly tenancy. It appears that Mark gave James a notice to quit in 1988, but that James stayed on, along with his wife, Cinzia, and son, David.

(b)   Mark had let the ground floor flat to Sarah in July 1987 for a fixed term of one year. Sarah wanted the flat as it was near to her office, but she has spent most weekends in her cottage in Wales.

(c)   The basement flat was let by Mark to a company called Acrecrest Ltd in December 1988. It appears that Mark was approached by George, who was looking for a place to rent. After taking legal advice, Mark insisted that George acquire Acrecrest Ltd, an 'off the shelf company', and Mark let the basement flat to Acrecrest Ltd for a fixed term of six months. George moved in and has been paying the monthly rent ever since with his own cheque.

James died last month, leaving his widow and son (aged 30) residing in the first floor flat.

Advise Susan as to the likelihood of her being able to recover possession of the three flats.

Commentary

This is a fairly typical problem question on the Rent Act 1977 which requires you to demonstrate an understanding of a number of different issues. Be careful not to linger too much on any one particular point — plan your answer and remember that your task is to advise Susan in relation to all three flats.

The subject of company lets is a favourite amongst examiners, and is likely to arise also in the context of the Housing Act 1988 since the 1988 Act specifically provides that an assured tenancy must be one granted to an 'individual'. Accordingly, a letting to a company will have the attraction of being completely outside the statutory provisions of the 1988 Act from the beginning of the tenancy. By way of contrast, a letting of residential premises to a company as a separate dwelling ranks as a protected tenancy under the Rent Act 1977, and consequently it will be entitled to the benefit of the fair rent provisions (*Carter* v *SU Carburreter Co.* [1942] 2 KB 288). For a good discussion of the company let device, see Radevsky, T., 'Sham Company Lets' (1990) 140 NLJ 620; Murdoch, S., 'Company Lets' [1989] EG 8907, 85; Waite, A., 'Dodging the Rent Acts' (1981) 131 NLJ 460, and Martin, J.E., 'Nominal Tenants and the Rent Act 1977' [1982] Conv 151.

Here again, the well prepared student should score very heavily!

Suggested Answer

(a)   First floor flat. The effect of serving a notice to quit on James in January 1988 was to terminate the contractual tenancy at common law. However, assuming James was a protected tenant of the flat immediately before termination, he would have remained in occupation as a statutory tenant of it (Rent Act 1977, s. 2(1)). James has now died, and the question arises whether his widow, who continues to reside in the flat, is entitled to the statutory tenancy by succession. The relevant provisions are contained in sch. 1 to the Rent Act 1977, as amended by the Housing Act 1988, s. 76. The schedule is further amended where the original tenant died on or after 15 January 1989 by virtue of the Housing Act 1988, s. 39 and sch. 4. Under these provisions, Cinzia is entitled to succeed as the widow of the original tenant if she resided in the flat immediately before James's death, provided that she occupied the flat as her residence. These preconditions appear to be met in the present case.

Moreover, as a spouse, her succession will remain a statutory tenancy under the 1977 Act. Accordingly, it is unlikely that Susan will be entitled to possession of this flat unless she is able to establish grounds for possession (under sch. 15 to the 1977 Act) or Cinzia ceases to reside (in which case she will lose her statutory tenant status).

As to James's son, David, the position is that a member of the family of the deceased statutory tenant cannot take the tenancy by succession if there is a surviving spouse. Subject to this, the family member claimant cannot obtain a succession unless he or she has resided in the dwelling-house immediately before the original tenant's death and for a minimum period of two years immediately before then. In these circumstances, the family member obtains an assured tenancy by succession under the Housing Act 1988.

(b)   Ground floor flat. Sarah's tenancy expired by effluxion of time in July 1988. Assuming she was a protected tenant under the 1977 Act, the question arises whether she qualifies as a statutory tenant under the Act. A statutory tenancy depends on continuing residence. But the courts have accepted that a tenant may have two homes. In *Langford Property Co. Ltd* v *Tureman* [1949] 1 KB 29, the owner of a cottage in the country resided there with his wife and family. His work was in London and he took the tenancy of a London flat where he slept, on average, for two nights a week. The Court of Appeal held that the tenant was in personal occupation of the flat as his home. See also, *Blanway Investments Ltd* v *Lynch* [1993] EGCS 8, where the tenant lived in Essex but was held to have retained his statutory tenancy of a London maisonette to assist in his business activities. By contrast, in *Walker* v *Ogilvy* (1974) 28 P & CR 288, the flat in question was used only occasionally at weekends and for holidays, and consequently was not held on a statutory tenancy. Thus, occupation merely as a convenience for occasional visits (e.g., for a holiday or as a temporary retreat) will not be classified as residence so as to entitle the tenant to protection under the 1977 Act (*Beck* v *Scholz* [1953] 1 QB 570).

We are told that Sarah wanted the flat as it was near to her office, but that she spends most weekends in her cottage in Wales. It seems evident that Sarah treats her London flat as her home and mere temporary absence at weekends will not deprive her of statutory tenant status (*Roland House Gardens* v *Cravitz* (1975) 29 P & CR 432).

(c)   Basement flat. If a company is made the tenant of residential premises, since it is inherently incapable of occupying the premises personally, it cannot claim a statutory tenancy and so has no security of tenure after the contractual tenancy has expired (*Hiller* v *United Dairies (London) Ltd* [1934] 1 KB 57 and *Carter* v *SU Carburreter Co.* [1942] 2 KB 288). Hence the legal advice to Mark that the tenancy should be placed in the name of Acrecrest Ltd. However, it is possible that a letting to a company may be viewed by the courts as a sham device to avoid the protection of the 1977 Act.

In *Hilton* v *Plustitle* [1989] 1 WLR 149, the landlord let a flat to a limited company for a six-month term with a view to enabling the defendant, who was a shareholder and director of the company, to occupy the flat without the right of becoming its statutory tenant. The Court of Appeal held that, although the purpose of the letting was to prevent the creation of a statutory tenancy, the letting was not a sham since it was the intention of both parties (knowing all that was involved) that the flat was to be let to the company. Although the defendant paid the rent with a personal cheque, the letting was clearly intended to be to the company. The same result was reached in *Estavest Investments Ltd* v *Commercial Express Travel Ltd* [1988] 49 EG 73 and *Kaye* v *Massbetter Ltd* [1991] 39 EG 129. In *Estavest*, the rents were paid by the tenant companies and there was no evidence that the amounts came out of the occupier's pocket. Where, however, there is a letting in which the company does not perform genuinely the obligations under the lease and in which a company has been put in as tenant solely as a cloak to avoid statutory protection, the argument that the letting is a sham becomes more persuasive. Ultimately, the issue is one of the genuineness of the transaction. The fact that George has been paying the rent with his own cheque points to the fact that he was intended to be the real tenant. If that is the case, George is now the statutory tenant of the flat who cannot be evicted without proof of Rent Act grounds.

The conclusion must be that all three flats are currently occupied by statutory tenants and that Susan is unable to recover possession without establishing grounds for possession.

QUESTION 3

'In considering the character of alternative accommodation not only the physical characteristics of the premises containing the accommodation fall to be considered but also such matters as neighbourhood, noise, smell and other considerations of a kind which one can, perhaps, best describe as environmental considerations.' (*Redspring* v *Francis* [1973] 1 WLR 134, *per* Buckley LJ)

Discuss this statement in the context of Rent Act case law.

Commentary

This essay question requires a general discussion of cases on the meaning of suitable alternative accommodation as a ground for possession under the Rent Act 1977, sch. 15, Pt IV. For further reading, see Wilkinson, H.W., 'Suitable Alternative Accommodation and the Environment' (1983) 266 EG 1166, and Williams, D.W., 'How Suitable is Suitable?' (1983) 268 EG 882.

Try to plan a structure before you start writing your essay — the examiner will be impressed by a well-structured answer which draws on cases to illustrate points of principle.

If you have revised this topic well, it should be plain sailing all the way!

Suggested Answer

The provision of suitable alternative accommodation is a ground for possession contained in the Rent Act 1977, sch. 15, Pt IV. In the absence of a certificate of the local housing authority that it will provide suitable alternative accommodation, the accommodation must fulfil various criteria. In particular, the accommodation must be either:

(a)   similar as regards rental and extent to local housing authority dwellings provided for persons having similar needs as regards space to the tenant and his family; or

(b)   reasonably suited to the means of the tenant and to the needs of the tenant and his family as regards extent and character.

In *Redspring* v *Francis* [1973] 1 WLR 134, it was held that the court is obliged to have regard to environmental factors where these render the alternative accommodation unsuitable as regards 'character'. In that case, the tenant occupied a flat under a protected tenancy. The flat was situated in a quiet residential road and the tenant had the use of a garden. The alternative accommodation offered was nearby and more spacious, but it had no garden and was in a busy traffic thoroughfare. The Court of Appeal concluded that what a tenant 'needed' was somewhere where he or she could live in reasonably comfortable conditions suitable to the type of life which he or she led. In so far as environmental factors affected the suitability of the proposed accommodation, it was proper to take them into account either as affecting the suitability of the accommodation as regards character, or as affecting the question whether it was reasonable to make an order for possession. In *Redspring*, the trial judge had failed to take the environmental factors into account, and accordingly had misdirected himself in making an order for possession.

The decision in *Redspring* may be contrasted with *Hill* v *Rochard* [1983] 1 WLR 478, in which an elderly couple held a statutory tenancy of a period country house in which they had resided for many years. The premises contained many spacious rooms, outbuildings, a stable, and one and a half acres of land, including a paddock, where the tenants kept a pony. The landlords offered the tenants a modern, detached, four-bedroomed house as alternative accommodation. The house was situated in a cul-de-sac on a housing estate in a nearby country village. The garden covered one-eighth of an acre and there was no stable or paddock. The Court of Appeal held that, in determining whether alternative accommodation was reasonably suitable to the needs of a tenant as regards extent and character, a court should have regard to the particular tenant's *housing need* and not to other ancillary advantages enjoyed by a tenant in his or her present accommodation. Thus, in considering a tenant's housing needs as regards character, it was permissible to compare the environment to which the tenant had become accustomed with that offered by the alternative accommodation. In the present case, the trial judge's finding that the new environment would permit the tenants to live reasonably comfortably in the style of life which they liked to lead was a crucial finding directed to the particular tenants which could not be faulted. Accordingly, the order for possession was upheld.

The upshot of the *Hill* case is that it is not necessary that the character of the alternative accommodation should be similar to that of the existing premises. The real question is whether the alternative accommodation is reasonably suitable to the tenant's *housing needs* as regards its character.

The decision in *Redspring* was also considered *Siddiqui* v *Rashid* [1980] 1 WLR 1018, in which the tenant, a Muslim, was the protected tenant of a flat in London where he had friends and attended a mosque and cultural centre. His place of work, however, was in Luton. The landlords offered him alternative accommodation in Luton near to his place of work. The Court of Appeal held that the word 'character' in sch. 15, para. 5(1)(b), was confined to the character of the property, and although that might be affected by environmental factors (such as noise and smell) which would directly affect the tenant in the enjoyment of the property, it did not extend to the society of friends or cultural interests of the tenant. Accordingly, it was not possible to say that the accommodation offered in Luton was not such that the tenant could not live there in reasonably comfortable conditions suitable to the style of life he had been leading in London.

Reference may also be made to *Roberts* v *Macilwraith-Christie* (1987) 1 EGLR 224 and *Battlespring Ltd* v *Gates* (1983) 268 EG 355. In the former case, the tenant had lived in the basement of a large, early 19th-century house and the alternative accommodation offered was in a modernised ground floor flat, smaller but in better condition than the basement, on a very low rent. The disadvantages were exchanging access to the public garden in Kensington Square for access to Shepherd's Bush Green, lack of room for the large amount of furniture which the tenant possessed, and lack of accommodation for a sub-tenant. Despite these disadvantages, the Court of Appeal upheld the trial judge's order for possession. In the latter case, an elderly widow was offered alternative accommodation in a flat similar in many respects to her maisonette, in the same road, at a slightly smaller rent, the alternative flat being at the more pleasant end of the road and, when renovated, probably more comfortable than her present accommodation. However, after 35 years, having brought up her family there, she was attracted to her present maisonette, with the memories it had for her, and did not want to move. The Court of Appeal held that it would not be reasonable to make an order for possession.

In assessing the character of a property, environmental considertions are of equal relevance to para. 5(1)(a) and para. 5(1)(b) of sch. 15, Pt IV to the 1977 Act, despite being specifically mentioned only in the latter (*Dawncar Investments Ltd* v *Plews* (1993) 25 HLR 639, where the flat was in a quiet road in Hampstead and the alternative accommodation offered was on a busy commercial road in Kilburn).

QUESTION 4

Martin purchased a block of three flats in April 1987.

(a) Flat 1 was unoccupied and Martin lived there for six weeks. He then let it on a weekly tenancy to David, giving notice under the Rent Act 1977, sch. 15, case 11, that he might wish to regain possession. During his six weeks in the flat, Martin spent two or three nights each week in his girlfriend's house where he kept most of his belongings.

(b) When he was staying in Flat 1, Martin granted a weekly tenancy of Flat 2, which was unoccupied, to Michelle, a single mother with two small children. Martin has recently found out that Michelle works as a prostitute, advertising her services and the flat's telephone number in the windows of local newsagents. He has also discovered that she has recently been convicted of possessing cannabis on the premises.

(c)   When Martin purchased the block, Flat 3 was occupied by Doris as a statutory tenant under the Rent Act 1977. When she fell ill in January 1990, her daughter Ellen, who had her own house nearby, moved in to look after her mother. Ellen has spent most nights at the flat, returning to her house every few days to make sure that everything was in order. Doris has just died.

Advise Martin, who wishes to obtain possession of the three flats with a view to a sale of the block.

Commentary

This is another fairly typical problem question raising a number of issues on the Rent Act 1977. Remember that there are, essentially, three parts to the question so you should not spend an undue amount of time on one part at the expense of the other parts. Here again, a good knowledge of the case law will pay dividends!

Suggested Answer

(a)   Flat 1. The question here is whether Martin can rely on case 11 in order successfully to obtain possession of the flat. Martin must show:

(i)   he let the flat on a regulated tenancy;

(ii)   before the letting, he occupied it as his residence;

(iii)   at the commencement of the tenancy, he gave notice in writing to David that possession might be recovered under case 11; and

(iv)   the flat is now required by Martin as a residence for himself.

As to the requirement of residence prior to the letting, occupation by the landlord immediately before the letting is no longer necessary (Rent (Amendment) Act 1985 reversing the decision in *Pocock* v *Steel* [1985] 1 WLR 229). A more obvious problem relates to the quality of Martin's residence prior to the letting to David. For the purposes of case 11, it is not necessary for the landlord to show that he has occupied the premises as a home but merely for the purposes of residence, which may be temporary or intermittent. In *Mistry v Isidore* [1990] 31 EG 43, the landlord slept in the flat five or six nights each week, spending the other night(s) in his brother's home where he kept most of his belongings. The landlord kept at the flat such clothes as he needed for work and such things as he required for daily living. There were no facilities for washing or cooking in the flat. He remained at the flat on this basis for some eight to nine weeks until he let the flat to the tenant. On these facts, the Court of Appeal held that the landlord had occupied the flat as his residence within the meaing of case 11. Similarly, in *Naishe v Curzon* (1984) 273 EG 1221, where the landlord had used the place as his home on only an intermittent basis prior to letting it out, the Court of Appeal held that whether or not a dwelling-house is occupied as a residence is a question of fact and that temporary or occasional residence can be sufficient.

Although very much a borderline case, given the courts' generous attitude to residence, it is submitted that Martin has occupied the flat as his residence for the purpose of case 11. In order to succeed, however, he must also show that he requires the flat as a residence for himself. In this connection, it has been held that a landlord seeking possession of a dwelling-house under case 11 need not show that he reasonably requires to occupy the house, but merely that he genuinely wants and intends to do so as a residence for himself (or for members of his family) (*Kennealy v Dunne* [1977] QB 837). Thus, Martin must establish a genuine desire and a genuine immediate intention to use the flat as his residence. An intention on his part to live in the flat until it can be sold would be consistent with occupying it as a residence under case 11 (*Whitworth v Lipton* [1993] EGCS 172). However, if all that he established was an intention to realise his interest in the premises as soon as possible and live in the flat temporarily until he was able to do so, then he would not be entitled to succeed (*Rowe v Truelove* (1977) 241 EG 533).

(b) Flat 2. There is no question of Martin relying on the resident landlord exclusion since, even though he may have been technically resident in the block at the time he granted the tenancy to Michelle, the requirement of continuing residence is not satisfied (Rent Act 1977, s. 12). It is likely, however, that Martin may have a ground for possession of the flat under sch. 15, case 2, to the 1977 Act. This case applies where the tenant, *inter alia*, has been guilty of conduct which is a nuisance or an annoyance to adjoining occupiers, or has been convicted of using or allowing the dwelling-house to be used for immoral or illegal purposes.

It is not necessary to show that the tenant has committed the tort of nuisance (see, e.g., *Shine* v *Freedman* [1926] EGD 376, where the tenant had persistently turned the landlord's customers away instead of directing them to the landlord's premises on the first floor). More to the point, it was suggested in *Frederick Platts Co. Ltd* v *Grigor* [1950] WN 194, that a tenant prostitute could be evicted on this ground without proof that adjoining occupiers were annoyed by her activities.

As to the conviction for possession of cannabis in the flat, the mere fact that drugs were on the premises and the tenant was there and had them in her immediate custody will not involve a 'using' of the premises in connection with the offence for the purpose of case 2. The premises must actually be employed as a storage or hiding place for the drugs for a conviction for being in possession of them to come within case 2 (*Abrahams* v *Wilson* [1971] 2 QB 88). See also *S. Schneiders and Sons Ltd* v *Abrahams* [1925] 1 KB 301 (conviction of receiving stolen goods at the demised premises).

The first step will be for Martin to serve Michelle with four weeks' notice to quit the flat, complying with the Protection from Eviction Act 1977, s. 5, thereby terminating her contractual tenancy. Since case 2 is a discretionary ground of possession, Martin must additionally prove that it would be reasonable to make an order for possession (s. 98). In considering reasonableness, the court may take into account the widest range of circumstances. Thus, the fact that Michelle is a single mother with two small children may be relevant. However, it has been held that the statutory protection given to residential tenants under the Rent Act 1977 was not intended to apply where the premises were being used for immoral purposes and, in such cases, therefore, an immediate order for possession is appropriate (*Yates* v *Morris* [1950] 2 All ER 577).

(c)   Flat 3. The problem here is that Ellen may wish to claim that she is entitled to succeed to her mother's statutory tenancy. Since her mother died after 15 January 1989, the relevant provisions are to be found in the Rent Act 1977, sch. 1, as amended by the Housing Act 1988, s. 76 and sch. 4. In the absence of a surviving spouse, a family member of the deceased may succeed if he or she resided with the deceased tenant immediately before his death and for a minimum of two years immediately before then.

Since there is no doubt that she qualifies as a member of the family, the central issue is whether Ellen has been 'residing with' her mother for the requisite period of time. The phrase 'residing with' in the statutory succession provisions requires some factual community of family living and companionship. In *Foreman* v *Beagley* [1969] 1 WLR 1387, the tenant was in hospital for the last three years of her life, and her son came to the flat to air the premises and eventually lived there for the last year of her life. The Court of Appeal held that he had not been 'residing with' her as he only moved in as a caretaker without any intention of establishing a joint household. Similarly, in *Swanbrae Ltd* v *Elliott* (1987) 281 EG 916, a daughter who moved in with her sick mother, sleeping three or four nights a week at the premises and spending the other nights in her own house where her son continued to live, was held not to be residing with her mother as she was only a regular visitor. The test, therefore, is whether the claimant had made his or her home with the deceased and had the intention of forming a family unit (*Morgan* v *Murch* [1970] 1 WLR 778; *Hildebrand* v *Moon* (1989) 37 EG 123 and *Hedgedale Ltd* v *Hards* (1991) 15 EG 107).

On the facts of the present case, it is debatable whether Ellen will be able to satisfy this test of residence. However, if she does qualify as successor, she will obtain an assured periodic tenancy of the flat under the Housing Act 1988 (see s. 39(5) and (6)).

10   Part I of the Housing Act 1988

INTRODUCTION

This chapter contains questions on the Housing Act 1988, Pt I (i.e., the assured and assured shorthold tenancy), which came into force on 15 January 1989. The assured tenancies scheme replaces that of the Rent Act 1977 in respect of tenancies created on or after 15 January 1989.

One of the basic aims of the new scheme was to enable landlords to grant tenancies to residential tenants at a market rent, with the ability more easily to regain possession of the premises at the expiry of the lease than was possible in the case of a Rent Act protected or statutory tenant.

Prior to the enactment of the Housing Act 1996, an assured shorthold tenancy had to be for a fixed term with a minimum duration of at least six months and the landlord must have served a notice on the proposed tenant before the tenancy began, informing the tenant that the tenancy was to be a shorthold. The court had no power to waive this requirement. Thus, if the requisite notice was not served, the tenancy would be an assured tenancy enjoying the full benefit of security under Pt I. The 1996 Act has changed the law by providing (in s. 96) that an assured tenancy post-dating the commencement date of the section (i.e., 28 February 1997) is to be automatically treated as an assured shorthold, unless it falls within any of the stated exceptions. The exceptions are narrowly defined to maximise the scope of shortholds and contain obvious exclusions such as, for example, where it is explicitly stated (either before or during the assured tenancy) that it is not to be an assured shorthold.

The upshot of these amendments is that a landlord is no longer required to serve any preliminary notice on the tenant, neither is there any requirement that the tenancy is of a fixed term. However, the landlord is not entitled to an order for possession until at least six months have elapsed from the grant of the tenancy (s. 99).

You will find that most of the questions on Pt I of the Housing Act 1988 will require you to delve into Rent Act case law since the provisions of the two Acts are similar (but not necessarily identical) in many respects. We would urge you, therefore, to look also at the questions featured in the preceding chapter on the Rent Act 1977.

QUESTION 1

Maud has just inherited a house converted into flats, with part vacant possession. She intends to use the house as a source of rental income rather than to sell it or grant long leases. Advise her to what extent she may ensure that future occupants do not enjoy security of tenure.

Commentary

This is a straightforward essay question on the exclusions to an assured tenancy and the mechanics of the assured shorthold tenancy. The sch. 1 exclusions (in the 1988 Act) bear a close resemblance to those of the Rent Act 1977, ss. 4–16, but they are not identical. In particular, a letting which includes payments in respect of board or attendance, exempt from protected status under the 1977 Act (see s. 7), is not prevented from being an assured tenancy on that ground. It should also be noted that, with the repeal of the restricted contract provisions (see s. 19 of the 1977 Act), there is no residual security of tenure for tenancies which are excluded from assured status by sch. 1 to the 1988 Act.

Suggested Answer

An obvious way in which Maud can ensure that her future occupants do not enjoy security of tenure is to grant assured shorthold tenancies of the flats under Pt I of the Housing Act 1988. Section 96 of the Housing Act 1996 (which came into force on 28 February 1997) has amended the 1988 Act by abolishing the requirement for a preliminary notice as a precondition for the grant of an assured shorthold tenancy. Moreover, the requirement of a minimum fixed term of at least six months has also been removed so that a shorthold tenancy can now be granted for any term (fixed term or periodic), although the landlord will not be entitled to obtain a court order for possession until at least six months have elapsed from the grant of the tenancy (s. 99). If the tenancy is made orally (i.e., if it is periodic or for a term not exceeding three years: s. 54(2) of the Law of Property Act 1925), the landlord is obliged to provide written terms of the tenancy (rent, duration, etc.) only if requested by notice in writing served by the tenant.

The effect of granting an assured shorthold tenancy is that once the fixed term has expired by effluxion of time (subject to s. 99), Maud can obtain possession of the flat without establishing any grounds for possession. She must, however, give the tenant two month's written notice, but this may be given before the fixed term has expired (s. 21(1) and (2)). By the time the action comes to court, the tenant may be holding over as a statutory periodic tenant (see s. 5(2)) but this will not prejudice Maud's right to possession. In fact, the court, on being satisfied of the above conditions, must order possession.

Instead of granting assured shorthold tenancies of the flats, Maud may be in a position to bring her tenancies within one or more of the exclusions contained in sch. 1 to the Housing Act 1988 and thereby avoid assured status altogether. One possibility is that she grants holiday lettings of the flats. A tenancy cannot be an assured tenancy (and, hence, an assured shorthold tenancy) if its purpose is to confer on the tenant the right to occupy the dwelling-house for the purpose of a holiday (sch. 1, para. 9). The word 'holiday' is not defined in the statute but, in the context of the Rent Act 1977, it has been judicially interpreted as 'a period of cessation of work or a period of recreation' (*Buchmann* v *May* [1978] 2 All ER 993). Although the onus is on the tenant to displace the prima facie evidence of the parties' true purpose which the written agreement provides, the courts are astute to detect shams, whose only object is to avoid statutory protection such as the Housing Act 1988.

Another possibility is for Maud actually to live in the house and thereby qualify as a resident landlord (sch. 1, para. 10). The first precondition for resident landlord status is that the flat let to the tenant forms part of a building which is not a purpose-built block of flats. The phrase 'purpose-built block of flats' is defined in sch. 1, para. 22. It must *as constructed* contain two or more flats. The date of construction is the relevant time to consider, and a distinction is drawn between conversions of existing buildings (which will not, generally speaking, constitute 'purpose-built blocks of flats') and constructions of new buildings which, if they consist of two or more flats, will be within the definition (see *Bardrick* v *Haycock* (1976) 31 P & CR 420 and *Barnes* v *Gorsuch* (1981) 43 P & CR 294). Assuming the house is *not* a purpose-built block of flats, then several further preconditions must be satisfied, namely:

(a)   the flats let to the tenants must form part only of the building;

(b)   Maud (being the person who granted the tenancies) must have been an individual and she must have occupied another dwelling-house in the same building as her only or principal home; and

(c)   she must continue to occupy part of the building as her only or principal home from the date of the tenancies to the date possession is claimed.

A further exclusion which Maud may wish to consider relates to the granting of licences (as opposed to tenancies) of the flats. An assured/assured shorthold tenancy under the 1988 Act must be a tenancy. The classic definition of a tenancy is to be found in *Street* v *Mountford* [1985] AC 809 (i.e., there must be a grant of exclusive possession for a term at a rent). It has been the common practice of landlords to grant 'non-exclusive occupation agreements', whereby a landlord issues joint occupiers with identical licence agreements under which each occupier agrees that he or she will share the dwelling-house with the other(s) or, in some cases, with whomsoever the landlord may nominate. The argument for upholding such agreements is that they do not confer on the occupants exclusive possession of the premises and therefore fall outside statutory protection. However, such agreements have been successfully attacked on the basis that they are shams or pretences in so far as the landlord does not genuinely intend them to be a true statement of the nature of the possession to be enjoyed by the occupiers (see, e.g., *AG Securities* v *Vaughan/Antoniades* v *Villiers* [1988] 3 WLR 1205). If, however, the true effect of the agreement is to confer on the occupiers a *joint* right of exclusive possession, then they will be joint tenants.

It may also be possible for Maud to utilise the company let device for avoiding security of tenure under the Housing Act 1988. A tenancy is assured only if and so long as the tenant is an individual (s. 1(1)(a)). Moreover, the tenant must occupy the dwelling-house as his home (*Hiller* v *United Dairies (London) Ltd* [1934] 1 KB 57). These provisions are intended to prevent companies from claiming the benefits of the legislation. In its simplest form, the company let involves the landlord letting the property to a limited company (which undertakes to pay the rent and comply with the tenant's covenants), and the company then allows a person into occupation as licensee. The company cannot be an assured tenant, as it is not an individual, and the occupier is not an assured tenant either (i.e., he may not be a tenant at all, or he may be paying no rent). Similar schemes have succeeded in avoiding Rent Act protection (*Hilton* v *Plustitle Ltd* [1988] 3 All ER 1051).

Lastly, it should be mentioned that a letting which includes payment in respect of board or attendance, exempt from protected status under the Rent Act 1977, is not prevented from being an assured tenancy on that ground.

QUESTION 2

Greenleaves and Brownleaves are two detached freehold properties in the ownership of Mr Wright.

In October 1989, Mr Wright granted an assured monthly tenancy of Flat 1 at Greenleaves to Tom, who is currently four months in arrears with his rent. Tom has had a history of late payment of rent over the past few years.

In January 1990, Mr Wright granted an assured tenancy for a fixed term of three years of Flat 1 at Brownleaves to Dick, who has recently separated from his wife and no longer lives at the premises with her.

In May 1993, Mr Wright granted an assured shorthold tenancy of Flat 2 at Brownleaves to Harriet. Since the expiry of this tenancy, Harriet has remained in occupation paying a weekly rent.

In order to run both properties efficiently, Mr Wright has (since acquiring both properties in 1985) spent three nights a week at Flat 2, Greenleaves, and four nights a week (including weekends) at Flat 3, Brownleaves. He has now decided to retire from the business and wishes to sell both properties with vacant possession. He seeks your advice as to whether he can successfully bring proceedings to evict Tom, Dick, and Harriet prior to the sale of the properties.

Advise Mr Wright.

Commentary

This is a factually complicated question and certainly not one for the faint-hearted! Although there are numerous issues to cover, be consoled by the fact that you cannot be expected to deal with all the issues in any great detail.

Before you start, draw up a rough plan showing which flats are situated in the two buildings, details of each tenancy and key issues arising. Our suggestion is to deal with each tenancy in turn and then consider the general point regarding the resident landlord exclusion.

Suggested Answer

Flat 1, Greenleaves, is occupied by Tom on an assured monthly tenancy. Because he occupies as a contractual periodic tenant, his tenancy cannot be brought to an end by Mr Wright except by obtaining a court order for possession (s. 5(1) of the Housing Act 1988). In other words, a notice to quit by the landlord in relation to such a tenancy will be of no effect.

Before proceedings are commenced, Mr Wright must serve on Tom a s. 8 notice in the prescribed form. This must inform Tom of the ground(s) on which possession is sought and set out the time-scale of the action (s. 8(3)). Once this s. 8 notice is served, Mr Wright must bring his proceedings within the time-limits set out in s. 8(3). Proceedings should not commence earlier than two weeks from the service of the s. 8 notice, unless possession is sought under grounds 1, 2, 5 to 7, 9 and 16, in which case proceedings should not commence earlier than two months from service and, if the tenancy is periodic, the date on which the tenancy could be terminated by notice to quit given on the date of service of the notice.

It seems that Mr Wright has three separate grounds for possession under sch. 2 — ground 8 (mandatory — at least three months' rent unpaid) and grounds 10 (some rent lawfully due) and 11 (persistent delay in paying rent), being both discretionary grounds — all relating to non-payment of rent. Accordingly, he may commence proceedings for possession after two weeks from the date of service of his s. 8 notice. It has been held recently that the terms of the 1988 Act expressly rule out a claim for forfeiture by the landlord (see s. 5(1) and s. 45(4)). In *Artesian Residential Investments Ltd* v *Beck* [1999] 22 EG 145, the Court of Appeal held that s. 7(3) is explicit in obliging the court mandatorily to order possession if the court is satisfied that any of the grounds in sch. 2 is established. There is no room, therefore, for an assured tenant applying for relief against forfeiture under s. 138 of the County Courts Act 1984.

So far as Flat 1, Brownleaves, is concerned, Dick's assured tenancy expired by effluxion of time in January 1993 and he has recently separated from his wife and no longer lives with her at the premises. The question, therefore, arises as to whether Dick's statutory periodic tenancy (which automatically came into being upon the expiry of the fixed term: see s. 5(2)) continues to be assured under the 1988 Act. If not, Mr Wright may simply determine the statutory periodic tenancy by giving Dick the appropriate notice for the period of the tenancy (i.e., one month's notice in the case of a monthly tenancy). If, on the other hand, Dick retains his assured tenancy status (despite no longer living at the premises), Mr Wright would only be entitled to evict him by seeking possession on any of the grounds in sch. 2 and by serving the appropriate s. 8 notice on him. For the purposes of security of tenure, there is no distinction made between assured contractual periodic tenancies and assured statutory periodic tenancies.

As to Dick's status, it is evident that an assured tenant must 'occupy' the dwelling-house as his 'only or principal home' (s. 1). The tenant husband who goes away for a time leaving his spouse in occupation will, as long as he intends to return to the house, remain an assured tenant (*Brown* v *Brash* [1948] 2 KB 247). The tenant who leaves with no intention to return (in other words, abandoning his wife) will also, nevertheless, remain an assured tenant (*Brown* v *Draper* [1944] KB 309, in the Rent Act context). The Matrimonial Homes Act 1983, s. 1(6), as amended by the Housing Act 1988, sch. 17, para. 33, provides that the occupation of the wife, in these circumstances, is to be treated as the occupation of the husband. Accordingly, as long as Dick's wife continues to occupy the flat (and as long as she continues to be Dick's wife), the assured tenancy will persist. She will be entitled to make rent payments herself (Matrimonial Homes Act 1983, s. 1(5)). She may fail to do this, in which case Mr Wright will have grounds for seeking possession (see grounds 8, 10 and 11, above).

Regarding Flat 2, Brownleaves, this was initially occupied by Harriet under an assured shorthold tenancy, which we are told has now expired, but Harriet continues to remain in occupation paying the weekly rent. Since the fixed term has expired by effluxion of time, Mr Wright can obtain possession of the flat by giving Harriet two months' notice (s. 5(2)). The fact that Harriet is holding over as a statutory periodic tenant (by virtue of s. 5(2)) will not prejudice Mr Wright's position (s. 21(3)). The court, on being satisfied that the tenancy was an assured shorthold, must order possession. One problem which may arise, however, relates to the continued payment of the weekly rent by Harriet. This may give rise to the inference that a *new* periodic tenancy has been created by agreement following the expiry of the assured shorthold. Normally, the expiry of the term will lead to the implication of a statutory periodic tenancy. If, however, Harriet can point to the grant of another tenancy on the coming to an end of the fixed term, that tenancy will not be a statutory periodic tenancy (s. 5(4)); it will almost certainly be an assured (shorthold) tenancy under the 1988 Act (s. 20(4)), and Mr Wright will have to satisfy the two months' notice requirement under s. 21(1) in relation to that tenancy.

It seems, therefore, that Mr Wright may have difficulties in recovering possession of Flats 1 and 2, Brownleaves. In order to avoid these difficulties, he may wish to consider arguing that he is a resident landlord in respect of the flats at Brownleaves, based on his residence of Flat 3 in that building for four nights a week (including weekends). Assuming that the building is *not* a purpose-built block of flats, Mr Wright must establish that he has occupied Flat 3 as his only or principal home. It has been held, in the Rent Act context, that a landlord may have two homes for the purpose of the resident landlord exclusion (*Wolff* v *Waddington* [1989] 47 EG 148) and that it is possible to occupy a flat as a home despite spending only two or three nights there (*Langford Property Co. Ltd* v *Tureman* [1949] 1 KB 29, involving a statutory tenant). In the Housing Act 1988 context, however, assuming Mr Wright occupies both flats as his home, the crucial question is whether he occupies Flat 3, Brownleaves, as his *principal* home. Only then will he qualify for resident landlord status.

QUESTION 3

To what extent does the assured tenancy permit landlords to charge their tenants a market rent? What is the position under an assured shorthold tenancy?

Commentary

This is an easy question if you have studied the relevant provisions on rent in the Housing Act 1988.

Some landlord and tenant syllabuses may concentrate quite heavily on the rental aspects of Pt I of the 1988 Act, although our experience is that lecture-time tends to be devoted more to security of tenure. Our advice is to be guided by your lecturer and the emphasis he or she places on different parts of the course.

Suggested Answer

The policy of Pt I of the Housing Act 1988 is to allow the landlord and tenant to enjoy freedom of contract to stipulate the level of the rent, to agree upon a rent review clause in appropriate cases, and to limit the degree of statutory intervention.

While a fixed term (assured) tenancy is continuing, the parties will be bound by the contractual rent. Thus, the landlord is not entitled to increase the rent unilaterally or to apply to the rent assessment committee for the rent to be increased (s. 13(1)). There may, however, be a rent review clause in the lease which may permit upwards (or downwards) rent reviews at stated intervals. Similarly, the tenant is bound by the terms of the lease and (in the absence of a review clause) has no right to apply for a rent reduction.

In the case of a statutory periodic tenancy (which will arise when an assured fixed-term tenancy comes to an end), the rent payable will continue at the same level as before (s. 5(3)). However, the landlord now has the right to propose a rent increase. The tenant, however, is given no corresponding right to propose that the rent be reduced.

In the case of a contractual (assured) *periodic* tenancy, the landlord is free (at any time) to invoke the Act's rent proposal provisions. These involve the landlord serving on the tenant a notice in prescribed form which proposes the new rent and the date it is to take effect. If the tenant wishes to contest the rent proposed, he must refer the notice to a rent assessment committee before the date on which the proposed rent is to take effect. If he fails to do so, the rent as proposed will take effect on the date shown in the notice (ss. 13 and 14).

Where the tenant refers the notice to the rent assessment committee, the committee must determine the rent at which they consider the dwelling-house might reasonably be expected to be let in the open market by a willing landlord under an assured tenancy having the same terms as the tenancy in question (s. 14(1)). In making the determination, the committee must disregard any effect on the rent attributable to the granting of a tenancy to a sitting tenant, any increase in value of the dwelling-house attributable to certain tenant's improvements (defined in s. 14(3)) and any reduction in value of the house attributable to the tenant's breach of covenant (s. 14(2)).

This formula is, of course, radically different from that which prevails in relation to Rent Act tenancies. In its attempt to free the private landlord from the shackles of letting at a 'fair rent' (which, by definition, was less than the market rent), and thereby revitalise the private rented sector, the 1988 Act places the responsibility in the hands of the rent assessment committees rather than rent officers. These committees must, in each case, consider the local market, the number of potential tenants for the particular property, and then assess the sum at which a 'willing landlord' (i.e., someone who wants to let, given a reasonable return on his or her property, being appraised of the market conditions) would reasonably expect the property to be rented. The committee may, in determining the rent under s. 14, refer to comparable assured tenancy rents in the vicinity, and the president of each rent assessment panel is placed under a duty to keep and make publicly available certain information with respect to rents under assured tenancies.

In the case of assured shorthold tenancies, the landlord has no right to seek an increase in rent during the initial fixed term. During that same fixed term, however, the tenant may apply to the rent assessment committee for a reduction in the rent. On such an application, the committee is required to determine the rent which, in its opinion, the landlord might reasonably be expected to obtain under the assured shorthold tenancy (s. 22(1)). If the tenant's application is successful, he may not apply again (s. 22(2)(a)). Moreover, once the initial fixed term has ended, the tenant no longer has the right to apply, even if he has not applied before and even if the landlord and tenant enter into a new fixed term assured shorthold agreement (s. 22(2)).

Under the s. 22 procedure, the committee is directed not to make a determination at all unless it considers that there is a sufficient number of similar dwelling-houses in the locality let on assured tenancies (whether shorthold or not) (s. 22(3)(a)). In other words, the committee is not expected to tamper with the rent payable by the tenant: unless it considers that the rent he or she pays is 'significantly higher' than those with comparable tenancies, it should not make any determination at all (s. 22(3)(b)).

When the initial fixed term has expired, the landlord may propose an increase of rent under s. 13 of the 1988 Act. However, if the committee has made a determination under s. 22 on the tenant's application, the landlord will have to wait 12 months before he can make a rent proposal (s. 22(4)(c)). When the landlord is free to propose an increased rent, the procedure to be followed will be the same as for any assured tenancy (i.e., the committee must determine the rent at which the dwelling-house might reasonably be expected to be let in the open market by a willing landlord under an assured shorthold tenancy).

The inference to be drawn from these provisions is that a landlord who lets on an assured shorthold should not reasonably expect to obtain as high a rent as a landlord who lets on an assured tenancy which is not shorthold. The price to the landlord of conferring no security of tenure is a return on the property lower than that otherwise obtainable. However, much will depend on the way the market operates. If there are more potential tenants than available properties, the level of rents under assured shorthold tenancies will not be substantially lower than that for assured tenancies with security of tenure. In either case, the rent will be a market rent for that particular tenancy.

11   Leasehold Enfranchisement

INTRODUCTION

By virtue of the Leasehold Reform Act 1967 and the Leasehold Reform, Housing and Urban Development Act 1993, certain tenants of long residential leases are conferred rights compulsorily to purchase the freehold reversion or compulsorily to acquire (for a premium) an extension of their lease.

Questions in this area may be of both essay and problem type. In this chapter, we have set out an example of each.

The Leasehold Reform Act 1967 confers on a tenant of a leasehold *house*, occupying the house as his or her residence, a right to acquire on fair terms the freehold or an extended (50-year) lease of the house, subject to certain conditions, most notably:

(a)   the tenancy must be a long tenancy at a low rent; and

(b)   the tenant must have occupied the house as his residence for the last three years or for periods amounting to three years in the last 10 years;

The Leasehold Reform, Housing and Urban Development Act 1993, Pt I, on the other hand, gives most owners of long leases of *flats* a right either to collective enfranchisement (i.e., a collective right to buy the freehold of a block of flats), or an individual right to acquire a new 90-year lease. It also amends the right to enfranchisement of house freeholds under the Leasehold Reform Act 1967 (above). In this connection, house tenants excluded from the 1967

Act enfranchisement machinery because their low rents were too high are now entitled to enfranchise if the rent is within the limits for the purpose of the new flat enfranchisement machinery under the 1993 Act. The provisions were brought into force on 1 November 1993 (see the Leasehold Reform, Housing and Urban Development Act 1993 (Commencement and Transitional Provisions No. 1) Order 1993 (SI 1993 No. 2134)).

Both Acts provide for notice procedures by which the enfranchisement/ leasehold extension machinery can be put into motion and lay down formulae as to price calculation. For general reading in this area, see Hague, N., *Leasehold Enfranchisement*, 3rd edn, London: Butterworths, 1999, and Mathews, P., and Millichap, D., *Guide to the Leasehold Reform, Housing and Urban Development Act 1993*, London: Butterworths, 1993. For a good summary of the new provisions, see Williams, D., 'Leasehold Reform, Housing and Urban Development Act 1993' [1994] EG 9402, 100.

The subject of collective enfranchisement is currently under review by the Government. The proposals are to relax the rules for qualification, amend the residency test and increase the permitted proportion of non-residential floor area which may be excluded. The proposals would also give the majority of tenants a new right to take over the management of a building without acquiring the freehold: see, further Marcus, D., 'Along the Right Lines' [1998] EG 9850, 78–79, Driscoll, J., 'A Fairer deal for Residential Long Leaseholders' (1998) 148 NLJ 1855–56 and Driscoll, J., 'Residential Leasehold Reform' (2000) 150 NLJ 285–86.

QUESTION 1

On 1 May 1990, the Earl of Westminster granted Tom a 25-year lease of a five-bedroomed terraced house in Central London. The ground rent is £550 per annum. Tom has always resided in the house during weekdays, spending weekends with his mother in Brighton. Since taking up the lease, he has also run a business from the two ground-floor rooms in the house. In July 1999, Tom inherited a family fortune and now wishes to acquire from the Earl the freehold title to the house.

Advise Tom as to whether he is able to claim a right of enfranchisement under the Leasehold Reform Act 1967. Assuming Tom is able to claim such a right, outline the procedure which must be followed under the Act.

Commentary

You should approach this question by, first, explaining the preconditions of enfranchisement under the 1967 Act in the light of the interpretative case law which has developed since the enactment of the statute, and, secondly, outlining the requisite procedures for enfranchisement (i.e., the tenant's notice, the fixing of the price and the execution of the conveyance).

Suggested Answer

The Leasehold Reform Act 1967, s. 1, confers on a tenant of a leasehold house, occupying the house as his residence, a right to acquire on fair terms the freehold (or an extended lease) of the house. This right, however, is subject to certain conditions. A claim under the Act can only be made in respect of a 'house and premises' which, under s. 2(1) of the Act, includes any building designed or adopted for living in and reasonably so called, notwithstanding that the building is not structurally detached, or was or is not solely designed or adapted for living in, or is divided horizontally into flats or maisonettes. The scope of this provision was explored in *Sharpe* v *Duke Street Securities* (1987) 2 EGLR 106. Here, a tenant, who had acquired the leases of both an upper and a lower maisonette in the same property, and who had lived in both, was held to be living in a 'house' for the purposes of s. 2 of the 1967 Act (see also, *Malpas* v *St Ermin's Property Co. Ltd* (1992) 24 HLR 537 and *Duke of Westminster* v *Birrane* [1995] 3 All ER 416, where a basement area was held to form part of the house).

Section 2(3) of the Act provides that the premises accompanying a house may, for the purposes of the Act, include garages, gardens, yards, outhouses and appurtenances which, at the relevant time, are let to the tenant with the house and are occupied and used for the purposes of the house or any part of it by him (*Gaidowski* v *Conville and Caius College Cambridge* [1975] 1 WLR 1066 and *Methuen-Campbell* v *Walters* [1979] QB 525).

Section 3 of the Act provides that the lease must have originally been granted for a period exceeding 21 years as from its actual date of execution and delivery (*Roberts* v *Church Commissioners for England* [1972] 1 QB 278).

If the lease in question commenced before 1 April 1963, the rent must be less than two-thirds of the letting value of the premises, or less than two-thirds of the rateable value on the appropriate day if the lease was entered into on or after 1 April 1963 but before 1 April 1990. If, on the other hand, the lease in question commenced on or after 1 April 1990 (as in the present case), the rent must be less than £1,000 per annum for properties situated in London, or less than £250 in relation to properties situated elsewhere (see, s. 4 and s. 4A, as amended by the Leasehold Reform, Housing and Urban Development Act 1933, s. 65).

Although the Housing Act 1996 (see s. 106 and sch. 9) has now removed the low rent test under both the Leasehold Reform Act 1967 and the Leasehold Reform Housing and Urban Development Act 1993, this amendment only affects leases of houses and flats over 35 years. The low rent test, set out above, continues to apply for leases (as in the present case) between 21 years and 35 years.

The house and premises must be used for residential purposes (i.e., the tenant must occupy the house as his only or main residence, whether or not he uses it also for other purposes: s. 1). Moreover, to qualify for enfranchisement, the tenant must occupy all or part of the property let as his residence (*Harris* v *Swick Securities* [1969] 3 All ER 1131). In *Poland* v *Earl of Cadogan* [1980] 3 All ER 544, it was held that a tenant could still be in occupation of a house as his residence, for the purposes of the 1967 Act, even though absent for substantial periods, provided such a tenant could establish that he had evidenced a clear intention to maintain his occupation. Ultimately, it is a question of fact whether the tenant occupies the house as his main residence. In *Tandon* v *Trustees of Spurgeons Homes* [1982] AC 755, the House of Lords held that a house used for mixed business and residential purposes could fall within the 1967 Act.

It must also be established that the house was the tenant's only or main residence either for the last three years, or for periods amounting to three years out of the last 10 years.

If all the above conditions are fulfilled, the tenant will be able to enfranchise under the 1967 Act. To this end, it seems that Tom has a qualifying lease which, as from its date of execution and delivery, exceeds 21 years. It also appears that, being granted after 1 April 1990, Tom's lease is a lease at a qualifying low rent (i.e., his ground rent is less than £1,000 per annum, the premises being situated in Central London). It would also seem that the property in question (a terraced house) falls within the statutory definition of 'house and premises' and that Tom has resided there for the past three years. (Despite his absences from the house at weekends, Tom will still be regarded as occupying the house as his main residence, unless it is shown that he treated his mother's house in Brighton as his main residence — see the *Poland* case, above.) What may cause some difficulty is the mixed business and residential user. However, the *Tandon* case (above) shows that it is possible for a house with mixed business and residential user to qualify under the 1967 Act. Much will depend on the nature and extent of the business user; if the business user is limited, Tom may still qualify for enfranchisement.

The facts do not show any grounds which might prevent Tom from enfranchising (i.e., the Earl is not an exempt landlord under the Act, nor is there anything to suggest that he has an intention to develop the property or that he requires possession for occupation by himself or an adult member of his family: see ss. 17 and 18 of the 1967 Act, respectively).

Provided the necessary qualifying conditions are fulfilled, Tom may at any time serve on the Earl a notice of intention, in prescribed form, to acquire the freehold of the house. As soon as the notice has been served, a binding contract of sale is deemed to have come into existence. Tom can register this contract either as a minor interest by way of a notice or caution (if the house is registered land), or (if the house is unregistered) as a Class C(iv) land charge, so as to bind any third-party transferees.

After service of the notice, Tom may seek a release from the agreement to enfranchise either freely or for a consideration payable to the Earl.

The price payable will be fixed with reference to the value which the house, if sold on the open market by a willing seller, might be expected to realise on the basis of certain assumptions detailed in s. 9 of the Act, as amended by the

Leasehold Reform, Housing and Urban Development Act 1993, s. 66 and sch. 15. In default of agreement, the price payable will be determined by a local Leasehold Valuation Tribunal, with a right of appeal to the Lands Tribunal.

By virtue of s. 8(1) of the 1967 Act, the Earl, once served with Tom's notice and after such time as the price has been agreed, is obliged to convey to Tom the house and premises in fee simple free from any incumbrances attaching to the freehold land, subject only to the lease and incumbrances thereon created by Tom (e.g., mortgages, underleases etc.).

By virtue of s. 9(4), Tom will be responsible for paying the Earl's legal and other professional fees incurred in investigating and verifying Tom's claim, the valuation costs and conveyancing fees.

QUESTION 2

To what extent has the Leasehold Reform, Housing and Urban Development Act 1993 enabled lessees of blocks of flats to enfranchise or acquire extended leases?

Commentary

This question requires you to explain (in some depth) the statutory provisions on collective enfranchisement and leasehold extension contained in the Leasehold Reform, Housing and Urban Development Act 1993. Your answer should demonstrate a working knowledge of Pts I and II of the 1993 Act — no doubt, a daunting prospect for many students in view of the complexity of the statutory provisions!

For a helpful summary of the law, see Greenish, D.J.W., 'Leasehold Reform, Housing and Urban Development Act 1993' (1994) vol. 14/2 RRLR 7. See also, Foinette, C., and Pinkerton, M., 'Seize the Moment' [1999] EG 9909, 170, on the Government's recent Consultation Paper on leasehold reform.

Suggested Answer

The Leasehold Reform, Housing and Urban Development Act 1993 received Royal Assent in the Summer of 1993 and, in relation to its enfranchisement provisions, came into force on 1 November 1993. One of the most fundamental reforming measures introduced by Pt I of the Act is to give most owners of long leases of flats either a right to collective enfranchisement (i.e., a collective right

to buy the freehold of a block of flats), or an individual right to acquire a new
90-year lease.

(i)   *Collective enfranchisement*

For a building to qualify under the 1993 Act, it must fulfil certain conditions,
namely, it must:

(a)   be an independent building or be part of a building which is capable of
independent development;

(b)   contain two or more flats held by 'qualifying tenants';

(c)   not have a resident freeholder if the building is not a purpose-built
block of flats and comprises less than five units;

(d)   be in single freehold ownership;

(e)   have at least 90 per cent of the internal floor space occupied or intended
to be occupied for residential purposes; and

(f)   have at least two-thirds of the flats held by 'qualifying tenants'.

To be a 'qualifying tenant', the lessee must have a long lease (i.e., a lease which,
when originally granted, was for a term exceeding 21 years) at a low rent (i.e.,
a rent which, during the first year of the lease did not exceed either two-thirds
of the letting value in that year (if the lease was granted before 1 April 1963),
or two-thirds of the rateable value in that year (if the lease was granted on or
after 1 April 1963 but before 1 April 1990), or £1,000 per annum for London
properties or £250 per annum elsewhere (in any other cases)). (These low rent
limits have been removed under the Housing Act 1996 but only for leases over
35 years.) The lessee must also not own three or more flats in the building in
question.

A qualifying tenant may give notice to his landlord requiring details of the
various interests in the block. This notice places no commitment on the tenant
but the response to the notice is intended to provide the tenant with the
information necessary for him to ascertain whether the building contains
sufficient numbers of qualifying tenants for it to qualify for collective
enfranchisement. A landlord has 28 days to reply to such a notice. If the
building qualifies, and in order for enfranchisement to take place, at least

two-thirds of the qualifying tenants must be prepared to participate in the purchase (i.e., the 'participating tenants') and the participating tenants must comprise, in any event, not less than one-half of all the flats in the building, and at least one-half of the participating tenants must have each lived in their respective flats as their only or principal home for at least one year, or periods amounting to three years out of the previous 10 years.

Once it is established that the building qualifies and that there are sufficient numbers of qualifying tenants who wish to participate, it will be necessary to establish what price should be paid by the participating tenants to purchase the freehold. This will be the aggregate of the building's investment value to the freeholder, not less than one-half of the marriage value (i.e., the increased value attributable to the freehold by virtue of the participating tenants being able to grant themselves extended leases at nil premium and a peppercorn rent), and compensation for loss in the value of other property owned by the freeholder. The participating tenants will also need to agree on the vehicle by which to effect the purchase (i.e., the nominee purchaser), which will usually be a management company set up by the tenants, and organise the financing of the purchase (e.g., by a loan from a building society or bank).

The next process which the participating tenants must follow is set out in some detail in the Act. First, the tenants must serve on the landlord a s. 13 notice containing specified information, including the premises involved in the purchase, the interests to be acquired, the names of those applying, the price proposed and a date for reply (being not more than two months after the service of the s. 13 notice).

Once the s. 13 notice has been served, there follows a succession of procedural notices and counternotices between the freeholder and the nominee purchaser to establish the right to enfranchise, the terms of sale, the price to be paid etc. If the purchase proceeds to completion, the participating tenants, through the nominee purchaser, will become the freeholder of the building, subject to the various flat leases. In effect, the tenants will replace the existing freeholder so as to put them in a position to grant themselves extended leases.

(ii)   *Individual right to extend*

All qualifying tenants of flats, subject to certain conditions, have an individual right to extend their leases under the 1993 Act. In order to qualify, the tenant must be a tenant of a flat which he holds on a long lease at a low rent (the tests are the same as for collective enfranchisement) and which he has occupied as his only or principal home for three years or for periods amounting to three years out of the last 10 years.

The extended lease will be for a term expiring 90 years after the end of the current lease and will reserve a peppercorn rent. The landlord is entitled to oppose a claim for an extended lease on redevelopment grounds.

The premium to be paid by the tenant for the new extended lease will be the aggregate of the diminution in the flat's investment value to the landlord, not less than 50 per cent of the marketable value (i.e., the additional value released by replacing the existing lease with the extended lease), and compensation for loss in the value of other property owned by the freeholder.

The procedure to be followed is very similar to that for collective enfranchisement. The qualifying tenant can serve a preliminary notice to obtain information. Thereafter, he must serve his notice of claim which, *inter alia* must state a description of the flat, sufficient particulars to establish that the lease and tenant qualify, the premium being offered, the terms of the new lease, and a date by which the landlord must respond to the notice (being not less than two months). As with collective enfranchisement, there then follows a succession of procedural notices and counternotices between the parties to reach agreement on the terms of the sale and on the price. Any dispute over the terms are resolved by the court, whereas disagreement on price is referred to the Leasehold Valuation Tribunal with appeal to the Lands Tribunal.

The 1993 Act provides no limit to the number of times that a qualifying tenant can exercise his right to a lease extension.

12   Business Tenancies

INTRODUCTION

Here again, the subject lends itself to problem questions, although you may also find essay-type questions which ask you to consider, for example, whether the Landlord and Tenant Act 1954, Pt II draws a fair balance between the parties, or whether the machinery of Pt II works well and what reforms might be introduced (see Question 4).

Most business tenants have the benefit of two quite distinct statutory codes:

(a)   the Landlord and Tenant Act 1954, Pt II (as amended by the Law of Property Act 1969), which affords

(i)   security of tenure, and

(ii)   compensation for disturbance in certain cases where the landlord is entitled to possession; and

(b)   the Landlord and Tenant Act 1927 (as amended by the 1954 Act), which entitles the tenant to compensation for improvements on quitting the holding.

Security of tenure under Pt II of the 1954 Act is afforded by:

(a)   automatic continuance of the tenancy notwithstanding expiry of a fixed term or service of a notice to quit on a periodic tenant (s. 24);

(b)   compelling a landlord who desires possession to establish one or more specific grounds (listed in s. 30(1)), having made a formal statement of the grounds relied on *either* by notice of termination complying with s. 25 *or* by notice of opposition to a tenant's request for a new tenancy under s. 26;

(c) giving the tenant a right to apply for a new tenancy *either* pursuant to a request for a new tenancy under s. 26 *or* pursuant to a counternotice in response to a landlord's notice of termination served under s. 25. The right accrues once either procedure is initiated (s. 24).

The 1954 Act leaves the parties free to agree extensions and renewals (s. 28) and imposes no restrictions on rent. The Act is, therefore, of no immediate importance to the parties unless and until either the landlord is opposed to a renewal (or continuation of a periodic tenancy), or negotiations for a renewal break down. In the former case, the landlord would normally take the initiative by service of a s. 25 notice of termination. In the latter case, the deadlock is invariably broken by either the landlord serving a s. 25 notice stating that he would not oppose an application for a new tenancy, or the tenant serving a request for a new tenancy under s. 26. This course, however, is not open to periodic tenants. Given that a tenancy continues under Pt II on the same terms as granted, it is usual for the landlord to take the initiative under s. 25. It would be otherwise if the tenant wished to regularise his position, for example, prior to selling his business.

For a good summary of recent case law on Pt II procedures, see Wilkinson, H. W., 'Termination of a Business Lease', (1999) 149 NLJ 1489 and 1521 and Higgins, S., 'The Continuation Conundrum: Part II of the Landlord and Tenant Act 1954' [1997] Conv 119.

We have included three problem and four essay-type questions in this Chapter. We have not included a question on the various methods by which a landlord may seek to avoid Pt II protection, although this is also a fertile source for a good examination question in this field. The reader is, however, referred to Pawlowski, M., 'Avoiding Protection under Part II' [1996] RRLR vol. 16/2, pp. 29–35 for a summary of the various ways in which Pt II may be excluded. See also, *Receiver for the Metropolitan Police District* v *Palacegate Properties Ltd* [2000] 13 EG 187 (CA), for a recent case on the workings of s. 38 exclusion orders.

Our general advice for all examinations holds good for this subject. Read the question carefully, prepare a rough plan, list the relevant cases and, above all, ANSWER THE QUESTION AS SET!

QUESTION 1

Nigel is the landlord of business premises, the lease of which expires on 25 December 2001. The tenant has on several occasions paid the rent a few weeks late and is using the premises for a purpose other than that specified in the lease. In addition, Nigel has vague plans to demolish and reconstruct the premises, or alternatively to let them to his son who wants to set up a video business. Explain to Nigel:

(a) Which of the grounds under the Landlord and Tenant Act 1954, s. 30, are available to him in order to claim possession. In the case of each ground, you should consider what he will have to substantiate and the financial consequences of his choice of grounds.

(b) What steps he should take (and when) in order to claim possession, and what steps you would expect the tenant to take in response (assuming that the tenant does not wish to leave) and how the matter may eventually be resolved.

Commentary

This is a fairly typical problem question on the subject. There is a lot of ground to cover so you cannot afford to dwell on one point for too long at the expense of others. Remember that there are two parts to the question and your time is limited!

For a summary of the Pt II procedures, see Pawlowski, M., *Leasing Commercial Premises*, Oxford: Chandos Publishing (Oxford) Ltd, 1999, Ch. 8. For a good overview of the workings of ground (f) (intention to redevelop), see Dean, B., and Clark, R., 'Into the Valley of Decision' [1996] EG 9644, 176 and Pawlowski, M., 'Three Bites at the Cherry?' [1996] RRLR vol. 16/3, pp. 7–13.

Suggested Answer

(a) Four possible grounds present themselves on the facts. First, Nigel may seek to rely on s. 30(1)(b) of the 1954 Act (i.e., persistent delay in paying rent). Here, Nigel must show that a new tenancy ought not to be granted in view of the delay. In *Hopcutt* v *Carver* (1969) 209 EG 1069, the tenant had been consistently late in payments of rent during the preceding two years, at one time delaying for five months. No offer was made by the tenant for payment in advance in the future, nor was any security offered. On these facts, a new lease was refused. In *Hurstfell Ltd* v *Leicester Square Property Co. Ltd* [1988]

37 EG 109, the Court of Appeal reiterated that there was an obligation on the tenant to explain the reason for past failures and to satisfy the court that, if a new lease was granted, there would be no recurrence of the late payments. See also *Horowitz* v *Ferrand* [1956] CLY 4843. In the present case, it is unlikely that Nigel would succeed on this ground bearing in mind that the rent was paid only a few weeks late and (presumably) not 'persistently' in arrears.

Secondly, the tenant is using the premises for a purpose not specified in the lease. Here, Nigel can rely on s. 30(1)(c) of the 1954 Act (i.e., substantial breaches of obligations under the tenancy or any other reason connected with the use or management of the holding). Once again, this is a discretionary ground in so far as the breach of covenant must be such that a new tenancy ought not to be granted (*Eichner* v *Midland Bank Executor and Trustee Co. Ltd* [1970] 1 WLR 1120). It may be that, in the present case, the breach is not serious enough to warrant a refusal of a new lease.

Thirdly, we are told that Nigel has vague plans to demolish and reconstruct the premises. This may afford a basis for opposing a new tenancy under s. 30(1)(f) (i.e., intention to demolish or reconstruct, or effect substantial work of construction on the holding). In order to succeed, Nigel would need to establish that he has the necessary intention to demolish etc. at the date of the hearing and that he requires legal possession of the holding (i.e., the work could not be done satisfactorily unless he obtains exclusive occupation). A bare assertion of intention is not enough and Nigel will fail if serious difficulties (e.g., obtaining planning permission or finance) lie ahead (*Betty's Cafes* v *Phillips Furnishing Stores Ltd* [1959] AC 20, adopting the test laid down in *Cunliffe* v *Goodman* [1950] 2 KB 237 with regard to the similar provision in the Landlord and Tenant Act 1927, s. 18). It has been recently held, however, that lack of planning permission for the development need not be fatal under ground (f). It is sufficient if there is a reasonable prospect of obtaining permission, which is not fanciful or one that would be sensibly ignored by a reasonable landlord: see *Cadogan* v *McCarthy & Stone Developments Ltd* [1996] EGCS 94 and *Aberdeen Steak Houses Group Ltd* v *Crown Estate Commissioners* [1997] 2 EGLR 107.

The landlord's intention must be to effect the work on the termination of the current tenancy. In Nigel's case, we are told that he has only 'vague plans' to carry out redevelopment work. Unless Nigel can avail himself of a declaration under s. 31(2) (i.e., the near-miss provisions), he will not, it is submitted, succeed under this ground because of the lack of the requisite intention on his part.

Fourthly, Nigel is considering letting the premises to his son who wants to set up a video business. It would seem that s. 30(1)(g) has no application here since Nigel does not intend to occupy the holding for his own business or residence. In this connection, the intended business must be the landlord's business to be carried on by him in the holding (*Hunt* v *Decca Navigator Co. Ltd* (1972) 222 EG 625), except where the landlord is a trustee and the business is to be carried on by a beneficiary (s. 41(2)), or where the landlord has a controlling interest in a company and it is intended that the company will occupy (s. 30(3)), or where the landlord is a company and the business is to be carried on by another company in the same group (s. 42(3)). None of these exceptions seems to apply in the present case.

The financial consequence of Nigel relying on grounds (b) and (c) is that he will not be obliged to pay the tenant compensation for disturbance under s. 37 of the 1954 Act. The position is otherwise if Nigel successfully objects on grounds (f) or (g). The obligation to pay compensation for tenant's improvements carried out during the tenancy under the Landlord and Tenant Act 1927 will, however, apply in either case.

(b)   Nigel will need to serve a s. 25 notice of termination on the tenant not more than 12 months and not less than six months before the termination date specified in the notice. The specified termination date must not be earlier than the date at which the tenancy would expire at common law (i.e., 25 December 2001). The notice must also require the tenant to notify Nigel in writing within two months whether or not he (the tenant) will be willing to give up possession at the date specified in the notice. Nigel's notice must also state whether he would oppose an application to the court for a new tenancy and, if so, on which grounds (mentioned in s. 30(1)).

There appears to be no provision for amendment and so a landlord cannot depart from the grounds stated in his notice. Moreover, the withdrawal of a notice with a view to serving a fresh notice stating different grounds seems to be excluded by s. 24(1). Nigel should therefore be advised to state his grounds carefully, although the court will excuse minor slips so long as the tenant has fair warning of the case he has to answer (*Barclays Bank Ltd* v *Ascott* [1961] 1 WLR 717).

Nigel's tenant will, no doubt, serve a counternotice in response stating that he is not willing to give up possession at the date specified in the s. 25 notice of termination. Assuming he serves the requisite counternotice in time, the tenant must then make an application to court for the grant of a new tenancy not less than two months and not more than four months after the giving of the s. 25 notice. These time limits are strict (*Meah* v *Sector Properties Ltd* [1974] 1 WLR 547), although the court does have power to enlarge the time available for service of a tenant's application (*Ali* v *Knight* (1984) 272 EG 1165 (county court); *Joan Barrie* v *GUS Property Management Ltd* (1981) 259 EG 628 (High Court)). The time limits are also capable of waiver by the landlord (*Zenith Investments (Torquay) Ltd* v *Kammins Ballrooms Co. Ltd (No. 2)* [1971] 1 WLR 1751). The assumption is that Nigel is the competent landlord for the purpose of these proceedings.

As to how the matter may eventually be resolved, this will depend on whether Nigel is successful in opposing the grant of a new tenancy. If so, the tenancy will end on the date specified in the s. 25 notice (25 December 2001), or three months after the final disposal of the application by the court, whichever is the later (s. 64). If Nigel is unsuccessful, the court will be obliged to grant the tenant a new tenancy of the holding (s. 29). If the parties fail to agree on the terms of the new tenancy, the court will decide having regard to the guidelines laid down in s. 32 (the property), s. 33 (the duration), s. 34 (the rent), and s. 35 (other terms).

QUESTION 2

'In order for a tenancy to fall within section 23 of the Landlord and Tenant Act 1954, the property comprised in the tenancy must include premises which are "occupied by the tenant and are so occupied for the purposes of a business carried on by him or for those and other purposes".' (s. 23(1)).

Discuss.

Commentary

Superficially this may appear a simple question, but in fact there is considerable opportunity for the well-prepared student to examine a number of different points and illustrate them by reference to the case law.

Apart from considering what constitutes 'occupation' for the purpose of s. 23(1), you should also examine the meaning of the word 'business' and, in particular, draw the distinction between bodies of persons where virtually any activity suffices, and an individual where engagement in a 'trade, profession or employment' is essential (s. 23(2)). The reference to 'those and other purposes' should also trigger a discussion of mixed business and residential user. Lastly, a brief reference to the meaning of the word 'premises' in s. 23(1) will gain additional marks.

You will obviously need to make reference to the House of Lords ruling in *Graysim Holdings Ltd* v *P & O Property Holdings Ltd* [1996] 1 AC 329, on the subject of 'dual occupation' of business premises.

The secret of a good answer, therefore, is to select the material which most directly addresses the question.

Suggested Answer

A tenant who wishes to qualify for protection under the Landlord and Tenant Act 1954, Pt II, must bring his tenancy within the requirements of s. 23(1). Thus, if the tenant ceases to occupy for the purposes of his business at the expiry of a fixed term, there can be no continuance of his tenancy under s. 24 (*Esselte AB* v *Pearl Assurance plc* [1997] 1 WLR 891 and *Webb* v *Sandown Sports Club Ltd* [2000] EGCS 13). If a business tenant temporarily vacates the premises while they are being repaired or following a fire, he will not lose his protection under Pt II provided that he has the intention to return as soon as the premises are fit for occupation (*Morrisons Holdings Ltd* v *Manders Property (Wolverhampton) Ltd* [1976] 1 WLR 533 and *I. and H. Caplan Ltd* v *Caplan (No. 2)* [1963] 1 WLR 1247). It is not necessary for him to establish that he has a reasonable prospect of bringing this about in that the premises will be reinstated in the near or reasonable future (*Flairline Properties Ltd* v *Hassan* [1998] 169 EGCS 169). In most cases the tenant will be in personal occupation of the premises, but it has been held that a tenant who occupies a building for the sole purpose of sub-letting parts falls outside the section (*Bagettes Ltd* v *GP Estates Ltd* [1956] Ch 290). Such an occupation, although for a 'business', is not one to which Pt II applies since it involves the progressive elimination of the holding. The position is otherwise, however, if the tenant retains a sufficient degree of control over the occupied parts (*Lee-Verhulst (Investments) Ltd* v *Harwood Trust* [1973] QB 204 and *William Boyer & Sons Ltd* v *Adams* (1976) 32 P & CR 89).

In *Graysim Holdings Ltd* v *P & O Property Holdings Ltd* [1996] 1 AC 329, the House of Lords ruled that intermediate landlords who are not themselves in occupation of the premises are not protected under Pt II because the 1954 Act makes no provision for dual occupation of premises (i.e., a business tenant and his sub-tenant cannot enjoy statutory protection under Pt II in respect of the same premises). The House of Lords, however, did not rule out the possibility that, in exceptional cases, the rights reserved by the tenant might be so extensive that he would remain in occupation of the property for the purposes of Pt II. The crux of the matter lies in the distinction between the two earlier cases (mentioned above), namely, *Bagettes* and *Lee-Verhulst*. In the former, the residential flats were let unfurnished and, although the tenant provided hot water for the sub-tenants and cleaned the common parts, the 'service' element was negligible: see also, *Bassairi Ltd* v *Camden London Borough Council* [1998] EGCS 27. By contrast, in *Lee-Verhulst*, the lettings comprised furnished rooms with substantial services (i.e., supply of bedlinen, daily cleaning of rooms and regular change of linen, and provision of light meals if required). The Court of Appeal held that, in view of the degree of control and extent of the services provided, the tenant 'occupied' the entire premises for the purposes of its business, namely that of 'providing furnished accommodation and services for those residing there'. In *Graysim* itself, it was suggested that where the letting takes the form of a *sub-tenancy*, the sub-tenant will be entitled to exclusive possession of the sub-let part and, hence, will be the 'occupier' to the exclusion of the tenant. At the other end of the spectrum, however, where the occupancy takes the form of a *licence*, there will often be more room for argument that the tenant retains occupation of the property because the rights granted by a licence will be less extensive than those comprised in a sub-tenancy. The key elements in the *Lee-Verhulst* case were the provision of services to the occupants (who were characterised as licensees) and the unrestricted entry to each room necessary to perform those services: see also, *Linden* v *Department of Health and Social Security* [1986] 1 WLR 164, to the same effect, involving eight self-contained flats managed by the district health authority. By contrast, in *Graysim*, neither the tenant nor his agents had any right of access to the units, nor did they have keys or means of access. All the occupants had exclusive possession and each was a sub-tenant in respect of his unit.

Occupation preparatory to carrying on business is sufficient (e.g., occupying a seaside cafe during the winter months) (*Artemiou* v *Procopiou* [1966] QB 878, *per* Salmon LJ at p. 890). Occupation by servants of the tenant may also be sufficient, provided the premises are occupied for a purpose necessary to the furtherance of the business and not merely for its convenience (*Chapman* v *Freeman* [1978] 1 WLR 129). It seems, however, that the tenant cannot occupy through a company unless it is the tenant's agent or manager (*Christina* v *Seear* (1985) 275 EG 898 and *Nozari-Zadeh* v *Pearl Assurance plc* (1987) 283 EG 457, where the 'alter ego' argument failed). However, where the tenancy is held on trust, occupation by all or any of the beneficiaries under the trust, and the carrying on of a business by all or any of the beneficiaries, falls to be treated for the purposes of s. 23 as equivalent occupation or the carrying on of a business by the tenant (*Frish Ltd* v *Barclays Bank Ltd* [1951] 2 QB 541, *per* Lord Evershed MR at p. 549).

In *Cafeteria (Keighley) Ltd* v *Harrison* (1956) 168 EG 668, Denning LJ expressly declared that business premises could be occupied by an agent or manager of the tenant. See also *Hills (Patents) Ltd* v *University College Hospital Board of Governors* [1956] 1 QB 90, where Denning LJ observed that while 'possession in law is, of course, single and exclusive . . . occupation may be shared with others or had on behalf of others'. In *Ross Auto Wash Ltd* v *Herbert* (1978) 250 EG 971, Fox J held that a tenant company could be in occupation of business premises even though another company was acting as its manager. Moreover, s. 42 of the 1954 Act provides, *inter alia*, that the occupation and carrying on of a business by one member of a group of companies of which the tenant is a member is deemed to be the occupation and conduct of the business of the tenant. For these purposes, a company is a member of another if it is a subsidiary of the other or of a third body corporate.

It is possible for the character of a tenancy to change from residential to business. A tenancy of residential premises will be a business tenancy if the tenant's business activity is a significant purpose of the occupation and is not merely incidental to the residential occupation (*Cheryl Investments Ltd* v *Saldanha; Royal Life Saving Society* v *Page* [1978] 1 WLR 1329). Contrast *Gurton* v *Parrott* [1991] 18 EG 161, where it was held that the tenant occupied the premises for the purpose of her residence only and that the running of the business of dog kennels was merely incidental, being something akin to a hobby (see also *Wright* v *Mortimer* (1996) 72 P & CR D36, where the business purposes were held not to be a significant element in the occupation).

The word 'business' is defined in s. 23(2). Where bodies of persons are concerned, 'any activity' suffices (*Addiscombe Garden Estates* v *Crabbe* [1958] 1 QB 513, lawn tennis club). However, it has been held that the activity for this purpose must be something which is correlative to the conceptions involved in the words 'trade, profession or employment' (*Hillil Property & Investment Co. Ltd* v *Naraine Pharmacy Ltd* (1979) 252 EG 1013). In that case, a company tenant who used premises simply for dumping waste building materials from another property was held not to be indulging in an 'activity' within s. 23(2).

On the other hand, where individuals are concerned, they must be engaged in a 'trade, profession or employment' (*Abernethie* v *A.M. & J. Kleiman Ltd*

[1970] 1 QB 10, carrying on of a sunday school held to be a gratuitous, spare-time activity). See also *Lewis* v *Weldcrest Ltd* [1978] 1 WLR 1107 (taking in of lodgers where no commercial advantage involved held insufficient).

It should be stressed that Pt II does not apply where the tenant is carrying on a business use in breach of covenant, unless the immediate landlord or his predecessor in title has consented thereto or the immediate landlord has acquiesced therein (s. 23(4) and *Bell* v *Alfred Franks and Bartlett Co. Ltd* [1980] 1 WLR 340).

Lastly, the word 'premises' in s. 23(1) has been held to include the letting of incorporeal hereditaments together with land (*Stumbles* v *Whitley* [1930] AC 544, fishing rights). In *Bracey* v *Read* [1963] Ch 88, it was held that premises were not confined to buildings but included the land on which the buildings were erected. Thus, the letting of gallops was held to come within Pt II. Contrast, however, *Land Reclamation Ltd* v *Basildon District Council* (1979) 250 EG 549, where it was held that a right of way, which stood by itself and was not the subject of a more comprehensive demise including a corporeal hereditament, fell outside Pt II.

QUESTION 3

John has a 10-year lease which will expire on 30 June 2001. The premises consist of a ground floor shop with a flat above and a basement. John occupies the shop for the purpose of his video rental business and lives in the flat. He has sub-let the basement to a nearby solicitor on a monthly tenancy for the purpose of storing old files. John's landlord, Bill, bought the freehold in 1998.

In August 2000, John received a notice in proper form in respect of the whole premises from Bill, specifying 30 June 2001 as the termination date and stating that he would oppose any renewal of John's lease under the Landlord and Tenant Act 1954, s. 30(1)(f) and (g). Bill intends to refurbish the property and has vague plans to turn it into a wine bar, which he hopes to run himself. John wants to remain in the premises.

(a) Advise John as to the steps he should take to protect his position and as to the likelihood of his obtaining a new lease. If he does so, what principles will govern the establishment of its terms?

[15 marks]

(b) How would your advice differ if John was the lessee but ran his business through a company, Visionhire Ltd, in which he owned all the shares?

[10 marks]

Commentary

This question should provide few problems for the student who has revised business tenancies thoroughly. Part (a) calls for a broad outline of the statutory machinery for termination, including the guidelines for determining the terms of a new tenancy by the court. Part (b) is more specific and requires you to consider whether a business tenant can occupy the premises through a company which is wholly owned by him. There are several cases dealing with this point, and unless you are familiar with this case law you should think twice before attempting this question.

For a summary of the cases on occupation through a company, see Pawlowski, M., 'Business Occupation Through Third Parties' [1988] EG 8840, 20.

Suggested Answer

(a) In order to preserve his position, John should respond to Bill's s. 25 notice of termination by serving a counternotice on him stating that he is unwilling to give up possession on the date specified in the notice. He must do this within the prescribed time limit (i.e., within two months of the giving of the s. 25 notice). This is a condition precedent to the tenant's application for a new tenancy under s. 24 of the 1954 Act (*Chiswell* v *Grifton Land and Estates Ltd* [1975] 1 WLR 1181). There is no prescribed form for the tenant's counternotice so a simple letter notifying Bill that he is not prepared to give up possession at the date specified in the notice will suffice.

John must also make an application to court for the grant of a new tenancy not less than two months and not more than four months after the giving of the s. 25 notice of termination (s. 29(3)). These time limits are strict (*Meah* v *Sector Properties Ltd* [1974] 1 WLR 547), although the court does have power to enlarge the time in exceptional circumstances (*Ali* v *Knight* (1984) 272 EG 1165 (county court) and *Joan Barrie* v *GUS Property Management Ltd* (1981) 259 EG 628 (High Court)).

As to the likelihood of John obtaining a new lease, this will depend on whether Bill can successfully object to the grant of a new tenancy on the ground specified in his s. 25 notice. In order to succeed under s. 30(1)(f), Bill must show that:

(a) he intends to demolish, or reconstruct or effect substantial work of construction on the *holding* on the termination of the tenancy; and

(b) he requires legal possession of the *holding* (i.e., the work could not be done satisfactorily unless he obtains exclusive occupation).

A bare assertion of intention is not enough and Bill will need to establish that he has a reasonable prospect of obtaining the requisite planning permission, finance, builders etc. in order to carry out his refurbishment plans (*Reohorn* v *Barry Corporation* [1956] 1 WLR 845, *Gregson* v *Cyril Lord* [1963] 1 WLR 41 and *Cadogan* v *McCarthy & Stone Developments Ltd* [1996] EGCS 94).

The word 'holding' is defined in s. 23(3) of the 1954 Act as meaning the property comprised in the tenancy, there being excluded any part thereof which is occupied neither by the tenant nor by any person employed by the tenant and so employed for the purposes of the business by reason of which the tenancy is one to which Pt II applies. Thus, it would seem that Bill would not be entitled to possession of the basement in any event since this does not form part of the holding for the purposes of s. 23(3).

It is surprising that Bill has relied on s. 30(1)(g) (i.e., intention to occupy the holding for landlord's business) in his s. 25 notice of termination. It is to be noted that Bill purchased the freehold during the last five years ending with the termination of the tenancy and thus falls foul of the exclusion to ground (g) under s. 30(2) (*Diploma Laundry Ltd* v *Surrey Timber Co. Ltd* [1955] 2 QB 604 and *VCS Carpark Management Ltd* v *Regional Railways North East Ltd* [2000] 1 All ER 403 (CA)). In any event, in order to have succeeded under this ground, Bill would need to have shown not only that he had a genuine *bona fide* intention to occupy the holding but also, on an objective test, that he had a reasonable prospect of bringing about this occupation by his own act or volition (*Gregson* v *Cyril Lord Ltd* [1963] 1 WLR 41). The wisdom or long-term viability of the landlord's proposed business are irrelevant in determining the requisite intention under s. 30(1)(g). Moreover, it appears that the absence of detailed plans, permissions and consents will also not necessarily denote lack of intention. The crucial factor in all cases is the reality of the landlord's intention to start the proposed business, not the likelihood of its ultimate success (*Dolgellau Golf Club* v *Hett* [1998] 34 EG 87 and *Gatwick Parking Service Ltd* v *Sargent* [2000] EG 11). As already mentioned, however, ground (g) is not open to Bill in view of his purchase of the freehold in 1998.

Assuming that Bill is unsuccessful in opposing John's application for a new tenancy, then the court must grant a new tenancy (s. 29). If the parties are unable to agree the terms of the new tenancy, the court will set them, subject to various limits as to property, duration, rent and other terms.

As a general rule, the grant must be of the *holding* as existing at the date of the order, nothing more and nothing less (s. 32). That being the case, John will be granted a new tenancy of the ground floor shop and flat only to the exclusion of the basement premises (*Narcissi* v *Wolfe* [1960] Ch 10). However, Bill may insist on the grant of the entire premises comprised in the current lease, if so minded (s. 32(2)). Unless the parties agree otherwise, John will be entitled to the re-grant of easements or profits enjoyed under the current lease (s. 32(3)).

As to duration, the court is empowered to grant such term as is reasonable, subject to an upper limit of 14 years (s. 33). However, the court has full discretion to order a short term where the landlord fails to establish grounds (d) to (g) but persuades the court that he is likely to be able to establish such grounds in the near future (see, e.g., *Upsons Ltd* v *E. Robins Ltd* [1956] 1 QB 131). Instead of granting a short term, the court may insert a break clause allowing the landlord to determine the lease when ready to redevelop (*McCombie* v *Grand Junction Co. Ltd* [1962] 1 WLR 581). This may be of relevance to Bill who may not be able to establish the requisite intention at the specified date of termination.

The rent to be determined is an open market rent disregarding prestige (or adverse image) attaching to the holding, goodwill and certain tenant's improvements (s. 34).

As to the other terms, s. 35 directs the court to have regard to the terms of the current tenancy and to all relevant circumstances in determining the terms of the new tenancy other than duration and rent. The basic principle is that the landlord is not entitled without justification to the insertion of terms in the new tenancy which are more onerous than the terms in the current tenancy (*Gold* v *Brighton Corporation* [1956] 1 WLR 1291 and *Cardshops Ltd* v *Davies* [1971] 1 WLR 591). The burden of persuading a court to change the terms of the current tenancy is on the party proposing them, and the court must be satisfied that they are fair and reasonable in all the circumstances (*O'May* v *City of London Real Property Co. Ltd* [1983] 2 AC 726).

(b) If John was the lessee but ran his business through a company in which he owned all the shares, it could be argued that he was not in occupation of the holding for the purpose of his business within the meaning of s. 23(1). In *Pegler v Craven* [1952] 2 QB 69, the plaintiff was the tenant of premises comprising living accommodation and a shop. The business of the shop was carried on by a company, half the shares of which were held by the tenant, and he was the managing director. The Court of Appeal held that he was not the occupier of the shop since the business of the shop was the business of the company and was not the tenant's business. Lord Evershed MR, however, left open the question whether, in some circumstances, it could be argued that a company in actual occupation was but the *alter ego* of the tenant, particularly where the tenant was the beneficial owner of all (or substantially all) the shares issued in the company so that the tenant remained in legal theory in occupation of the premises.

The point was taken up in *Christina v Seear* (1985) 275 EG 898, where the tenants owned all the shares in the company and therefore controlled it. They argued that the premises were occupied by them for the purposes of a business carried on by them within s. 23(1), in that the company was a mere vehicle or *alter ego* through which the business was carried on by them. The Court of Appeal, rejecting this argument, held that the tenants did not bring themselves within s. 23(1). The same result was reached in *Nozari-Zadeh v Pearl Assurance plc* (1987) 283 EG 457, where it was intimated that the position might be different if the company in question was merely the agent or manager of the tenant. In this connection, it has been expressly declared that business premises could be occupied by an agent or manager (*Cafeteria (Keighley) Ltd v Harrison* (1956) 168 EG 668, *per* Denning LJ). In *Ross Auto Wash Ltd v Herbert* (1978) 250 EG 971, Fox J held that a tenant company could be in occupation of business premises even though another company was acting as its manager.

Lastly, reference may be made to s. 41 of the 1954 Act, which provides, *inter alia*, that when a tenancy is held on trust, occupation by all or any of the beneficiaries under the trust, and the carrying on of a business by all or any of the beneficiaries, shall be treated as equivalent occupation or the carrying on of a business by the tenant. This provision, therefore, may successfully be used to overcome the difficulty that arose in the *Pegler, Christina* and *Nozari-Zadeh* line of cases; but it should be noted that s. 41 can be used only if the terms of the tenant's lease permit the actual entry into occupation and carrying on of the business by the company.

QUESTION 4

'The Law Commission's analysis of the workings of Part II of the 1954 Act supports the view that both abolition, at one extreme, and changing to a different scheme of statutory protection at the other are undesirable. Instead, the proposals address areas of the 1954 Act, both substantive and procedural, which have caused difficulties or anomalies.'

What areas have caused 'difficulties or anomalies', and how does the Law Commission seek to deal with them?

Commentary

This question seeks to test your knowledge of the broader issues governing the workings of the Landlord and Tenant Act 1954, Pt II.

You should be aware that the Law Commission published its final proposals for reform in this area in 1992: see, 'Business Tenancies: A Periodic Review of the Landlord and Tenant Act 1954 Part II', Law Com. No. 208 (1992). Prior to this, the Commission published a working paper on Pt II of the 1954 Act (Working Paper No. 111, 1988). For a review of the Law Commission's proposals, see Martin, J., 'Business Tenancies — The Proposed Reforms' [1997] RRLR vol. 17/1, pp. 26–33, Balance, G., 'A Review of the Workings of Part II of the Landlord and Tennt Act 1954' [2000] 1 RRLR, pp. 3–11 and [2000] 2 RRLR, pp. 75–83, Murdoch, S., 'Law Commission Proposals for Reform' [1993] EG 9303, 106; Ballaster, R., 'The Law Commission White Paper (No. 208): Periodic Review of the Landlord and Tenant Act 1954 — Part II' [1993] RRLR vol. 13/4, p. 29; Williams, D., 'The Law Commission's Proposals' [1988] EG 8848, 61, and Fogel, S. and Freedman, P., '1954 Act — Some Thoughts on Reform' (1985) 275 EG 118 and 227.

Remember that you are asked to examine the problem areas *and* to consider the Law Commission's proposals for dealing with them.

Suggested Answer

The Law Commission published its final proposals for the amendment of the Landlord and Tenant Act 1954, Pt II, in November 1992. Prior to that (in 1988), it published a Working Paper on the subject analysing the practical problems of the 1954 Act's operations and procedures.

The Commission has taken the view that the principles of Pt II are acceptable but that its central procedures need some re-examination. Most of the proposals are, therefore, of a detailed and technical nature, although some (e.g., on interim rent) are more substantive.

The Commission recognised that anomalies arise in the current interpretation of the occupation of property for the purposes of a business. The existing provisions do not work consistently since an individual tenant has no protection if a company which he controls trades on the premises (*Christina* v *Seear* (1985) 275 EG 898), while an individual landlord can oppose renewal on the basis that a company that he controls is intending to trade from the premises (s. 30(3)). It is, therefore, suggested that s. 23(1) be extended so that it confers protection both where a tenant is an individual and the business is run by a company which he controls, and where the tenant is a company and the business is run by the individual who controls the company.

The Commission also recommends that there should be an additional ground of opposition to allow a company landlord to oppose renewal where an individual who controls the landlord company intends to use the premises for *his* business (i.e., a new para. (h)). It is also proposed that the five-year rule (currently applicable to ground (g)) be extended to cover the new para. (h)).

In order to tidy up a number of other anomalies in this area, it is proposed that the statutory definition of a group of companies should be extended to cover the situation where companies are controlled by the same individual (whereas at present they must be controlled by a holding company).

It was also recognised that the current provisions regarding contracting-out are unnecessarily complicated by the need to make a court application. Thus it is suggested that this requirement be abolished and replaced by compliance with a series of formalities, including the need to endorse the agreement to contract out of the tenancy agreement coupled with a statutorily prescribed statement explaining the nature of the tenant's statutory rights and a declaration (signed by the tenant) that he has read and understood the terms of the agreement and the statement. The Commission also proposes that agreements to surrender should be subject to the same formal requirements as contracted-out leases.

Another area of current dissatisfaction lies in the workings of s. 40 of the 1954 Act. It is suggested that this section be extended to oblige a tenant to reveal whether any subtenancies are contracted out, and both sides would be required to reveal (where known) the identity of the owner(s) of a split reversion. The party who provides information in response to a s. 40 notice would also be under a duty to update that information for six months following the service of the notice. A failure to provide the required information would give rise to a civil action for breach of statutory duty. This would make clear that there was a sanction for non-compliance.

Apart from various minor amendments to other statutory notices, the Commission concluded that no practical purpose would be achieved by the retention of a tenant's counternotice indicating whether he is willing to give up possession. In reality, this is served virtually automatically by tenants regardless of their plans. On the other hand, it can work unfairly to deprive ill-advised or disorganised tenants of statutory protection. For these reasons, it is proposed that the tenant's counternotice be abolished.

The view was also expressed in the Commission's Working Paper that steps should be taken to reduce the number of court applications which were commenced simply to safeguard the tenant's rights. It is proposed, therefore, that a *landlord* should be able to make an application under the Act and that this may take one of two forms. The landlord may apply simply for the termination of the current tenancy, a procedure that would be adopted in cases where the landlord was opposing renewal on one of the statutory grounds. Alternatively, a landlord could apply for the renewal of the tenancy, a process which would mirror the tenant's right to make a similar application. Coupled with this, the Commission proposes to make extendible the time limits for any court application.

A crucial change proposed to the current law relates to interim rent. The changes recommended by the Commission are based on the belief that interim rent provisions which are fair will prevent both the manipulation of the current notice provisions to achieve a rental advantage and undue protraction of the negotiation process. Accordingly, it is proposed that either a landlord or a tenant should be able to apply for interim rent. This, it is hoped, will eradicate the unfairness which currently enables a landlord to drag out the statutory procedures in order to ensure that the tenant continues to pay a contractual rent which exceeds current market levels.

In order to prevent the prolonging of liability to pay the contractual rent, it is further recommended that interim rent should be payable from the *earliest* date which *could have been specified* in the s. 25 notice or s. 26 request, wherever it is the *other* party who is applying for interim rent. Coupled with this is the proposal that, in cases where there is no serious doubt that the tenant will be able to renew, the level of interim rent should be fixed at the level of the new rent payable at the commencement of the lease. In such an instance, the tenant will thus be paying the market rent under the new lease from the date specified in the s. 25 notice or s. 26 request and (possibly) from the earliest date which could be specified therein. In other cases, the existing rules, which allow for a variety of discounts to the market rent, would continue to apply subject to one amendment. This is that, when determining the rent, regard should be had to the rent payable under any subtenancy. This is designed to prevent the adverse effect which can result where a tenant is required to pay an interim rent of the whole of the property to his landlord in circumstances where he cannot extract an interim rent from his subtenant.

No doubt, the proposal that in incontrovertible applications for renewal the new market rent can be backdated to the term date of the current tenancy, will be most attractive to landlords. Indeed, the Commission's proposals are generally to be welcomed as simplifying the procedures for renewal.

QUESTION 5

In what circumstances will a business tenant be eligible for compensation for improvements undertaken to the demised premises? How does this form of compensation differ from compensation for disturbance?

Commentary

This is a relatively easy essay question on a business tenant's compensation rights. It is the sort of question which should leave you in no doubt as to whether it is 'on' or not. The subject matter is immediately clear and you have either revised this topic or not! If you are lucky enough to have studied the subject prior to the exam, this is a 'give-away' question and you should have no difficulty in scoring high marks.

Notice that there are really two parts to this question — you must, therefore, give a *balanced* answer which shows the examiner that you understand the differences between the two types of compensation.

The rules governing the amount of compensation payable for disturbance are quite complex. For a good summary, see McLoughlin, P., 'Compensation for Disturbance of Business Tenants' [1990] EG 9033, 22. On the subject of compensation for improvements, see Pawlowski, M., 'Compensation for

Improvements' [1992] RRLR vol. 13/2, p. 110 and, more recently, Anyamene, R., 'Recovery Programme' [1999] 9926 EG 148, containing a useful diagram of the relevant procedures.

Suggested Answer

The right to compensation for improvements is governed by the Landlord and Tenant Act 1927, Pt I (as amended by the Landlord and Tenant Act 1954). In relation to improvements, Pt I applies to any premises held under a lease used wholly or partly for carrying on any trade, profession or business (except a lease of agricultural holdings), mining leases, or written leases where the tenant is expressly the holder of an office or employment under the landlord (s. 17).

The tenant is entitled to compensation only at the termination of the tenancy and upon quitting the demised premises. In addition, the tenant must have complied with a number of pre-conditions. First, the tenant must show an 'improvement' on his holding made by him or his predecessors in title. In order to qualify, the improvement must:

(a)   be of such a nature as to be calculated to add to the letting value of the holding at the termination of the tenancy;

(b)   be reasonable and suitable to the character of the holding, and

(c)   not diminish the value of any other property belonging to the same landlord or to any superior landlord.

Secondly, the tenant must have served on the landlord a notice of intention to effect the improvement. The notice of intention must be served on the landlord prior to the commencement of the works and contain a specification and plan showing the proposed improvement and the part of the premises affected. If the landlord makes no objection to the proposed improvement, the tenant may go ahead and carry out the works without recourse to litigation. If, on the other hand, the landlord, within three months after service of the tenant's notice, serves on the tenant a notice of objection, the tenant must then apply to the court for a certificate that the improvement is a proper one if he wishes to proceed with the works. The landlord may object to the proposed improvement on a variety of different grounds. For example, he may seek to argue that the proposed works do not comprise an 'improvement' within the meaning of the 1927 Act, or that the tenant is outside the scope of the Act. In particular, the landlord may object on the ground that he has offered to execute the improvement himself in consideration of a reasonable increase in rent, or of an increase to be determined by the court. If the landlord carries out the works, no compensation is payable under the 1927 Act, but if he defaults the court may then issue a certificate that the improvement is a proper one and compensation will be available.

Thirdly, the tenant must have completed the improvement within the time agreed with the landlord or fixed by the court. Once the tenant has executed the improvement, he is entitled to request the landlord to furnish him with a certificate that the improvement has been duly executed. If the landlord fails or refuses, the court may grant the certificate.

Lastly, the tenant must give notice to the landlord of his claim for compensation. There are detailed time limits specified in s. 47 of the 1954 Act as to the service of the tenant's notice. The amount of compensation is fixed by agreement between the parties or, in default of agreement, by the court.

The right to compensation for disturbance differs in a number of respects. This form of compensation is essentially intended to compensate the tenant for the loss of goodwill attached to the holding. It is available to the tenant where the landlord successfully objects to the grant of a new tenancy on grounds (e), (f) or (g) of s. 30(1) of the 1954 Act (s. 37(1)). The compensation is recoverable from the landlord from the date that the tenant quits the holding.

There are complicated rules for determining the amount of compensation. In the case of existing tenancies where the landlord's s. 25 notice of termination was served before 1 April 1990, the level of compensation remains at three times the rateable value of the holding, or (if the tenant can show continuous occupation as a business tenant over a period of 14 years immediately preceding termination of the tenancy) six times the rateable value (at the date of the service of the notice). Personal occupation during the 14-year period is not, however, essential where all the previous occupants were predecessors in the same business (s. 37(2)).

On 1 April 1990, the rating revaluation of commercial properties came into effect resulting in an average increase in rateable values of eight times. To coincide with this change, the multiplier used to compute compensation for disturbance was reduced from three to one. Thus now, where the s. 25 notice is served after 31 March 1990, the level of compensation is one or two times the rateable value of the holding at the date of service of the notice. However, some tenants have the option to require compensation at eight (or 16) times the rateable value of 31 March 1990 instead of one (or two times) the current rateable value.

It is apparent that the 14-year period of occupation has to be satisfied up to the date of termination of the tenancy specified in the landlord's s. 25 notice. In *Sight & Sound Education Ltd* v *Books etc. Ltd* [1999] 43 EG 161, the tenant gave up possession by the contractual term date (thereby ceasing to enjoy Pt II protection) and, consequently, was not entitled to compensation based on twice the rateable value.

As a result of a 1969 amendment to the 1954 Act, it is not necessary for the tenant to go through the motions of applying for a new tenancy to preserve his claim for disturbance. For example, if the landlord specifies grounds (e), (f) or (g) in his s. 25 notice or opposition to a s. 26 request, and the tenant sees little chance of a successful application, his claim under s. 37 will be unaffected by a decision to quit the holding on the specified termination date (cf. *Lloyds Bank Ltd* v *City of London Corporation* [1983] Ch 192).

Agreements restricting or excluding compensation for disturbance are void except where, looking back from the date that the tenant quit the holding, there was less than five years' continuous business occupation by the tenant or his predecessors in business (s. 38). When determining whether the business tenant has occupied for the whole of the five-year period, the courts are reluctant to find that a business occupancy has ceased where the business premises are empty for only a short period, whether mid-term or before or after trading at either end of the lease, provided always that during that period there existed no rival for the role of business occupant and that the premises were not being used for some other non-business purpose. However, if the premises are left vacant for a period of months, the courts are more likely to conclude that the reason for that period of closure was not an incident in the ordinary course of business life and that the 'thread of continuity' had been broken (*Bacchiocchi* v *Academic Agency Ltd* [1998] 2 All ER 241, where the tenant was held to have been in business occupation despite the premises standing empty for 12 days prior to termination of the lease). The decision has been the subject of much criticism: see, for example, Bennion, F., (1998) 148 NLJ 953 and 986.

Equally, the right to compensation for improvements cannot be excluded by contract unless it was made before 9 February 1927. However, the court may give effect to a contract depriving the tenant of the right to claim compensation for improvements provided it was made between 8 February 1927 and 10 December 1953, and for valuable consideration.

QUESTION 6

In 1965, Property UK Ltd acquired the freehold of a block of 25 flats in Chelsea. Daniel has, since 1992, held a fixed-term lease of the premises, which he uses for his property business. He lives in one of the flats in the block and lets out the rest on six-month assured shorthold tenancies. Daniel retains a key to each of the flats and cleans the common parts, landings and stairwells once a week.

Last month, Daniel read through the terms of his head lease and realised that it is due to expire in two years' time. He is keen to keep his lucrative letting business and does not wish to give up possession of the block.

Advise Daniel as to what rights (if any) he may have under Pt II of the Landlord and Tenant Act 1954.

Commentary

This question is concerned primarily with the recent House of Lords decision in *Graysim Holdings Ltd* v *P & O Property Holdings Ltd* [1996] 1 AC 329, on the meaning of business occupation under Pt II of the 1954 Act. A good answer will outline the relevant qualifying conditions for statutory protection under Pt II and consider specifically whether Daniel's business of sub-letting the flats within the block precludes him from seeking a statutory renewal of his tenancy. For further reading, see: Haley, M., 'Business Tenancies: Parting with Occupation' [1997] Conv 139, Higgins, S., 'The Continuation Conundrum: Part II of the Landlord and Tenant Act 1954' [1997] Conv 119 and Pawlowski, M., 'Business Occupation under Part II — An Update' [1998] RRLR vol. 18/3, pp. 239–46.

Suggested Answer

A business tenant under Pt II of the 1954 Act enjoys the benefit of a large measure of security of tenure following the expiry of his contractual lease. Under s. 24(1) of the 1954 Act, a tenancy to which Pt II applies cannot come to an end except in the manner provided by the Act. The most important effects are that a fixed term continues after its contractual expiry date and a periodic tenancy cannot be determined by a normal notice to quit. A business tenancy which is continued in this way (i.e., under s. 24) can be assigned and is capable of transmission on death (and bankruptcy) in the normal way. The only feature which is changed is the mode of termination. The continuation tenancy can be terminated only in accordance with the statutory machinery for termination prescribed by the Act.

This machinery is complex. A landlord who desires possession must establish one or more specific grounds (listed in s. 30), having made a formal statement of the grounds relied on either by notice of termination complying with s. 25 or by a notice of opposition to a tenant's request for a new tenancy under s. 26. A tenant who wishes to renew his business tenancy must apply for renewal either pursuant to a request for a new tenancy under s. 26, or pursuant to a counter notice in response to a landlord's notice of termination served under s. 25. If he is successful, the court is bound to order the grant of a new tenancy and will determine the terms of the new tenancy in default of agreement between the parties. If, on the other hand, the tenant is unsuccessful in his application to renew, he will be eligible to be paid compensation for disturbance and for tenant's improvements to the premises in certain circumstances.

The qualifying conditions for Pt II security are set out in s. 23 of the 1954 Act, which provides that Pt II applies to any tenancy where the property comprised in the tenancy is or includes premises 'which are occupied by the tenant and are so occupied for the purposes of a business carried on by him . . .'. Where the tenant is an individual (as in the present case), he must be engaged in a trade, profession or employment in order to qualify under Pt II. There is no doubt that Daniel is engaged in a business within the meaning of s. 23. However, it has been held that a tenant occupying a building for the sole purpose of sub-lettings parts neverthless falls outside s. 23(1). In *Graysim Holdings Ltd* v *P & O Property Holdings Ltd* [1996] 1 AC 329, the House of Lords held that intermediate landlords who are not themselves in actual physical occupation of the premises are not within the class of persons protected by Pt II, which is concerned to protect tenants in their occupation of property for the purpose of their business, not to give protection to tenants in respect of income from sub-lettings. Moreover, Pt II makes no provision for 'dual occupation' of premises. In other words, it looks through a sub-letting to the occupying sub-tenant and affords him statutory protection (assuming he is in business occupation), not the mesne landlord.

Although the *Graysim* case involved the letting of a market hall, it has since been applied in the context of residential sub-lettings. In *Bassairi Ltd* v *Camden London Borough Council* [1998] EGCS 27, the existence of the sub-lettings (which were, significantly, assured shorthold tenancies) was enough to prevent the tenant from being able to claim it occupied the premises for the purposes of a business under Pt II.

It is important, however, to bear in mind that the House of Lords did not rule out the possibility that, in exceptional cases, the rights reserved by the tenant might be so extensive that he would remain in occupation of the property for the purposes of Pt II. In *Lee-Verhulst (Investments) Ltd* v *Harwood Trust* [1973] 1 QB 204, for example, the occupancies comprised furnished rooms with substantial services (i.e., supply of blankets, bed linen and towels, daily cleaning, regular change of linen and provision of light meals if required). The Court of Appeal held that, in view of the degree of control and extent of the services provided, the tenant 'occupied' the entire premises for the purpose of its business, namely, that of 'providing furnished accommodation and services for those residing there'. By contrast, in *Bagettes Ltd* v *G.P. Estates Ltd* [1956] Ch 290, the residential flats were let unfurnished and, although the tenant provided hot water for the sub-tenants and cleaned the common parts, the 'service' element was negligible. Not surprisingly, the tenant was held not to be in occupation of the holding.

In *Graysim* itself, it was suggested that where the letting takes the form of a *sub-tenancy*, the sub-tenant will be entitled to exclusive possession of the sub-let part and, hence, will be the 'occupier' to the exclusion of the tenant. At the other end of the spectrum, however, where the occupancy takes the form of a *licence* to occupy, there will often be more scope for argument that the tenant retains occupation of the property because the rights granted by a licence to the occupier will be less extensive than those comprised in a sub-tenancy. The key elements in the *Verhulst* case were the provision of services to the occupants (who were characterised as licensees) and the unrestricted access to each room necessary to perform those services: see also, *Linden* v *Department of Health and Social Security* [1986] 1 WLR 164, involving eight self-contained flats managed by a district health authority. By contrast, in *Graysim*, neither the tenant nor his agents had any right of access to the units, nor did they have keys or means of access. All the occupants had exclusive possession and each was a sub-tenant in respect of his unit.

Central, therefore, to the application of Pt II is the notion that a business tenant must be in *occupation* of the premises for the purposes of his business at the contractual expiry date of the lease. If he does not occupy at that date, there can be no continuance of his tenancy under s. 24 (see *Esselte AB* v *Pearl Assurance plc* [1997] 1 WLR 891). Daniel will, therefore, need to satisfy this requirement of s. 23 in order to qualify for protection under Pt II.

Unfortunately for Daniel, as we have seen, the authorities do not assist him in his current position. Although he clearly carries on a business, this is not one to which Pt II applies since it involves the progressive elimination of the holding. By sub-letting all the flats in the block, he has effectively excluded the sub-let accommodation from the holding and thus cannot be said to be *occupying* any significant part of the holding for the purposes of a business. In the present context, the term 'occupation' connotes some business activity by the tenant on the property in question; in other words, some physical use of the property for the purposes of a business carried on by him.

Exceptionally, however, where the tenant grants a genuine licence, the rights reserved by the tenant may be so extensive as not to rule out the possibility of statutory protection under Pt II. In the residential context, it may be open to a tenant to argue that its degree of control over third-party occupants is sufficiently great to come within the *Lee-Verhulst* ruling, referred to above. As things stand at the moment, Daniel clearly does not fall within this exception, but he may be well-advised to alter the nature of his business so as to do so. This would involve granting licences (as opposed to tenancies) in the future and ensuring that he has a right of unrestricted access to the flats in question in order to provide requisite attendance and services. If he alters his business in this way over the next two years, he will be in a good position to argue that he is in business occupation for the purposes of Pt II and, hence, be eligible to renew his lease under s. 26 of the Act.

QUESTION 7

What is meant by PACT? What is the contemporary significance of the PACT scheme in the light of Lord Woolf's recent reforms to the English civil justice system?

Commentary

This essay question is concerned with the recently developed PACT system for settling disputes as to new lease terms in the context of lease renewal proceedings under the Landlord and Tenant Act 1954, Pt II. A good answer will consider the nature of the PACT scheme in the context of the changes recently brought about by the Civil Procedure Rules (CPR). For further reading, see King, Vivien M., 'The 1954 Act Goes PACT' [1997] RRLR vol. 17/4, pp. 322–27, Myers, A., 'Justice on a Faster Track' [1999] 9912 EG 160 and 'Renewals under Woolf', [1999] 9914 EG 147, Webber, G., 'Lease Renewals and the CPR', (2000) 144 SJ 136 and 170, pp. 136–37 and 170–72, Hindle, A., 'Forcing the Issue', Estates Gazette, January 22, 2000, pp. 124–25, Thomas, M., 'Alternatively Speaking', Estates Gazette, February 5, 2000, pp. 136–37, Herbert, A., 'Changing the Rules', Estates Gazette, February 5, 2000, p. 139, and Francis, P., 'The Woolf Reforms — How Will They Impact on Property Disputes under the Landlord and Tenant Act 1954?' [1999] RRLR 237.

Suggested Answer

PACT stands for 'Professional Arbitration on Court Terms'. It is a method of alternative dispute resolution which was put forward by the RICS and Law Society to be used in the context of business tenancy renewal proceedings under the Landlord and Tenant Act 1954, Pt II. At present, the scheme provides a means by which disputes over the terms of a new lease (which has been renewed in accordance with Pt II of the 1954 Act) can be dealt with by way of arbitration or the use of an independent expert, rather than litigation. The scheme does not currently apply to an application for a new lease which is opposed by the landlord on one of the grounds contained in s. 30(1)(a)–(g) of the 1954 Act (although it may be so extended in the future). The appointment of a PACT arbitrator or expert may be made by either the Royal Institute of Chartered Surveyors (RICS) or Law Society upon the application of both the landlord and tenant. Such arbitrators and experts are specialists in the area of commercial leases and the workings of the 1954 Act and have been specifically trained under the PACT scheme. It is estimated that there are approximately 60 PACT appointees to date, appointed from the ranks of both solicitors and surveyors.

In essence, the PACT scheme vests in a PACT appointee the same statutory discretion as a judge has in court when determining lease terms under ss. 29–35 of the 1954 Act. In this regard, PACT represents a system of dispute resolution which is an alternative to litigation.

The stated aim of the scheme is to increase the effectiveness and flexibility of the legal system and to give a greater choice both to landlords and tenants and to their legal advisers. The scheme is very much in keeping with the spirit of Lord Woolf's civil law reforms as contained in his Report, *Access to Justice*. In this vein, the scheme encourages parties to view litigation as a last resort, and to view professional arbitration as a cheaper and speedier option for settling disputes over new lease terms.

PACT system is intended to be more flexible than the current court system, in that the parties are able to adapt their own rules to their very specific requirements and choose whether the adjudicator is to be a solicitor or surveyor sitting as an arbitrator or expert. It is intended that the PACT system will avoid delays — which have been a common complaint about the system of settling lease terms under the current renewal procedures. If PACT proves more speedy, then it is hoped that wasted costs will be avoided. In this connection, under PACT, the parties have a choice as to the type of PACT dispute resolution method to use, namely, arbitration with an oral hearing, arbitration on paper submissions, or the use of an independent expert.

It is noteworthy, however, that PACT can be adopted as a mean of settling a dispute as to new lease terms only where *both* parties consent to the referral. In this context, PACT can be used in one of two instances: first, where the landlord does not *per se* oppose the lease renewal but the parties cannot reach agreement over the terms of the new lease; and, secondly, where the landlord has sought, but failed, to obtain possession and the parties (having failed to reach agreement over the new lease terms) decide to adjourn matters so as to allow a PACT appointee to determine the lease terms. The adjournment of the court proceedings and reference of the matter to a PACT appointee would ordinarily be done by a consent order.

When using PACT, the parties are free to choose their own type of appointee (i.e., solicitor or surveyor). Either type of appointee is feasible. If the dispute regarding the new lease terms is valuation or rental based then a surveyor would probably be the more appropriate expert. If the dispute relates to the wording of new clauses in a renewed lease then a solicitor would be more suitable.

The parties may present their submissions to the PACT appointee by way of either written or oral submissions. If agreement cannot be reached on these procedural matters, the appointee may choose the relevant route as to how to determine the case and directions as to how matters should proceed. The parties can represent themselves, or have professional representation in the form of a lawyer or surveyor.

If the parties choose to engage a PACT appointee as an arbitrator then he will sit in a quasi-judicial capacity and will be bound by the provisions of the Arbitration Act 1996. A PACT appointee sitting as an expert, on the other hand, will not be so bound, and the rules of evidence do not apply to expert determinations. Conversely, an arbitrator has, by virtue of the 1996 Act, a discretion as to whether to apply the rules of evidence (s. 34(2)(f) and s. 34(2)(d)). An arbitrator also has power to decide whether any, and if so what, documents or classes of documents should be disclosed by the parties. In contrast, experts have no power to order disclosure, and can only decide matters on the documents presented to them by the parties.

Once a decision has been made as to the new lease terms, the PACT appointee must formally record his decision, and in so doing apply the criteria as set out in the appropriate sections of the 1954 Act as regards the property to be comprised in the new lease, the rent to be paid, duration, and other terms of the new lease. In this connection, the starting point for determining the terms of the new lease will be the terms of the old lease, and the burden of showing any detraction from the old terms is on the party seeking change (see *O'May* v *City of London Real Property Co. Ltd* [1983] 1 AC 726).

The PACT scheme has attracted a new significance in the light of Lord Woolf's changes to civil justice. The recommendations for reform of the civil justice system have largely been embodied in the Civil Procedure Rules (CPR) which came into force on 26 April 1999. The rules have sought to effect a change in the culture of dispute resolution and there are two broad objectives: (i) to make litigation a matter of last resort and to make the courts more accessible for those who genuinely need assistance; and (ii) to make litigation quicker and cheaper. By virtue of the rules, the courts are obliged to promote settlement of disputes wherever possible. The PACT scheme, as we have already seen, already operates in the context of uncontested 1954 Act lease renewals, where the main source of dispute is the terms to be included in a new lease. Thus far, PACT has not been widely used, the main problem being that its use depends on the consent of *both* parties. It is often in one party's interest to delay the resolution of matters and not resort to the quicker and cheaper facility of the PACT scheme. However, since the introduction of the Woolf reforms, with their emphasis on speed, cost effectiveness and alternative dispute resolution, it is likely that a party who chooses not to use the PACT facility will be regarded by the court as having unreasonably refused to comply with the aims of the CPR and be penalised in costs. In this respect, it may be worthwhile for the party seeking to use PACT to write formally to the other party suggesting use of the scheme, while reserving the right to refer the matter to the court on the issue of costs in the event of the other party refusing consent.

Although there is, as yet, no pre-action protocol in relation to lease renewal cases, the parties are, nevertheless, required 'to act reasonably in exchanging information and documents relevant to the claim and generally in trying to avoid the necessity for the start of proceedings' (CPR, PD Protocols, para. 4). The inherent difficulty, however, with applying this latter principle in the context of business renewal is that the 1954 Act requires the tenant to commence his application for the grant of a new tenancy at an early stage of negotiations for renewal in order to preserve his security under Pt II. Under CPR, once proceedings are issued, there are limited options for the parties to adjourn pending negotiations for renewal of the lease. Strictly speaking, the parties may only adjourn for up to a period of 28 days to enable such negotiations to proceed. The court may, however, be persuaded to grant a further adjournment of 28 days by joint application of the parties. But a general stay is unlikely to be granted once proceedings have been issued. There is no doubt that the potential difficulties with adjournments in the lease renewal content have yet to be fully resolved. One solution may be for the parties to agree a general extension of time for the actual *issuing* of the tenant's application for the grant of a new tenancy. Although this practice has been rare thus far, it may be that we shall see such general extensions becoming more popular.

13 Agricultural Holdings and Agricultural Tied Cottages

INTRODUCTION

In this chapter, you will find four questions — two on agricultural holdings, one on agricultural tied cottages and one on the Agricultural Tenancies Act 1995.

The subject of agricultural holdings is complex in so far as it is regulated by highly detailed statutory provisions. The legislative code which continues to apply in respect of agricultural tenancies granted before 1 September 1995 is the Agricultural Holdings Act 1986, which consolidated a number of earlier enactments. On 1 September 1995, the Agricultural Tenancies Act 1995 came into force and introduced the farm business tenancy. The Act does not generally apply to any tenancy granted before this date, so that rights acquired by agricultural tenants under the 1986 Act remain intact.

Most landlord and tenant courses do not deal with this topic in any great depth and, consequently, exam questions tend to be of the essay type, requiring only a broad knowledge of the area. For a good summary of the 1986 statutory code, see Evans, D. and Smith, P. F., *The Law of Landlord and Tenant*, 4th edn, London: Butterworths, 1993, Chs 29–33.

The subject of agricultural tied cottages tends also to be given little emphasis, and hence we have included only one question on this topic. Occupiers of agricultural tied cottages who are agricultural workers are governed, in principle, by one of two statutory codes. If the occupation arose under an agreement entered into before 15 January 1989, it will be governed by the Rent (Agriculture) Act 1976. If, on the other hand, the occupation arose under an agreement entered into on or after this date, it will be an assured agricultural occupancy under the Housing Act 1988, Pt I, Ch. III. Essentially, this latter form of occupancy is treated as an assured tenancy under the 1988 Act.

QUESTION 1

'An agricultural holding is defined in s. 1(1) of the Agricultural Holdings Act 1986 as being the aggregate of the land (whether agricultural land or not) comprised in a contract of tenancy which is a contract for an agricultural tenancy . . .'

Discuss.

Commentary

This is a highly technical question on the definition of an agricultural holding for the purposes of the 1986 Act. To score high marks, you need to refer not only to the appropriate statutory provisions but also the relevant case law interpreting the same.

Essentially, you should cover three main areas, namely:

(a)   the meaning of 'agricultural land';

(b)   the definition of 'contract of tenancy'; and

(c)   the two main exceptions to s. 2 of the Act (i.e., grazing/mowing agreements and licences).

Suggested Answer

Essentially, the Agricultural Holdings Act 1986 applies to contracts of tenancy of agricultural holdings. The term 'agricultural holding' is defined in s. 1(1) of the 1986 Act and, in simple terms, means the aggregate of the agricultural land comprised in a contract of tenancy which is not a service tenancy.

It may be convenient to begin with the phrase 'agricultural land'. This is defined by s. 1(4) as meaning land used for agriculture which is so used for the purpose of a trade or business. The word 'agriculture' is further defined in s. 96(1) as including horticulture, fruit growing, seed growing, diary farming, livestock breeding and keeping, market gardening and the use of land as grazing or meadow land.

Where there is a mixed use, the test is one of dominant user so that the tenancy must be in substance agricultural. There is no question of severance, so that the

Act either applies to all of the land or to none of it (*Howkins* v *Jardine* [1951] 1 KB 614). In *Blackmore* v *Butler* [1954] 2 QB 171, a cottage and garden (let for use in connection with a farm) were held to constitute 'land used for agriculture'. The same test is applied where there is a mixed agricultural and business use. For example, in *Dunn* v *Fidoe* [1950] 2 All ER 685, an inn, which was used both as an inn and as a farmhouse let with 12 acres of agricultural land, was held to be an agricultural holding. (See also, *Bracey* v *Read* [1963] Ch 88 and *Monson* v *Bound* [1954] 1 WLR 1321).

Given that the land is used for agriculture, it is immaterial that the business is not agricultural (*Rutherford* v *Maurer* [1962] 1 QB 16). In this case, the Court of Appeal held that the words 'trade or business' in the Agricultural Holdings Act 1948, s. 1(2) (predecessor to the 1986 Act) could not be limited in their meaning to any specific trade or business such as agriculture. Hence, since the field in question was used for grazing (and, therefore, for agriculture) and was so used for the purpose of a trade or business (namely, a riding school), it was agricultural land within s. 1(2) of the 1948 Act. (See also, *Gold* v *Jacques Amand Ltd* [1992] 27 EG 140).

However, an agricultural tenancy will cease to be agricultural if, during the tenancy and before service of any notice to quit, agricultural activity is wholly or substantially abandoned, regardless of the landlord's consent (*Wetherall* v *Smith* [1980] 1 WLR 1290).

The phrase 'contract of tenancy' is defined by s. 1(5) of the 1986 Act as meaning 'a letting of land, or agreement for letting land, for a term of years or from year to year'. For the purposes of this definition, a lease for life or lives within the Law of Property Act 1925, s. 149(6), is deemed to be a letting for a term of years.

Under s. 2 of the 1986 Act, if land is let for agricultural use for an interest less than a tenancy from year to year (s. 2(2)(a)), or a person is granted a licence to occupy land for agricultural use (s. 2(2)(b)), the agreement is *deemed* to be for a tenancy from year to year. In order, however, for a licence to fall within s. 2(2)(a), it must confer exclusive possession of the land on the licensee (*Bahamas International Trust Co. Ltd* v *Threadgold* [1974] 1 WLR 1514).

A tenancy for more than one year but less than two is a tenancy for a 'term of years' within the meaning of s. 1(5) of the 1986 Act. It is not, however, a tenancy for a term of 'two years or more' (within s. 3 of the 1986 Act), nor does it qualify as an 'interest less than a tenancy from year to year' (within s. 2(2) of the 1986 Act) (*Gladstone* v *Bower* [1960] 2 QB 384). The consequence, therefore, is that such a tenancy is not protected against termination either by the Landlord and Tenant Act 1954, Pt II (dealing with business tenancies), or by the Agricultural Holdings Act 1986 (*EWP Ltd* v *Moore* [1992] 1 QB 460). By contrast, in *Bernays* v *Prosser* [1963] 2 QB 592, it was held that a tenancy for one year certain was less than a tenancy from year to year, so that a tenant holding under such a tenancy fell within s. 2 and the tenancy took effect as if it were a tenancy from year to year. In *Calcott* v *J. S. Bloor (Measham) Ltd* [1998] 40 EG 180, the landlord entered into an agreement to let the land for a term of 13 months from 1 November 1992. The agreement was not, however, signed until 11 June 1993, by which time there was less than a year to run. Because a term cannot be granted retrospectively (see *Keen* v *Holland* [1984] 1 EGLR 9), the agreement was converted into a yearly tenancy. Moreover, that yearly tenancy was held to run from 11 June (when the agreement was signed) and not 30 November (when the purported 13-month term came to an end).

Section 2 of the 1986 Act will also not apply to an agreement for the letting of land (or the granting of a licence to occupy land) which is made:

(a)   in contemplation of the use of the land only for grazing or mowing (or both) during some specified period of the year (s. 2(3)(a)); or

(b)   by a person whose interest in the land is less than a tenancy from year to year and has not taken effect as such a tenancy by virtue of s. 2 (*Rutherford* v *Maurer* [1962] 1 QB 16).

Where a tenancy is granted for one year (less one day) of agricultural land which is to be kept as grassland and is partially used for ploughing and raising crops, the tenancy is not made 'in contemplation of the use of land only for grazing . . . during some specified period of the year' within s. 2(3)(a) of the 1986 Act, and accordingly the tenancy will take effect as a tenancy from year to year of an agricultural holding under that section (*Lory* v *Brent London Borough Council* [1971] 1 WLR 823). However, an agreement for grazing rights only during the grazing season (i.e., from April to October) will fall within the exclusion contained in s. 2(3)(a) (*Stone* v *Whitcombe* (1980) 40 P & CR 296, where it was held that it was not necessary for specified dates to be agreed for the agreement to relate to 'specified' periods if the parties have agreed exclusive occupation of the land only during a particular season). Similarly, in *Watts* v *Yeend* [1987] 1 WLR 323, it was held that a licence granted in contemplation of the use of land for grazing was a seasonal grazing licence which was understood in agricultural circles as referring to a period of less than a year.

Lastly, it may be mentioned that for the protection of the 1986 Act to apply, the agricultural holding must be comprised in a single contract of tenancy (*Blackmore* v *Butler* [1954] 2 QB 171).

QUESTION 2

(a) To what extent is it possible to contract out of the security of tenure provisions of the Agricultural Holdings Act 1986? (Illustrate your answer by reference to decided cases.)

(b) How may an agricultural tenant oppose a landlord's notice to quit the holding?

Commentary

The first part of this question is quite specific and requires you to consider several important cases on devices for avoiding security of tenure under the 1986 Act. The leading case is now the House of Lords decision in *Barrett* v *Morgan* [2000] 1 All ER 481.

The second part of the question is much wider in scope and should give you no problems provided you have a good working knowledge of the security of tenure provisions of the 1986 Act. Since this is only half the question, you will need to be succinct in your answer — the examiner will not expect you to go into great detail.

Suggested Answer

(a) The Agricultural Holdings Act 1986 does not in terms expressly prohibit contracting out of the right to serve a counternotice, but s. 26(1) of the Act (which confers security of tenure on the tenant) has been held to be mandatory and to override any contrary stipulation in the tenancy.

Thus, a covenant in a lease of an agricultural holding purporting to prevent a tenant from serving a counternotice in response to a landlord's notice to quit under s. 25(1) of the Agricultural Holdings Act 1986 will be invalid as being contrary to public policy. This was established by the House of Lords in *Johnson* v *Moreton* [1980] AC 37, where a clause in the lease provided that the tenant was to give up possession of farm premises to the landlords upon the determination of the term, and not to serve a counternotice or take any other steps to claim the benefit of any statutory provision granting security of tenure.

The House of Lords concluded that the policy of the Agricultural Holdings Act 1948 (predecessor to the 1986 Act) made it clear that an agricultural tenant could not by agreement deprive himself of the option to serve a counternotice in advance. Accordingly, the clause was held unenforceable.

Reference may also be made to *Featherstone* v *Staples* [1986] 1 WLR 861. In this case, it was held that, where an agricultural tenancy is granted to joint tenants, including a company wholly owned by the landlord, who farm the land as a partnership, a clause in the partnership agreement purporting to prevent the joint tenants serving a counternotice without the consent of the company will be void and unenforceable. The general rule, however, is that a valid counternotice cannot be served without the concurrence of all the joint tenants (*Newman* v *Keedwell* (1977) 35 P & CR 393).

Most recently, the House of Lords have held that a notice to quit an agricultural holding served by the landlord on the head tenants with their agreement not to serve a counternotice under the 1986 Act took effect as notice to quit (and not as a surrender) and consequently was effective to terminate a sub-tenancy of the holding. In *Barrett* v *Morgan* [2000] 1 All ER 481, the claimant freeholders were seeking possession of farm land from the defendant sub-tenant. A head-lease of the farm had been granted by the claimants' predecessor to his two sons. As part of a scheme to evict the sub-tenant, the claimants, as head landlords, served a notice to quit on the two sons, who then abstained from exercising their statutory right to serve a counternotice. In this way, it was argued, the claimants had effectively determined the head-lease which, in turn, gave them the right to possession against the defendant sub-tenant.

The point was addressed in the earlier case of *Sparkes* v *Smart* [1990] 2 EGLR 245, where on very similar facts, the Court of Appeal concluded that the actions of the tenant were collusive with the freeholder with a view to putting an end to the sub-lease and giving the freeholder vacant possession. The upshot of the *Sparkes* decision was that the notice to quit effectively determined the head-lease but not the sub-lease. In the Court of Appeal in *Barrett* ([1998] 4 All ER 179), their Lordships followed the *Sparkes* decision and held that the mechanism employed by the claimant freeholders of serving a notice to quit on the footing that no counternotice would be served was tantamount to a consensual surrender and could not, therefore, result in the determination of the defendant's sub-tenancy.

The House of Lords, on appeal, has now reversed this finding. According to Lord Millett, who gave the leading speech, service of a notice to quit by either a tenant or a landlord by pre-arrangement with the other was *not* tantamount to surrender of the tenancy, as unlike a surrender it did not need the consent of the receiving party to have effect. In the *Barrett* case, although the tenants had consented to the service of the notice to quit, their consent was unnecessary and the freeholders were only doing with their consent what they were entitled to do without it. In his Lordship's view, it would be an extraordinary result if a tenant could determine a sub-tenancy by the unilateral act of serving a notice to quit on the landlord but could not achieve the same result by telling the landlord that he would not object to a notice to quit served by him. The defendant's sub-tenancy was, therefore, determined, not by any collusive agreement but by the natural expiry of the tenancy from which the defendant's sub-tenancy was derived.

In reaching this conclusion, the House essentially applied the earlier Court of Appeal decision in *Pennell* v *Payne* [1995] QB 192, where it was held that an immediate tenant who serves notice to quit on the head landlord does an act which on the expiry of the notice to quit will determine not only his own tenancy but also any sub-tenancy that he may have granted. The upshot of the House of Lords ruling is, therefore, that if the termination of the head tenancy is brought about by a *unilateral* act (i.e., notice to quit), this will destroy the sub-tenancy. If, on the other hand, the head tenancy is determined by the *consensual* act (i.e., by surrender) then the sub-tenancy is unaffected. The decision in *Sparkes* is, accordingly, no longer good law.

(b) Where a notice to quit is served on the tenant, he or she may within one month serve a counternotice on the landlord requiring that the notice to quit shall not take effect unless the Agricultural Land Tribunal consents to its operation (s. 26). If no such counternotice is served in time, the consent of the Tribunal is not required. In this connection, the landlord is under no statutory or implied duty to the tenant to set out his (or her) right to serve a counternotice (*Crawford* v *Elliott* [1991] 13 EG 163).

The right of the tenant to serve a counternotice is excluded if the notice to quit is given on any of the Cases set out in sch. 3, Pt I to the Act (i.e., Case A (smallholdings); Case B (planning consent); Case C (certificate of bad husbandry); Case D (non-compliance with notice to pay rent or to remedy breaches); Case E (irremediable breaches); Case F (insolvency); Case G (death of tenant) and Case H (ministerial certificates): s. 26(2)).

Where a notice to quit is given specifying Case A, B, D or E, a tenant who wishes to contest the reason stated may refer the notice to arbitration. The tenant's notice requiring arbitration must be given within one month of the service of the landlord's notice to quit (see, e.g., *Parrish* v *Kinsey* (1983) 268 EG 1113, where it was held that the time limit was inflexible). This procedure is somewhat modified if the tenant has committed a breach of the terms of the tenancy (e.g., a failure to repair) and has been served with a notice to do work as a prerequisite to a notice to quit served under Case D. Here, the tenant, if he wishes to contest a reason stated, must, within one month of service of the landlord's notice to do work, serve a written notice specifying the items in respect of which he denies liability and requiring arbitration. In addition, despite non-compliance with a notice to do work, the tenant may, under s. 28, by counternotice within one month of the landlord's notice to quit under Case D or an arbitration award, require consent of the Tribunal to the Case D notice. By s. 28(5), the Tribunal must consent to the operation of the notice unless it appears to them that a fair and reasonable landlord would not insist on possession, having regard to:

(a)   the extent of the tenant's failure to comply with the notice to do work;

(b)   the consequences of his failure to comply in any respect; and

(c)   the circumstances surrounding the failure.

Where the tenant is entitled to serve a counternotice and does so, the Tribunal will consent to the operation of the landlord's notice to quit if satisfied that one of the grounds in s. 27(3) exists, unless it appears that, in all the circumstances, a fair and reasonable landlord would not insist on possession (s. 27(2)). The grounds may be summarised as follows:

(a)   that the carrying out of the purpose for which the landlord proposes to end the tenancy is desirable in the interests of good husbandry as repects the land to which the notice relates, treated as a separate unit;

(b)   that the landlord's purpose in ending the tenancy is in the interests of sound management of the estate of which the land in question forms part;

(c)   that the landlord's purpose in ending the tenancy is desirable for agricultural research, education, experiment or demonstration, or for the purpose of enactments relating to smallholdings or allotments;

(d)   greater hardship would be caused by withholding than by giving consent to the operation of the notice; and

(e)   that the landlord intends to end the tenancy for the purpose of the land being used for a non-agricultural use not falling within Case B.

The Tribunal has power, under s. 27(4), to impose such conditions as appear to them requisite for securing that the land to which the notice relates will be used for the purpose for which the landlord proposes to terminate the tenancy.

Lastly, it may be mentioned that a landlord's notice to quit will be invalid and unenforceable if it contains a false statement made fraudulently by the landlord (*Rous* v *Mitchell* [1991] 1 All ER 676).

QUESTION 3

What security of tenure is available to an occupier of an agricultural tied cottage?

Commentary

This is a 'give-away' question if you have revised this particular topic for the exam. You should refer both to the Rent (Agriculture) Act 1976 (which continues to apply to agreements entered into before 15 January 1989) and to the Housing Act 1988, Pt I, Ch. III (which applies to agreements entered into on or after this date) as amended by the Housing Act 1996 (which applies to agreements made on or after 28 February 1997). Note that you are not asked to specify the conditions which must be satisfied in order to come within the statutory codes. The question is directed solely at the *security of tenure* provisions of the two Acts.

Suggested Answer

The Rent (Agriculture) Act 1976 conferred on agricultural workers security of tenure (and a considerable degree of rent protection) with respect to their tied cottages. Largely modelled on the provisions of the Rent Act 1977, the 1976 Act was necessary as many agricultural workers would be excluded from being Rent Act protected tenants, their tenancies either being at a low rent or being within the agricultural holding exemption. Indeed, many would not be tenants at all but mere licensees.

The 1976 Act continues to apply in respect of agreements entered into before 15 January 1989, However, the Housing Act 1988, Pt I, Ch. III, phased out the statutory scheme of the 1976 Act in respect of agreements entered into on or after this date. The 1988 Act seeks to retain security of tenure for agricultural workers, while allowing the landlord to charge a market rent. The new tenure which was introduced to cater for these persons was the assured agricultural occupancy.

The 1976 Act confers security of tenure in a similar manner to that conferred on protected and statutory tenants by the Rent Act 1977. Thus, upon the termination of the tenancy or licence, a protected occupier under the 1976 Act automatically becomes a statutory tenant in his or her own right (s. 2(4)) provided that he or she occupies the dwelling-house as his or her residence at all material times (s. 4(1)). Generally speaking, all burdens and benefits of the original (contractual) agreement will continue to apply to the statutory tenancy. However, by agreement the parties have the right to vary many of the terms of a statutory tenancy.

A single succession to a tenancy or relevant licence is allowed under the 1976 Act (ss. 3 and 4). If, however, the original occupier dies after 15 January 1989, leaving no surviving spouse but a family member who has resided in the dwelling-house for two years before death, then the succession of the family member is to an assured agricultural occupancy under the 1988 Act. If more than one family member qualifies, the county court is to choose one in default of agreement. Moreover, common-law spouses are entitled to succeed and will have priority over other members of the occupier's family.

A statutory tenancy will also come into being where a notice of increase of rent is served on the occupier (s. 16 of the 1976 Act).

The landlord of a protected occupier is able to recover possession only on proof of one or more statutory grounds (s. 6 and sch. 4 of the 1976 Act). The grounds for possession are, as with the Rent Act 1977, divided into discretionary and mandatory grounds. As with the 1977 Act, in the case of a discretionary ground, the court cannot make an order for possession under the 1976 Act unless it is reasonable to do so (s. 7(2)). The discretionary grounds resemble corresponding Rent Act 1977 grounds. In the case of the mandatory grounds, there is, as with the 1977 Act, no overriding discretion in the court to refuse to make an order for possession once a ground is made out by the landlord. These grounds are:

   (a)   recovery of possession by the landlord as an owner-occupier following a notice to quit to the tenant;

   (b)   a retirement ground; and

(c)   an overcrowding ground.

The landlord may also recover possession under a discretionary ground (Case 1) where he is able to show that suitable alternative accommodation is available to the tenant.

Where the landlord wishes to obtain possession of the dwelling-house with a view to housing an employee of his in agriculture and that person's family, and no other suitable accommodation can be provided by the landlord by reasonable means, he may apply to the relevant housing authority for alternative accommodation to be provided for the occupier under s. 27. If satisfied of the above, and that it ought, in the interests of efficient agriculture, to provide the alternative accommodation, the authority will be under a statutory duty, enforceable by an action for damages, to use its best endeavours to provide the accommodation.

Under the Housing Act 1988, the assured agricultural occupancy is treated as if it were an assured tenancy even though it may not be a tenancy at all (s. 24(3)). If the assured agricultural occupancy is for a fixed-term tenancy, it will become a statutory periodic tenancy once the fixed term comes to an end (s. 25(1)(b)). That statutory periodic tenancy will, however, remain an assured agricultural occupancy so long as the agricultural worker condition is fulfilled (i.e., the occupier must be either a qualifying worker, or someone who is incapable of work in agriculture in consequence of a qualifying injury or disease, and the dwelling-house must be in qualifying ownership).

The recovery of possession of an assured agricultural occupancy differs only in two respects from other assured tenancies. First, the discretionary ground of possession in ground 16 of sch. 2 (tenant having ceased to be in the landlord's employment, dwelling-house having been let in consequence of his employment) would, if available, make a nonsense of the protective code. Accordingly, the landlord cannot use it (s. 25(2)). Secondly, the rehousing provisions of Pt IV of the 1976 Act will apply to a dwelling-house let on an assured agricultural occupancy (see above). If the landlord is able to use this procedure to secure suitable alternative accommodation for the occupier, he will be able to argue that it is reasonable for the court to order possession of the dwelling-house, producing a certificate from the local authority as conclusive evidence of the availability of the suitable alternative accommodation for the tenant when the order takes effect (s. 7(4) of the 1988 Act).

Substantial amendments to Pt I of the Housing Act 1988 were made by the Housing Act 1996 (which came into force on 28 February 1997). In respect of tenancies granted after this date, a landlord is no longer required to serve a notice of assured shorthold on a tenant and it is no longer a requirement that the assured shorthold tenancy be for at least six months. Essentially, the emphasis has been reversed so that, in most cases, new tenancies granted on or after 28 February 1997, and which fall within the provisions of the Housing Act 1988, will be assured shortholds. However, the 1988 Act (see para. 9 of sch. 2A) provides that one of the circumstances in which a tenancy will not automatically take effect as an assured shorthold is where the agricultural worker condition is 'for the time being' fulfilled. It seems, therefore, that if at the commencement date of the tenancy the agricultural condition is *not* fulfilled, the tenancy will start and (presumably) continue as an assured shorthold. It has been suggested, however, that any tenancy granted to an agricultural worker who subsequently satisfies the agricultural worker condition will switch to being an assured agricultural tenancy (Johnstone, M., 'Countryside Contradictions [1997] EG 9709, pp. 150–51). This is because, it is argued, a tenancy cannot be an assured shorthold tenancy if 'for the time being' the agricultural worker condition is satisfied. One way of avoiding this difficulty is for the landlord to ensure that there is a written agreement containing an express statement that the tenancy is to be an assured shorthold. If this is done, the tenancy will not switch in the way described above.

QUESTION 4

To what extent has the Agricultural Tenancies Act 1995 altered the law in respect of the statutory regulation of agricultural tenancies? What were the main objectives of the new legislation?

Commentary

This question requires you to give a discursive account of the workings of the 1995 Act with particular reference to the principal objectives of the new law. You will gain more marks if you approach your answer from a comparative standpoint — to what extent is the 1995 Act an improvement on the 1986 Act regime? You may find the following literature helpful in answering this question: McNully, S. and Evans, D., 'The Agricultural Revolution' [1995] EG 9530, 82–85; Yates, R., 'Pastures New', (1995) 145 NLJ, pp. 1372–74; (Mainly for Students) 'Agricultural Lettings' [1995] EG 9525, 153–54 and Jessel, C., 'Drafting Farm Business Leases' [1995] EG 9545, 126–27. See also, generally Evans, D., *The Agricultural Tenancies Act 1995* (London: Sweet & Maxwell), and Sydenham A., and Mainwaring, N., *Farm Business Tenancies* (London: Jordan Publishing Limited).

Suggested Answer

The Agricultural Tenancies Act 1995 received Royal Assent on 1 September 1995 and introduced the novel concept of the farm business tenancy. Agricultural tenancies granted before this date remain within the Agricultural Holdings Act 1986 regime and are unaffected by the 1995 Act changes. The 1986 Act will also continue to apply to any tenancy which is a succession tenancy on death or retirement pursuant to the Act.

The main aims of the new legislation were to: (i) deregulate the number of agricultural lettings and to simplify agricultural legislation; (ii) increase the number of agricutural lettings and allow them to be freely negotiated between the parties; and (iii) provide a statutory framework which would enable farmers to adapt to future changes in policy and market conditions.

The basic rationale of the new legislation is, therefore, to permit the parties freely to negotiate a contract of tenancy upon terms which are acceptable to both landlord and tenant, but within a statutory framework which provides some degree of security of tenure to the farm tenant. This is in sharp contrast to the old regime under the Agricultural Holdings Act 1986, where an agricultural tenant can expect (subject to limited exceptions) lifetime security of tenure and succession rights on death and retirement for up to two generations (in respect of tenancies granted before 12 July 1984). Moreover, a landlord, under the 1986 Act, has very limited scope for recovering his property and the complexity of the notice procedures gives rise to unfairness and expensive litigation for both parties. The statutory regime was regarded by many as contributing to a reluctance on the part of landlords to make land available on anything other than specific short-term lettings outside the security of tenure provisions of the 1986 Act. The new scheme sought to address this difficulty.

The central feature of the 1995 Act is the farm business tenancy. To qualify as such, the tenancy must meet the business conditions and *either* the agricultural condition *or* the notice condition. The business conditions are that all or part of the land in the tenancy is farmed for the purposes of a trade or business and has been so farmed since the tenancy began. The agricultural condition requires that the character of the tenancy is primarily or wholly agricultural having regard to the tenancy terms, use of the land, the nature of any commercial activities conducted on the land and any other relevant circumstances. The alternative notice condition is that the landlord and tenant each gave the other written notice before the tenancy began stating that they intended the tenancy to be and remain a farm business tenancy and identifying the land concerned (so long as at the beginning of the tenancy its character was primarily or wholly agricultural).

There is no specific minimum term for a farm business tenancy, unlike under Pt I of the 1986 Act in relation to agricultural holdings. Whereas the 1986 Act converts licences into tenancies within the scope of the Act, the 1995 Act does not, leaving scope for a genuine licence outside the Act. A tenancy at will is expressly excluded from the 1995 Act's definition of a tenancy.

The tenant's security of tenure is radically different from that under the 1986 Act. The tenant of a farm business tenancy does not have enduring statutory protection. Instead, a tenant of more than two years has merely the certainty of one full agricultural cycle's notice that his tenancy is to be terminated. He is entitled to at least 12 months' (and not more than 24 months') notice in writing from his landlord to take effect at the end of a year of the tenancy unless it has been given to take effect on the term date of the tenancy itself. The tenant has a similar right to give written notice of termination on his landlord. Significantly, no grounds are needed by the landlord to regain possession. Until terminated by notice, the tenancy will continue from year to year at the expiry of the contractual term. If the farm business tenancy is for two years or less, its termination is governed solely by the parties' agreement or, in the absence of express provision for termination, by the common law.

Another significant feature of the new law relates to repairing obligations. The 1986 Act contains substantial controls that limit the repairing obligations of both the landlord and tenant. By contrast, under the 1995 Act, repairing obligations are left to the agreement of the parties. So far as rent is concerned, a statutory review machinery applies unless expressly excluded by the tenancy, or the tenancy provides for the variation of the statutory rent review by fixed amounts or in accordance with a formula, provided that the formula allows the possibility of the rent going down as well as up and does not require or permit anyone to exercise a discretion or judgment in determining the rent (s. 9). The rent review procedure in the Act sets out the machinery for a statutory review notice and the appointment of an arbitrator. Undoubtedly, these provisions bring the determination of rent review or into line with commercial rent determinations. For example, the parties are free to agree the frequency of rent reviews (otherwise they will be three-yearly).

The 1995 Act also provides for a non-excludable right to compensation for improvements made by the tenant with the landlord's consent. In addition, the tenant is entitled, subject to certain exceptions, to remove any fixtures erected by him during the tenancy or at any time after when he remains in possession as a tenant. The tenant is not obliged to give notice to his landlord that he intends to remove a fixture, neither is he obliged to comply fully with the conditions of the tenancy before he is entitled to remove a fixture.

There is no doubt that the 1995 Act represents a marked shift away from the heavy statutory regulation of the 1986 Act towards a system which encourages free negotiation of terms as between agricultural tenant and landlord. The original aims of the Agricultural Holdings Act 1948 which preceded the 1986 Act (and which sought to safeguard tenants and enhance food production in post-war Britain) have little relevance today where the emphasis is on encouraging diversification of business by tenants and making more farmland available for letting on commercial terms.

Although the 1995 Act has been welcomed by most, the continuing application of the 1986 Act alongside the 1995 Act has given rise to some anomalies. For example, an agricultural tenant under the 1986 Act may be able to claim substantial compensation for disturbance on quitting the holding pursuant to his landlord's notice to quit (s. 60 of the 1986 Act), but a tenant of a farm business tenancy is unable to claim such compensation unless specifically provided for in the tenancy. Such anomalies, however, will eventually disappear as 1986 Act agricultural holdings become fewer in number.

The radical reduction in legislative interference reflected in the 1995 Act has prompted both lawyers and surveyors to rethink the way in which they negotiate and draft agricultural tenancies: see Jessel, C., 'Drafting Farm Business Leases' [1995] EG 9545, 126–27. Undoubtedly, the trend is to produce agreements for farm business tenancies which resemble leases for other forms of investment property without the former strictures of a complex statutory agricultural regime.

14 Secure Tenancies

INTRODUCTION

Most tenants (and some licensees) of public sector residential accommodation are conferred security of tenure by virtue of the Housing Act 1985, Pt IV. The Housing Act 1985 also deals with other important areas of housing law (e.g., homelessness, right to buy etc.) which are outside the scope of this book. For an excellent work on these subjects, see Partington, M. and Hill, J., *Housing Law: Cases, Materials and Commentary*, London: Sweet & Maxwell, 1991.

By s. 79(1) of the 1985 Act, a tenancy under which a dwelling-house is let as a separate dwelling is a secure tenancy at any time when both the landlord and tenant conditions are satisfied. The landlord condition is that the interest of the landlord belongs to one of the authorities or bodies listed in s. 80 of the Act (i.e., a local authority, a new town corporation, the Development Board for Rural Wales, the Housing Corporation, a housing trust which is a charity, and certain housing associations and housing cooperatives). The condition will not be satisfied where only one of two joint landlords complies with it (*R v Plymouth City Council and Cornwall City Council, ex parte Freeman* (1987) 19 HLR 328). The tenant condition is that the tenant is an individual and occupies the dwelling-house as his or her only or principal home, or, where the tenancy is a joint tenancy, that each of the joint tenants is an individual and at least one of them occupies the dwelling-house as his or her only or principal home (s. 81 and *Crawley Borough Council v Sawyer* (1987) 20 HLR 98).

The provisions of Pt IV of the 1985 Act apply in relation to a licence to occupy a dwelling-house (whether or not granted for a consideration) as they apply in relation to a tenancy (s. 79(3)). However, security does not apply to a licence granted as a temporary expedient to a person who entered the dwelling-house (or any other land) as a trespasser (whether or not, before the grant of that licence, another licence to occupy that or another dwelling-house had been granted to him) (s. 79(4)). A licence will not be secure if there is no exclusive possession of the subject premises (*Family Housing Association* v *Miah* (1982) 5 HLR 94; *The Royal Borough of Kensington and Chelsea* v *Hayden* (1985) 17 HLR 114; *Westminster City Council* v *Clarke* [1992] 1 All ER 695 and *Shepherds Bush Housing Association Ltd* v *HATS Co-operative* [1992] 24 HLR 176). In addition, a number of tenancies and licences are not secure, and these are listed in sch. 1 to the 1985 Act.

In this chapter, you will find two questions dealing with security of tenure, terms of a secure tenancy and succession rights.

QUESTION 1

In 1998, the Burberry District Council granted Mark and his wife, Michelle, a weekly tenancy of a flat in a block of flats on its housing estate at a rent of £50 per week. Upon their taking up possession of the flat, the Council provided them with a rent book detailing the terms of their tenancy. Condition 2(a) provides '... the tenants covenant at all material times to use the premises in a tenant-like manner'.

The couple's marriage is an unhappy one and Mark and Michelle frequently row. They have broken the door, smashed a front window and damaged the bathroom. They have also been abusive to other tenants on the estate, engaging in anti-social behaviour including the revving of their car engine and slamming of the car doors in the early hours of the morning. Mark and Michelle have also fallen into rent arrears. At present, six months' rent arrears are outstanding. Despite their estrangement, the couple continue to live in the flat with their 19-year-old daughter, Yvette.

The Council has plans in the near future to demolish the block of flats to make way for a new housing estate.

Advise the Council which wishes to evict Mark and Michelle.

Commentary

This is a straightforward question on the security of tenure provisions of the Housing Act 1985, Pt IV. You should begin your answer by outlining the requisite preconditions for a secure tenancy and then consider what grounds (under sch. 2 to the Act) are available to the Council to obtain possession of the flat. The relevant statutory procedures for obtaining possession should also be mentioned.

Suggested Answer

It would seem from the facts that Mark and Michelle have a secure periodic tenancy under the Housing Act 1985, Pt IV. By s. 79(1) of the 1985 Act, a tenancy under which a dwelling-house is let as a separate dwelling is a secure tenancy at any time when both the landlord and tenant conditions are satisfied. The landlord condition requires that the interest of the landlord belongs to one of the bodies listed in s. 80 of the Act, and this includes a local authority. The tenant condition requires that the tenant is an individual and occupies the dwelling-house as his or her only or principal home, or, where there is a joint tenancy (as in the present case) that each of the joint tenants is an individual and at least one of them occupies the dwelling house as his or her only or principal home (s. 81). Both these conditions appear to be satisfied in the present case. Moreover, the couple's tenancy does not appear to fall within any of the excluded tenancies listed in sch. 1 to the 1985 Act.

A periodic secure tenancy cannot be brought to an end by a landlord's common law notice to quit (s. 82(1)). Instead, the landlord must serve a statutory notice, under s. 83(2) of the Act, on the secure tenant(s). Moreover, the landlord must obtain an order for possession and the secure tenancy will end only on the date specified in the court order. The statutory notice (which must be in prescribed form) must be in force when the proceedings for possession are issued and must specify the ground(s) for possession relied on.

There are three categories of grounds, which are contained in sch. 2 to the 1985 Act. Grounds 1–8 (contained in sch. 2, Pt I) are subject to an overriding requirement that it must be reasonable to make an order for possession. The term 'reasonable' means reasonable having regard to the interests of both the parties and the public (*London Borough of Enfield* v *McKeon* (1986) 18 HLR 330). An example of a ground falling within this category relates to rent arrears or breaches of obligation of the tenancy (ground 1). Grounds 9–11 (contained in sch. 2, Pt II) are subject to a requirement that when the order takes effect suitable alternative accommodation will be available to the tenant and his family (s. 84(2)(b) and sch. 2, Pt IV). Ground 10 (in this category) gives the landlord a ground for possession where demolition or reconstruction works are intended to the premises. Grounds 12–16 (contained in sch. 2, Pt III) are subject to both the requirement of reasonableness and the availability of suitable alternative accommodation. This last category is not relevant to the problem.

In this case, Mark and Michelle, by deliberately damaging the premises, are in breach of their express covenant to use the premises in a tenant-like manner. The phrase 'tenant-like manner' has been judicially defined as giving rise to an obligation to take proper care of the property and not to damage it, wilfully or negligently (*Warren* v *Keen* [1954] 1 QB 15, *per* Denning LJ, at p. 20). We are also told that Mark and Michelle have fallen into rent arrears. Both these breaches of covenant provide the Council with a discretionary ground for possession under ground 1 (above). If the Council is successful, the court may make an immediate order for possession, suspend the order, or adjourn matters generally. In *Haringey London Borough Council* v *Stewart* (1991) 2 EGLR 252, the tenant's poor record for persistent late payment of rent, coupled with no proposals for paying off the arrears, justified an order for possession. By contrast, in *Woodspring District Council* v *Taylor* (1982) 4 HLR 95, the amount of arrears of rent (£557) was not considered substantial enough to justify an outright possession order. In the present case, much will depend on how the county court judge views the damage to the property (i.e., its extent and cost of repair) and the reasons why the arrears have fallen due. On balance, a suspended order for possession is the most likely outcome (i.e., a possession order suspended on terms that Mark and Michelle make good the damage to the property and pay off the arrears by instalments, within a specified time-scale).

In addition, the Council should seek to invoke ground 2 of sch. 2 (as replaced by s. 144 of the Housing Act 1996) based on the conduct of the tenants which causes (or is likely to cause) a nuisance or annoyance to 'persons residing, visiting or otherwise engaging in a lawful activity in the locality'. This new terminology replaces the former reference to 'neighbours' under the 1985 Act: see *Northampton Borough Council* v *Lovatt* [1998] 07 EG 142. We are told that Mark and Michelle have been abusive to other tenants on the estate and engaged in various acts of anti-social behaviour. It is evident, therefore, that their conduct falls within this ground, but here again, it is unlikely that the Council will obtain an outright possession order: see *Woking Borough Council* v *Bystram* [1993] EGCS 208 (complaints by neighbours relating to abusive and foul language by the tenants — suspended possession order granted).

In view of the unlikelihood of obtaining an outright possession order under grounds 1 and 2, the Council should consider relying on ground 10 as an additional basis for obtaining possession of the house. Ground 10 is mandatory in the sense that it is not subject to the overriding requirement of reasonableness (see earlier). However, the Council must show that, when the possession order takes effect, suitable alternative accommodation will be available to Mark and Michelle and their family.

One difficulty with relying on this ground is that the Council must establish the requisite settled intention to carry out development work within a reasonable time of obtaining possession of the flat (*Wansbech District Council* v *Marley* (1988) 20 HLR 247). Although a resolution of the Council passed by its appropriate committee is not essential, there must be clear evidence proving a definite intention (*Poppet's (Caterers) Ltd* v *Maidenhead BC* [1971] 1 WLR 69 and *Betty's Cafes Ltd* v *Phillips Furnishing Stores Ltd* [1959] AC 20, applying *Cunliffe* v *Goodman* [1950] 2 KB 237). In addition to showing the requisite intention, the Council must establish that it cannot reasonably carry out the demolition and reconstruction works without obtaining possession of the flat.

Lastly, regarding the requirement of suitable alternative accommodation, since the court cannot make an order for possession under ground 10 unless it is satisfied that suitable alternative accommodation will be available for 'the tenant and his family', it follows that Mark and Michelle's daughter, Yvette, who is 19 and living in the premises, is a person with a potential interest in the possession proceedings and must be joined as party to those proceedings (*Wandsworth London Borough Council* v *Fadayomi* [1987] 3 All ER 474).

QUESTION 2

(a)   What terms are imposed in a secure tenancy under the Housing Act 1985?

[15 marks]

(b)   Mary, a widow with two (foster) boys, Derek and Ian, was granted a monthly secure tenancy of a three-bedroomed family house by the local authority in 1986. In 1988, Mary invited her gay lover, Judy, to move into the house with her. Derek got married in 1989 and moved away. Mary has recently died, leaving Ian, now aged 16, and Judy living in the house.

Advise Derek, Ian and Judy whether any of them has any rights in relation to the house.

[10 marks]

Commentary

This two-part question requires you to demonstrate your knowledge of the terms of a secure tenancy and succession rights under the Housing Act 1985. Part (a) covers familiar ground and should not pose any real problems. Part (b), on the other hand, raises a number of issues, not all of which may be readily apparent even to the well-prepared student. Your answer should, of course, refer to the recent House of Lords ruling in *Fitzpatrick* v *Sterling Housing Association Ltd* [1999] 4 All ER 705 on succession rights of same-sex partners. See further, Pawlowski, M., 'Succession Rights: The House of Lords' Ruling in *Fitzpatrick*' (2000) JHL 21 and Thompson, M. P., 'Gay Equality in the Lords' [2000] Conv. 153. The reference to the two children being foster boys seems a little unsporting since the point has been judicially considered only at county court level (*Reading Borough Council* v *Isley* [1981] CLY (Current Law Year Book) 1323).

Suggested Answer

(a)   The Housing Act 1985 imposes a variety of terms into secure tenancies. Sections 91–101 contain complex provisions which place varying levels of restrictions on the ability of secure tenants to take in lodgers, to sublet or assign their leasehold interests to third parties, or to exchange their lettings with other secure tenants, and to carry out repairs or improvements to the premises. The aim of these provisions is to establish a framework so as to enable secure tenants to carry out various activities which, prior to the legislation, often amounted to a breach of covenant.

Save for a few limited exceptions (e.g., where there is an exchange, or where a succession has occurred on the death of a secure tenant, or where the tenancy is transferred to the spouse of a secure tenant following divorce or judicial separation), s. 91 prohibits assignments of all or part of the dwelling-house: *Burton* v *Camden London Borough Council* [2000] EGCS 23 (HL). Section 92, however, provides that it is a term of every secure tenancy that the tenant may, with the written consent of the landlord, assign the tenancy to another secure tenant. In such cases, only limited grounds for refusal exist. These grounds are set out in sch. 3 to the 1985 Act and include situations where:

(a)   one of the tenants is being evicted for non-payment of rent or breach of any other obligation of the tenancy; or

(b)   one of the tenants would be acquiring premises which were substantially greater than his or her own family's needs; or

(c)   one of the tenants does not intend to use the premises for housing purposes; or

(d)   the landlord in question provides accommodation for people with specific needs and the exchange would bring in occupiers outside this purpose.

Section 93(1)(a) is concerned with the ability of secure tenants to take in lodgers. The subsection provides that it is a term of every secure tenancy that the tenant may allow any persons to reside as lodgers in the dwelling-house.

It is also a term of every secure tenancy that the tenant will not, without the written consent of the landlord, sub-let or part with possession of *part* of the dwelling-house (s. 93(1)(b)). If the tenant parts with possession of the dwelling-house or sublets the *whole* of it, the tenancy ceases to be a secure tenancy. The landlord cannot unreasonably withhold his consent, and the onus is on the landlord to show that the withholding of consent was not unreasonable (s. 94(2)). In determining this question, the fact that consent would lead to overcrowding of the dwelling-house, or that the landlord proposes to carry out works on the dwelling-house which would affect the accommodation likely to be used by the proposed sub-tenant, may be taken into account. If a landlord fails to reply to a tenant's request, this is deemed to be an unreasonable refusal.

Section 96(1), as re-enacted by the Leasehold Reform, Housing and Urban Development Act 1993, provides for the Secretary of State to formulate a scheme whereby secure tenants may serve a notice informing the landlord of repairs the landlord is responsible for. The current repair scheme requires that the tenant serves a notice on the landlord stating that 'qualifying repairs' need to be carried out. The landlord must respond with a counternotice specifying the nature of the proposed repair, the name of the contractor who will undertake the work and the date when it will be carried out. If the work is not completed in time, a second contractor must be nominated by the landlord. If the second contractor fails to execute the works, the landlord is liable to pay the tenant compensation, enforceable in the county court.

Sections 97–101 are concerned with the issue of improvements. As a general rule, a secure tenant cannot cary out improvements (including alterations, additions and external decorative work), unless consent has been obtained from the landlord. Here again, as with the rules governing partial sub-letting, the landlord must not unreasonably withhold his consent, and if unreasonably withheld it is treated as given (s. 97(3)). There is also provision for the landlord to reimburse the tenant the cost of his improvements (s. 100).

Both the landlord and the tenant may vary the terms of the secure tenancy (ss. 102–103).

Part V of the Housing Act 1985 confers on secure tenants who have been in occupation of their properties for over three years, the right either to purchase the freehold of their house, or to acquire a long lease of 125 years, subject to generous discounts.

   (b)   The succession rights on the death of a secure tenant are contained in the Housing Act 1985, ss. 87–90.

Under s. 87, a person is qualified to succeed if he or she occupies the dwelling-house as his or her only or principal home at the time of the secure tenant's death and either:

(a) he or she is the tenant's spouse; or

(b) he or she is another member of the tenant's family and has resided with the tenant throughout the period of 12 months ending with the tenant's death (*Peabody Donation Fund Governors* v *Grant* (1982) 264 EG 925).

Section 113(1) of the 1985 Act defines the phrase 'member of the tenant's family' as including a person living with the tenant as husband and wife, the tenant's parent, grandparent, child, grandchild, brother, sister, uncle, aunt, nephew or niece.

The House of Lords in *Fitzpatrick* v *Sterling Housing Association Ltd* [1999] 4 All ER 705 has recently held that a same-sex partner may be entitled to succeed to a statutory tenancy under the Rent Act 1977 on the ground that he (or she) was a member of the original tenant's family, provided that the relationship was stable and permanent. The House, however, also confirmed the earlier case of *Harrogate Borough Council* v *Simpson* [1986] 2 FLR 91 (involving a lesbian couple) decided under the provisions of the 1985 Act, that a same-sex partner could not succeed to a tenancy as the surviving spouse of the original tenant. This is because the word 'spouse' meant a person who was legally the husband or wife of the original tenant, and the extended definition (of a person living with him 'as his or her wife or husband') only applied to those persons who, though not legally husband and wife, lived *as such* without being married. Such words were gender specific, connoting a relationship between a man and a woman, so that the man had to show that the woman was living with him as 'his' wife, and the woman had to show that the man was living with her as 'her' husband.

Judy, therefore, will be entitled to succeed to Mary's secure tenancy as a member of her family (but not as a surviving spouse), provided that their relationship was a stable, close and loving one. This seems apparent from the fact that Mary and Judy had lived together for a number of years prior to the former's death.

We are told that Derek got married in 1989 and moved away from the house. He, clearly, cannot succeed to his mother's secure tenancy because he cannot fulfil the necessary 12-month residence requirement. Ian, on the other hand, appears to qualify as a successor, having lived in the house at all material times. The fact that Ian is a foster child should not affect this conclusion. In *Reading Borough Council* v *Isley* [1981] CLY 1323, three foster boys, who were never formally adopted by the tenant, were held entitled to succeed to a secure tenancy. The undisputed evidence was that they had always been treated in all respects as the natural children of the tenant (and her husband). Although Ian is still a minor, he may still hold an equitable tenancy of the property (*Kingston upon Thames RLBC* v *Prince* [1998] EGCS 179 (CA), where it was held that the security provisions of the 1985 Act did extend to minors.

15 Pick and Mix Questions

INTRODUCTION

In this chapter, we have set out six questions which mix a number of different topics in landlord and tenant law.

Most students tend to shy away from such questions because they are perceived as being more complicated than single topic questions. Our experience is that most students will have revised *some* of the topics covered in the question but, invariably, not all. If you are faced with a mixed topic question and cannot answer all the areas, it is best not to attempt it — move on to another question which covers more familiar ground which you have revised more fully.

If you do decide to attempt such a question, our advice is to read the question very carefully and pick out all the various issues before putting pen to paper. If you feel you can take on all the topics, then you will need to structure your answer so that the various areas are dealt with in a logical, coherent whole. One advantage to mixed topic questions is that the examiner will not expect you to cover each topic in the same detail as you would a single topic question, but you should, nevertheless, be able to display a command of a wide area of knowledge, not superficially, but incisively and with depth in the given area.

QUESTION 1

(a)   To what extent is the classification of tenancies into specific and periodic an over-simplification?

(b)   Explain the legal position of a tenant who withholds payment of rent on the ground that his landlord has failed to execute repairs for which he (the landlord) is responsible.

Commentary

This is a good example of a two-part question where the two parts are wholly unrelated in subject-matter.

Part (a) requires you to consider those tenancies which do *not* fall neatly into the two-fold classification of specific or periodic. In other words, you should examine (i) the tenancy at will, (ii) the tenancy at sufferance, and (iii) the tenancy by estoppel. If you merely give a list of the different types of fixed-term and periodic tenancies, you are not answering the question.

Part (b) requires you to examine equitable set-off against rent (*British Anzani (Felixstowe) Ltd* v *International Marine Management (UK) Ltd* [1980] QB 637) and the common law right to deduct repairing costs from rent (*Lee-Parker* v *Izzet* [1971] 1 WLR 1688 and *Asco Developments Ltd* v *Gordon* (1978) 248 EG 683). For further reading, see Rank, P. M., 'Repairs in Lieu of Rent' (1976) 40 Conv 196, and Waite, A., 'Repairs and Deduction from Rent' (1981) 45 Conv 199. This is a topical question in view of a number of recent cases where the right to set-off and to make a deduction was considered in the context of an express exclusion that rent should be payable 'without any deduction' (*Connaught Restaurants Ltd* v *Indoor Leisure Ltd* [1994] 4 All ER 834 (CA); *Famous Army Stores* v *Meehan* [1993] 09 EG 114; *Electricity Supply Nominees Ltd* v *IAF Group Ltd* [1993] 1 WLR 1059; *Star Rider Ltd* v *Inntrepreneur Pub Co.* [1998] EGLR 53; and *Unchained Growth plc* v *Granby Village (Manchester) Management Co. Ltd* [1999] EGCS 116 (CA)).

Suggested Answer

(a)   Not all tenancies fall neatly into the two-fold classification of specific (i.e., fixed term) or periodic. For example, a tenancy at will creates a relationship of tenure without estate and arises where the occupier is more than a licensee (i.e., he enjoys exclusive possession with the consent of the owner) but the conduct of the parties allows for no inference as to quantum of interest. Because the permitted occupation is for an uncertain period, it is not a 'term of years absolute' within the Law of Property Act 1925, s. 205(1)(xxvii), so that a tenancy at will may be determined at any time by a demand for possession or by any other act which, by implication of law, negates any continuing consent given by the landlord.

Such a tenancy may arise:

(a) by express agreement (see, e.g., *Manfield & Sons Ltd* v *Botchin* [1970] 2 QB 612 and *Hagee (London) Ltd* v *Erikson (A.B.) and Larson* [1976] QB 209);

(b) where the tenant holds over with the landlord's consent and a periodic tenancy has not yet arisen (see, e.g., *Wheeler* v *Mercer* [1957] AC 416, where there was a holding over pending agreement on the new rent);

(c) where the tenant takes possession under a void lease; or;

(d) where a purchaser is let into possession before completion. The courts, however, are generally disinclined to infer a tenancy at will from an exclusive occupation of indefinite duration (*Heslop* v *Burns* [1974] 1 WLR 1241).

A tenant at will is entitled to the protection of the Rent Act 1977 where applicable (*Chamberlain* v *Farr* [1942] 2 All ER 567), but a tenant at will of business premises cannot claim the protection of the Landlord and Tenant Act 1954, Pt II (*Hagee (London) Ltd* v *Erikson (A.B.) and Larson* (express tenancy at will) and *Wheeler* v *Mercer* (implied tenancy at will)).

Another example of a tenancy not falling within the two-fold classification is a tenancy at sufferance. This donates the relationship of owner and occupier where the tenant holds over on the expiry of his lease and the landlord has neither consented to nor expressed objection to the occupation. The absence of the landlord's consent negatives any relationship of tenure. The legal effects of this relationship will depend on subsequent events, namely:

(a) if the landlord requires the tenant to quit, the tenant becomes a trespasser and (by the doctrine of trespass by relation) the landlord can claim mesne profits from the date that the tenant's possession ceased to be lawful until possession is given up; or

(b)   if the landlord signifies his consent (e.g., by a demand for rent) the tenant becomes a tenant at will, and if rent is paid with reference to a particular period the tenant becomes a periodic tenant; or

(c)   if the landlord simply acquiesces, he will be statute barred if he fails to re-assert his title within 12 years from the date that the tenant's possession ceased to be lawful (Limitation Act 1980, s. 15).

Reference may also be made to a tenancy by estoppel. The doctrine of estoppel precludes parties, who have induced others to rely upon their representations, from denying the truth of the facts represented. For the purposes of landlord and tenant law, this means that neither the landlord nor the tenant can question the validity of the lease granted once possession has been taken up. Thus, even if the landlord is not the lawful owner of the estate out of which the tenant is granted his lease, the tenant cannot deny any of his leasehold obligations to the landlord by arguing that the grant was not effectively made. In other words, the tenant is estopped from suggesting that, due to the defect in the landlord's title, he is released from his leasehold obligations (*Industrial Properties (Barton Hill) Ltd* v *Associated Electrical Industries Ltd* [1977] QB 580). Similarly, the landlord cannot set up his want of title as a ground for repudiating the lease (*EH Lewis* v *Morelli* [1948] 2 All ER 1021 and *Mackley* v *Nutting* [1949] 2 KB 55).

If, after the purported creation of a tenancy by means of the estoppel doctrine, the landlord acquires the legal estate out of which the tenancy could be created (e.g., as where he purchases the freehold), this feeds the estoppel and the tenancy becomes good in interest. On this occurrence, the tenant acquires a legal tenancy founded upon the landlord's newly acquired legal estate (*Church of England Building Society* v *Piskor* [1954] Ch 553).

A tenancy by estoppel may be a protected tenancy under the Rent Act 1977 (*Stratford* v *Syrett* [1958] 1 QB 107) and a business tenancy subject to protection under Pt II of the Landlord and Tenant Act 1954 (*Bell* v *General Accident Fire & Life Assurance Corporation Ltd* [1998] 17 EG 144).

(b)   A tenant has two distinct arguments he can put forward to justify his withholding of rent in this type of case.

By way of self-help, the tenant may decide to do the repairs himself and deduct the expense from current or future rent. On being sued for unpaid rent by his landlord, the tenant will be able to rely on his own counterclaim against the landlord for breach of the landlord's repairing covenant as effecting a complete defence by way of an equitable set-off to the claim for rent (*British Anzani (Felixstowe) Ltd* v *International Marine Management (UK) Ltd* [1980] QB 137). Equitable set-off can be used to pay for the cost of repairs the landlord is required to carry out but fails to, and for any reasonable consequential losses arising from the landlord's default. Set-off will, therefore, be important to a tenant where the failure to repair has led to expenditure, not only to get the work done but also to put right damage caused to the tenant's property as a result of the failure to repair.

Alternatively, the tenant has a common law right to deduct the repairing cost from the rent where, having given notice to the landlord, the tenant carries out the repairs which are the landlord's responsibility. In *Lee-Parker* v *Izet* [1971] 1 WLR 1688, Goff J held that there is an 'ancient common law right' to recover the cost of repairs out of rent payable and, in any action for non-payment of rent, to raise the withholding of rent as a defence because, as a matter of law, that money is not owed to the landlord. The principle was approved by Sir Robert Megarry VC in *Asco Developments Ltd* v *Gordon* (1978) 248 EG 683, who allowed the cost of repairs to be recovered by reduction of rent arrears already in existence.

The ancient common law right can be used only to recover the cost of repair, whereas set-off is wider (as mentioned above) because it enables the tenant to get back, for example, the cost of repairing or replacing furniture damaged by water coming into the premises because of the landlord's default. In *British Anzani* (above), Forbes J suggested that the ancient common law right was appropriate for claiming ascertainable sums spent on repairs which the landlord could not really dispute, whereas the wider right of set-off should be used if more than the basic cost of repair is claimed.

The right to set-off and to make a deduction will not be excluded even where the obligation to pay rent is expressly stated to be 'without any deduction' (*Connaught Restaurants Ltd* v *Indoor Leisure Ltd* [1994] 4 All ER 834, where the Court of Appeal held that the expression 'without any deduction' was insufficient by itself, in the absence of any context suggesting the contrary, to operate by implication as an exclusion of a tenant's equitable right of set-off against rent). Contrast *Famous Army Stores* v *Meehan* [1993] 09 EG 114, which was disapproved. However, such an exclusion, where operative (e.g., by the use of words 'without any deduction *or set off whatsoever*'), does not fall foul of the Unfair Contract Terms Act 1977 since sch. 1, para. 1(b) to the Act expressly states that the provisions of the Act are not applicable to 'any contract so far as it relates to the creation or transfer of an interest in land or the termination of such an interest'. In *Electricity Supply Nominees Ltd* v *IAF Group Ltd* [1993] 1 WLR 1059, it was held that the words 'relates to' in sch. 1 to the 1977 Act were sufficiently wide to contemplate the inclusion of all the lease covenants which were integral to the lease which itself created the interest in land. See also, *Star Rider Ltd* v *Inntrepreneur Pub Co.* [1998] EGLR 53 and *Unchained Growth plc* v *Granby Village (Manchester) Management Co. Ltd* [1999] EGCS 116 (CA).

However, reference must also now be made to the Unfair Terms in Consumer Contracts Regulations 1999, which came into force on 1 October 1999 and apply to any terms entered into on or after 1 July 1995. The Regulations apply to a 'seller or supplier' acting in a business capacity and to a 'consumer' acting for purposes which are outside a trade, business or profession. Whilst, therefore, this definition appears to exclude business tenants, it will cover all residential tenants. If a particular term falls to be characterised as unfair, it will be unenforceable against the consumer (reg. 8(1)). It is evident that a number of leasehold terms may potentially fall foul of the Regulations. For example, an absolute prohibition against assigning, sub-letting or parting with possession or occupation of the premises could be treated as unfair in so far as it causes a significant detriment to the tenant who may have good reasons for assigning or sub-letting. Similarly, a forfeiture clause which entitles the landlord to determine the lease without any prior warning when the rent is, say, only 14 days late, is likely to be struck down. Clauses which fetter the tenant's right of set-off or deduction could also be held unenforceable on similar grounds: see para. 1(b) of sch. 2 to the 1999 Regulations, which specifically refers to 'inappropriately excluding ... the option of offsetting a debt owed to the [supplier] against any claim which the consumer may have against him'.

QUESTION 2

In 1980, Dracula Properties Ltd (Dracula) demised a newsagent's shop to David for a term of 21 years from 25 December 1980. By the lease, David covenanted (*inter alia*):

(a)   not to assign, underlet or part with possession of the premises or any part thereof;

(b)   not to use the premises (nor suffer or permit the same to be used) for any unlawful or immoral purposes;

(c)   not to make any alterations or additions to the premises.

It has come to Dracula's attention that:

(a)   David's wife, Sarah, has recently been in trouble with the police for selling obscene magazines and videos in the shop. David has actively encouraged his wife in this new venture. Dracula became aware of these facts in early May 2000;

(b)   Miss Smith is occupying the basement of the premises as a sub-tenant. There is strong evidence that she is using this accommodation for the purpose of prostitution and that David and his wife have turned a blind eye to this. These facts came to light in August 2000;

(c)   The frontage of the premises has been substantially altered. This fact came to light only last week.

The rent due on 24 June 2000 in advance was duly paid by Sarah on behalf of her husband. No other rent has been demanded or accepted.

Advise Dracula on the legal consequences of these events under common law and statute.

Commentary

This question combines the topic of forfeiture with the termination of a business tenancy under the Landlord and Tenant Act 1954, Pt II. Notice that the lease is due to expire on 24 December 2001, which makes it possible for the landlord to invoke the statutory machinery for termination under Pt II instead of bringing an action for forfeiture.

For further reading, see Williams, D., 'Landlord and Tenant Act 1954 Part II — The Operation of Sections 30(1)(b) and (c)' [1990] EG 9049, 40 and Brown, J., 'Waiver' [1997] EG 9702, 119.

Suggested Answer

The fact that David's wife, Sarah, has been selling obscene magazines and videos in the shop prima facie constitutes a breach of the user covenant in the lease under which David (as lessee) covenanted not to suffer or permit the premises to be used for any unlawful purposes. But does the acceptance of rent for the June quarter preclude Dracula from forfeiting the lease for this breach? A waiver by acceptance of rent is sufficient if payment is accepted from a person on behalf of the tenant in satisfaction of the rent under the lease (*Pellatt v Boosey* (1862) 31 LJ CP 281). The fact, therefore, that the rent has been accepted from David's wife on his behalf will constitute an act of waiver of forfeiture. However, a breach of a user covenant is classified, as a matter of law, as a *continuing* breach (*Doe d Ambler* v *Woodbridge* (1829) 9 B & C 376 and *Segal Securities Ltd* v *Thoseby* [1963] 1 QB 887), so that despite the acceptance of rent in June 2000 with knowledge of the breach, there will be a continually recurring cause of forfeiture and the waiver (by the acceptance of rent for the June quarter) will operate only in relation to past breaches. Because the breach is continuing, a fresh right of forfeiture will arise after the next rent day (i.e., 29 September 2000).

In order to pursue its remedy of forfeiture, Dracula must serve on David a notice pursuant to the Law of Property Act 1925, s. 146, specifying the breach complained of and, 'if the breach is capable of remedy', requiring the tenant to remedy it within a reasonable period of time (s. 146(1)). A breach of a negative covenant which leaves a stigma on the demised premises is generally incapable of remedy (*Governors of Rugby School* v *Tannahill* [1935] 1 KB 87). Thus, if the breach is irremediable (as in the present case), the landlord does not have to stipulate in its s. 146 notice that the breach be remedied and may proceed to execute its right of forfeiture (whether by action or physical re-entry) with little delay (*Dunraven Securities Ltd* v *Holloway* (1982) 264 EG 709 and *DR Evans & Co.* v *Chandler* (1969) 211 EG 1381, use of premises for the sale of pornographic material). In *Van Haarlam* v *Kasner Charitable Trust* [1992] 36 EG 135, a case involving a breach of covenant not to use the premises for any illegal or immoral purposes, 30 days' notice was held reasonable. Furthermore, since the breach is technically incapable of remedy, David's only recourse is to seek relief from forfeiture under s. 146(2) of the 1925 Act. Whether such relief will be granted is debatable in view of the fact that relief from forfeiture is normally refused where the tenant has permitted immoral or illegal user of the premises (*Egerton* v *Esplanade Hotels, London Ltd* [1947] 2 All ER 88). In an appropriate case, however, where the tenant is genuinely ignorant of the facts, relief may be granted (*Glass* v *Kencakes Ltd* [1966] 1 QB 611 and *Ropemaker Properties Ltd* v *Noonhaven Ltd* (1989) 2 EGLR 50).

Miss Smith's occupation of the basement as a sub-tenant is also in clear breach of the terms of David's lease. The lease contains an absolute covenant against assignment, sub-letting etc., so that the provisions of the Landlord and Tenant Act 1927, s. 19(1) (which impose a proviso that the landlord's consent shall not be unreasonably withheld) do not apply (*FW Woolworth and Co. Ltd* v *Lambert* [1937] Ch 37, *per* Romer LJ at pp. 58-59). Assuming the basement premises are being used for prostitution, this will also constitute a breach of David's covenant not to suffer or permit any part of the premises to be used for an immoral purpose.

We are told that these facts came to light in August 2000, so that there is no question of Dracula waiving these breaches by the acceptance of rent in June 2000 when it had no knowledge of the same. In this connection, a waiver of forfeiture can only occur where the landlord does some unequivocal act recognising the continued existence of the lease with knowledge of the facts upon which its right of re-entry arises (*Matthews* v *Smallwood* [1910] 1 Ch 777, at p. 786 and, more recently, *Cornillie* v *Saha* (1996) 28 HLR 561 (CA)). Here again, Dracula will need to particularise the breaches complained of in his s. 146 notice as a preliminary to forfeiting the lease by physical re-entry or proceedings for possession. Moreover, because a breach of a covenant not to assign, underlet or part with possession is an irremediable breach (*Scala House & District Property Co. Ltd* v *Forbes* [1974] QB 575), David is not in a position to avoid the forfeiture by ceasing the action which constitutes the breach. Once again, his only recourse is to seek relief from forfeiture under s. 146(2) of the 1925 Act, which (as mentioned earlier) is problematical in view of the immoral nature of the breach.

The alteration to the frontage of the shop also constitutes a breach of the covenant not to make any alterations or additions to the demised premises. As Dracula became aware of this only last week, no question of waiver arises. It will be necessary, however, for Dracula to include particulars of this breach in its s. 146 notice. In *Savva* v *Houssein* [1996] 47 EG 138, the Court of Appeal held that all breaches of covenant were capable of remedy if the mischief caused by the breach can be removed. In the case of a covenant against alterations, the mischief can be removed by restoring the property to the state it was in before the alterations. Dracula's s. 146 notice, therefore, must require David to remedy the breach.

Since David's lease constitutes shop premises, it is likely that it qualifies as a business tenancy under the Landlord and Tenant Act 1954, Pt II. Section 24 of the Act expressly preserves various common law methods of termination, including forfeiture of the lease. Alternatively, Pt II of the Act prescribes statutory machinery for termination of a business tenancy. In this case, it would be open to Dracula, as an alternative to forfeiting the lease, to serve on David a notice of termination of his tenancy under s. 25 of the 1954 Act. This must be in a prescribed form (or substantially to like effect) and must specify the date at which the existing tenancy is to come to an end. The notice itself must be given not more than 12 months and not less than six months before the termination date specified in the notice, which must not be earlier than the date at which the tenancy would expire or could be brought to an end by the landlord at common law. In David's case, the earliest termination date is the date of the expiry of his lease (i.e., 24 December 2001). In addition, Dracula's notice must require David to notify it in writing within two months whether or not he will be willing to give up possession at the date specified in the notice, and must state whether Dracula would oppose a tenant's application to the court for the grant of a new tenancy and, if so, on which of the seven grounds specified in s. 30(1) of the Act.

On the facts, Dracula may rely on ground (c) of s. 30(1), namely, substantial breaches of obligations under the tenancy. The ground (like grounds (a) and (b)) is discretionary in the sense that, although proof of a breach of covenant is essential, the landlord must also show that a new tenancy ought not to be granted by reason of the substantial breaches of obligations. In this connection, the court is entitled to consider the whole of the tenant's conduct and not merely matters specified in the landlord's notice of opposition (*Eichner* v *Midland Bank Executor and Trustee Co. Ltd* [1970] 1 WLR 1120). If Dracula is successful in opposing David's application for a new tenancy, the existing tenancy will come to an end on the date specified in the s. 25 notice (i.e., 24 December 2001), or three months after the final disposal of the application by the court, whichever is the later (s. 64). It is important to bear in mind that the tenant's right to compensation for disturbance is limited to cases where the landlord successfully objects to the grant of a new tenancy on grounds (e), (f) or (g) of s. 30(1) (s. 37(1)). The tenant's right to compensation for improvements, however, will not be affected.

QUESTION 3

In March 1995, Joshua granted Peter (who runs a car parking and vehicle storage business) a 15-year lease of a two acre car parking and vehicle storage area. The lease provided that the rent was £15,000 per annum payable quarterly in advance and that Joshua would 'keep in good repair and structural condition' the boundary wall surrounding the demised premises.

In 1998, Peter discovered that the boundary wall was subsiding due to inadequate foundations. In the same year, the entrance to the car park was shut off by building contractors employed by the local water authority who were carrying out major excavations to a local sewage system. Peter wrote to Joshua in relation to both these matters requesting that Joshua repair the boundary wall and put pressure on the authority to reorganise their works so as to free up the entrance to the car park. Joshua ignored both these requests.

As a result of the water authority's works, the entrance to the car park remained blocked for two years, rendering the car park inoperable during this period.

In March 2000, Peter eventually abandoned the premises. Joshua has now written to Peter demanding the outstanding rent for the June and September quarters.

Advise Peter.

Commentary

The essential issue in this question is whether Peter is still bound under the terms of his lease to pay the rent. One approach is to argue that Joshua was guilty of a repudiatory breach by failing to remedy the defective boundary wall and that Peter, by accepting the repudiation by quitting the premises in 2000, effectively terminated the lease. But does the remedial work to the wall constitute a work of repair within the meaning of the landlord's repairing covenant? Moreover, are the defects sufficiently fundamental to constitute a repudiatory breach? Even assuming the facts warrant a repudiatory breach, does this doctrine apply to a business tenancy governed by the Landlord and Tenant Act 1954, Pt II?

Alternatively, it may be possible to argue that the lease was discharged by frustration (i.e., by the actions of the water authority denying Peter the substantial benefit of the letting). Here again, it is doubtful on the facts whether the event in question was sufficiently serious to warrant the operation of the doctrine.

A third possibility is that the lease was effectively surrendered upon Peter abandoning the premises.

The likelihood of Joshua forfeiting the lease for non-payment of rent should also be considered.

See also, Question 4, **Chapter 8**.

Suggested Answer

The question whether Peter is bound to pay the rent will depend on whether or not the lease has effectively been brought to an end. One possibility is that the lease has been terminated by operation of the doctrine of repudiatory breach. It was once thought that this doctrine had no universal application to leases. In *Total Oil Great Britain Ltd* v *Thompson Garages (Biggin Hill) Ltd* [1972] 1 QB 318, Lord Denning MR was of the opinion that because a lease was a demise conveying an interest in land, it did not come to an end like an ordinary contract on repudiation and acceptance. This view no longer represents the law. In *Hussein* v *Mehlman* [1992] 32 EG 59, it was reaffirmed that a lease could come to an end by the tenant's acceptance of his landlord's repudiatory conduct. In that case, the defendant landlord granted the plaintiff tenants a three-year assured shorthold tenancy of a dwelling-house subject to the covenants to repair implied on the part of the landlord by the Landlord and Tenant Act 1985, s. 11. From the commencement of the term, the plaintiffs made several complaints to the defendant regarding the disrepair of the premises. The defendant refused to carry out these repairs and eventually the plaintiffs returned the keys and vacated the dwelling-house. On the evidence, the court held that the defendant had been guilty of a repudiatory breach (in so far as the defects were such as to render the house as a whole unfit to be lived in) and the plaintiffs, by vacating the premises and returning the keys, had accepted that repudiation as putting an end to the tenancy. The decision in *Hussein* was treated as apparently correct, without argument, by the Court of Appeal in *Chartered Trust plc* v *Davies* [1997] 2 EGLR 83, where, although the lease had still about 20 years left to run, the landlord's conduct in derogating from grant resulted in substantial interference with the tenant's business driving her to bankruptcy. This, in itself, was considered sufficient to deprive the tenant of the whole benefit of her contract and constitute a repudiation of the lease regardless of the unexpired term of the lease.

In the present case, we are told that the boundary wall was subsiding due to inadequate foundations. Does this come within Joshua's covenant to repair? Although the term 'repair' includes the obligation to remedy inherent defects in design or construction of the premises, the question in all cases is one of fact and degree (*Brew Bros Ltd* v *Snax (Ross) Ltd* [1970] 1 QB 612 and *Ravenseft Properties Ltd* v *Davstone (Holdings) Ltd* [1980] QB 12). In *Smedley* v *Chumley & Hawke Ltd* (1981) 261 EG 775, for example, the lease of a restaurant contained a landlord's covenant to keep the main walls and roof in good structural condition and repair throughout the tenancy. A few years after the commencement of the lease, it became evident that the foundations of the restaurant were defective. There were no piles under part of the concrete raft on which the building was constructed, with the result that the raft tilted, causing damage to the walls and roof. The Court of Appeal held that the landlords were liable under their covenant.

Assuming that remedial work to the boundary wall constitutes repair, are the defects sufficiently fundamental to constitute a repudiatory breach? In *Hussein v Mehlman* (above) the defects in question rendered the dwelling-house uninhabitable, thereby depriving the tenant of the essential part of what he had contracted for, namely, a house in which all rooms were usable and in which ceilings were not collapsed or collapsing and into which rain, wind and cold did not penetrate through the various defects in the structure. It is submitted that the present case is distinguishable in that the car park was capable of operating without hindrance despite the defects to the boundary wall. Another distinguishing feature is that in *Hussein v Mehlman* there was clear evidence that the tenant had accepted the repudiation by vacating the premises and handing back the keys. In the present case, we are told that Peter merely abandoned the premises after two years. This delay may constitute an affirmation of the contract and deny Peter the right to terminate for its breach.

A more fundamental difficulty lies in the fact that it may be open to question whether the doctrine of repudiatory breach applies at all in the context of a business tenancy protected under the Landlord and Tenant Act 1954, Pt II. In this connection, s. 24 of the Act is quite specific in setting out certain non-statutory (common law) methods of termination (i.e., notice to quit given by tenant, surrender, forfeiture, agreement for a new tenancy etc.). It is doubtful whether termination by acceptance of a landlord's repudiatory breach falls within any of these heads.

Alternatively, it may be possible to argue that the lease was discharged by a frustrating event, namely, the actions of the water authority in shutting off the entrance to the car park. In *National Carriers Ltd v Panalpina Northern Ltd* [1981] AC 675, the House of Lords held that the contractual doctrine of frustration was applicable to leases, but the actual circumstances in which a lease could be frustrated would be rare. In that case, access to a warehouse demised to the defendants for a term of 10 years was closed up for a period of 20 months by the local authority in order for essential works to be carried out to a neighbouring warehouse. During that period, the demised warehouse was rendered useless for the tenants' purpose and they claimed that the lease had been frustrated by the events which had happened. The House of Lords held that, having regard to the likely length of continuance of the lease after the interruption of user in relation to the term originally granted, the tenants had failed to raise a triable issue. A similar conclusion would, it is submitted, be reached in the present case. Although the disruption was for a period of two years, it is important to bear in mind that the lease has another 10 years left to run before its expiry in March 2010.

It has been suggested by one commentator that there is a doctrine of 'frustratory mitigation' which may apply to leases: see Morgan, J. [1995] Conv 74. In contrast to frustration, an event giving rise to frustratory mitigation merely *suspends* the operation of the relevant covenant until such time as it can be performed, or it becomes evident that performance will never be possible and it is properly frustrated. It is unlikely, however, that this doctrine (if it exists) would provide a defence for an action for non-payment of rent against Peter. Despite the fact that he may not be getting what he bargained for as a result of the water authority's works, the payment of rent will still be possible even if the anticipated use of the premises is not.

Another possibility is that the lease was effectively surrendered by operation of law. Although a mere temporary abandonment of possession by the tenant will not of itself justify an inference that the lease has been impliedly surrendered, a permanent abandonment of possession will suffice, particularly where the tenant having left with the unequivocal intention of not returning, the landlord accepts his implied offer for a surrender by changing the locks and re-letting the premises to another person (*R* v *London Borough of Croydon, ex parte Toth* (1986) 18 HLR 493). The position, however, may be otherwise if the tenant (as in the present case) simply abandons possession but the landlord has not formally accepted the surrender and ended the lease nor re-let the premises (*Preston Borough Council* v *Fairclough* (1982) 8 HLR 70).

It seems, therefore, that Peter continues to be liable to pay the rent until such time as the lease is formally ended. One possibility is that Joshua will seek to forfeit the lease for non-payment of rent. Abandonment of the premises by the tenant does not of itself entitle a landlord to forfeit the lease unless it amounts to a breach of a covenant (e.g., non-payment of rent) or condition in the lease. Apart from relying on the law of forfeiture, Joshua may have resort to the Distress for Rent Act 1737, s. 16, which provides a means by which a landlord may, in certain circumstances, recover possession of premises left uncultivated or unoccupied. In view, however, of the cumbersome nature of this procedure, the landlord's remedy of forfeiture is to be preferred.

QUESTION 4

(a) What are the essential attributes of rent? What is meant by the doctrine of certainty of rent?

[10 marks]

(b) In August 1992, Norman granted Harriet an assured weekly tenancy of a dwelling-house known as 'The Mews'. At that time, the property was occupied by Harriet and her husband, Nick. In October 1993, Norman assigned his reversionary interest to Sheila subject to Harriet's tenancy. In December 1999, Harriet divorced Nick and, in the course of the proceedings for ancillary relief, she undertook to transfer the tenancy to Nick. Nothing, however, was done to implement the undertaking, and in fact Harriet continues to occupy the property. Nick has recently moved out and found accommodation elsewhere.

Since the divorce proceedings, no rent has been paid under the tenancy. Sheila now wishes to obtain possession of the property and recover the arrears of rent.

Advise Sheila.

[15 marks]

Commentary

This is a two-part question which raises a mixed bag of topics.

Part (a) requires you to write a mini-essay on the meaning of 'rent' and the doctrine of certainty of rent. To score good marks, you should illustrate your answer, wherever possible, by reference to case law.

Part (b) is more complicated since it requires you to assimilate the various issues and produce a coherent, succinct piece of advice in a relatively short time-span. The danger is that you will run out of time before completing your answer. There is quite a lot of ground to cover:

(a) the ability of an assignee landlord (Sheila) to sue upon breaches of covenant occurring after the assignment;

(b) the requisite legal formalities for the assignment of a weekly tenancy; and

(c)   the statutory machinery for termination under the Housing Act 1988, Pt I.

Note that part (b) of the question carries more marks than part (a). Your answer should, therefore, reflect this imbalance.

Suggested Answer

(a)   Rent is a profit issuing out of and derived from land payable by a tenant to a landlord as a compensation or consideration for possession of the land demised during a given term. In paying rent, a tenant implicitly acknowledges his landlord's title. In *CH Bailey* v *Memorial Enterprises Ltd* [1974] 1 WLR 728, Lord Denning cited with approval Holdsworth's *History of English Law* (1900), Vol. VII, p. 262, which states that '. . . in modern law, rent is not conceived of as a thing, but rather as a payment which a tenant is bound by his contract to make to his landlord for the use of the land'. Similarly, in *Bradshaw* v *Pawley* (1980) 253 EG 693, Sir Robert Megarry V-C observed (at p. 695) that rent was essentially the periodical monetary compensation payable by the tenant in consideration for the grant of a lease of land.

Rent is, accordingly, a contractual sum which the landlord is entitled to receive from the tenant in return for the latter's use and occupation of his land. Rent may be contrasted with a rentcharge, the latter being charged on land in perpetuity or for a term, with an express power of distress, but the owner of the rentcharge has no reversion on the land charged. By the Rentcharges Act 1977, s. 2, rentcharges cannot generally be created after 22 August 1977. Rent may also be contrasted with a premium or fine. These are capital sums payable as a lump sum (or in instalments) at or from the commencement of a lease, or on its subsequent assignment.

The House of Lords has recently ruled that money paid under a mistake of law can be recovered by the payer even where payment had been made under a settled understanding of the law at the time, or where payment had been received by the payee under an honest belief of an entitlement to retain the money (*Kleinwort Benson Ltd* v *Lincoln City Council* [1998] 3 WLR 1095 (HL)). The case has huge potential consequences in respect of overpayments of rent, service charges and other periodical payments payable under a lease. For example, in *Nurdin & Peacock plc* v *DB Ramsden & Co. Ltd (No. 2)* [1999] 1 All ER 941, the Court of Appeal held that various overpayments of rent under a commercial lease were paid under a mistake of law and, hence, under the *Kleinwort* principle, recoverable by the payer. (See also, *Universities*

Superannuation Scheme Ltd v *Marks & Spencer plc* [1990] 04 EG 158, involving underpayments of service charges made by the tenant.)

The doctrine of certainty of rent requires that the rent payable by a tenant to his landlord is calculable with certainty at such time as payment becomes due. In *Greater London Council* v *Connolly* [1970] 2 QB 100, the plaintiff Council increased the rents of the tenants of some quarter of a million houses by amounts averaging 7s 6d a week. The rent books of the tenants contained printed conditions of the tenancies. By condition 2, the rent was 'liable to be increased or decreased on notice being given'. The Court of Appeal held that although the amount of rent was dependent on an act of the landlord, it could be calculated with certainty at the time when payment became due and so was not uncertain. A rent calculated by reference to the index of retail prices has also been held as sufficiently certain: (*Blumenthal* v *Gallery Five Ltd* (1971) 220 EG 483). Similarly, a sum representing 10 per cent of the turnover of a business has been upheld as certain (*Smith* v *Cardiff Corporation (No. 2)* [1955] Ch 159).

In regard to rent review clauses, the rent does not necessarily have to be certain when it falls due, provided that it is ascertained in due course under a rent review procedure (*CH Bailey Ltd* v *Memorial Enterprises Ltd*, above).

(**b**)   We are told that in October 1993 the reversionary interest was assigned to Sheila subject to the benefit of Harriet's tenancy. Despite the assignment, Harriet's liability will have continued because the rent reserved under the tenancy and the benefit of every covenant having reference to the subject-matter of the tenancy will have passed with the reversionary estate under the Law of Property Act 1925, s. 141(1). The effect of s. 141(1) is that once the reversion has been assigned it is only the assignee of the reversion (Sheila) who can sue on the real covenants contained in the tenancy, whether the breach took place before or after the assignment (*Re King, Deceased, Robinson* v *Gray* [1963] Ch 459 and *London & County (A. & D.) Ltd* v *Wilfred Sportsman Ltd* [1971] Ch 764, at pp. 782–4).

We are also told that in December 1999, Harriet divorced Nick and undertook to transfer the weekly tenancy to him, but this was never implemented. A similar situation arose in *Crago* v *Julian* [1992] 1 WLR 372, where the Court of Appeal held that, although the Law of Property Act 1925, s. 54(2) excepted the creation of a lease for a term not exceeding three years at a full market rent from the requirement of s. 53(1)(a) that the creation of an interest in land had to be in writing, it did not extend to the *assignment* of such leases which, therefore, had to be in writing. Moreover, the exception in s. 54(2) from the requirement of a deed for leases not required to be in writing applied only to their creation, and subsequent dispositions by assignment (or otherwise) had to be by deed unless otherwise exempted. The upshot of the foregoing so far as the present case is concerned is that, since there has been no formal assignment of the weekly tenancy in writing, Harriet continues to remain the tenant of the property. (Interestingly, had Harriet's tenancy been a secure tenancy under the Housing Act 1985, any purported transfer of her interest to Nick would have been ineffective under s. 91(1) of the 1985 Act, which provides that a secure periodic tenancy is not capable of being assigned (*Burton* v *Camden London Borough Council* [2000] EGCS 23 (HL).)

Since the rent is in arrears, Sheila should be advised to commence proceedings against Harriet in the county court under the Housing Act 1988, Pt I (to which the tenancy is subject), for possession of the premises and recovery of the arrears. Since the assured tenancy is periodic, it cannot be brought to an end except by obtaining an order from the court (s. 5(1)). A notice to quit by the landlord in relation to such a tenancy will be of no effect.

Before proceedings are commenced, Sheila must serve on Harriet a notice under s. 8 of the 1988 Act, informing her of the ground(s) on which possession is sought and setting out the time-scale of the action (s. 8(3)). The proceedings should not commence earlier than two weeks from the service of the s. 8 notice.

The court is restricted in the granting of a possession order in relation to a dwelling let on an assured tenancy. It must not make a possession order unless it is satisfied that certain grounds, listed in sch. 2, have been established. In the present case, Sheila should be advised to rely on grounds 8, 10 and 11. Ground 8 is a mandatory ground which would entitle Sheila to an order for possession as of right (i.e., the court does not have a discretion to adjourn proceedings or suspend the operation of the possession order once it is satisfied that the ground has been established). To succeed under ground 8, Sheila must show that at least three months' rent is unpaid both at the date of the service of the s. 8 notice and at the date of the hearing. In this connection, there is always the danger that Harriet will pay off all the arrears prior to the hearing.

Grounds 10 and 11 are discretionary grounds which will not entitle Sheila to possession as of right; the court may only make an order for possession if it considers it reasonable to do so, and has wide powers to adjourn proceedings or suspend the operation of a possession order. Ground 10 requires Sheila to establish that some rent lawfully due from Harriet is unpaid on the date on which proceedings for possession are begun and was in arrears at the date of the service of the s. 8 notice. Here again, Harriet may thwart the proceedings by paying off the arrears before the hearing. However, ground 11 will apply whether or not any rent is in arrears on the date on which proceedings for possession are begun, provided Sheila can show that Harriet has persistently delayed paying rent which has become lawfully due.

QUESTION 5

You have been asked by a client landlord to draft a short lease for use in respect of residential premises.

(a) Outline the form and contents of your draft.

(b) Explain what obligations would be imposed by law (including statute) if your client chose to proceed in the absence of such a lease.

Commentary

This is a question which requires you to draw on a number of different areas of landlord and tenant law. The danger is that you will concentrate on one or two topics in detail at the expense of other areas. Try to give a broad outline of the contents of your draft, referring to the more important landlord and tenant covenants as appropriate. The question also asks you to describe the various implied obligations in the absence of express agreement. Here again, you are only expected to give a broad outline of the legal position.

You may assume that the two parts of the question carry an equal distribution of marks. Bear this in mind, when writing your answer.

Suggested Answer

(a) Although no precise form is required by law for a lease, a fairly standard layout is invariably adopted as a matter of conveyancing practice. A lease by deed usually consists of five parts.

The 'premises' comprises the date of the lease, the names and description of the parties, the recitals (if any), the rent or premium, the operative words of demise, the description of the parcels demised, and any exceptions and reservations. My client may wish to limit the physical extent of the grant by excluding from it some part of the premises (e.g., the garden). This can be done by means of an exception. On the other hand, the landlord may wish to reserve some right newly created out of the subject-matter of the demise. For example, he may wish to reserve himself a right of way over the demised premises.

The 'habendum' specifies the quantity and quality of the estate demised and is usually identified by the words 'to hold' or 'to have and to hold'. The habendum fixes the commencement date and duration of the term.

The 'reddendum' fixes the rent payable under the lease and indicates with certainty that rent is payable by words such as 'yielding and paying'. Invariably, the rent will be reserved throughout the term or for a fixed period, followed by a reference to a rent review provision. Because a short lease is envisaged in the problem, I would not consider inserting a rent review clause in my draft.

The 'covenants' are the various obligations of the landlord and tenant, and these will be set out after the reddendum. So far as the tenants covenants are concerned, I would envisage including the following:

    (a)   covenant to pay rent;

    (b)   covenant to repair;

    (c)   covenant against assigning, sub-letting, charging or parting with possession. Such a covenant would take a fully qualified form (i.e., not to assign, underlet etc. 'without the landlord's consent such consent not to be unreasonably withheld') so as to anticipate the provisions of the Landlord and Tenant Act 1927, s. 18(1);

    (d)   user covenant limiting user of the demised premises to a private dwelling-house and residence only;

    (e)   a qualified covenant against the making of alterations or additions to the demised premises without prior consent of the landlord;

    (f)   covenant permitting the landlord and his agents to enter upon the premises for the purpose of inspecting the state and condition thereof. This would be coupled with a provision entitling the landlord to serve notice on the tenant to effect repairs, and the right of the landlord to execute such repairs himself (in the event of a failure to repair by the tenant) and to claim the cost from the tenant as a debt or rent arrears. Such a clause would permit the landlord to recoup the cost of the repairs without the necessity of serving a notice under the Law of Property Act 1925, s. 146(1), or complying with the procedures contained in the Leasehold Property (Repairs) Act 1938 (*Colchester Estates (Cardiff)* v *Carlton Industries plc* [1986] Ch 80) and *Jervis* v *Harris* [1996] 1 EGLR 78 (CA).

(g) covenant to insure.

So far as the landlord's covenants are concerned, I would limit these to just the covenant for quite enjoyment.

Following the covenants, I would insert an appropriate proviso for re-entry for non-payment of rent or other breaches of the tenant's covenants. The proviso (or forfeiture clause) provides the landlord with a contractual remedy against the tenant whereby he can terminate the lease.

Lastly, my draft would contain a number of schedules dealing with various matters, for example, a detailed description of the premises demised, a list of fixtures and fittings, and a set of regulations regarding the tenant's use of the premises (e.g., a prohibition on keeping animals on the premises, committing acts of nuisance etc.), and a schedule of condition in connection with the tenant's covenant to repair which obliges him to keep the premises in repair to a defined standard.

(b) In the absence of a written lease, a number of covenants will be implied under the common law and by statute into an oral tenancy. (Presumably, it is envisaged that such a tenancy would be either periodic or for a term not exceeding three years at a full economic rent with immediate possession so as to fall within the exception of a formal deed under the Law of Property Act 1925, s. 54(2).)

A covenant to pay rent will be implied from the mere contractual relationship of landlord and tenant. There is also an implied liability on the part of the tenant to pay charges in respect of the property (e.g., council tax, water rates and sewerage charges). It is also an implied condition of every lease, fixed term or periodic, that the tenant is not expressly or impliedly to deny the landlord's title or prejudice it by any acts which are inconsistent with the existence of the tenancy.

So far as the landlord is concerned, there is implied into every lease a covenant entitling the tenant to the quiet enjoyment of the demised premises. Under this covenant, the tenant is entitled peacefully to enjoy the premises without interruption from the landlord or persons claiming under him. The implied covenant, however, terminates with the landlord's interest (*Baynes & Co.* v *Lloyd & Sons* [1895] 2 QB 610). A landlord is also subject to an implied covenant not to derogate from his grant (*Harmer* v *Jumbil (Nigeria) Tin Areas Ltd* [1921] 1 Ch 200 and *Aldin* v *Latimer Clark, Muirhead & Co.* [1894] 2 Ch 437).

In addition to the above, a number of obligations relating to the state and condition of the premises will be implied on the part of the landlord. At common law, in relation to furnished lettings, there is an implied condition that the premises will be fit for human habitation at the commencement of the tenancy (see, e.g., *Smith* v *Marrable* (1843) 11 M & W 5). Where the essential means of access to units in a building in multiple occupation are retained in the landlord's control, the landlord is also impliedly obliged to maintain those means of access to a reasonable standard (*Liverpool City Council* v *Irwin* [1977] AC 239). This principle, however, appears to be confined to the special circumstances of a high-rise building in multiple occupation where the essential means of access to the units are retained in the landlord's occupation (*Duke of Westminster* v *Guild* [1985] QB 688).

An obligation to repair may also be implied on the landlord in order to match a correlative obligation on the part of the tenant (*Barrett* v *Lounova (1982) Ltd* [1990] 1 QB 348; but see *Adami* v *Lincoln Grange Management Ltd* [1998] 17 EG 148, in which the Court of Appeal concluded that the *Barrett* case was decided on its own special facts and contained no general principle requiring the implication of an obligation on a landlord to keep the structure of a building in good repair.).

There are also a number of repairing obligations imposed on a landlord by statute. The Landlord and Tenant Act 1985, s. 8 (formerly the Housing Act 1957, s. 6), implies terms as to fitness for human habitation throughout the term of the tenancy. However, the section applies only to residential lettings within certain specified rent limits (see s. 8(4)). More importantly, the Landlord and Tenant Act 1985, s. 11 (formerly the Housing Act 1961, s. 32), as amended by the Housing Act 1988, s. 116, implies covenants on the part of the landlord in relation to residential lettings under seven years, to keep in repair the structure and exterior of the dwelling-house and to keep in repair and proper working order the installations in the dwelling-house for the supply of water, gas and electricity, and for sanitation and space and water heating. If the lease is of a flat, the landlord's duty extends to any part of the structure or exterior of the building in which the landlord has an estate or interest (s. 11(1A)(a)). In the case of installations, where the landlord lets only part of the building, the landlord must keep in repair and proper working order an installation which directly or indirectly serves the flat, provided that the installation is in part of a building in which the landlord has an estate or interest, or which is owned or controlled by him (s. 11(1A)(b)). These extended obligations apply only if the disrepair or failure to maintain affect the tenant's enjoyment of the flat or common parts (s. 11(1B)).

So far as the tenant is concerned, his implied obligations in relation to the state and condition of the premises are limited to not committing waste and using the premises in a tenant-like manner (*Warren* v *Keen* [1954] 1 QB 15).

QUESTION 6

Janet and Arnold hold the freehold title to a four-bedroomed house in Sussex. Last year, they decided to move to another property in Cornwall. Eleven months ago, the couple allowed Stanley to take up occupation of the Sussex property. Stanley duly entered into occupation of the property and, upon being handed the front door keys, signed an agreement entitled 'Occupation Agreement'. This agreement stated, *inter alia*, that Stanley would pay Janet and Arnold £450 per month and that the latter could nominate a third party to share occupation with Stanley, if they so chose.

Three months ago, Janet and Arnold fell into a disagreement about the property in Sussex. Janet wished to sell the property with vacant possession, being keen to use the proceeds of sale for her own business purposes. Arnold, however, was very resistant to the idea of any sale because he felt that the property was producing a good financial return. Two months ago, without Arnold's concurrence or consent, Janet served on Stanley a month's written notice to quit, purportedly terminating the Occupation Agreement. The notice was duly served by Janet on the relevant monthly anniversary date.

Stanley immediately telephoned Arnold complaining about the notice. Arnold told Stanley that he should keep paying the £450 per month as normal, as Arnold took the view that Janet did not really mean to end the agreement. To date, Stanley has made one payment of £450 since the notice was served, but his cheque for this amount was promptly returned by Janet.

Advise Stanley as to his rights in relation to his occupation of the Sussex property, in particular, as to the validity of Janet's notice both at common law and under statute.

Commentary

This question is concerned with the law relevant to the lease/licence distinction, and the common law and statutory rules governing the validity of notices to quit. Although there is no direct authority dealing with the service of a notice by one joint landlord, reference should be made to the analagous position in respect of joint tenants: *Hammersmith and Fulham London Borough Council v Monk* [1992] 1 AC 478 and *Crawley Borough Council v Ure* [1995] 1 FLR 806. For further reading, see: Goulding, S. [1992] Conv 279, Dewar, J. (1992) 108 LQR 375 and Shorrock, K. [1995] Conv 424.

A consideration of the statutory code relating to assured shorthold tenancies under the Housing Act 1988 is also essential, especially in the light of the amendments introduced by the Housing Act 1996.

Suggested Answer

It is first necessary to determine whether Stanley holds a tenancy or a contractual licence of the Sussex property. Whereas a tenancy of residential property attracts some measure of statutory protection, a licence will not. If Stanley has been granted a tenancy, it is likely that this will be an assured shorthold under the Housing Act 1988 (as amended by the Housing Act 1996). If he has a licence then the Act will not apply.

The agreement itself does not provide any clues as to the nature of the arrangement. In any event, since the House of Lords' ruling in *Street v Mountford* [1985] AC 809, the labels placed on the agreement are not of real importance in determining the legal relationship between the parties. According to *Street*, the test as to whether an occupancy agreement is a tenancy or a licence is whether, on the true construction of the agreement, the occupier has been granted exclusive possession of the accommodation, for a fixed or periodic term, at a stated rent. If these conditions are satisfied, the agreement will be held to create a tenancy, except where the circumstances surrounding the relationship negate the inference of a tenancy (e.g., where the occupier falls to be classified as a 'lodger' in the sense that the landlord provides attendance or services which require the landlord to exercise unrestricted access to and use of the premises, or where, from the outset, there is no intention to create legal relations, or where possession is granted pursuant to a contract of employment or sale).

Does Stanley have exclusive possession of the property, for a term, at a rent? Clearly, Stanley has a term, albeit periodic in nature, since the payment of £450 is treated by the parties as being referable to a monthly period. It is monthly by virtue of the fact that, in the absence of any contrary agreement, the payment is tendered and accepted on a monthly basis (see *Adler* v *Blackman* [1952] 2 All ER 945). He clearly pays a consideration, which falls to be construed as rent. But does Stanley have exclusive possession? The central aspect of any landlord and tenant relationship is the notion of exclusive possession (i.e., the occupier has the legal right to exclude everyone, including the landlord, from the demised premises). In this connection, the nomination clause reserved in the agreement in favour of Janet and Arnold suggests, at first glance, that Stanley lacks the requisite 'monopoly of control' over the property so as to confer exclusive possession on him. However, such clauses have been held to be shams if not genuinely exercised by the grantor. For example, in *Antoniades* v *Villiers and Another* [1990] 1 AC 417, a nomination clause in an occupation agreement was held to constitute a sham and a pretence. It was seen by the court as merely an attempt to deny the occupier exclusive possession and permit the owner to circumvent the statutory protection afforded to residential occupiers. In the present case, if the nomination clause has been *genuinely* exercised by Janet and Arnold then it may be valid. On the facts, however, there is no such suggestion and, therefore, I would conclude that the clause is of no effect and that Stanley falls to be characterised as a monthly tenant.

Being a monthly tenancy granted in possession, for a term not exceeding three years, at the best rent available without taking a fine, it will be valid despite the absence of a deed (s. 54(2) of the Law of Property Act 1925). Moreover, despite the potential for the tenancy to continue for more than three years before being determined, it falls to be treated as being within s. 54(2) because the length of each period of the tenancy (i.e., one month) is less than three years (see *Ex Parte Voisey* (1882) 21 ChD 442). Accordingly, Stanley holds the Sussex property on a valid monthly periodic tenancy.

Periodic tenancies continue until such time as either the landlord or the tenant serves a valid notice to quit bringing the tenancy to end. The basic rule, at common law, is that one full period of notice must be given. Moreover, where there are joint tenants so that there is co-ownership at law of the leasehold estate (in the sense that the joint tenants hold the estate collectively as one legal unit), a valid notice to quit can be served on the landlord by *one* tenant alone so as to determine the tenancy (see *Hammersmith and Fulham LBC* v *Monk* [1992] 1 AC 478 (HL) and *Greenwich London Borough Council* v *McGrady* (1982) 6 HLR 36 (CA)). The notice must, however, be a genuine notice to quit terminating the tenancy at the end of a period of the tenancy, otherwise it may be construed as a surrender which requires the concurrence of all joint tenants (*Leek and Moorlands Building Society* v *Clark* [1952] 2 QB 788 (CA) and *Hounslow London Borough Council* v *Pilling* [1994] 1 All ER 432 (CA)). Although the *Monk* and *McGrady* cases both dealt with secure tenancies under the Housing Act 1985, there is no reason to suppose that they do not apply in the context of assured tenancies under the Housing Act 1988. In this connection, it seems also that the common law position regarding the service of a notice to quit by one joint assured tenant is unaffected by s. 45(3) of the Housing Act 1988, which provides that any reference in the Act to the landlord or tenant is a reference to all persons jointly constituting the landlord and/or tenant. There is no case, however, directly in point so the matter remains an open one.

The decision in *Monk* was applied by the Court of Appeal in *Crawley Borough Council* v *Ure* [1995] 1 FLR 806, which also considered the related issue of whether the joint tenant who serves notice is under a duty to consult his co-tenant under s. 26(3) of the Law of Property Act 1925, which provides that statutory trustees for sale 'shall so far as practicable consult the persons of full age for the time being beneficially interested in possession . . .'. The Court of Appeal concluded that s. 26(3) did not apply to the service of a notice to quit and, therefore, there was no obligation of consultation.

In the present case, the notice to quit served by Janet (as joint landlord) on Stanley is for a full period and *prima facie* seems valid at common law. In the light of the *Monk* ruling, referred to above, and by parity of reasoning, it is probably valid at common law despite the fact that it was served by Janet without Arnold's concurrence. As Janet has accepted no rent since Stanley received the notice, it is also likely that no waiver of the notice to quit has occurred.

However, this does not conclude the matter since Stanley is almost certainly an assured shorthold tenant entitled to statutory protection under the Housing Act 1988 (as amended by the Housing Act 1996). The 1996 Act has substantially altered the assured shorthold tenancy scheme originally set up by the Housing Act 1988. As from 28 February 1997 (being the date when the relevant provisions of the 1996 Act came into force), any tenancy which before this date would have been an assured tenancy under the 1988 Act is now deemed to be an assured shorthold unless the parties otherwise agree. In order to qualify as an assured shorthold tenancy, there must be a letting (as opposed to a licence) of a dwelling, which is let as a separate dwelling, to an individual (or group of individuals) who occupies the dwelling as his/her only or principal home and it is not a tenancy which falls within one or other of the exceptions set out in sch. 1 of the Housing Act 1988. These exceptions include tenancies entered into before the commencement of the 1988 Act, tenancies of high rateable value (or if granted after 1 April 1990, high rents in excess of £25,000 per annum), tenancies after 1 April 1990 at an annual rent of less than £250 per annum, business tenancies, students lettings, holiday lets, tenancies granted by resident landlords, Crown lettings, and lettings by public sector landlords. None of these exceptions, of course, applies to Stanley's tenancy. The upshot of the foregoing, therefore, is that Stanley's tenancy, being created after 27 February 1997, will be an assured shorthold.

Under the 1988 Act, landlords are given an automatic right to possession of assured shorthold tenancies on giving two months' written notice of seeking possession (see s. 21 of the 1988 Act as amended by s. 96 of the Housing Act 1996). Under s. 21(1)(b), it is permissible for one out of joint landlords to serve the requisite s. 21 notice on the tenant so no difficulty arises from the fact that, in the present case, Janet has served notice without the concurrence of her co-owner, Arnold. It is evident, however, that Janet has only given one month's notice requiring possession. Her notice is, accordingly, invalid under the Act and a fresh two months' notice will need to be given by Janet, on the relevant anniversary day, in order to determine Stanley's assured shorthold tenancy properly. If, upon expiry of the notice, Stanley refuses to vacate, it will be necessary for Janet to bring proceedings for possession of the Sussex property in the local county court. She will not be entitled to evict him without a court order.

15 Index

Abandonment of premises   155, 263, 266
Access, maintenance of   90, 274
Agreement to lease   6–7, 15–16, 24–5
Agricultural holdings   227
  'agricultural land' meaning   229–30
  Agricultural Tenancies Act 1995   239–42
  'contract of tenancy'   230–1
  counternotice   232–6
    contracting out of right   232–4
    right to serve   234
  definition   229–32
  dominant use   229–30
  grassland   230, 231
  grounds for possession   235–6
  mixed use   229–30
  notice to quit   234–6
    pre-arrangement   233–4
  security of tenure avoidance   232–4
  sub-tenancies   233–4
'Agricultural land' meaning   229–30
Agricultural tied cottages   227–8
  assured agricultural occupancy   237, 238–9
  grounds for possession   237–8
    overcrowding   238
    retirement   237
  housing authority alternative
    accommodation   238
  rent protection   236
  security of tenure   236–9
  single succession   237
Alteration covenants   116–18, 122–5, 272
  'alteration' defined   123
  forms   124
  improvements   124, 126

Alternative accommodation
  agricultural tied cottage tenants   238
  damages for costs of   59
  protected tenancies   170–3
Anti-social behaviour   247
Arbitration, PACT system   222–6
Assignment of lease   71–3
  authorised guarantee agreement
    30, 37–9, 46–9, 72–3
  covenant not to assign   65, 71, 272
  enforceability of covenants and   32–7
  equitable lease benefits   16
  forfeiture remedy   85
  free surrender before   72
  indemnity for arrears of rent   35
  injunction remedy   86–8
  Landlord and Tenant Act 1988   81–4
  landlord's remedies   84–8
  non-payment of rent   41, 43–6
  original tenant
    authorised guarantee agreement
      30, 37–9, 46–9, 72–3
    notice   29, 45–6
    release from liabilities   30, 37–9, 46–9
    rent liability   41, 43–6
  overriding lease   29–30, 48–9
  privity of contract   30, 39–40, 42
  qualified covenant   77–80
  renewal options and   126, 127, 130
  rental deposit   77, 80
  statutory continuation of tenancy   32–3, 37
  subsequent variation of terms   34–5
  suing on covenants   34
  surety

Assignment of lease — *continued*
    consent   77–80
    covenant   35
    surrender of sublease   88
    third party benefits   31, 49–53
    unauthorised   84–8
    withholding of consent   74–7
        burden of proof   74
        grounds   74–7
        occupation for efficient management of
            estate   76
        reasonable   76
        reasons in writing   83–4
        subject to conditions   77–80
        unreasonable   72, 74–7
Assured agricultural occupancy   237
    recovery of possession   238–9
Assured shorthold tenancies   160, 178–9
    expiry by effluxion of time   185
    Housing Act 1988   278–9
    Housing Act 1996   278–9
    notice abolition   178, 180
    notice to quit   185
    rent   187–8
    resident landlord   185–6
Assured tenancies   160, 178
    bringing to end   183–6
    company lets   182
    court order for possession   183
    exclusions   178, 180–2
    expiry by effluxion of time   180, 184
    holiday letting   181
    individual tenant requirement   182
    licences and   182
    non-exclusive occupation   182
    'only or principal home'   184
    'purpose-built' block of flats   181
    qualification for   180
    rent   186–7
    resident landlord and   181
    s.8 notice   184
    spouse's occupation   184–5
    statutory continuation of tenancy   175, 184
Authorised guarantee agreement   30, 37–9,
        46–9, 72–3
    consent of landlord   38–9, 46, 72–3

Break clauses   156–9
    defective notice   158
    incorrect date   156, 157
    validity of notice   156
Bruton, lease or licence distinction   9, 10–11
Business tenancies   198–226
    assured tenancies   182

Business tenancies — *continued*
    'business' definition   206
    civil procedure rules   225
    continuation tenancy   219
    contracting-out   213–14
    demolition or reconstruction   201, 209
    farm business tenancies   239–42
    forfeiture of lease   261
    grounds for possession
        delay in rent payment   200–1
        demolition and reconstruction plans
            201, 209
        required for family of landlord   202
        use not specified in lease   201
    'group of companies' definition   213
    improvements   215–18
        compensation for disturbance   215, 216,
            217, 218
        completion within time   217
        'improvement' description   216
        notice of intention to effect   216–17
        rating evaluation   217–18
    individuals   206–7
    intermediate landlords   204–5
    Landlord and Tenant Act 1927   198
    Landlord and Tenant Act 1954 Part II
        198–208, 219–22
        PACT system   222–6
        qualifying conditions   220
        sub-tenancy   220–1
    Law Commission proposals   212–15
    licence   205
    occupation
        Graysim Holdings   204–5, 219–22
        preparatory to carrying on business
            205–6
        for sub-letting purpose   204
        temporary absence   204
        through third parties   211, 213
    PACT system   222–6
    'premises' meaning   207
    procedure for possession   202–3
        application for new grant   202–3
        counternotices   202–3, 208
        service of s.25 notice   202, 208–10
    protected tenancies   168, 169–70
    qualification of tenant   203–7
    rating evaluation   217–18
    rent   210
        interim rent   214
        prolonging liability for contractual
            214–15
    security of tenure   198–9
    split reversion   214

Business tenancies — *continued*
    Street v *Mountford* test application   10
    temporary absence   204
    termination   202–3, 208–10, 261–2

Certainty of rent   269
Certainty of term   6, 17, 19–22
    periodic tenancies   25–8
Collective enfranchisement   189–90, 194–7
Company lets *see* Business tenancies
Concurrent lease   22, 23–4
Condensation   101, 102–4
Construction defects   94–5, 101–5, 109
Covenants
    alteration   116–18, 122–5, 272
    assignment of lease
        covenant against assignment
            65, 71, 272
        qualified covenant   77–80
    breach *see* Forfeiture of lease
    denial of title   64, 66–7
    derogation from grant   70
    enforcement *see* Enforceability of covenants
    entry by landlord   65
    express   116–33
    insurance   116, 118, 131–3, 273
    non-derogation from grant   54–5
    nuisance   55, 60–2, 67–70
    option to renew   116, 118, 126–30
    payment of rates and taxes   64
    payment of rent   64, 272, 273
    quiet enjoyment   54, 57–60, 62, 63, 64, 70,
        273–4
    re-entry for non-payment of rent   65
    rent review   116, 119–22
    repairs *see* Repairing covenant; Repairs
    sound insulation   55, 60–2, 67–70
    Southwark LBC   55, 60–2, 69
    state of property   55, 60–2, 67–70
    surety covenant   35–6
    unlawful eviction   57–60
    user covenant   116, 117–18, 122–3, 125–6,
        272
        forfeiture for breach   259–62
    usual   64–5
    waiver *see* Forfeiture of lease

Damages
    alternative accommodation costs
        59
    disrepair remedy   97, 98, 99–100
    harassment   59
    unlawful eviction   59
Decorative repairs   96, 141

Defective Premises Act 1972
    dilapidations   105–8
    liability in tort   90
Defects in design or construction
    94–5, 101–5, 109
Demolition   209
Denial of landlord's title   64, 66–7
    waiver of notice to quit   66–7
Derogation from grant   70
Design defects   94–5, 101–5, 109
Development intention   246, 247–8
Dilapidations   89–115
    access maintenance   90, 274
    compensation   111
    concrete steps   105, 107–8
    condensation   101, 102–4
    decorative repairs   96, 141
    Defective Premises Act 1972   105–8
    enforcement of obligations   109, 110–11
    Environmental Protection Act 1990   104
    express covenants   89–90
    fit for human habitation   90, 110, 274
    gutters   105, 106–7
    inherent defects in design or
        construction   94–5, 101–5, 109
    Law Commission proposals   91, 108–12
    negligence   90, 103–4
    notice of defects   90
    notice requirement   112–15
    remedies for disrepair   90, 96–101
        damages   97, 98, 99–100
        forfeiture   97, 98
        landlord's   97–9
        receiver appointment   99, 100–1
        self-help   100
        specific performance   99, 100
        tenant's   99–101
    renewal and improvements   89, 93–4, 109,
        110–11
    'repair' meaning   93
    Rimmer principle application   103
    safety from personal injury   107–8
    specific performance   111, 112
    standards   110–11
    structure and exterior of dwelling-house
        104–5
    subsidiary portion of building   95–6
    tort liability
        Defective Premises Act 1972   90
        Environmental Protection Act 1990   90
        negligence   90, 103–4
        waste   90
    waste doctrine   111
Disclaiming a lease   36

Displaced residential occupier   59
Doctrine of certainty
  rent   269
  term   6, 17, 19–22, 25–8
Doctrine of repugnancy   25, 27–8
Doctrine of subrogation   33, 36
Drafting lease   271–3

Enforceability of covenants   29–53
  assignment of lease and   32–7
  liability of surety under guarantee
    covenant   41, 42–3
  non-payment of rent, original tenant
    and   41, 43–6
  privity of contract   50
  repairs   109, 110–11
  subrogation doctrine   33, 36
  third party benefits   31, 49–53
Enfranchisement   189–97
  absence   193
  collective enfranchisement   189–90, 194–7
    notice   196
    qualifying tenant   195–6
  costs payment   194
  Leasehold Reform Act 1967
    189, 191–4
  Leasehold Reform, Housing and Urban
    Development Act 1993
    individual right to extend   196–7
    see also collective enfranchisement
  low rent test   192
  notice of intention   193
  price payable   193–4
  registration of minor interest   193
  rent value   192
  residential purpose use   192
  statutory   127
Environmental Protection Act 1990
  dilapidations   104
  liability in tort   90
Equitable leases   13–16
  assignment of benefits   16
  enforcement against third parties
    15, 18–19
  proprietary estoppel   15
  specific performance   15, 18, 24
  Walsh v Lonsdale rule   23, 24–5
Estoppel
  proprietary   15
  tenancy by   256
Eviction
  reinstatement   60
  self-help remedy   58–9
  wrongful   55–6, 57–60

Exclusive possession   17
  re-entry as trespass   56, 58

Farm business tenancies   239–42
  conditions   240–1
  improvements   242
  repairing obligations   241
  security of tenure   241
  term   241
Fit for human habitation   90, 110
  at commencement of lease   274
  throughout term   274
Fixtures   134, 150–4
  agricultural fixtures   152, 153
  chattels   152
  degree of annexation test   151–2
  domestic fixtures   152, 153
  purpose of annexation test   151, 152
  trade fixtures   152, 153
Forfeiture of lease   134–5, 136–46
  breach of covenant
    non-payment of rent   139, 141–2, 145–6,
      266
    repair   139, 140–1
    user covenant   259–62
    see also waiver of breach
  business tenancies   261
  disrepair remedy   97, 98
  Law Commission's proposals
    142–6
  re-entry   143–5
    by   134–5
    lease end at time of   143, 144
    time lapse before   139
    as trespass   136, 139
  waiver of breach   145, 261
    continuing breach   137
    demand for rent   137–8
    once and for all breach   137
Frustration   134, 135, 147–8, 263, 265–6
  circumstances of   148
  lease and contract   148
Frustratory mitigation   266

Graysim Holdings, business tenancy
  occupation   204–5, 219–22
Gutters   105, 106–7

Harassment   58, 59
  restricted contract occupier
    162, 167
Holiday lets
  assured tenancies   181
  protected tenancies   164, 166

Housing Act 1985 Part IV
  licence to occupy 243–4
  public sector accommodation *see* Secure
    tenancies
Housing Act 1988
  assured agricultural occupancy
    237, 238–9
  Part 1 *see* Assured shorthold tenancies;
    Assured tenancies
  security of tenure 57–60
Housing authority, rehousing from agricultural
  tied cottages 238

Illegal purposes use 175–6, 260
Immoral purpose use 175–6, 260
Improvements
  alterations and 124, 126
  business tenancies 126, 215–18
    compensation for disturbance 215, 216,
      217, 218
    completion within time 217
    'improvement' description 216
    notice of intention to effect
      216–17
    rating evaluation 217–18
  farm business tenancies 242
  repair and 89, 93–4, 109, 110–11
  secure tenancies and 250
Inherent defects 94–5, 102–4, 109
Insurance covenants 116, 118, 273
  application of moneys 132, 133
  burden of cost 131
  joint names 132
  landlord's veto on insurer 132

Joint tenants, notice to quit 278–9

Landlord and Tenant Act 1927, business
  tenancies 198
Landlord and Tenant Act 1954 Part II *see*
  Business tenancies
Landlord and Tenant Act 1988, assignment of
  lease 81–4
Law Commission proposals
  business tenancies 212–15
  dilapidations 91, 108–12
  forfeiture of lease 142–6
Leasehold dilapidations *see* Dilapidations;
  Repairs
Leasehold enfranchisement *see*
  Enfranchisement
Leasehold extension 189, 190
Leasehold Reform Act 1967, enfranchisement
  see Enfranchisement

Leasehold Reform, Housing and Urban
  Development Act 1993
  collective enfranchisement
    189–90, 194–7
  individual right to extend 196–7
Leases
  agreement to grant 6–7, 15–16, 24–5
  certainty of term 6, 17, 19–22, 25–8
  concurrent 22, 23–4
  contractual only interest 11
  disclaiming 36
  drafting 271–3
  enforcement against third parties
    15, 18–19
  equitable *see* Equitable leases
  exclusive possession 17
  formalities 6–7, 16–19
    certainty of term 17, 19–22
    deeds 17
    exclusive possession 17
    rental payment 17
  joint exclusive possession
    12–13
  licence distinction 6, 9, 276–7
    Bruton 9, 10–11
    intention 10–11
    object of charity 11
    short term agreements 12–13
    special circumstances 10, 11
  of the reversion *see* concurrent lease
  oral agreement 18
  parties
    privity of estate between 23
    separate 20
  termination *see* Termination of tenancy
  void 13–14
  see also Tenancies
Licences
  assured tenancies and 182
  Housing Act 1985 Part IV 243–4
  joint exclusive possession 12–13
  leases distinguished from
    6, 9, 276–7
    Bruton 9, 10–11
    intention 10–11
    object of charity 11
    short term agreements 12–13
    special circumstances 10, 11
  'licence agreement' 9, 10–11
  non-exclusive occupation 182
Lodgers 249

Negligence 90, 103–4
Noise nuisance 55, 60–2, 67–70

Non-payment of rent
  forfeiture of lease for   139, 141–2, 145–6,
    266
  grounds for possession   270–1
  original tenant and assignees   41, 43–6
  payment of arrears before proceedings   270
  re-entry for   65, 273
  secure tenancies   246–7
  suspended possession order   142
Notice to quit
  agricultural holdings pre-arrangement
    233–4
  joint tenants   278–9
  waiver by denial of title   66–7
Nuisance   55, 60–2, 67–70

Option to renew *see* Renewal options
Overcrowding
  agricultural tied cottages   238
  secure tenancies   250
Overriding interest registration   18
  former tenant   29–30, 48–9

PACT system   222–6
Part performance   15
Parties to lease
  privity of estate between   23
  two separate parties   20
Parting with possession *see* Assignment of
  lease
Periodic tenancies   277–8
  certainty of term and   25–8
  partial fetter on right to serve quit notice   27
  repugnancy doctrine   25, 27–8
Possession
  non-payment of rent *see* Non-payment of
    rent
  order   270
  parting with *see* Assignment of lease
  protected tenancies *see* Protected tenancies
Privity of contract
  assignment of lease and   30, 39–40, 42
  covenant enforcement   50
Privity of estate   23
Professional Arbitration on Court Terms
  (PACT)   222–6
Proprietary estoppel doctrine   15
Protected tenancies
  alternative accommodation provision
    170–3
    character of property   172
    similarity   171
    suitable to means and needs of tenant
      171–2

Protected tenancies — *continued*
  company lets   168, 169–70
  continuing residence   160–1, 169
  exclusions
    board or attendance   162–6
    holiday lets   164, 166
    resident landlord exclusion   164, 165–6,
      175
  forced absence   160–1
  grounds for possession
    alternative accommodation provision
      170–3
    discretionary   161, 176
    landlord's   161
    residence for landlord or his family
      175
    use for immoral or illegal purposes
      175–6
  possession   173–7
    grounds *see* grounds for possession
    residence prior to letting requirement
      174–5
  qualification for   161
  relevant date   162
  Rent Act 1977   160–77
  restricted contracts   162, 167
  separate dwelling   163, 164
  statutory tenancy continuation
    160
    succession   168–9, 176–7
  succession   168–9, 176–7
    after death of tenant   168–9
  'two-homes' occupant   160, 169
Public sector accommodation *see* Secure
  tenancies
'Purpose-built' block of flats   181

Quiet enjoyment   54, 62, 63, 64, 70, 273–4
  nuisance   55, 60–2, 67–70
  remedies available   57–60

Rates, covenant to pay   64
Re-entry
  breach of covenants   272–3
  forfeiture by   134–5
  forfeiture of lease and   139, 143–5
  lease end at time of   143, 144
  non-payment of rent   273
  notional   144
  to carry out repairs   108
  as trespass   56, 58, 136, 139
Receiver appointment, disrepair remedy
  99, 100–1
Reconstruction   209

Registration
  enfranchisement right   193
  options to renew   130
  overriding interest   18
Renewal, repairs and   89, 93–4, 109
Renewal options   116, 118
  assignment of estate   126, 127, 130
  breach of contract for refusal   128–9
  certain and unequivocal in terms   128
  conditional estate contract   128
  material date for compliance with conditions
      129–30
  registration of option   130
  vague wording   128
Rent
  attributes of   268
  business tenancies   210
    interim rent   214
    prolonging liability for contractual
        214–15
  covenant to pay   64, 272, 273
  deposit for consent to assign   77, 80
  doctrine of certainty   269
  equitable set-off   256–8
  'fair rent'   187
  Housing Act 1988 Part I   186–8
  increasing   57–8
  interim rent   214
  let on open market by willing landlord   187
  mistaken payment   268
  non-payment see Non-payment of rent
  Rent Act tenancies   187
  repairs and deductions from   100, 257
  'willing landlord'   187
Rent Act 1977   160–77
  see also Protected tenancies
Rent assessment committee   57–8, 187
Rent review
  clauses   269
  covenants   116, 119–22
  'subject to contract' notices
      119, 120, 121–2
  trigger notices   119, 120, 121–2
  'upwards only'   119, 121–2
  'without prejudice' notices
      119, 120, 121–2
Repairing covenant   65, 74–5, 272
  decorative repairs   96, 141
  enforcement   109, 110–11
  farm business tenancies   241
  forfeiture of lease for breach   139, 140–1
Repairs
  compensation   111
  concrete steps   105, 107–8

Repairs — *continued*
  gutters   105, 106–7
  inherent defects in design or construction
      94–5, 102–4, 109
  meaning   93–4
  notice requirement   112–15
  re-entry right to carry out   108
  remedies for disrepair   90, 96–101
    damages   97, 98, 99–100
    forfeiture   97, 98
    landlord's   97–9
    receiver appointment   99, 100–1
    self-help   100
    specific performance   99, 100
    tenant's   99–101
  renewal and improvement   89, 93–4, 109,
      110–11
  safety from personal injury   107–8
  secure tenancies and   250
  specific performance   111, 112
  standards   110–11
  structure and exterior of dwelling-house
      104–5
  waste doctrine   111
  see also Dilapidations; Repairing covenant
Repudiation   135, 147, 148–50, 263–6
  contractual tenancy   149–50
Repugnancy doctrine   25, 26–8
Resident landlord
  assured shorthold tenancy   185–6
  assured tenancies   181
  protected tenancies   164, 165–6, 175
Restricted contracts   162, 167
Restrictive user covenants   125–6
Reversion, lease of the reversion see
      Concurrent lease
Rimmer principle   103

Secure tenancies   243–52
  alternative accommodation offer
      246, 248
  anti-social behaviour   247
  breach of covenant   246
  conduct   247
  damage to property   246
  development intention   246, 247–8
  failure to pay rent   246–7
  grounds for possession   246–7
  improvements   250
  landlord condition   243, 245
  licence to occupy and   243–4
  lodgers   249
  notice to quit   246
  overcrowding   250

Secure tenancies — *continued*
  periodic   246
  purchase of freehold   250
  qualifying repairs   250
  repairs   250
  security of tenure   245–8
  sub-letting   249–50
  succession   250–2
  tenant condition   243, 245–6
  terms imposed   248950
Security of tenure *see individual forms of*
  tenancy
Self-help
  disrepair remedy   100
  termination of tenancy remedy
    58–9
Sound insulation   55, 60–2, 69
Specific performance
  disrepair remedy   99, 100
  equitable leases   15, 18, 24
  repairs   111, 112
Statutory continuation of tenancy
  assignment of lease and   32–3, 37
  assured tenancies   184
  continuing residence   169
  protected tenancies   160
  succession   168–9, 176–7
Statutory enfranchisement   127
Street v *Mountford* test   10
Sub-letting *see* Assignment of
  lease
Subrogation doctrine   33, 36
Succession
  agricultural tied cottages   237
  death of statutory tenant
    family member   169
    spouse   168–9
  protected tenancies   176–7
  secure tenancies   250–2
    foster children   251–2
    same-sex partner   251
Sufferance, tenancy at   255–6
Surety covenant   35–6
Surrender of lease   134, 154–6, 263
  abandonment   155, 263, 266
  agreement to surrender   154–5
  by operation of law   155, 157, 266
  express   154–5
  future surrender   154–5
  implied   155
  past breaches of covenant   156
  rent paid in advance   156
  subtenants   156
  third parties   156

Taxes, covenant to pay   64
Tenancies
  at sufferance   255–6
  at will   254–5
  assured *see* Assured shorthold tenancies;
    Assured tenancies
  business *see* Business tenancies
  by estoppel   256
  periodic *see* Periodic tenancies
  protected *see* Protected tenancies
  see also Leases
Tenant's right to fixtures   134, 150–4
  agricultural fixtures   152, 153
  chattels   152, 153
  degree of annexation test   151–2
  domestic fixtures   152, 153
  purpose of annexation test   151, 152
  trade fixtures   152, 153
Term of lease
  certainty   6, 17, 19–22, 25–8
  variation after assignment   34–5
Termination of tenancy   134–59
  assured tenancies   183–6
  break clauses   156–9
  business tenancies   202–3, 208–10,
    261–2
  civil remedies
    damages   59
    self-help   58–9
  fixtures, tenant's rights to   134, 150–4
  forfeiture *see* Forfeiture of lease
  frustration   134, 135, 147–8, 266
  harassment   58, 59
  Housing Act 1988   57–60
  notice to quit, waiver by denial of
    title   66–7
  repudiation   135, 147, 148–50, 263–6
  surrender   134, 154–6, 263, 266
  unlawful deprivation of occupation
    58, 59
  waiver of notice   66–7
Third parties
  enforceability of covenants   31, 49–53
  enforcement of lease against   15, 18–19
Title, denial of   64, 66–7
Tort
  Defective Premises Act 1972   90
  Environmental Protection Act 1990   90
  negligence   90
  waste   90
Trespass, re-entry as   56, 58, 136, 139

Unfair terms in consumer contracts   258
Unlawful eviction   55–6, 57–60

User covenants   116, 117–18, 122–3, 272
    forfeiture for breach   259–62
    improvements   124
    restrictive   125–6

Void lease   13–14

Waivers
    notice to quit   66–7
    see also Forfeiture of lease
Walsh v *Lonsdale* rule   23, 24–5
Waste doctrine   111
Will, tenancy at   254–5